Tales of the Rails

Tales of the Rails

John Fletcher
Main line footplateman

Cliff and I pose in front of our steed being held in Oubeck loop due to a tanker train derailment at Morecambe barring our passage to Heysham Harbour. *Sunday Times*

First published in 2017
Reprinted 2017
Reprinted 2018
Reprinted 2019

British Library Cataloguing in Publication Data

A catalogue record for this book is available from the British Library.

ISBN 978 1 85794 507 2

Silver Link Publishing Ltd
The Trundle
Ringstead Road
Great Addington
Kettering
Northants NN14 4BW

Tel/Fax: 01536 330588
email: sales@nostalgiacollection.com
Website: www.nostalgiacollection.com

Printed and bound in the Czech Republic

Acknowledgements

This book would not have been possible to compile over the last three years without the patience and understanding of my first love, my wife Jacqueline, and our three sons. My second love is railways, which over the years has brought me into contact with so many like-minded people, some of whom have become good friends and work colleagues and who I must mention for their help and assistance. My mentor has been David Idle, for helping with my grammar, punctuation and proofreading. A close second has been family friend Caroline Stewart and her husband Ray, who unlike myself are both computer-literate. Many facts and figures have been forwarded to me by Adrian Scales regarding steam specials visiting his home town of Scarborough, particularly the 'Scarborough Spa Express'. Many of the photographs used are from my own somewhat puny collection, but other more gifted cameramen have kindly allowed me to show off their handiwork in this book – my sincere thanks to you. Mention must also be made of Peter Townsend at Silver Link publishing for guiding me along with his professional advice freely given to this amateur author. I cannot close without expressing my gratitude for a happy life over the years spent in the company of fellow footplate staff and railway enthusiasts.

John Fletcher
Grosmont
August 2016

Contents

Introduction

I must admit to not having had a lifelong love of railways. I certainly wasn't interested in them in my early days; I would have been at least 18 months old before getting hooked, after being presented with a plastic steam engine rattle by my mother, which she tied to the side of my Silver Cross pram, giving me an early opportunity to noisily announce an affection for my new-found interest, and I have been rattling on about them ever since!

My childhood was one of happiness in our small terraced house in 1950s Preston and, looking back on those days I feel fortunate to have been brought up in a generation where people had little of monetary value, but a mixture of discipline, love and respect did exist in most working-class households. The great outdoors gave us freedom to play and pursue a variety of interests and, influenced by my uncle, Bob Fletcher, who drove steam locomotives for a living, I became an avid trainspotter, and from then on my life's ambition was to follow in his footsteps and work on the footplate.

In February 1962 my five years of dreaming became reality when I began my railway career at 24C Lostock Hall on the bottom rung of the ladder as an engine cleaner with clock number 287. It was a case of being in the right place at the right time, as in some areas of the country steam had been superseded, but not here in the North, where steam still ruled supreme – and I was going to be part of it! We were the last generation of BR steam footplatemen,

and during those 6½ years it was steam all the way for most of the time, which saw me accumulate more than 1,600 footplate turns and graduate to become one of the senior firemen. Such was my enthusiasm for the job that the only thing I looked forward to after finishing work for the day was going back again the day after!

Unlike in the age of steam, computers can never create characters. The job has changed so much over the years, but fortunately for me the railways of my generation seemed to attract a whole host of varying personalities to perform the many now obsolete manual jobs then in existence. With name changes to protect the innocent – or guilty – some of these men feature prominently in this book.

I left the railways at the end of steam before returning after a brief interlude for another five-year spell. But I had no real love of the diesel locomotive, my opinion being that a complete layman could generate the same power from the machine as any experienced driver could. The electric locomotive had even less appeal, particularly when electrification of the West Coast Main Line was completed in 1974, the 'chicken mesh' obliterating those beautiful Westmorland Fells. I decided that my time on the railways was finally up.

Running our family business ate up all my time for a number of years before discovering the world of preserved railways in the early 1980s, first at the fledgling West Somerset Railway, followed shortly after by our discovery of the North Yorkshire Moors Railway, where I became a driver in 1985. This was followed in 1998 by a return to operating steam on the main line, spending 15 years as a fireman with both West Coast Railways and Merlin Rail, during which time I fired almost every main-line-registered steam locomotive over the length and breadth of the country. This would have been impossible to achieve working for BR in the steam era, and I personally doubt if anyone would be able to cover these journeys again due to the ever increasing restrictions imposed on the routes available to the steam locomotive.

Looking back, I suppose that I have had three railway careers – first with British Railways, followed by preserved railways, then West Coast and Merlin Rail – during which time I calculate that I have fired more than 60 different classes of steam locomotive. My long career on the footplate is now over for health reasons, and I have been withdrawn from traffic, but have not yet gone for scrapping! I do hope that you enjoy reading these memoirs as much as I have in writing them and reliving many of the journeys again. Please forgive any mistakes or errors that may have crept in, bearing in mind that some of these events took place more than half a century ago.

I Early years

Many years ago, when steam locomotives roamed the earth, a 10-year-old lad in Preston, Lancashire, bought his first Ian Allan *abc* engine number book, and so began an interest in railways that is still with him some 60 years later.

I lived near the Preston Dock branch and in those early days I would lie awake at night listening to the sounds of ex-

LNWR 'Super D' engines working trains off this busy branch, pounding their way up the 1 in 29 gradient to Preston station. A sleeper fence separated us from the engines awaiting a path across the busy Strand Road leading to the busy dock sidings, and one day the impossible happened when we were summoned onto the footplate of 'Super D' No 49196 by the kindly driver. However, my real mentor in life was my Dad's brother, who also drove these machines, being based at the former Lancashire & Yorkshire Railway engine sheds at Lostock Hall near Preston.

Robert Fletcher, or Uncle Bob as he was to me, would visit us about once a month, usually on a Saturday when he was on the right shift. He and my Dad would give each other a haircut in the afternoon and at night off they would go into Preston for a few pints. Looking back to those days, I'll bet that Uncle Bob was glad to get out of our house at times, having faced a barrage of questions from me about railways and the type of engines that he worked on and how good or bad they were. All of this inside information would be passed on to my trainspotting mates at school. Then a couple of years later I became the envy of them all when he took my father Tom and me on a footplate trip from Preston to Todmorden, with a passenger train hauled by an ex-L&Y 2-4-2 tank, convincing me of what I probably already knew, that the footplate was going to be the life for me when I left school. So there you have it, and 'Bob's your uncle'!

My father worked as a ploughman in the

Curly-haired innocence, aged 4 in 1950 in River Street, Preston. *Author's collection*

Me and Dad at the Vale of Rheidol Railway, Aberystwyth, in 1981. *Author's collection*

1920s and '30s in charge of a team of horses on Longton Moss adjacent to the railway line, and would often wave to his brother when he passed by on the footplate of a Preston to Liverpool express. Over the years I have often thought about having a painting commissioned depicting the combined scene of shire horses alongside the iron horse.

My enthusiasm for trainspotting reached its peak about this time with endless hours spent number-snatching either perched on a high wall in Pitt Street overlooking the entire array of lines covering the north side of Preston station, or sometimes on the glass bridge at the south end, which was a magnet for railway enthusiasts. Thirty feet below the wall, the footpath leading from the station to the engine sheds was a busy thoroughfare with loco crews going back and forth to the depot. The wall was often referred to as Spit Street wall by these men, because

some of the spotters were guilty of spitting, it sometimes landing on the men walking below. It was probably their way of getting their own back on some of the local footplate crews who made a habit of covering up the cabside number with a rag as they passed by going light engine to the shed. Let me state quite clearly that none of our gang engaged in this activity, and I personally witnessed a vengeful driver and fireman attack some spotters after scaling the wall, which dropped down to 6 feet in height around the corner out of sight of the spotters.

Around this time some of us decided to buy an ex-Army tent to provide overnight accommodation on weekend spotting expeditions. For the first couple of weekends we stayed locally and the weather was fine; the tent slept four quite comfortably. Then we became a little more ambitious and it was decided to camp out in a field alongside the West Coast Main Line at Brock, some 8 miles north of Preston, the bonus being able to observe locos taking on water from Brock troughs. Unfortunately it transpired that it wasn't just the locos that took on water, but the tent as well, which proved not to be very waterproof. Our first two weekends using the tent had been dry and warm, but what a transformation at Brock where it started raining on the Friday evening just after we had pitched the tent, and rained continuously until the early hours of Sunday morning, by which time everything and everybody was soaked. I warned my friends that it might be a mistake to take all the food out of the carrier bags and place it around the tent, showing off how much grub they had with them, and sure enough when we awoke on the Saturday morning all the food was swimming in water and everything – the cakes, bread, biscuits and toffees, together with two *Eagle* comics – had to be thrown away. Luckily there was a small village shop nearby and more sensible items like soup and beans were purchased by four shivering spotters. In fact, the lovely lady owner took pity on us and warmed the soup and lent us a flask. Needless to say we didn't 'cop' many locos over the weekend, nor did we derive much pleasure from standing near the troughs as the novelty of watching tenders, overflowing with more water, soon lost its appeal.

We packed up on the Sunday morning, and it took two of us to carry the sodden tent in its holdall across the field and to the bus stop on the nearby A6. A Ribble double-decker turned up eventually, and we hadn't the strength to go upstairs, so we left the tent in the centre aisle between us. Water started to run out of the holdall, making its way to the front, and the conductor gave us a good rollocking. To cap it all, two of us developed the flu and missed school the following week.

We four enjoyed our hobby and visited other steam depots, including the three sheds at Carlisle, once the home to seven different railway companies and where it was possible to see locos in black, red, green, blue and brown liveries, although I hasten to add a little before my time! It was here that we noted trains going to Newcastle, so a few weeks later we actually managed to get round Heaton shed, only being thrown out after copping everything and giving the irate shed foreman some fictitious Sunderland addresses. For some reason this made him even angrier and, no, he would not tell us the time of the next train to York! There we had no trouble bunking the shed before catching an evening train home to Preston via Manchester, spending the journey time underlining the day's cops in our Ian Allan 'Combined Volumes'. Ah, heaven! We also enjoyed taking car and bus numbers and looking in at the dashboard of the cars to see how fast the speedometers read on the wide variety of vehicles. In those days almost every car was British-made, with just a sprinkling of Yankee gas-guzzlers. Looking back to that time, I am sure that my later interest in classic cars must have begun around then.

Another interest was canals and canal fishing. The Lancaster Canal originated on our doorstep, and horse-drawn boat rides on a Sunday afternoon became a passion. After arriving back at the Leighton Street basin it was but a short walk to the ice-cream parlour down the street, where I was always given a free ice-cream for helping them unload the ice on Saturdays. Some of the lads enjoyed fishing, but sitting there drowning worms was not for me! One of the lads was given a really expensive carbon-fibre rod for Christmas; it was his pride and joy, and he persuaded me to go fishing with him for the day. I turned up with my converted broomstick handle with a float and hook tied on it and – you've guessed it – at the end of the day I had very nearly filled the keep-net with roach, tench, perch, etc, while he managed only a small pike. We threw the lot back in the cut. What a waste of a day – we could have gone spotting and copped something. And how was it that, when you next saw your mates, they would take great delight in telling you that the only engine you needed to complete the class had just gone through a few minutes before you arrived!

I was also friendly with another Lostock Hall driver, George Kay, whose wife Maud ran a small sweet shop in the front room of their terraced house just around the corner from where we lived in Bow Lane. I used to take pop bottles back to earn a few coppers to purchase sweets from boxes on the counter. These ranged from the penny box up to the sixpenny box. If George wasn't at work on shifts he would help Maud in the shop. He was about the same age as my Uncle Bob and he knew that I was an avid trainspotter and keen on the railway. Later in life I did work with him at the shed, but he had to retire early due to a bad chest. I think the Woodbines got to him in the end.

About this time I had taken on an evening paper-round after school and a couple of my lady customers stick out in my mind for different reasons. The first lady had a most unusual, and not very pleasant, job that took her to most schools in the area at that time, examining children's hair for lice, biddies, nits, etc. She was known to us as 'Nitty Norah the biddy explorer', but no one dare call her that to her face. The other lady was like an angel to us; if we had a sick pet, we would turn up on Mrs Fothergill's doorstep and she would take the animal into the back room while you waited in her parlour. I don't think she was a trained vet but just had a natural way with animals and birds. The only payment she would take was for pills or medicines. My mother used to tell that when she was younger and someone in the street died, another local woman would lay them out for the undertaker.

About this time I began my first paid job delivering newspapers, which gave me an opportunity to try and save up some money from my weekly 10-shilling wage to buy a few Triang model railway items from our local model railway shop, 'Harry Welch, the Modellers Mecca', in Church Street, Preston. In the side window of this shop was a coin-operated model railway; it cost 1 penny, which you placed in a slot at the side of the window. This was a big draw for youngsters, to be able to go down in the evenings or Sundays when the shop was closed and operate the trains; and I think it must have been a good money-spinner for the owner. I did eventually build a small layout of my own; all the rolling-stock was from the American range that Triang produced at the time. I had always been fascinated by American railroads and the sheer size and power of their locomotives. I vividly recall reading of engines with wheel arrangements of 4-6-6-4 dragging loaded coal trains of 14,000 tons up steep grades; the same locos were also capable of running at 75mph with passenger trains, or varnish trains, as the Yanks call them. I also tried to imagine just how the fireman managed to shovel enough coal into these monsters to keep them on the move. It was only in later years that I became more knowledgeable about the operation of these giants of steam, and realised that it was actually a mechanical stoker doing all the work, feeding pulverised coal or oil into the huge fireboxes, the fireman himself never needing to get up off his backside, as all the stoker and injector controls were within easy reach, directly in front of him. How I would have loved to have witnessed those engines in action, and I may yet have this privilege should I still be around when the restoration of the world's biggest steam locomotive, the Union Pacific 4-8-8-4 'Big Boy' No 4014, is completed at its former home in Cheyenne, Wyoming.

My own layout wasn't much when compared to the one that my friend's father bought for him, which occupied a medium-sized bedroom in their house. The control panel was made up of ex-Second

World War RAF electrical equipment, including voltmeters, etc. These enabled you to have extra-fine control of the locos. As an example, we applied minimum power to a 'Prairie' tank, then left it and went downstairs for tea, returning some 30 minutes later to find that the engine had travelled less than 6 feet. That was in the 1950s, but I would challenge any present-day model railway controller to better that ex-RAF equipment. We also had loads of fun with my Mamod traction engine, steaming it up with methylated spirits and nearly setting the kitchen table on fire; it's not the same fun now using the fuel cubes supplied with these models. Speaking of hot water, Sundays was always bath night in our little back-to-back terraced house, and how can you ever forget the experience of bathing in a tin bath with the front room coal fire blazing away on a cold winter's night? Sheer bliss!

My father did not have much holiday time in the 1950s – I don't think many of their generation did. When he was off we would go away on day trips to Rhyl, New Brighton or Windermere, usually by coach. One of the local companies that we travelled with was 'Bon Chaunce', from the French for 'good luck'. It operated a fleet of Bedford OB buses, and I always tried to get the front seat for I loved listening to the sound of that petrol engine when going through the gears or labouring up the hills on the A6 heading for the Lake District, and seeing the reflection of our bus in shop windows.

Another vehicle engine sound that fascinated me was that of the Thames 4D diesel. Our neighbour drove one of these wagons for a small company in Preston called Ideal Wonder Wash, and he would take me along occasionally. The engine had a governor, or cut-out, and when on tick-over or idling I could listen to it all day long. Victor, the driver, was a friendly Scottish lad about ten years older than me; his job was to collect from hotels and bed & breakfast

My favourite bus, a Bedford OB, on the Isle of Man. *Author's collection*

places all bedding, sheets, etc, contained in bulky cotton bags, transport them to the industrial laundry in Preston and return them after washing. Some of these hotels were situated in quite isolated places down single-track roads, and I would be allowed to do a bit of the driving. About a year later he and his young family moved away and he changed jobs to driving an ice-cream van. I missed my driving lessons with him and shortly afterwards he was tragically killed in a road accident that wasn't his fault. I went with my parents to his home to pay our respects on the night before his funeral. I was allowed to see Victor in his coffin in the dimly lit parlour, half of his face being covered due to the crash injury. I remember touching his forehead and him being so cold. I had never seen a dead person before and it took me a long time to get over his loss.

At school, sport was my main interest, football in particular. We practised mainly at night or weekends in the streets near home. I did fancy myself as a footballer and became the captain of the school team; my hero was, of course, Preston North End's Tom Finney. Many players from that era had a little business as a sideline, including Tom Finney (later, Sir Tom) who had his own plumbing company. I often think just how fortunate I was being brought up in an era of steam trains, Tom Finney and rock 'n' roll music. Sadly, as I write this news has just broken that Sir Tom Finney has passed away aged 91. Among the many tributes to him was one that for me really sums up the man: 'He could talk about football all day long, but he would never mention himself.' Also, throughout his entire career he was never booked or sent off. He was a true gentleman in every sense of the word.

On Church Street at that time was the sports shop owned by Preston North End and Scotland international captain Willie Cunningham, a tough craggy ex-miner whom Preston signed from Airdrieonians for

A proud Captain at Christ Church School, Bow Lane, Preston, 1961. *Author's collection*

Sir Tom Finney CBE, of Preston North End, was Footballer of the Year in 1954 and 1957, the first player to win the award twice. *Lancashire Evening Post*

£10,000. He followed a long line of Scottish internationals in the team, including Bill Shankly and Tommy Docherty. Willie captained Scotland in the 1954 World Cup Finals, so as you can imagine I hung on to his every word of advice when buying my football gear from his shop. It is difficult to imagine any of today's Premiership players running a little sports shop and flogging you a pair of shin pads or football socks; they would probably be offering you advice about players' wages instead!

In one memorable weekend in March 1958 I copped my last 'Lizzie', No 46226 *Duchess of Norfolk*. Then in the afternoon I was off on my bike to Deepdale, home of my beloved Preston North End, to watch another magical display by the greatest footballer of all time, Tom Finney. We had an easy 3-0 win over Sunderland in front of 24,000, with no segregation of supporters, and no aggro either. Looking back to those days, if Tom had picked up an injury the week before and there was some doubt about him being fit, the Friday night local paper would never have revealed whether he would be playing. Supporters walking to the ground would be asking one another whether Tommy was playing. 'Have you heard?' You didn't get to know until the team was announced just before kick-off. 'And at number 7 we have Anders, replacing Finney.' A huge groan would go around the ground. Clearly the real reason you were never told beforehand of Finney's fitness doubt was because the attendance would have been affected, with the resultant loss of gate money. Many fans idolised him and stayed away if they knew he would not be fit to play. Preston North End is steeped in football history. Formed in 1881, becoming one of the founder members of the Football League in 1888, the team has been League and Cup double winners and has the distinction of being the oldest Football League club still playing at its original ground at 'Deepdale'.

Some cynics say that it seems as though it is still playing with the original team when results go against us!

However, the day after the Sunderland match there was something not to be missed on our flickering black-and-white telly. Appearing on *Sunday Night at the London Palladium* that night was my rock 'n' roll hero Buddy Holly, a guy whom I have always maintained would have gone on to become a true musical genius. We all sat around the telly that night as Holly treated us to three of his self-penned hit songs. *That'll be the Day*, *Oh Boy* and *Peggy Sue*. He wrote nearly all of his own music, and played a magical guitar that none of us had ever seen before, a red and white Fender Stratocaster, later adopted by the Shadows on their instrumental hits of the 1960s. The Beatles idolised him, giving

The Buddy Holly wheel cover on my N4YMR. Sister plate N3YMR was on our Chrysler Crossfire. Note a typical July day in Whitby! *Author's collection*

themselves a name similar to his group, the Crickets. Paul McCartney now owns all of Holly's music and organised the annual Buddy Holly week in London. The tribute musical *Buddy* is now the longest-running rock 'n' roll show of all time – not bad going for a kid who was only with us for 270 months.

Holly has been described as the single most influential creative force in rock 'n' roll music. I am still a member of the Buddy Holly Fan Club despite losing him in that plane crash in Iowa, North Dakota, on that snowy Monday night of 3 February 1959, together with the Big Bopper and Ritchie Valens – 'The day the music died' according

Jacqueline and myself meet Buddy's group, the Crickets, at the Southport Theatre in 1984. *Author's collection*

to the Don McLean song. I think it to be more than a coincidence that the Buddy Holly Center is actually situated in the former railroad station in his home town of Lubbock, Texas. A good friend of mine, Stevie Shields, recently visited the memorial to the three stars in Clear Lake, Iowa, and brought me back some seedlings from the cornfield crash site!

On a brighter note, what did amuse me about the pop scene at the time was the names adopted by some of the British male artists; seemingly you had to be a Steel, Fury, Tempest, Storm or Wilde to further your

music career. Every other Saturday morning in the winter it was off to the ABC cinema in town for three of us pals, as we were ABC Minors. But as we hadn't much money, only one of us usually paid to get in, then off down to the toilets he must go, to open the emergency exit door and let the other two in for a free morning's viewing of the latest cowboy or comic films.

Another ruse we had was during the film interval, when the compère invited on to the stage those whose birthday it was that week, then everybody sang 'Happy Birthday to you' and you were given a present, had your photo taken, and were given free admission to the next show. I got to liking having 'Happy Birthday' sung to me for a few weeks, before the manager spoiled it all by producing three recent 'birthday' photographs he had of me on stage. As he escorted me out by the ear I remember him jokingly telling me that I'd had more birthdays than the Queen that year.

Across the road from the ABC cinema was the Fishergate Baptist Church, and here one Monday night I saw a crowd of boys in uniform standing at the side entrance waiting to get into the church hall. I asked one of them who they were. 'The Boys Brigade,' he replied. 'Would you like me to introduce you to Mr Hughes, who is in charge?' And so began my association with the 5th Preston Company of the Brigade. I enjoyed the companionship, including the religious aspect, being a member of my local church choir. We also helped the other companies in putting on shows and displays in front of the Mayor and other Preston dignitaries, and taking part in jamborees on the local park – all now gone. Well, not quite, as I still have my leather Boys Brigade belt, not that it fits me any more. My mother used to work as a cleaner on Monday and Thursday evenings at Rainfords butchers just up the road from the church, and after the Brigade meeting I would walk up to the shop and wait outside for her, then we would walk home together via the sweet shop. Her wage was only 10 shillings a night, but I was always treated to a bar of chocolate; my sister would be at home waiting for her treat, but she would always accuse me of being mummy's pet and getting spoiled!

When I was about ten years of age my mother underwent a serious operation, and a lengthy stay in hospital ensued. My father couldn't get time off work to look after my younger sister and me, nor were there any near relatives to look after us, so we spent a few weeks in the Harris Orphanage in Garstang Road, Preston. Dad visited us most nights after his work, then he would cycle to the hospital nearby to visit Mum. I hated being away from home and parents; my only companion was Bruce the black Labrador dog that lived at the orphanage and I was allowed to take it for a walk. In truth, the dog was friendly with all the kids.

One morning in November 1961, after finishing one of my pocket-money jobs helping the local milkman at 8.30am, I set off to walk to school, which just five weeks later I was to leave at the age of 15. That morning I had decided to call in at Preston motive power depot, about half a mile from my home, to enquire about any footplate vacancies. Arriving there, I knew the layout pretty well, having sneaked in many times snatching engine numbers. I gave the foreman's door a good knock and was told to come in. He was a bit surprised to see me standing there, as I didn't have an appointment! I told him that I was looking for a job. He said that the depot would not be taking on any staff and would be closing soon because of the disastrous fire a year earlier, which had engulfed most of the wooden roof, making the whole structure unsafe. He advised me to report to Lostock Hall shed where most of the staff had transferred.

So I left it at that for a few weeks,

as Christmas was approaching, and concentrated on my unofficial part-time job on the milk round at Preston Dairies in Bow Lane, which was just around the corner from my home and down the road from my school, Christ Church. This was probably the largest private dairy in Preston. The Co-op was another large concern, but was looked upon as a rival. I worked with various milkmen over a two-year period prior to leaving school. Some of the men I remember are Frank Blow, Raymond Shaw and inspector Gordon Birtle. I also worked with a lady milk woman called Margaret; she was quite a good looker and an accomplished jazz singer, well known in the Preston area. We would often have a singsong during the morning milk round – *Big Rock Candy Mountain*, *Cindy* and *Lay Down Your Arms* were our favourites at the time. She used to sing in the

The wooden roof of Preston shed (24K) on fire in June 1960, believed to have been caused by sparks from 'Super D' No 49104. *Tony Gillette*

Railway Hotel in Butler Street adjacent to the railway station, where the landlord was jovial cockney jazz enthusiast Wally Wallen, who played base in the jazz trio. Somebody once asked him what his favourite music was and, pointing across to the till on the bar, he replied in his best cockney accent, 'The sound o' that bleedin' till bell ringing!'

The pub nearest to Preston shed was in Wellfield Road, the Ribble View Inn, but fondly referred to as 'Dirty Dicks'. It's worth mentioning that the pubs in Preston in the late 19th century totalled more than 800, with almost one on every street corner. It will come as no surprise when I tell you that the Temperance movement was begun in Preston by Mr Joseph Livesey. Some further useful information is that one Charles Dickens spent time in Preston in the 1850s when writing *Hard Times*, and that the fictitious 'Coketown' is believed to be Preston. As kids we did quite well financially from the local pub trips; we would stand outside watching the beer crates being loaded into the hold at the back of the coach, then it was the turn for the trippers to board and, as they were leaving, money would be thrown to us from the open windows of the departing coach. We would often spend this on a treat such as fish and chips bought from one of the local chippies – as with the pubs, seemingly almost every street had its local grocer's shop and a chippy.

I never seemed to be short of a few bob when I was a kid, with income from the milk job topped up by the evening paper round. One of my customers on both duties was Broadgate Cycles, where I saw a magnificent Claud Butler racing cycle in the front window. It had Reynolds 531 tubing, Campagnolo Derailleur gears, and was priced at £19 19s 11d, a lot of money in 1961. The owner of the shop saw me looking at the bike on a number of occasions, so he then came up with the suggestion that if I could raise a £10 deposit, I could pay the other £10 at 10 shillings per week, because, as he said, 'You are here in the morning with the milk and back in the evening with my *Lancashire Evening Post*, so I know you are earning enough money to pay for it.' So off I went home with a definite spring in my step to approach father with a letter from the shop outlining the proposed deal.

Now it just happened to be a few weeks away from my birthday, and the following Saturday afternoon when Dad came home from work (everybody worked a Saturday morning in those days) he said, 'Come on, John, we'll take the dog for a walk on the park.' So off we went with Susie, our corgi. Now by pure coincidence – well, I thought it was at the time – we had to pass the cycle shop on our 2-mile walk to Avenham Park. I think you can guess the rest of the story. The bike became my pride and joy and I paid it off as agreed and used it, of course, on the paper round. In fact, I kept the bike until I was 18, then sold it to my future brother-in-law for £25. I still ride a Claude Butler bike, albeit a modern hybrid of a racer and a road bike, again purchased from Broadgate Cycles, the family business now firmly established near our former home in Penwortham.

Now that I had transport, and having just left school before Christmas, I decided on a visit to Lostock Hall sheds. Incidentally, the only qualification I had upon leaving school was my Cycling Proficiency certificate – I still wear my badge. I had another for swimming 10 yards in good freestyle. But, unlike some of today's youth, I could read, write, add up, subtract, multiply, divide, and I knew where Kuala Lumpur was. Present-day kids seemingly need a calculator to add up a couple of simple sums! But what do you expect when a maths teacher friend informs me that most schools have abandoned using the proven method of maths education and no longer use the unforgettable times tables! Anyway, when I arrived at the former L&Y

depot, having being advised by my Uncle Bob to present myself there in person, I was disappointed to be told that no vacancies existed at present, but to try again in a few months.

Now, never being one to allow the grass to grow under my feet, I was encouraged by the Youth Employment Officer to obtain a trade. I managed to secure a job as an apprentice fitter and turner at Blezards Millwrights in Marsh Lane, starting my real working life on New Year's Day 1962, which coincided with a house move on the same day. My parents moved some 2 miles out of town to a brand-new council house with three bedrooms, bathroom and garden in Oldfield, Penwortham, not very far from Lostock Hall engine shed. By another quirk, the millwright's premises were adjacent to the West Coast Main Line, just 300 yards north of Preston station, so when I looked up through the windows from the machinery, which was all belt-driven from an overhead line shaft, I could see and hear the northbound steam engines just getting into their stride on the 1 in 90 climb away from the busy station. As you can imagine, seeing all this on a daily basis was just purgatory.

Lostock Hall shedmaster Harold Sedgebeer, the last steam shedmaster under British Rail. *Bill Ashcroft*

I stood it for about three weeks before taking an afternoon off to try my luck at gaining the real employment that I wanted. Well, this time I got a quick audience with the shedmaster, Mr Harold Sedgebeer. All right, I did mention that my Uncle Bob was a top-link driver at the shed and that this was my third attempt at gaining railway employment. I think by this time he was probably getting a bit fed up of listening to me, so he handed me a job application form to fill in and give to his Chief Clerk, Mr Jim Walmsley.

About a week later I got a reply requesting me to attend a medical and to report to Dr Reed, the railway doctor, on No 9 platform at Preston station. The doctor was an avid collector of railwayana, each step on the staircase of his house having attached to it a smokebox number plate from a withdrawn engine! After completing a successful examination he gave me a letter to take back to the depot. I jumped on the first Liverpool train that stopped at Lostock Hall station, riding on the footplate for the 4-mile journey after telling the driver that I had just passed a medical and was going to be a driver one day. He said, 'You'd better ride with us and see how it's done!'

2 Cleaning days: sand, phones and detonators

On Monday 5 February 1962 I started my railway career as an engine cleaner at Lostock Hall. My boss at the engineering company wished me well, as he could see my heart wasn't in that job. I did not know it at the time but I had gained employment at what would later become the very last depot to service a BR steam locomotive, No 70013 *Oliver Cromwell*, which left on Sunday night, 11 August 1968.

Originally 'the Hall' had been a dangerous level crossing, replaced in 1856 by a bridge. The booking hall was built into the bridge, and the station was constructed in 1888, followed by the engine shed in 1892. The shed was situated in a triangle bounded by the West Coast Main Line, the ex-L&Y Liverpool to Blackburn line, and a spur from Farington Junction that joined the Blackburn line and also continued on to Preston via Todd Lane Junction, renamed from Preston Junction due to passengers confusing it with Preston station, 2 miles down the line.

On my first morning of railway work at the now 70-year-old engine shed, coded 24C, I was told to read all the instructions in the notice cases regarding performing tasks around the depot. Some of it was the Offices, Shops & Railway Premises Act, which I suppose was a forerunner of the present-day Health & Safety Regulations. Also on my first working day on the railway I was approached by the ASLEF rep, Paddy. He was keen to get in first and recruit new starters, as the depot was well represented by the NUR. 'The early bird catches the worm' as they say, and Paddy duly signed me up into the ASLEF union, at the same time giving me a short lecture regarding the importance of solidarity in the event of any industrial action or strikes. The following day I was collared by Bill the pension man, promoting the Provident Mutual scheme. His opening words on only my second day at work were, 'Now, son, you need to start thinking about your retirement and pension – it's surprising how quickly

This photograph of Lostock Hall shed was taken from the top of the coal hopper on my first day at work there, 5 February 1962. *Author's collection*

This similar view was taken on my last day, 4 August 1968. The ashpits and hoist are clearly visible, and the sand pot is the brick structure between 8 and 9 roads. The Railway pub stands behind the right-hand arched bridge. *Author's collection*

it comes upon you.' There was some truth in what he said to me that day because, looking back 50 years later, time does seem to have flown by. So I did take Bill's advice and signed up to pay 5 shillings a week out of my paltry pay as an engine cleaner.

That afternoon I was photographed wearing my newly issued cap and badge, the overalls coming a few days later! I remember an elderly fitter doing a few maintenance jobs on the locos, and he asked us later if we would give him a push with his van to get it started when he had finished work. About four of us met him outside with his head under the bonnet of this ancient Bradford Jowett van. We told him to jump in and we would push. When he opened the van door there was such a flurry and commotion as half a dozen startled hens leapt on him! Apparently this was their mobile home, according to one of his fitting staff mates

who had been watching. He then told us that it was an almost daily ritual pushing old Ezra's van, but we did get half a dozen eggs between us for our efforts!

In the first year at the shed I did very little engine cleaning; most of my work was labouring, working on the coal hopper, emptying the ashpits, and working as a

My railway career begins at Lostock Hall. The coal stacks used to be here in the outside roads. The 3F tank is on shed shunt duties. *Author's collection*

fitter's mate and bar lad's mate. I became quite skilled at this and eventually could build the firebox brick arches myself. The plus side to all this non-cleaning work was that we received the adult labouring rate, earning nearly as much as booked firemen. I took every opportunity to gain footplate experience as I wanted to know as much as I could about how a steam engine worked, and what the vast array of controls did – all the levers, dials, handles, wheels and gauges. I suppose I became quite fanatical, particularly when I was unofficially allowed to operate the controls, having once bribed the preparing crew into letting me have a go. It therefore came as no surprise that before long I was given a nickname befitting my role, 'Fingers'. On the railway once you are given a nickname it usually sticks with you for life, hence at 70 years of age a lot of my former workmates still address me as 'Fingers'. But nowadays it is often 'Fletch', or Aunty Wainwright – at least, those are two of the more printable ones.

During the first 13 months prior to being passed for firing duties I spent as much time as possible gaining actual footplate experience, having befriended a number of drivers and firemen who would take me along with them on some of the late-afternoon jobs, both passenger and freight. I couldn't go during the day, of course, but after cleaning/labouring duties finished at

4.30 off I would go out on the main line, sometimes not getting back home until after midnight or later, then up and back at the shed for 8.00am. Our depot had regular work on the Preston-Southport line, so I would travel home on the footplate to my home station, which was the first on the line at Penwortham Cop Lane, or I remained on shed and helped the men on disposal duties. Here I was warmly welcomed in helping out with the arduous task of fire-cleaning, raking out ashpans and emptying smokeboxes. The plus side of all this hard graft was being allowed to drive the engine into the shed or turn it ready for its next duty All this was unofficial, of course, and only certain crews would take me on the ride-outs.

With the amalgamation of Preston and Lostock Hall sheds, the latter became extremely busy. Steam still ruled supreme and I gained valuable firing experience on most classes of locomotive, including 'Clans', 'Britannias', 5XPs, 'Scots', 'Baby Scots', 9Fs, 8Fs and 'Black 5s', as well as the shunting locos. When referring to the classes of steam locomotives, I quickly realised that the names I had for them from my trainspotting days bore no resemblance to what locomen called them. For instance, none of them knew what I was talking about when I mentioned a 'Jub' or a 'Pat' or a 'Duchess': it was a '5X', or a 'Baby Scot' or a 'Lizzie', the 'Princess' Class being called 'old Lizzies'.

Penwortham Cop Lane was my home station, seen here from the footplate of Standard Class 2 No 78040 on the 1.17pm Southport-Preston service on 6 September 1964, the day before closure of the line. *Alan Castle*

I particularly hate the name 'Jub', and do wonder when my generation is extinct whether the footplate terminology we used for some locomotives will disappear with us.

The transfer of 'Wessy' men from Preston to our 'Lanky' shed was not without its complications. Some of the men displayed open hostility, particularly when in the mess room, often exchanging poetic banter with each other such as, 'You scratch my back mate, and I'll stick a knife in yours,' 'If you kick one of them they all limp,' 'Be quiet in here – walls have ears,' 'If you Preston men lose sight of St Walburge's steeple you're asking for a conductor,' 'Aye, but none of you Lanky man will sign the Whelley route,' and so on. I could listen to their bitching all day long.

Cleaning and labouring duties did have the lighter moments, and when you put a gang of boisterous youths together some fun and games are bound to take place, so do please read on. New starters in the cleaning grade were always given a pretty torrid time; because of their innocence and inexperience they became the victims of a wide variety of pranks and initiations by the senior hands. A favourite among them was oiling up – no, not a locomotive, but the poor victim's privates. Having first been stripped of his britches, he was lubricated with thick steam oil, then a scattering of gritty sand was rubbed in. With no showering facilities at the depot, you had to clear up this fine mess in the bath at home, which would occasionally result in a

visit to the shed the following morning by the poor lad's irate mother, complaining of how long it took to clean him up, and maybe leaving him with the distinct possibility of being unable to father any children!

Mentioning gritty sand reminds me of when it would arrive on a regular basis by rail in a purpose-built 8-ton sand wagon, to keep the depot's supply topped up, sand being a very necessary item on a locomotive to assist adhesion between wheel and rail. Four cleaners were usually allotted the task of emptying the sand wagon, two of them shovelling the sand up from the wagon through the open cavity of the sand pot 6 feet above them, where the other two cleaners shovelled again up to another level above the sand furnace itself. The fire grate of this was kept alight 24 hours a day to keep the sand dry. The sand was more than 3 feet deep once the wagon was empty. The sand pot itself was on the second floor of a two-storey building; underneath was a storeroom and a mess room, unofficial sleeping quarters for the shed's three-man team of boiler-washers.

Also ensconced in this building was the bar lad, Ken, whose duties involved working in fireboxes most of the time, replacing fire bars and damaged rocking grates, building and/or repairing brick arches, and cleaning any scale off tube

The rear and side of the sand pot building at Lostock Hall, with on the extreme left a sand wagon attached to a loco. Unloading was by hand, shovelling the sand into the raised middle section. *M. D. Lloyd*

ends and firebox stays. Ken combined these exacting duties with that of bookie's runner for the shed, a most important role requiring a quick mathematical brain to be able to work out, to the nearest penny, some of the complicated betting odds and winnings. Many were the sixpence each way or shilling roll-ups left for him each day, written on the back of torn-up fag packets, wagon labels, drivers' notices or the borders of newspapers – no official betting slips, of course, as betting was illegal. Every day at 1 o'clock he would leave the shed and cycle the 5-mile round trip to the bookies in Leyland, with his leather bag containing all the punters' bets left for him by the shed staff on early and late shifts, together with a not inconsiderable amount of money. On his return journey he would bring back the winnings from the previous day's racing – but of course nobody beats the bookies, and I rarely recall Ken returning with more money than he set out with.

For the three boiler washers, Brendan, Bob and Tommy, an hour in the afternoon was siesta time while the locomotive boilers slowly filled prior to the fires being lit up again. Having completed the task of washing out the boilers during the morning, they retired to the purpose-built bunks for a lie-down on the cushions suitably borrowed from a 1st Class carriage, the heat from the sand pot furnace soon inducing slumber. However, when four noisy cleaners were on the floor above, having

completed the task of emptying the sand wagon, and looking to have a bit of fun, they made sure that the three didn't get much rest. However, aggravating them was not without its risks – all three were biggish blokes, particularly the easy-going southern Irishman Brendan, who often gave the fitting staff a lift when they were changing engine springs, carrying and lifting the spring into place! But we did have the advantage of being able to out-run the three of them if need be.

This was put to the test one afternoon when they finally snapped, after becoming fed up of listening to our noisy antics and cocky threats to sort them out, daring them to come up the stairs and take us on. It had to happen and, following a bout of bravado from us, all of a sudden the big wooden door to the sand pot was kicked off its hinges to reveal the immense bulk of Big Bob, Tommy and Brendan blocking the exit, and any light

Big Bob Dixon (*top*) and Tommy Forrest, boiler washers at Lostock Hall. *Author's collection*

behind it . We all made a frantic dash to escape through the big gap in the loading bay and leap down 6 feet into the empty sand wagon and freedom. Well, three of us just made it, and I nearly did, but my 15-year-old 10-stone body was unable to withstand a rugby-style flying tackle from the 6ft 2in 16-stone frame of spring carrier Brendan. Thankfully it was a cushioned landing in the sand! I came round to hear the three of them discussing my fate. It didn't do me any good threatening them that I was going to get my Dad to come and sort them out, because they recognised me as the one who had been doing most of the gobbing-off as usual.

'Right, Tommy – get that bloody shovel and dig a hole in the sand while I keep hold of the little bugger,' said Brendan.

When he'd finished, the pair of them sat me in the hole and shovelled until the sand buried me up to my neck, with only my head sticking out. Fortunately I was sitting down, but they compacted the sand so I couldn't move, although I could breathe. They got to the door to go out and leave me when Bob turned around, demanding to know my name. I told them John Fletcher, or 'Fingers'. They looked at each other and laughed, then came back and pushed the shovel into the sand behind my head, carefully placed my grease-top cap on top of the shaft, and in the sand in front of my almost buried body they scrawled 'HERE LIES FINGERS REST IN PEACE'. Then they cleared off and left me looking like a casualty from a spaghetti western shoot-out, with the body buried on Boot Hill.

After a while I began to get a bit worried. I couldn't hear anybody. It was not much good shouting for someone because the sand furnace was away from the main shed building, and as it was Friday afternoon it wasn't very busy. I could only guess at what time it was. It couldn't be far off finishing time at 4 o'clock. Surely somebody would come looking for me. I was beginning to get

a bit warm with all this sand on top of me on a summer afternoon. A short while later, I heard a door opening downstairs and some footsteps.

'Up here!' I shouted. 'Get me out please!'

To my relief I heard someone coming up the stairs in a pair of clogs. He walked into the sand pot and saw my head above the sand. He didn't recognise me at first until he read the epitaph written in the sand. But if there was one person I didn't want to see that afternoon it was the foreman cleaner; he was another 70-year-old fit-as-a-butcher's-dog retired driver who stayed on at work just to keep out of the wife's way.

'Get up and out of here!' he shouted.

'I can't! I'm stuck!'

'I'll bloody well get you out of there,' he said, and strode forward, grabbing hold of all my hair and pulling and pulling with both his hands. I could hardly move and it hurt like hell, so he got the shovel and eventually dug me out. To this day I blame him for premature hair loss in my 30s! He gave me a right good rollocking, and as usual threatened to tell the shedmaster, and get all us bloody useless cleaners the sack. He was actually a bit soft-hearted with us all but, if pushed, those clogs he wore came to good use and certainly hurt when coming into contact with your rear. I later found out that Bob and Tommy had gone to tell the foreman before they went home that a cleaner was up in the sand pot.

I eventually became good friends with all of them, including Ken; because of the shortage of labourers, some of us deputised and gained useful experience when working with them, helping on boiler washouts and tube-cleaning. Ken trained me to erect brick arches – no concrete arches then – and I became his regular mate on bar lad duties, combined with assisting boilersmith Freddie Craig, once I had become used to working with carbide lamps.

After about three months' service,

cleaners were issued with two pairs of overalls (bib and brace and jacket), and a locoman's grease-top cap and badge. But we can't have cleaners looking too smart and tidy, can we? So some of them fell foul of another favourite stunt. While hiding on a footplate away from the foreman cleaner, the new starters among them, one would be asked to show the others how to break up a cob of coal using the loco's pointed coal pick. He would be given the advice to look for the grain on the cob and hit it along there. This usually did the trick and split the cob, the cleaner would be congratulated on his skills, and began to feel quite confident. But what if the train went into a tunnel where it was dark? Could he do the same again? To simulate this, the poor unsuspecting lad had a scarf tied over his eyes. After having his new cap suitably removed, because it would get in the way, he was then helped into position and told to keep on hitting the cob for all he was worth until it broke up into small pieces. His cap, of course, had been neatly placed on the cob of coal and, with the pick doing its job, with each blow the cap was mutilated beyond any future use. 'How am I doing?' the cleaner would usually ask, but received no reply, of course, for his mates had crept off the footplate and disappeared into the shed for safety. Removing the blindfold and seeing the total destruction of his newly issued grease-top cap by his own hand usually left the victim bitter and twisted and feeling unbelievably stupid.

Some days on labouring duties we were sent to assist on the coal hopper, first picking up coal spillage that had dropped from over-filled tenders or bunkers. This we loaded into an empty 8-ton coal wagon. Other duties were to help the two old boys who were in charge of coaling duties. We would be attaching and detaching the capstan rope used to draw wagons on and off the lifting cradle that hoisted the wagons up some 60 feet, where the coal was tipped

into the massive bunker. About halfway through the morning it was bagging time, and we were usually allowed in the cabin with the two regular old boys who worked on hopper duties. But when they were on holiday leave for a couple of weeks they were replaced by two miserable old gits hired in from elsewhere, who would not let us into the comfy little hut with its coal fire blazing away. So we had to sit out in the open to have our food, which on a winter's day wasn't very enjoyable. But come lunchtime the two of them used to disappear to the pub for a liquid lunch. So into the cosy cabin we went, making sure we were out of it before they returned. But, as you might have guessed, one afternoon we mistimed it and they came back a bit early and told us to clear off out of there quick! The next day they put a lock on the door to keep us out.

Anyway, about mid-afternoon, when all duties were complete, it was back in the warm and cosy cabin for them, and soon the dual effects of heat and alcohol had them snoring away in the small 6-by-4-foot brick cabin, the chimney of which protruded about 3 feet through the roof. Now, to this day I can't remember whose idea it was to fill an old baked bean tin full of urine, but we then slowly emptied it down the chimney, at the same time leaning over the edge of the roof and looking through the little windows to see their reaction. It wasn't long before the aroma from their medication had its effect on their nostrils, resulting in much twitching and spitting out, especially when we emptied the entire contents of the can down the chimney, which caused a blowback on the fire, sending a fine blend of hot ash and urine everywhere. This was enough to bring them to life and they made a dash for the door and some fresh air. But yes, you've guessed it, the door had been mysteriously locked with the new padlock that they had bought to keep us out. This brought on abuse and threats of suspension, the sack, P45s, castration, etc, but after some negotiations carried out through the closed door a truce and compromise was reached. In future they agreed to let us eat our bagging in the warmth of the cabin, and we would keep our mouths shut about their lunchtime visits to the boozer.

Needless to say I did not get allocated many more labouring turns on the coal hopper until the regular old boys returned from leave! Instead I was put on the locomotive depot's two-road ashpits. The job involved working in the pits with wheelbarrows, transporting ash and tipping it through a grid into the ash plant bucket 10 feet below the pit level. When this was full, the electric winch then lifted the bucket from below ground into the air on runners, then it arched over and tipped the contents into an 8-ton steel wagon on the adjacent ashpit road. As the wagons gradually filled up, a heavy metal pinch bar was placed under the wheel sets and, after taking off the wagons' brakes, it was possible to move them into position without the use of a locomotive. A few weeks went by during which time we had become quite friendly with the two shed labourers who worked full-time on the ashpit. They were actually supposed to be in charge of us but, unlike us on regular day work, they worked shifts from 6.00am to 2.00pm or 2.00pm to 10.00pm.

During the busy summer months more locomotives were placed into traffic working holiday extras, which meant that the ashpits were in almost continuous use with engines arriving for fire-cleaning and disposal. This required extra help, but the man appointed was a senior cleaner who turned out to be a complete know-all and clever sod – worse than that, he was a bully. We hated working with him but he was a big lad and, as we would have come off the worse in a fight, something else needed to be done to bring him down to size – and I was the one chosen to do it! On the 6.00am to 2.00pm shift it

was his job to first pinch-bar the wagons into place directly under the ash tipper. So the plan was to give bully-boy a rather loud awakening when he started his 6.00am shift. This meant me cycling down to the sheds at 10.30 the night before. No one saw me creeping up to the ashpit road clutching four detonators that we had 'borrowed' from an engine that was in for a washout. These I slipped under the wheels of the first ash wagon, then cleared off sharpish back down the station platform the same way as I had come in, jumped onto my trusty Claud Butler bike hidden behind the porters' room, and off home I went.

Returning the following morning at 8.00am, our starting time for ashpit duties, there was no sign of bully-boy, but one of the other labourers met us, excitedly telling us, 'Fingers, you missed it all at 6 o'clock this morning! Some kind person had put detonators under all the wheels on the ash wagon, and when clever-arse, standing three feet away, moved them down with the pinch bar they exploded, which scared the shit out of him and he took off at top speed towards the foreman's office 300 yards away, bursting in there still clutching the 6-foot-long heavy iron pinch bar. Apparently he was as white as a sheet, shaking and couldn't speak for a good few minutes. The night staff in the foreman's office had heard the big bang, but obviously they hadn't heard it as loud as bully-boy had. They made him a cuppa and he eventually settled down. "What actually happened?" the foreman had asked him. "Some lousy twat put them there deliberately – it was no bloody accident," he said.'

Anyway, he had to go home for the day to recover. The following day when he returned he hadn't much to say for himself – perhaps he had gone deaf! The outcome of it all was that the foreman cleaner rounded up all the usual suspects and frog-marched us up to the ashpits, asking if we had seen any of them hanging about suspiciously around the ashpits. We put on our best innocent faces and shook our heads, for we were squeaky clean of course, having gone home at 4.00pm the day before the big bang, and the wagons had been moved about before we had signed on duty. Oh! Such sweet innocence!

Another little stunt that usually brought a laugh involved the telephone situated in the dust-and-muck-filled cabin adjacent to the coal hopper at footplate height. You literally stepped off the footplate and into the cabin to work the hopper and 'ring the engine on shed'. All users were instructed to use the phone when bringing their engine on shed, and it was the older type of telephone with a separate earpiece. The foreman's assistant on the other end would enter the engine details in his book. This cabin was always filthy, which accounts for nobody really noticing that the telephone earpiece had been smeared with a mixture of thick oil and black dust mixed in together by some joker. This brought many a laugh when the innocent victim walked into the mess room or foreman's lobby completely unaware of his filthy black ear, nobody telling them, of course, and off home they would go. Or it was better still if they had decided to call in for a pint on the way, standing at the bar with an ear full of muck.

Meanwhile, back in the mess room the

No 2 ash pit road at Lostock Hall, scene of the detonator incident. 'Black 5' No 44683 has its fire dropped while adjacent on the left is a 'KEEP THAT SMOKE DOWN' sign, one of many placed about the depot. *Win Wall, Strathwood Library Collection*

cleaning gang sat around their own table at break times and it wouldn't be long before some new plot was hatched to create mayhem. Our table was situated in one corner next to the huge old gas cooker where it was quite easy on the way out to slip an unopened tin of beans onto the stove, or to lift the heavy mess room door off its hinges and prop it against the frame, making it look as though it was still closed. We would then hide and await results. And didn't that heavy door hit the ground with a real bang when someone tried to push it open! The victim usually walked over the door into the mess room as if nothing had happened. A few minutes later we would reappear from one of our bolt-holes, drift off back into the mess room and settle down again looking completely innocent, the bean tin having exploded its contents over anyone within 3 feet of the cooker. I don't suppose our popularity increased when one day an old-hand driver put his weight behind the unhinged door, then kept hold of the door handle; this resulted in his appearance in the mess room with an almighty crash and with him lying full length on top of the door. Fortunately only his pride was hurt. He picked himself up, dusted himself down and asked around if anybody knew who was responsible. 'Cleaners! Who else?' came the reply. Not long after this the door was refitted with modern hinges screwed to the frame. Anyway, it was a bit of fun while it lasted.

Lostock Hall's coal hopper with the telephone cabin below. Always remember to check the earpiece! *M. D. Lloyd*

3 A foot on the learning curve!

With almost everyone at the shed working on shifts apart from the cleaners, it took a while to get to know some of the drivers and firemen – those who would actually speak to, or acknowledge, someone as low as us. Some did, and being an outgoing type I soon made a few friends among the higher ranks, often helping them to prepare their engines. I learned such a lot from these men. Some of the less agile drivers would reward me with a fag after oiling up the motion on an inside-cylinder engine, and I was soon able to name every moving part of the Walschaerts, Stephenson and Caprotti valve gears. Incidentally, I have carried on this practice into preservation as a driver on the NYMR; I nearly always allow my fireman to oil up the loco, then afterwards walk around the engine with him, asking him to point out and name all the oiling points, for how else is he going to progress without some actual practical experience? My hands-on approach has benefited many an up-and-coming fireman. Some of them had been firing for years and were due to go for their driving exam, and I find it incredible when they tell me that they have never actually oiled up and prepared a steam locomotive, and how much they have appreciated being given the opportunity.

One of the firemen at Lostock Hall with whom I became quite friendly was Colin Potter. He had started his railway career at Tebay, then after a spell at Cricklewood he transferred to our place, where he took me under his wing. Often when he was on the

Me and, Standard 2-6-4T No 80135 at Grosmont MPD – I'm not actually oiling up, just posing for the camera. *Author's collection*

evening 6.00pm Preston -Warrington fitted freight, he and driver Roy (Golly) Gorton would take me along, with Colin supervising my attempts at trying to keep enough steam and water in the 'Britannia' Class engine that regularly worked this train.

Oh! How I loved blowing that lovely melodious chime whistle at every opportunity. The loco crew often remarked that if I laid off the whistling then perhaps I would have a bit more steam showing on

'Britannia' 'Pacific' No 70029 *Shooting Star* just fits on to the turntable at Lostock Hall. The small 'ringing-out' box and Engine Shed signal box are visible in the distance. Note the Western Region lamp on the tender. *Author's collection*

the pressure gauge! The diagram for this job showed us as relieved at Warrington Arpley Sidings, then we remanned a Crewe-Preston freight as our return work. We usually had a couple of hours to kill waiting for this to make its way from Crewe and come jangling into view from the West Coast Main Line down the gradient to Arpley. If he was running a bit early it was to no benefit because the shunting staff were having their evening meal break about this time. Some of them had disappeared, having hitched a lift on the yard's shunting engine to the local pub; I say local, but it must have been three-quarters of a mile away in the direction of Bank Quay station, but that was no deterrent to those thirsty lads and I have personally witnessed nine of them crammed into the 'pub taxi', usually an ex-LMS 0-6-0 tank engine.

A nice surprise occurred one night with this return working when one of the last 'Baby Scots', No

45543 *Home Guard*, rolled up on the job from Crewe. Boy, was I looking forward to having a go with this old girl! After relieving the incoming crew we hooked off and stood in the shunting neck adjacent to the huge Manchester Ship Canal bridge while our train was re-marshalled by the now pleasantly lubricated shunting gang. Roy and Colin had left me alone on the footplate, having retired to the shunters' cabin for tea and sandwiches. This gave me the opportunity to appraise our steed, the firebox being quite a lengthy one to me. The Fowler tender was a bit off-putting, the fire irons being positioned on the tender top, half-buried in coal, and there were no side windows to the cab to keep out the weather – the later rebuilds mysteriously also lacked this facility. The rest of the footplate layout was quite familiar to engines of that period, and a working pressure of 200lb was increased to 225 on the rebuilds, with driving wheels of 6ft 9in, the same as the 5XPs. I spent the rest of the time on this warm summer evening giving the controls a good cleaning, finishing off by polishing the two *Home Guard* nameplates.

With departure time of 9.40pm now

'Baby Scot' No 45543 *Home Guard* at Lostock Hall with driver Tommy Parr and fireman Frank Finney. *Tony Gillette*

approaching, we backed down onto our re-marshalled train. The guard waved his paraffin lamp from side to side, displaying first a white then a green aspect, then a red as we buffered up. And while Colin hooked her up I started to build up the fire. Our guard asked Roy if he was all right taking a Class 6 load with our 6P5F engine ('5F' meaning Class 5 Freight).

'Go on then. After all, I have two firemen on board!' said Roy. 'But do inform Control that if we go via the Whelley line we shall need a banker.' (The 'Whelley' was the steeply graded goods route bypassing the main line through Wigan.)

Two long blasts on *Home Guard*'s ex-LNWR shriek whistle brought a response of a green light from the yard foreman, allowing us to draw forward with our freight on to the main line, up to the starting signal controlling the section from the goods to the main lines that pass through Warrington Bank Quay. It was a heavy pull and an immediate test for any engine on this first stretch of track leading up to the junction. You wouldn't be given the starter unless the junction signal was also clear – too many heavy trains had stuck on the bank, stopping the job.

We waited for a few minutes at the bottom, No 45543 biting the bit for the challenge ahead. Then Roy shouted across to us, 'We're going! We'll need to give her everything here before the really steep bit and the junction.'

He slammed on the front sanders then lifted the regulator, carefully feeling for the steam – no heavy-handedness here as we gradually took up the stretch of 43 wagon couplings, then we were on the move. It pleased us to see that No 45543 was steam-tight at the front end as she burst into song. 'One two – three four – five six, one two – three four – five six' went the three-cylinder beat from her single chimney. Roy then gave her the lot with full regulator and one

turn back on the reverser as we attacked the bank. The gradient immediately dragged us down to less than 10mph, and with the junction in sight my firing over the flap and around the box and hitting the front end was keeping the steam pressure right up on the mark. From the glare of the fire I could see how Roy was using both hands to grip the regulator in case she went into a sudden slip, then in one swift move he pushed back the reverser locking pin and wound the cut-off that last turn he'd kept in reserve.

'I've given her the lot,' Roy told us, raising his voice above the din of a steam engine working to near its capacity. I had the privilege of sticking my head out of the cab and listening to this old girl displaying her power in the twilight of her hard-working life. And I was not the only one whose attention she had attracted as we cleared the crossover and out onto the main line at a speed where you could almost count the ballast stones. Bank Quay station was just ahead of us and the engine was still working at its limit, as we still hadn't dragged the whole of the train off the gradient. Then as we approached the busy platform Roy eased her back, otherwise I think we would have lifted the roof off the place. I remember some of the waiting passengers giving us a short round of applause for the entertainment value as we headed out into the dusk and on through the suburbs of Warrington.

We stayed on the down fast to Golborne Junction, where we were switched across onto the slow line until the approach to Bamfurlong Junction. Roy whistled for banker assistance after seeing the left-hand bracket signal displaying a green to take us over the 'Whelley' line, to bypass the busy route through Wigan station. Not all drivers signed the road over this difficult route; many of them would only sign for the 'main line only' from Bamfurlong Junction, which kept them on the much easier West Coast route through to Standish. In some parts of the 'Whelley' your train could be on three different gradients, demanding thorough route knowledge on this goods-only line, particularly when working a loose-coupled freight train; this definitely sorted out the men from the boys among the drivers. Most will agree that it was a whole lot easier flying about on a passenger train with the benefit of a continuous brake than working a 500-ton loose-coupled freight job, with just the engine and the guard's brake van to control all that weight.

After a few minutes the banker came behind our 43 wagons. One class of engine ruled supreme over this railway, the former LNWR 0-8-0 'Super D' Class, sometimes jokingly referred to as a 'Wigan Scot'. We had one of Springs Branch's finest whistling up behind us, telling us that he was ready to push and heave together with us over this steeply graded line, so driver Gorton exchanged the correct whistle code with him, bringing *Home Guard* to attention and ready for action. Now all this took place some 55 years ago, but in my mind I can still hear both engines, LNWR whistles, echoing away into the dark, still night. Once on the move Colin did the firing, demonstrating his skills to me with the shovel and keeping the pressure just off the red mark. I just wish that I could have recorded those two machines giving their all. I love listening to a single-chimney, three-cylinder engine working at low speed, and what a contrast with the unique exhaust beat from our hard-working 'Super D' banker: two barks, a chuff and a wheeze meant that she was on song, as you rarely got four even beats with a 'D'. And if that did happen it usually meant that the Joy valve gear was out and the beast wouldn't steam. That wasn't a problem with our 'Baby Scot'. In fact, she lifted her valves when nearly over the line's last long gradient, where the 'Super D' said 'Goodnight' – as did the locals that I could see coming out of the adjacent Railway Hotel. (Pubs shut at 10.30

then!) Colin remarked that a nice cool pint of best bitter would have been very welcome as we breasted the summit of this diverging route, having left the banker behind.

We rejoined the West Coast Main Line at Standish Junction, coinciding with the safety valves lifting, eventually closing at the 170lb mark – only a minor handicap, otherwise the engine had given us a faultless display of power. The remainder of the run to Preston Ribble Sidings was on the slow line and once over the summit at Coppull it's downhill to Preston, so I was back on the shovel for the rest of our trip down through both Coppull and Leyland stations, the rhythmic sound of the three-cylinder motion echoing back off the buildings as we drifted down at a gentle pace in the darkness before finally arriving behind another freight on the Permissive Block-signalled down through line at Ribble Sidings. That train was soon shunted out of the way and we dropped down before hooking-off and setting sail tender first on the 2-mile run up to our depot at Lostock Hall There we coaled up *Home Guard*'s tender and left her for the disposal crew on one of the ashpit roads, our night's work over at just after midnight. I had actually been at work since 8 in the morning, but I was young and daft and foolish in those days and the only thing I looked forward to was getting back to work again the day after. Incidentally, when the foreman asked Roy if he was booking any repairs to the loco, he said he wasn't and duly completed the required 'No Known Defects' card, handing this to the running foreman before signing off duty.

1962 was to be the swansong for many of the 'Baby Scots', including No 45543, but it wasn't to be my final association with the engine, for shortly after it was withdrawn it was brought with some other members of the class to Lostock Hall shed to prepare them for their last journey to the scrapyard. This included emptying coal from the tenders, and I was involved in this work, as well as helping the fitting staff with any mechanical and lubrication work required. It was one of the fitters who handed to me a final souvenir to remind me of my involvement with *Home Guard* when he removed the engine's whistle – 'Just as a safety precaution,' as he put it.

Another fireman at the shed with whom I became quite good pals was Tony Gillette. He was a talented and versatile lad who always carried his camera with him, and you can see a lot of his handiwork in many railway publications over the years. He also played the trumpet and was a member of the National Youth Orchestra. Although English by birth, he spoke some Welsh. Latin was another of his many subjects, and to top it all he was a registered psychiatric nurse, which came in very handy working at the loco sheds. He had a very dry sense of humour, and always referred to me as 'Digits' instead of 'Fingers'. He later passed for driving and I fired for him on his very first driving turn, the story of which is referred to in a later chapter.

My first trip with him as an apprentice fireman was on a Liverpool-Skipton afternoon job; in days gone by this was a 'slip' train, which dropped coaches at the small country station of Midge Hall, the last

station from Liverpool before Lostock Hall. After slip-working ceased, the 11-coach train, usually hauled by one of Liverpool Bank Hall's 5XPs, stopped at the station, split the train and worked forward to Blackpool with six coaches. After travelling on Ivatt 'Mogul' No 46501 tender-first for the 3 miles from our shed to Midge Hall, we backed on to the remaining five. The job was still known as the Midge Hall slip train. Our loco was usually an Ivatt Class 2 or the less popular BR Standard Class 2, but either way you had to be on top of the job with plenty of hill-climbing in front of you before reaching Skipton. The train was tightly timed, with Blackburn the first stop after surmounting the 5-mile 1 in 100 climb up Hoghton Bank beyond Preston, then stopping at principal stations to Skipton.

It was a tradition with this job to get the little Class 2 warmed up before the climb ahead by giving it a good thrashing on leaving Midge Hall and trying to get it up to about 60mph when going past the shed and station at Lostock Hall, hanging on to the whistle and waving to your mates as you sped through before braking sharply for the 40mph through the junction. Then the serious bit started for the fireman, as you had an engine with a small firebox pulling its maximum load; extra care and skill was required with this combination, for just a few shovelsful placed into the wrong areas of the box could see the pressure gauge start to fall, but get it right and just listen to that little Ivatt chop them off on full regulator and 50% cut-off! This meant that you had to be able to fire against the injector all the time when working the engine as hard as this. We had at least three of these fine machines – Nos 46449, 46501 and 46452 – but when one wasn't available a Standard Class 2 deputised. Now these were not as popular with the crews, the exhaust being very muffled and restrained at the front end; they certainly didn't chop them off like the Ivatt,

Tony Gillette and myself alongside Southern 'S15' No 841 at Grosmont. *Stan Withers*

although they steamed well, again provided you fired them properly. Three of these were allocated to Lostock Hall, the now preserved No 78022 and Nos 78036 and 78037. I have since renewed my acquaintance with No 78022 on the lovely Keighley & Worth Valley Railway, footplating it again courtesy of Driver Graham Hartley ('Tiny').

Anyway, back to 1962, and we were slowing for the Blackburn stop. To use footplate terminology, we were in good nick, with our driver, the redoubtable Dick Kay, bringing us to a right-time stop in the station. Just a word or two here about Dick. He was one of the senior drivers at that time, and if there was one person who wouldn't tolerate fools it was him. Things had to be done right both on and off the footplate. Woe betide anybody, whatever rank they held, trying to cut corners where Dick was concerned. But if you were interested in doing the job properly and professionally, you had his respect. He had another side to him, his dry humour, which appealed to me, and we got on fine considering our age gap. He knew I was keen and willing and I actually became one of his regular firemen just before he retired. He appreciated you keeping the footplate clean and tidy – no coal on the floor, all the controls cleaned before we went off the shed, keeping the dirt down with the slacker pipe when running bunker- or tender-first. He rolled his own fags and, yes, I used to scrounge these off him. But he never bought any matches – he would roll a sheet of newspaper into a long taper and keep this handily placed across the injector steam valves, placing it in the fire whenever he wanted to light his fag.

If I might just digress a little here, I knew some firemen who were actually quite frightened of going with him. One of them (let's call him Mike) was marked up to fire for Dick for the duration of the summer workings. He wasn't the brightest of lads, but Dick did his best in trying to help him

improve on his firing skills. After a few weeks of extra tuition Mike felt confident enough to inform Dick that he had now developed a technique for firing the Class 2 engines. The following week they were on the same tricky Midge Hall slip job. This was always going to test Mike's new-found technique. So they set sail with a Standard 2, Dick keeping a careful eye on proceedings. But halfway up Hoghton Bank Mike was struggling to keep steam and water in the boiler and they started to lose time. The engine was having to be eased and nursed all the way to the Blackburn stop, arriving some 4 minutes late, whereupon Dick dryly asked, 'Mike, which pressure gauge are you using?'

'What do you mean?' asked Mike.

'Well, you've got more showing on the carriage heating gauge than the one for the boiler,' joked Dick.

It was the same story all the way to Skipton. Mike couldn't make it steam; time was being lost and using the fire irons didn't help. He had the pricker dart and paddle in the fire but to no avail. They finally limped into Skipton station some 12 minutes late, where Dick exclaimed, 'Mike, I am going to have the line searched from here, back to where we started from.'

'Why, whatever for?' replied a perplexed Mike.

'To see if they can find that technique you've lost between Midge Hall and here!'

So, back to my run with Tony Gillette, where he had given me the shovel for the rest of the run to Skipton. I was being extra careful with my firing in this small box. Seven or eight shovels of coal at a time in the right places, firing over the flap, kept No 46501 and, more importantly, the driver happy. I was being carefully watched by Tony. It was a pleasure to be on board one of my favourite class of engines, as we three Lancastrians crossed over the border into Yorkshire with our train, to make a punctual arrival at the market town of Skipton. Here

Tony went to hook the engine off the train, telling me to go to the front and put up the right headcode for light engine to Skipton shed. But what did I find as well as lamps on the front of the engine? The ultimate put-down, an 'L' plate, put there by Tony and Dick for my benefit before we had departed from Midge Hall! So that's why some loco crews were pointing and laughing as we passed the engine sheds at Rose Grove!

One of the Standard Class 2s that featured occasionally on the Skipton job was No 78037. This loco had been one of the casualties of the disastrous fire at Preston shed, when sparks from the chimney of 'Super D' No 49104 had ignited the wooden roof of the shed. The fire spread quickly and soon engulfed the entire roof. Men risked their lives to couple up and drag a lot of the locomotives out into the open, among them 'Black 5s', 5XPs and a 'Lizzie'. Legend has it that when it was brought to the foreman's attention that three 'Super Ds' were still

Discovered upon arrival at Skipton with Ivatt 2-6-0 No 46501, the 'L' plate had attracted much attention on our 50-mile run. *Author's collection*

inside the shed, his words were, 'Leave them in there – best end to the buggers.'

Once the fire had been extinguished, all the damaged locos were towed across into the goods yard at Maudland opposite the shed to await their fate. We visited the footplates in the evenings and I 'drove' 5XP No 45675 *Hardy* and 'Scot' No 46161 *King's Own* all the way to Glasgow and back in my imagination before being kicked out of the yard by the night watchman! Some of the locos did return to traffic following a visit to the works. Almost all the 'Ds' had been withdrawn by the time I became a fireman, but I just managed a few turns on them working the local trip jobs, or 'targets' as they were known. The engines were originally saturated, as the LNWR 'D' Class, but were later superheated, thus becoming the 'Super Ds', although other not so polite names were given to them at various depots. For instance, Carnforth men always referred to them as 'Night Fighters', possibly because of the large amount of night freights they dragged up Grayrigg and Shap at a heady 10 miles per hour.

4 Nervous Norman and schoolboy pranks

Keeping with the 'Super D' theme, my mate on a few occasions was Preston driver and gifted comic Andy. Now he could tell a tale. One that I remember was about his firing days to his regular driver at the time, whom he called Nervous Norman. He had been driving the shunts for years due to his disposition. One of his habits was double-checking everything with his fireman before he would even move the engine; nothing was done until he was assured by his fireman, including any hand signals relayed from the shunter or the guard, asking, 'Are we clear ahead?' even though he could see for himself that it was. So you get the gist of it, and can imagine the scenario that took place early one morning while preparing their 'Super D' engine inside Preston shed. Norman began to go through the ritual of double-checking everything to ensure all was correct with the preparation before leaving the shed.

'Right, Andy, have we all the fire irons on board – paddle, dart and pricker?'

'Yes, Norman – paddle, dart and pricker.'

'Then have we four spanners including the gauge glass spanner?'

'Yes, Norman, we have four spanners including the gauge class spanner.'

And so it went on to include one gauge lamp, two headlamps trimmed and filled, one firing shovel, one coal pick, one bucket, one tin of detonators examined for contents, two red flags, one oil feeder, one bottle cylinder oil, one bottle engine oil, all of which Andy duly followed the ritual and repeated every one back to Norman.

'Right then, Andy, I am satisfied that everything has been done. Take off the handbrake.'

'Handbrake taken off, Norman.'

'Then are we clear at your side, Andy, to set back out of the shed?'

'Yes, all clear at my side to set back out of the shed.'

On hearing this Norman blew the engine whistle and pulled down the regulator on the 'Super D', which immediately shot off in the forward direction, and before he could stop it the engine hit and demolished the brick wall just in front of them with the front end of the loco entirely covered in engineering bricks, debris and dust. Norman instructed Andy to go forward and inform the fitting staff what had happened, to which Andy replied, 'Going forward to tell the fitting staff what has happened, Norman, but I think they might already have an idea something's up – isn't that them running towards us now through that gap you have just made in the wall?'

What had actually happened, you might ask, to cause ultra-careful Norman to take up demolition work with his 'Super D', instead of using it to shunt the goods yard? Well, so concerned was he that Andy had got the job right, that he failed to notice that he had left the engine in forward gear and, as anybody will tell you who is familiar with the handling of 'Super Ds', you must not, you shall not, you will not give them a lung full of steam and expect to be able to bring them to a sudden stop – this was just not in their make-up. The 'Ds' had a mind of their own. They liked nothing better than a set of buffer stops to flatten, or to dive head-first into some turntable pit. God bless Peter Waterman for having the courage and determination to rescue and restore the only living example. I once told Peter what one driver had said to me about them: 'In the beginning there were steam engines – and then they built "Super Ds".'

'The culprit' and the wooden roof. 'Super D' No 49104 is seen leaving Preston shed to work No 11 Target. *R. J. Buckley*

One day, after booking on duty, our foreman cleaner, Harry Bridge, asked some of us if we would go to Carnforth shed to help them out with a shortage of engine cleaners. I didn't really fancy it, but I stuck my hand up and volunteered to go. No one else followed suit until Harry elaborated, saying that the job involved cleaning engines for the Royal Train. With that I was nearly knocked over in the rush, but in the end four of us were selected to be dispatched to Carnforth for three days the following week.

Monday morning arrived and we caught the local to Preston from Lostock Hall, then gathered ourselves on No 3 platform to await the 8.15am Windermere train, a job worked by Lostock Hall men, so we were able to scrounge a footplate ride on

each day from Preston to Carnforth. This train always carried a fair number of well-heeled schoolboys travelling to Lancaster Grammar School, some of them joining the train at the Garstang & Catterall stop. On one of the mornings, when we arrived at Carnforth and were walking past one of the non-corridor coaches of the train, we could hear someone earnestly pleading for help. However, looking through the windows the compartment looked empty, and the train was about to pull away from the station when we looked up on to the luggage rack and saw this lad up there. We told the guard to hold the train while we opened the carriage door and jumped in to see what was up. We discovered a distressed youth securely bound to the rack with his belt and tie, his schoolmates having jumped ship three stops earlier at Lancaster. We released him just as the station inspector arrived on the scene.

'The devils are always up to something,' he said, as the lad straightened himself up and, putting on his blazer, ran off to catch the next train back to Lancaster and school detention no doubt. We had a laugh about it, especially when the inspector told us that the week before they had done the same thing, but had left the lad with no clothes on, and he had to give him a blanket from the first-aid locker to cover himself until his father came to collect him some 2 hours later.

Anyway, over at the shed we worked hard on the two 'Black 5' engines. The first day we cleaned the frames and motion, then attacked the boilers the day after, finally finishing off with giving the tenders our attention. So by the end of our three-day task we had two gleaming locomotives fit for any Royal Train. It was only after we had finished the job that the foreman revealed to us that our engines were to act as stand-by locos in case of failure of the two rostered diesel locos! We were disappointed at not being told that at the beginning but, when you think about it, he knew that if he had told us that at the start we might not have had as much enthusiasm for the job. However, we parted as friends. He had actually been quite benevolent to us, treating us all to a fish and chip dinner each day at the High Street chippy. It's still there today, but yes, you've guessed it, it's now a Chinese chip shop.

Returning home to Lostock Hall each day from Carnforth we caught the afternoon Barrow-London express to Preston. The train was usually double-headed, and I waited at the south end of the Barrow platform for its arrival in the hope of a footplate ride back to Preston. The other three lads had decided to ride back home in the stock. The first day saw the train piloted by 5XP No 45671 *Prince Rupert*, the train engine being No 46107 *Argyll and Sutherland Highlander*. I quickly approached the crew of the 5XP and said the first thing that came into my head with the intention of being obliging.

'Would you like some coal knocking down mate?' I said.

'Who the hell are you?' they asked.

'I'm a passed cleaner from Preston looking for a lift back home,' I fibbed.

'Aye, just for your bloody cheek come on and get cracking in the tender,' said the driver. So that was it, in the tender I went clutching the coal pick and began bringing the coal forward as we departed from Carnforth out on to the main line.

'Keep your bloody head down, kid, and mind the bridges!' hollered the fireman.

The Lancaster stop saw me sharing a fag given to me by the crew. We whistled away to attack the climb up to Lancaster No 1, then it was back into the tender for me with the added bonus of a grandstand display of power emitted from the double chimney of *Argyll and Sutherland Highlander* less than 9 feet behind us, in contrast to our own single-chimney steed, but *Prince Rupert* was giving it everything. Oh, how privileged I was to

be in the presence of these three-cylinder machines and witnessing their daily toil! We must have been approaching Garstang when I stepped back onto the footplate from the tender, a couple of tons of coal now within the reach of the Barrow-based fireman.

'Put me a back end on, kid, for the pull out of Preston up to Coppull!' he shouted above the din.

I think he was putting me to the test and I began to regret telling him that I was passed for firing, but I had no intention of backing out as he handed me his shovel. Now, the 'back end' on a 5XP meant filling up about the first 3 feet of the firebox under the door, which I seemed to be managing at first until we hit a bad rail joint and she rolled and pitched about, throwing the tea can right off the warmer plate. But I struggled on and filled her up under the door, then lifted the flap and filled up that space, just leaving enough to fire over the top to the front end. It took about 5 minutes to pick up all the coal on the footplate that hadn't quite made it into the firebox! But very importantly, I had swept the floor and driver's corner with the brush, finally swilling down the whole footplate with the slacker pipe just as we came to a stand at the main southbound No 6 platform at Preston.

I thanked the driver and fireman, who slipped me another fag. As I was getting off the footplate he remarked, 'Thanks for your help, kid – you didn't shape too bad for a cleaner!'

So I left the two of them chuckling to each other, having obviously sussed out what my rank was. I made my way across to the L&Y side of the station and our train back to Lostock Hall, feeling quite satisfied with myself and excitedly relating my experience to the other lads – or maybe I was boring them to death all the way to Lostock Hall as we sat in the compartment of the Liverpool-bound train.

The following day it was back to normal.

All the labouring turns had been taken while we were away, so it was back to cleaning. I paired up again with my mate Don (Snowy) Harrison; while I had been away he had got his girlfriend to taper his bib and brace trousers in keeping with the fashion of tight trousers and jeans worn by the pop stars and Teddy boys of that era. Of course, later on I had to have mine altered so as not to feel 'square' and, as we knew most of the songs from the Top 10, a good singsong was in order while we worked underneath, cleaning the frames of 5XP No 45635 *Tobago*. We went through the whole repertoire, our favourites being *Runaway* by Del Shannon, *Running Scared* by Roy Orbison, the Everly Brothers' *Ebony Eyes*, as well as Gene Pitney and others.

'My, what big wheels you have!' 5XP No 45635 *Tobago* with myself and Donald (Snowy) Harrison at Lostock Hall.

During the summer seasons we had actually seen some of these stars on stage at Blackpool. We had their autographs and I had managed to persuade them to pose for a photograph with us. This was such a great time to be around in the early 1960s, because those guys could actually sing! I remember catching the last train back from Blackpool Central to Preston one Saturday night after watching and later meeting Don and Phil

Everly following their performance at the ABC Theatre. The perfect harmonies from those two brothers could pull out all your heartstrings. I had gone with a girlfriend, my sister and her boyfriend, who was a fireman at Lostock Hall. Our engine for the trip back home was 2-6-4 tank No 42436, with a Lostock Hall crew on board. The girls decided that they wanted to have a look at the engine while we lads joined the train clutching a few cans of beer. Next thing we are away – but where were the girls? Yes, you've guessed it, up on the footplate with our mates, and it was next stop Preston. Upon arrival we met the girls as they climbed down from the cab. They were a bit mucky, but in high spirits, blurting out that they had been doing a bit of the firing and driving after encouragement from the crew, who remarked that they had shaped much better than us lads would have done.

While writing about my sister's boyfriend, the time has now come to own up and plead guilty after being a little economical with the truth when a certain incident took place. One of the stupid things we used to get up to in the confines of the gloomy shed was to hide on a footplate and wait until some unsuspecting cleaner happened to be passing, then leap out, screaming, onto his back and scaring the living daylights out of him. Which is just what my sister's boyfriend did to me late one Friday afternoon. Unfortunately I overbalanced and spun round to the ground in a crumpled heap. We both heard the crack of my left ankle breaking. He panicked and cleared off, leaving me on the floor. Luckily another cleaner happened to hear my howling and brought the foreman out of his office.

His first words were, 'What have you pillocks been up to now?'

'He fell getting off that engine there,' said my saviour, a lad named Austin, pointing to No 47413.

'Are you a witness?' asked the foreman.

I gave Austin an anxious look. 'Yes, yes, I saw everything,' he said. 'He fell off the steps.'

'Right then, go and fetch Billy the first-aid man – he's in the fitting shop.'

A few minutes later Billy appeared. 'What's up, son?'

But before I could answer, the foreman told him that I had fallen off an engine and gone over on my ankle. Billy took off my boot and, seeing the swelling and realising the pain I was in, decided to take me to the hospital himself rather than go to the trouble of calling an ambulance. He helped me outside and into his car. Away we went at top speed to cover the 6 miles to Preston Royal Infirmary. I say 'at speed' because Billy's 'car' was a Reliant Robin, which we called a 'Rubber Duck', or a 'Three-Pin Plug'.

Billy stayed with me while my ankle was plastered, afterwards taking me home that night. My Dad had no idea what had happened and had just assumed that I had cleared off on another ride out on an engine.

We both thanked Billy; he was the sort who would do anything for anybody, a credit to mankind, and spent a lot of his spare time as manager/trainer of the Preston MPD football team. I subsequently had to fill in an accident form and spent six weeks off work in January and February 1963, but looking on the bright side I missed most of that winter's atrocious weather. So now you know the truth about that afternoon, but please keep quiet about it or it might go on my railway record!

While I was off work my father collected my sickness benefit each week from the shed on a Friday. When I could manage without my crutches I would go myself, but quickly realised just how dirty a steam locomotive depot was in those days. I would go there in my 'civvies', walk through the shed entrance then down No 1 road to the stores window to be given my brass pay check, No 287 (which I still have), and proceed to the clerk's office window hatch, hand in my pay check, and draw my wages contained in a half-slotted small round tin. The sum had been calculated manually and was usually correct to the last penny. Coming out, I put the empty tin in the basket and made my way out of the depot. The point I am making is that I walked for about 200 yards and never went near any steam engines, yet my hands and my jacket were mucky!

Going back to Bill's 'Rubber Duck', this car came to rather a sad end. He regularly

My 'accident' report form. *Author's collection*

used to park it adjacent to the fitting shop in a corner out of the way of all vehicular traffic, but unfortunately not out of the way of railway traffic, as it turned out one Sunday morning. 'What happened was…' as that Cornish comedian always says. On Sunday the shed yard was always busy with dead engines being shunted out and put in the correct position ready for lighting them up again for Monday morning. It was not unusual for the shed pilot engine to have three or four engines in tow, dispatching them down various roads. On this particular Sunday the shed shunt driver had recently transferred to Lostock Hall, so was perhaps a little unfamiliar with the length of the shed roads. Anyhow, he was propelling three engines into the shed down No 2 road, which comfortably held two engines under cover. But due to a mix-up with his fireman,

who was on the ground guiding him in, when he shouted 'Right!' the driver, being three engine lengths away, didn't hear him and carried on. The first loco overrode the safety rail and demolished the shed entrance wall, resulting in the bricks landing on Billy's 'Three Pin Plug', and a new radiator that had just been delivered for use on one of the shed's 170hp diesels. Such was the force of this heavy impact on the car that the plastic body was shorn off, but amazingly, once all the debris was cleared off, Billy jumped into the chassis and it started first time. Fortunately no one was hurt that morning apart from Billy's pride. The gap was not rebuilt until long after steam had finished at the shed, making it a pretty draughty area in which to work.

Quite a few of the staff owned three-wheeler cars, as they could be legally driven without a full car licence, provided you had passed your test on a motorbike, so Reliants were popular. Better still, why not prove an allegiance to your home town and drive a Preston-built three-wheeler, the Bond Mini. This had been designed by Laurie Bond and constructed at a factory in the town (which is now a city, by the way). The firm later manufactured the Bond Equip and the now much-sought-after Bond Bug.

I suppose I should elaborate and tell you more about my boss, Mr Harold Sedgebeer, the shed master during my time at the depot. His very name should give you a clue that he was not a fellow Lancastrian, but was actually what we call someone from his part of the world, a 'Worzel', having served his apprenticeship at Highbridge works on the famous Somerset & Dorset Railway. In a nutshell he had a job understanding our Lancashire dialect, just as much as we had with his Somerset burr. I would describe him as being more of a mechanical man than someone who enjoyed being surrounded by paperwork. He left most of this to be dealt with by our ever-patient Chief Clerk Jim

My mounted L&YR brass pay check, No 287.
Author's collection

Walmsley.

Looking back to my memories of Harold (Good God, I wouldn't dare call him by his first name in those days!), his real pleasure in life was when his pride and joy, the Lostock Hall breakdown train, was called into action under his supervision to attend some incident. Many times I have been fortunate enough to witness his skilful judgement when in charge of some tricky situation clearing up the mess after a serious collision or derailment, such as the runaway at Windermere, or the overnight sleeping car express at Hest bank, which took days to clear up. But at the end of the operation the tradition was always drinks on Mr Sedgebeer down at the local Railway Hotel bar. He was actually the very last serving shed master from the steam age, for his retirement coincided with the ending of steam at Lostock Hall, which became the very last steam depot to service and turn off a steam locomotive on 11 August 1968.

I did actually get to know him a little better after he retired, as he took up another responsible job as a 'lollipop man' in his home village of New Longton, just a couple of miles from my home. I would stop and have a brief chat with him. I don't think he knew my name, as I was just another fireman who had worked at the shed. I do regret not knowing at the time that he had served his apprenticeship at Highbridge locomotive works, on my all-time favourite railway, the Somerset & Dorset. It was years later when I found this out. How I could have quizzed him for his knowledge and experience working in that environment! I did once remind him of an incident that took place shortly before he retired when the shed was visited by ex-GWR 'Castle' Class No 7029 *Clun Castle* prior to working a railtour in October 1967 over Shap to Carlisle, then back via the Midland. Harold met the loco upon arrival at our shed and immediately insisted on both sets of name and number plates being removed for security purposes, and the placing of these in his office overnight for safe keeping. This was a wise precaution because the shed seemed to have been plagued by some naughty lads removing items as mementos, or selling them to railway enthusiasts. And, what with a nickname like mine, I didn't come under suspicion – honestly!

I will finish on a funny story involving Mr Sedgebeer and a well-known fireman at the shed. The background to the story is that

In October 1967, No 7029 *Clun Castle* heads north from Preston with an LCGB special from Liverpool to Carlisle with a 10D crew, driver Peter Norris and fireman John Roach. This picture provides a good view of the Pitt Street wall and the signal gantry. *Jack Hodgkinson*

during the latter days of steam working the authorities became very keen on clamping down on footplate crews who allowed their engines to emit black smoke, particularly in built-up areas or the confines of stations and loco sheds. Large notices were erected displaying 'KEEP THE SMOKE DOWN' or 'WATCH THAT SMOKE'. They even went to the extent of appointing staff who had some knowledge of the workings of the steam locomotive to assess the severity of the emissions and, if justified, to warn persistent offenders of disciplinary action. In reality these little Hitlers tended to overstep their authority. They would hide behind station hoardings or pillars, just keeping out of sight and waiting for the chance to pounce, should some poor sod of a fireman have the misfortune to put a few shovels of coal in the wrong place in the firebox and make a bit of smoke. Speaking as a fireman, if you were leaving Preston with a heavy train heading north or south you were faced with some hard labour on the shovel, so you had to be prepared, and that meant building up a good fire beforehand. Anyhow, I digress a little.

Having got that off my chest, it's back to the warning boards, all eight of them, erected on lamp posts, telegraph poles, buildings, etc, throughout our depot, including one right outside Harold's front office. His office was situated about 20 yards from No 1 shed road, and standing there one day more or less outside Harold's front door was loco No 42815, a 2-6-0 Horwich 'Crab'. The fire had been lit a few hours previously and it was just about beginning to make some steam, being due off the shed in about 3 hours. However, due to an engine failure No 42815 was needed urgently, so fireman Tom climbed aboard. Now, Tom was not the brightest of lads – we all used to say that the only useful purpose of his head was that it kept his ears apart. He first spread the fire, followed by a good helping of Yorkshire coal

all over the firebox, then he opened the front damper, put on the blower (but this was ineffective due to the lack of steam), and to finish off his efforts in blackening out the entire village he then closed the firehole doors and plonked himself in the fireman's seat, making even more smoke from the fag in his mouth, while awaiting the results of his steam-raising skills. You only have to imagine just what was trickling out of the chimney – dense acrid choking smoke, forming itself into a thick layer covering the entire front of the shed building and office. I think Harold did very well to stick it out for about 5 minutes before fighting his way out of the office with a handkerchief covering his nose and mouth.

He felt his way along to the barely visible cabside of No 42815, looked up and could just make out fireman Tom leaning out of the cab with the fag in his hand. 'Hey! You, fireman – what the hell are you playing at? I have been near to passing out in my office with all this damn smoke. What about all these signs we've had put up?'

Tommy instantly earned himself a Form 1 disciplinary with his reply of, 'I'm sorry, Sir, but I can't see them for all this smoke!'

Some of the staff, including Mr Sedgebeer, used to come to work on motorbikes, and these bikers would sometimes gather in the bike shed for a good natter regarding the capabilities of their various machines and, just as important, the riders. I recall seeing BSA Road Rockets, AJSs, Triumphs, Nortons, Velocettes and the two-strokes. The guy who owned the Road Rocket was a bit of a daredevil. The entrance to the shed was in a dip between two hump-backed bridges, and people swear that they saw him going so fast that he went from one bridge to the other with his bike, never touching the dip in between!

5 Widening horizons

One of the firemen, Brian, owned a Sunbeam with a sidecar. He took me for a spin in it one day and we became mates. I spent an enjoyable week riding out with him and his driver, the previously mentioned ASLEF rep Paddy, on the afternoon 4.48 Preston-Southport train with engine No 42298 and me on board as apprentice fireman. We returned from Southport with the 7.13pm train. This was very handy for me as the last stop before Preston was my home station at Penwortham Cop Lane, and I would leave the train there to walk the half-mile to my home. On the Friday of that week Brian asked me what I was doing the next day. He told me that he was going to Minehead. Oh great, I thought – that will be some firing turn, going all that way. No, he explained, he had booked a holiday at the newly opened Butlin's camp with his wife and their four kids, and his plan was to take down all his luggage by train the previous Saturday. He invited me to go with him to keep him company on the lengthy round trip.

I did want to go with him, but there was one problem. As a cleaner you were not really entitled to free passes. This meant a visit to the office and a request for a pass to be issued by Chief Clerk Jim Walmsley. It was going to be tricky, but I felt slightly confident as I wasn't entirely unknown to Jim; a few weeks previously I had been called upon to deputise for the office cleaner for a week. This had involved a 6.00am start, clearing and relighting the office fire,

then the fire in the shed master's office, some dusting down, window cleaning, floor mopping, etc. It all had to be done by 9.00am when the four office staff arrived. Incidentally, one of the office staff who dealt with the issuing of disciplinary forms, or Form 1s, was a lady named Martha. A popular song doing the rounds at that time was Adam Faith's *A Message To Martha*, and anyone having the misfortune to be issued with an 'explanation' form could expect to be serenaded with this song by their mates. I might just mention that, before starting the office cleaning job, I was lectured about using my discretion regarding any personal files or paperwork that might be on view. (I have always been able to keep any secret – it's those that I tell them to who can't keep their mouths shut, as the old joke goes.)

Anyway, I just managed to catch Jim before he left for home and he readily agreed to my request, as it was railway-related, and duly gave me the free pass to travel from Preston to Minehead and return. When I told Brian he was naturally pleased and we agreed to meet at Preston station to get the early train to Birmingham.

'But don't forget to bring your overalls tomorrow,' he said as I jumped down from the footplate at Cop Lane. This set me thinking as I walked home from the station. Why would I want my overalls when we would be travelling down 'on the cushions'?

A dry and sunny Saturday greeted us at Preston station as we made our way down the slope to the main southbound platform, No

This is the 'Lanky' side of Preston station, with the bay platforms and through roads in view. A car park and shopping mall later replaced all of this. *Author's collection*

6, at this 13-platform station, carrying with us the six large suitcases packed by Brian's missus. It seemed as though she had packed everything they owned, and I wondered just what they had left at home to wear.

'I've booked our seats right through to Taunton – we're in the front coach to Birmingham,' Brian said to me as we waited opposite where we knew our coach would be upon arrival of the Glasgow-Birmingham express. The train soon rolled into the station behind rebuilt 'Royal Scot' No 46125 *3rd Carabinier* of Crewe North, coming to a stand with the tender opposite the water column. Brian opened the carriage door, saying, 'Take all the cases in – I'll be back in a minute.'

He returned to find that I had loaded all the suitcases into the empty compartment, and said, 'Be quick and get your overalls on. I've had a word with the driver and you're up front till they come off at Crewe.'

This was an unexpected surprise, so overalls on and out onto the platform I went. The crew still had the bag in, taking water. The driver said to me, 'Your mate said you're a dab hand at bringing the coal forward, so off you go up into the tender.'

Climbing on board No 46125, I looked back along the lengthy Platform 6 but couldn't see the end of the train. Hell, I thought, how many have we got on? When I saw what was left of the coal in the tender it soon made me realise that this engine and crew had been working hard from Glasgow. They joined me a couple of minutes later and I noticed that the fire had been built up ready for the 15-mile climb ahead of us to Coppull.

'Keep bringing the coal forward, kid,' the fireman instructed me in his deep Glaswegian accent as we departed from Preston. 'We've 15 on, and are next stop Crewe. We need to bring forward what's left of the coal to see us through to Crewe where the engine comes off.'

And that's how it was with No 46125 working almost to its capacity, me bringing the coal forward and Jock skilfully shovelling it around the lengthy firebox until in what seemed no time at all we had gone through Wigan, then Warrington, and climbed up over the Ship Canal. I then deemed it advisable to clamber out of the tender onto the rolling footplate.

'Take ma seat, kid, and here's a fag for ye.'

I looked at Jock – how I admired his strength and skills. It's a long way from Glasgow to Crewe, and the tender was now almost devoid of its 8 tons of coal.

'Do you wanna work the scoop, kid? We are gannin near the troughs at Moore. I'll tell ye when to dip, my wee bonny lad – we only need about 2,000 gallons, so we'll dip about halfway along the troughs.'

I wound the scoop down, watching the tender water gauge rise rapidly. I was ready to pull her out when we reached the end of the troughs, so it required little effort to bring the scoop up, not having to fight the water pressure. Jock had judged it perfectly – he now had a total of 3,000 gallons on board.

'Go on, cleaner boy, give her the last rites,' said Jock, passing me his prized firing shovel. 'She'll need about another 40 around the box and under the door to get us to Crewe.'

I must admit that my limited experience of firing a long-box engine, particularly at around the 80mph mark, did mean a few shovelsful going astray. When I had finished I looked at Jock, who gave me some professional advice. 'Always remember this – the only way you will learn this job is by actually doing it yourself. You can watch someone else doing it, you can sit in a classroom learning about it, you can read books about it, you can listen to others telling you how to do it, but the only real way that you will learn is when someone puts the shovel in your hand, or lets you have hold of the regulator.'

I thanked him for that and have tried to remember his words throughout my footplate life.

The Crewe North signalman ran us down the long Platform 1 and journey's end for our Polmadie men, and a return back home for No 46125. Quick handshakes all round, then I hot-footed back to the coach, but Brian barred my way into the compartment

'You can't come in here with all that muck on you. Take a look in the mirror!'

Goodness! My face was as black as a smokebox door. So off with the overalls and into the toilet for a hosing down. Three face-washes later I emerged to be greeted by Brian holding out a bacon and egg butty he had brought from the buffet car.

'Bet you enjoyed that!' he said as we got on the move out of Crewe for the next leg to Stafford and Birmingham New Street with a fresh engine and crew up front.

'I missed the engine change – what's on the front?' I asked.

'You have to guess – listen to it and tell me,' he replied.

Being in the front coach you could hear the exhaust loud and clear. 'It's another "Scot",' I told him.

'You're nearly right,' he said.

'Well, if it's not a "Scot" then it's got to be a "Baby Scot" with that beat,' was my reply.

'Go on, I'll let you off then – we've got 5534. Do you know it's name?'

'Me? Yes of course I do – it's *E. Tootal Broadhurst*.'

'You are definitely a railway billy,' laughed Brian, which was footplate jargon for a trainspotter. Also, I have not wrongly written the engine number – locomen invariably dropped the '4' London Midland Region prefix, as the vast majority of loco numbers we worked on had numbers beginning with a 4.

I am ashamed to admit this, but I was fast asleep before Stafford, and it was only the jolt of the Birmingham New Street stop that woke me. There was a quick change of trains here for us and the cases; fortunately our onward train was arriving on an adjacent platform. This soon filled with passengers, including our compartment. We had three young ladies for company to Taunton, and I must say that I did fancy one of them: I kept giving her the eye, hoping she might respond, but to no avail. Brian saw what was going on and whispered to me, 'Have another look at yourself in the mirror.' Oh dear! No wonder I got the cold shoulder, for my face was still dirty, both my eyes were still black from the effects of an hour's graft amongst the coal dust of a steam engine tender. We had a further engine change at Bristol, a box on wheels taking us forward to Taunton. I think it was a 'Warship' diesel-hydraulic, but I couldn't be bothered to record the number.

We changed trains again at Taunton and lugged the cases over to the Minehead bay platform, where waiting to take us forward was 'Large Prairie' tank No 6113, which brought us into Minehead in the late afternoon. We borrowed two of the station barrows and made a dash for the nearby camp. Following a check-in at the reception, we dashed back to the station in time to board the same train that had brought us from Taunton, and Brian repeated his request for me to have a footplate ride, this time with the Taunton crew. I just had time to get the overalls on before we set sail, and upon chatting to the driver I remarked that his accent reminded me of my shed master at Lostock Hall, Mr Harold Sedgebeer. He was quite taken aback when I told him that Harold was from this part of the world and had served his time at Highbridge Works. I was soon offered the shovel for a stint at firing the 'Prairie'. Fortunately I could fire reasonably well either left- or right-handed. Although this was my first attempt at firing a Western engine, I was able to manage this lightly loaded train ambling along the single line through the lush and beautiful Somerset countryside on this early summer evening. The novelty of having two whistles on the engine and the working of the vacuum pump, not needing the ejectors, intrigued me. All too soon we were gliding into Taunton station, where I thanked the crew and said my goodbyes. I wasn't to know it then, but this wouldn't be the last time I would fire steam on the Taunton-Minehead line.

As we waited on the platform at Taunton we watched the 'Prairie' tank shunt its train and amble across to its home shed for disposal. We hadn't long to wait before our connecting train drifted in behind No 5094 *Tretower Castle*. This time I didn't wait for Brian to go up and ask – I told the crew that I was a fireman from Preston who loved Western engines and was there any chance of a ride to Bristol? I would work my passage. As the guard was now blowing his whistle for departure and I was already on the top step of the engine, the driver just nodded his head to come aboard. The fireman put me on his seat as we headed out of Taunton on this strange steed. My initial thoughts were just how primitive and dated things appeared to be – for instance, there was only one boiler gauge frame. I had noticed this on the 'Prairie' but assumed that the express engine would have two gauges. There were no doors or safety chains between engine and tender. Footplate promotion must have been quite rapid on the Western! The fireman's coat was hanging behind the front cab window, partially obscuring the view ahead, instead of being stowed in the locker, and he was picking coal up off the floor, the tender itself having no shovelling plate. I was sitting on what felt like a splintered piece of 3-by-2 timber – no comfort here for the fireman! If you put your head out of the spartan cab there was no side window spectacle plate to protect you from the slipstream. The tender was hardly self trimming, and my offer to bring some coal forward was readily accepted by our fireman. I was able to look

Lostock Hall cleaners trainspotting at Cricklewood, London. From the left, they are Melvin Rigby, Joseph Booth, Dennis Chatwin, Eric Ashton and apprentice fitter Peter Whelan. *Author's collection*

his pipe and jokingly remarked, 'You won't have many of these at Preston, will you, boy?'

I left them and thought to myself that I wouldn't mind having another go on one of these machines; a bit primitive it might have been, but it certainly seemed up to the job. But some 42 years were to pass before I would get the opportunity to fire a four-cylinder Western engine on the main line out of Bristol.

We finally arrived back home at Preston

back and count a 12-coach train on our tail, which was proving to be no trouble at all to our steed, and she was certainly riding well enough.

When I came back down out of the tender the fireman was having a minute enjoying a fag. I pointed to his shovel.

'Be my guest!' he shouted above the usual footplate din common when running at speed. I had watched him carefully and copied his technique, keeping a good back end and not neglecting the middle of the fire and filling up the front as required. He must have been reasonably satisfied at my attempts, encouraging me to carry on while he attended to the injectors and coal trimming. All too soon I felt a tap on my shoulder to tell me, 'That's enough mate – she's coming off at Bristol, so let the fire run down.'

What a shame – I was just beginning to enjoy myself! The magnificent Brunel masterpiece of Temple Meads station was also our changing point, so I exchanged a quick handshake with the driver, who hadn't spoke a word to me until now. He removed

in the early hours of Sunday morning, a bit tired and weary, but I had plenty to tell my mates at the shed on Monday. Brian stayed with steam until 1968, when I believe he emigrated to Australia.

As 1962 progressed plenty of other young lads started as engine cleaners. Some of them shared my enthusiasm for the railways and we soon made friends and began travelling around the country visiting other engine sheds and main-line stations. The regular gang was Dennis Chatwyn, Eric Ashton, Joe Booth, Melvin Rigby, apprentice fitter Peter Whelan, and me.

We made London our destination on a number of occasions. We did King's Cross, Old Oak Common, Nine Elms, Stewarts Lane and Paddington and Waterloo stations all in the day. Just occasionally another pal and I would set off late on a Friday night with our overalls and grease-top caps packed up in our bags and travel on an overnight train to anywhere it took us. One weekend we did all the sheds in the Midlands, then spent the whole of the Sunday on Wolverhampton Low Level station photographing Western locomotives with my newly acquired Halina Pet camera, bought from the chemist's shop in Lostock Hall.

The Great Western pub at Low Level was the venue for lunch, just as it was to be some 50 years later when I visited it in 2013 with my Birmingham-based train driver son. The track has long since gone from the station itself, but a lot of the buildings have been preserved, including the Great Western pub with its choice of some excellent real ales, including the magnificent Bathams bitter, which was so nice it was a shame to drink it! With a coal fire in the hearth, a great display of railwayana and excellent food, this pub is not surprisingly a regular gathering place for steam railwaymen and enthusiasts from all over the country.

A few weeks after that trip I decided that Bristol must be worth a visit following my brief stop there en route to Minehead. So it was decided to take an overnight train to London, then the first one out of Paddington down to Bristol. We fell asleep for most of this second leg and woke up just as we were approaching Bath, where we made a snap decision to bail out and take a look around. After a couple of hours observing engines sporting only four numbers, we were looking to move on when Roy, my companion for the trip, pointed out on our railway map that another station existed in Bath. So, after being given some directions by a friendly station inspector, we made our way across town to arrive at Bath Green Park station some 15 minutes later, in the early afternoon. The gloomy, two-platform station initially left us feeling slightly disappointed, but a visit to the nearby engine shed soon restored our enthusiasm and, being in railway uniform, we had no problems in wandering around the place after a brief chat with the shed foreman. We footplated some of the locos in the shed, including one of its S&D

2-8-0 freight locos, the crew telling us that the engine would be working a passenger train to Bournemouth and back.

'How far is that from here?' I asked.

'About a 150-mile round trip,' he said.

I thought he was kidding me! I could not imagine a 2-8-0 freight engine working that distance with an express passenger train.

'When are you going off shed?' I enquired.

'After that engine hooks on to the front of us,' he said, pointing to a Midland Class 2 on the next road. 'Fancy a ride down to Evercreech Junction, do you?'

And to this day I regret not taking him up on his offer, for we could not have got back home had we gone with them – but we did see them depart from Green Park station, with me still in doubt that Bournemouth and back with a goods engine could be possible. At a later date I did of course become aware of the outstanding capabilities of these locomotives in hauling long heavy trains over the steeply graded Mendip Hills. Perhaps that was where my love for the Somerset & Dorset Railway began. Twice I have walked the entire length of the line and, thanks to Sustrans and others, it is now possible to walk or cycle on the tarmac surface from the outskirts of Bath to Midford via Devonshire and Combe Down tunnels, both of which are illuminated throughout. I have also been a member of the Somerset & Dorset Railway Society for many years and have reopened the long-closed Edington Junction to Bridgwater branch, albeit via my O-gauge garden railway, helping to keep alive the unique character and charm of this most sadly missed 'railwayman's railway'. Nor did I neglect the railways of North Yorkshire when, together with modelling colleague and railway artist Stuart Rowell Hudson, we had our OO-gauge model of 'Sandsend' featured in that esteemed journal *Railway Modeller*.

6 Firing days

18 March 1963 is a very significant date in my life, for on that day I was passed for firing duties by the footplate inspector after attending the firing school, at the end of which I was given a practical exam on a freight to Heysham Harbour. I had met the inspector at Preston station and he informed me that my firing exam would be on the next northbound freight, and what turned up on the job was only a Midland 4F with a full load behind the tender! Fortunately the driver was an old hand, and experienced in the handling of these temperamental machines.

So here I was at 16 years of age, faced with keeping this ancient piece of kit hot enough to pull its maximum load without causing any delay along the busy West Coast Main Line. OK, so I probably did have about 50 unofficial firing turns under my belt by this time; that was experience, but not with one of these machines, which I had never fired before. I was glad of the advice given by the driver, who passed on to me the golden rule when firing a 'Derby 4', not to over-fire the front end of the box or there would be trouble ahead. Another plus factor for me was that even at this early stage of my career I could handle the shovel, having been taught by some of the top firemen at the shed. Looking back on my exam all these years later, I probably did make a few errors, but we got there to time with enough steam and water, then worked another freight from Heysham to Carnforth, leaving the engine on the shed there. The inspector must have seen enough and, following my rules exam later in the afternoon, he informed me that I was now a passed cleaner available for firing duties.

I think it is worth a mention that during the

A prized possession, my hard-earned BR firing certificate, signed by shedmaster Mr Sedgebeer on 18 March 1963. *Author's collection* previous few weeks that we had spent with the inspector at the firing school, he related to us details of numerous incidents involving train safety, including the report into the Harrow crash that had happened a decade earlier. I had a particular interest in this as a relation of a friend of mine was one of those killed when the Liverpool express mounted the platform. Our inspector was involved with some of the clearing-up work, and one of the points he made was how the British ambulance and emergency services lacked much of the advanced facilities of their American counterparts, who had been called in from their base nearby to assist with the rescue work; our ambulances were basically just large vans with a couple of stretchers inside. This terrible disaster led to a complete overhaul of our emergency services and their responses to a major incident. Finally, I always remember him mentioning a black American nurse who had worked alongside our own angels of mercy. She had the unforgettable name of Abbie Sweetwine, and had worked tirelessly in saving many of the seriously injured.

So now that I was passed for firing I began to get a foothold up the promotional ladder, and didn't really do any cleaning/labouring duties from that date. My first firing turn was with Driver Ernie Heyes, moving engines about the shed and disposing of about three of them. Ernie, who passed away in 2010, has his place in railway history as the driver of the last BR steam-hauled passenger train on the night of 3 August 1968, working the Glasgow-Liverpool express forward from Preston with 'Black 5' No 45318. The rest of my first week firing for him was a 4.00am engine preparation turn, which involved getting six engines ready. I found this work to be harder than the 4.00am disposal turn, due to the fact that you spent most of the time looking for tools, fire irons, shovels, coal picks, etc, to equip the engines – it was a case of robbing Peter to equip Paul! The

system did eventually alter and was much better when it became compulsory that, after disposal duties and before shedding the engine, all spanners, detonators, gauge lamps, etc, were to be put into the engine bucket, and taken into the stores together with engine lamps, coal pick and the firing shovel, with the engine number chalked on the back of same.

The standard of loco preparation could vary greatly; it was not unknown for engine oiling to consist of little more than pouring oil over the corks, or throwing a little ash under the smokebox door to make it look as though the smokebox had been emptied of ash. The height of laziness with some firemen when watering tank engines was when they could not be bothered to climb up to throw out the bag when the tank was full, preferring to move the engine forward or back and let the bag drop out; this was always a bit risky as the bag might become jammed, and then what happened if you didn't stop the engine in time? That's right, you pulled the entire water column down, and that is exactly what did happen on one occasion.

Remaining with the theme of 'owt for the easiest', the depot operated a three-shift shed shunt turn, whereby a driver and fireman would be responsible for locos being shedded in the right order for departure or repairs, boiler washout, etc. Lostock Hall was an 11-road engine shed, eight inside and three outside, and a full 70-foot turntable. So, as you can imagine, we were kept quite busy, particularly on the day shift. Movement of engines was almost constant, and if one had been stationary in steam for a few days extra care was needed when first moving it to ensure that the cylinder drain cocks remained open to clear excess steam or water from the cylinders. This was not always done, as was the case with No 45730 *Ocean*. The driver, or in this instance the fireman, closed the drain cocks too soon, resulting in a damaged right cylinder and a badly bent connecting rod. This engine spending many weeks standing inside No 1 road awaiting a visit to the works. Every steam depot had a small number of staff who always seem to be involved in some misdemeanours, but the majority of footplatemen at Lostock Hall were dedicated and conscientious staff.

The next week I was sent on loan to Preston as fireman on the station shunts. Preston was a former LNWR depot with different working methods from those at our ex-L&Y shed. For instance, the senior passed firemen at Preston acted as firemen on all the shunt and trip jobs, so if they were required for driving duties the turn could be covered by a relatively inexperienced passed cleaner or fireman. Another difference was regarding engine disposal; ex-LNWR depots employed men as fire-droppers, whereas on the 'Lanky' we dropped our own fires. Our engine for the week on the south-end station shunt was No 47472, unofficially named *City of Preston*. This loco was a bit of a rarity in its class, having been built with a screw reverser

and steam heating facilities for passenger working, similar to members of the class built exclusively for the Somerset & Dorset Railway. Actually one of these S&D engines, No 47314, came to Lostock Hall to work out its last days, although I cannot recall ever being on it.

Now, as a rule it was usually me setting someone up for a laugh or a prank, but that week I became the victim of one. It happened thus. When I looked on the roster to see who my driver was for the week I did not recognise his name, so I asked another Preston driver just who my mate was.

'You've got old Isaiah as your driver. He's not a bad old stick,' he told me.

'Oh, right, thanks for that,' I replied.

So early on Monday morning, as I climbed up the steps onto the dimly lit footplate of our engine at Preston station, I could just see him in the corner of the cab, so I politely said, 'Morning, Isaiah – I am your fireman for the week.'

Well, he flew into an immediate rage at me. 'Who the hell told you to call me that?

0-6-0T No 47472, fitted with a screw reverser, stands on No 9 road at its home depot of Lostock Hall. This engine was a regular on station pilot duties for some years at Preston, and was unofficially named *City of Preston. I. Vaughan*

My name is Sid, or Sidney to you, and don't you bloody well forget that.'

I went over to apologise to him, and it was only then that I got a proper look at him, and quickly realised why they called him Isaiah. He had a terrible squint, and one eye was definitely higher than the other!

'And just remember another bloody thing, son,' he continued. 'In our day it was a case of wooden seats and iron men. With you cheeky devils today, it's the other way around.'

As the week went by he simmered down to normal working pressure, and said to me on the Thursday, 'Right, son, you've seen the moves and know what time we do them. Get over to this side and let me see how you shape.'

I must have put his mind at rest with my engine handling, for on the Friday (payday) he spent half the shift with a couple of his mates having a drink in the refreshment room, keeping his good eye on me as I passed up and down the station piecing up trains, adding a van or a coach, with the shunter on board acting as my fireman. I think what gave me the greatest feeling was that he was trusting me to do the job, and no way on earth was I going to let him down.

My one regret regarding the timing of the closure of Preston shed was the withdrawal of its allocation of ex-Midland 4-4-0 Class 2 passenger engines, gone before I had an opportunity to work on these long-legged machines, sporting 6ft 9in driving wheels. However, listening to some of the guys who manned them on assisting jobs their pulling powers were often brought into question when, for instance, double-heading with a 'Scot' to Carlisle with a Manchester-Glasgow express. After hooking up at Preston, the guard would come up and give the 'Scot' driver his revised load, informing him that he had 13 coaches behind him, and equal to three coaches now attached to the front of him!

From the day I started at the shed I nurtured an ambition to act as fireman to my dear Uncle Bob before he retired in 1964 with 44 years' service. He had served in the First World War, during which he suffered gas attacks at Passchendaele. It was not going to be easy persuading management to relax the strict rules regarding the rostering together of close relatives due to the possibility of an accident, or being involved in an incident demanding an enquiry whereby it was felt that one might cover up for the other. However, having a good mate and fellow Preston North End supporter as the senior roster clerk did help somewhat, and strings were pulled accordingly. Vinny arranged for us to crew a summer Saturday special empty stock from Lostock Hall carriage sidings to Blackpool Central for an excursion to Windermere, with relief at Preston after traversing the circular curve through Todd Lane and Lostock Hall for a northbound departure from Preston.

Our loco was No 45226, a newly allocated 'Black 5'. We signed on at 5.30am and prepared before leaving the depot at 6.30. Waiting for us in the adjacent carriage sidings was our guard Horace Stewart, brother of driver Bert Stewart who had transferred to Crewe and later became the regular driver of No 60007 *Sir Nigel Gresley* in its early preservation days. I dropped down and hooked up to a nice and handy 10-coach train for the job, returning to the footplate to be told that I was to be the driver to Blackpool. So, after completing a brake test we whistled up and were given the road for our journey to the seaside.

I was familiar with the road to Blackpool, but of course my uncle knew every sleeper end of the journey. It was a joy to watch my veteran fireman working the shovel. On approaching Kirkham, instead of taking the coast route via St Annes we were routed via Marton to Blackpool South. I had been over this railway numerous times with the

ROF (Royal Ordnance Factory) jobs and we eventually came to a stand in the carriage sidings, where I got a pat on the back for my handling of the locomotive. After detaching us from the train, Bob took over his duties, first moving us onto the electrically operated turntable, followed by a visit to the water column, then back onto our train to await being called out to propel the stock into Central Station for our 9.50am departure. Shortly afterwards the carriage siding foreman gave us our headboard with the special reporting number, which I attached to the smokebox door; he then instructed us to propel back into the station. There it was a case of preparing ourselves with a fresh can of tea followed by a sandwich then 'be prepared' for take-off.

It was a very anxious nephew on the return journey doing his utmost to put on a good display and not disappoint his Dad's brother! So much so that I remember very little of the journey except that we traversed the coastal route to Kirkham and I recall relaying signals to him around Lostock Hall before coming to a stand in Platform 4 at Preston and being relieved by driver Teddy Aspin and fireman Tony Holman. Arriving back at the shed, we shook hands and he wished me good luck in my career. Shortly afterwards, as a finale to his 44-year career, he was presented with the standard 45-year service watch upon retirement.

Next week saw me on the 8.00am shed shunt job with driver George – a nice little job this, with a good start time. Speaking of time, a few years later I was to be George's fireman on the day that he retired, and when he signed off duty for the last time one Friday early afternoon I took him along to his favourite pub, the Victoria, and stayed with him for a couple of drinks. When I stood up, I asked him the time. He pulled out his silver Waltham pocket watch from his waistcoat.

'It's two minutes to three, and if you give me thirty bob the watch is yours!'

He would not take no for an answer, saying that he had no further use for it now that he was retired. Luckily for me it was pay day, so out of my £11 fireman's wage I paid up and for years kept his watch as a memento.

On this shed shunt turn you first sorted out the empties on the coal hopper road, then in with the full coal wagons, doing the same on the ashpit road – first checking for any detonators under the wheels! Then you kept hold of an empty 8-tonner, and shovelled up the coal spillage under the two hoppers. The man in charge of the shunting was a tough craggy character named Bill; he was ex-footplate, having had to give it up after being knocked down by not one, but two, express trains, surviving both incidents – so he was one person you would want on your side if any trouble started. Looking back, I can hardly remember seeing him without a pipe in his mouth, even when using his 'toothpick' (or shunting pole to you) – hooking on or hooking off, he never let go of his pipe. I will never forget the day when he was standing waiting for the pilot engine to buffer up to the wagon so he could lift the coupling onto the engine hook with his shunt pole. As the engine buffer came into contact with the wagon buffer, he failed to pull back clear with the pipe and it got crushed – but he wouldn't let go of it, and out of the corner of his mouth he was telling the driver to 'Ease off, ease off, mate!' while still gripping in his mouth what was left of the pipe!

I had George as my driver on a regular basis. He enjoyed his snuff, which left traces around his nostrils and waistcoat; he sometimes offered it to me, but I only tried it once and never again, although it was still quite popular with men of his generation. Unusually, he always wore a pair of red rubber gloves when driving. He had been a keen motorcyclist in his day, but apparently never wore the proper gear, always riding about in an open-neck shirt, which may have

This general view of the goods yard at Lostock Hall shows the shunters' hut on the left, the wagon repair shops on the right, and the station and engine shed in the distance. The local tripper, 63 Target, heads off towards Preston while another tripper makes its way to Farington Junction and the West Coast Main Line. *David Idle*

contributed to his chest problems later in life and subsequent demotion to the shunting link, which was what we were doing that day in the goods yard and wagon shops at Lostock Hall. During the break we gathered for tea in the wooden hut with the shunting staff.

One of these old boys was Arthur, a real character who could tell a tale or two. His teacup was his prized possession – you couldn't mistake it for that of one of his mates. It didn't really need tea putting in it to make a brew, just hot water would have sufficed, such was the density of tea stains inside and outside of it. Just as a joke, one of his shunting mates spent ages cleaning the cup and removing the stains using the strongest of bleaches. He made such a good job of it that when it was the next bagging time, Arthur did not recognise his own

cup among the others on the drainer, and accused everybody of nicking it. Peace was only restored when he eventually recognised on the side of the cup a long-forgotten faded image of Her Majesty the Queen's 1953 Coronation.

On one particular afternoon break, when the shunting staff and engine crews were all gathered in the small wooden shunters' hut, with the fire blazing and the cast-iron kettle on constant boil, Arthur was in story-telling mood, so 'If you are all sitting comfortably I will begin,' said Arthur. He then regaled us with a little gem from his days as a 16-year-old junior rating in the Navy during the Second World War. He was on watch aboard this cruiser patrolling the Baltic when they came across a German warship. Arthur began to demonstrate his role by standing on a chair looking through a rolled up newspaper acting as his telescope. Heavy firing began on both ships but, much to Arthur's annoyance, the shells from his ship were landing short of or beyond the German warship. After a while he had seen enough, and went amidships to remonstrate with the gun crew.

'Come down here and let some bugger else have a go!' he shouted up to the gun crew.

'Come up here if you think that you can do any better!' was their reply.

With that Arthur was straight up there and, pushing the lead gunner out of the way, he took up his position (by the way, he is still standing on the chair, but is now holding a three-legged stool rotating it like a gun turret). The audience were of course still sitting spellbound.

'Give me the range, mate,' Arthur demanded. 'Right, I now have him nicely in my sights. Load the shell,' he commanded. 'Prepare to fire – *fire!*'

Bang, and away it went, and with just the one shot it was a direct hit, the ship sinking with no survivors! This brought immediate applause from all and sundry gathered in the shunters' hut.

A few years later, when the yards closed to traffic, Arthur transferred to become the station foreman at Todd Lane Junction, the next station down the line to Preston from Lostock Hall, and the junction for the line to Blackburn and Skipton. He was much remembered for his amusing array of station announcements. Standing on the platform he would holler out, 'The next train to arrive is for Blackburn, Accrington, Colne, and beyond.' Now, where 'beyond' was nobody knew – I don't think he could remember the station names after Colne. He wouldn't need to these days, as the line closed in the 1970s.

Interestingly, the last time I met Arthur was a few years later in the now demolished Boatmans Arms in Preston. I was playing darts for the opposing team and Arthur was doing the marking, giving a running commentary on the scores. I wasn't doing very well, so I said to him, 'I wish my aim was as good as yours when you sank that German warship.'

His mates immediately asked him, 'What's all this about then, Arthur?'

He came back with a classic one-liner. 'Military secrets, boys, military secrets!'

Incidentally, it was at this pub in Marsh Lane that, when we were kids, an old boy by the name of Curly Helm kept a horse and landau in the stables and at weekends and holiday times used to ply his trade around the local streets giving rides for sixpence each. My mother also worked at the pub as a cleaner, which guaranteed a free ride for me and my little sister.

7 Enter Jacqueline, and sea lions

A few pleasant changes in my life occurred in the early spring of 1963, and it is important that I get them in the right order, otherwise the lady who is at present sitting across the table from me, busily spending every hour of her spare time typing out this lengthy manuscript, may go on strike and down tools – for it came to pass that our lives came together at this time.

At that time I was still hobbling about on crutches, recovering from the broken ankle, the real cause of which I have explained previously, but I had somehow managed to make it to the local pub, the Plough Inn at Penwortham, and it was leaving there when

John Fletcher and Jacqueline Woodburne, later to become Mr & Mrs Fletcher on 18 March 1967 – four years to the day since another important occasion, the passing of my firing exam! *Author's collection*

I first met Jacqueline, who was out exercising Kim, her family's pet dog. She was talking to a pal of mine, who introduced us, and we discovered that we lived near to each other. She accepted my invitation to walk me home; being on crutches, I think that she must have felt a little sorry for me, or perhaps I had spotted an early sign of what was later to become her career in nursing. Anyway, I quickly became aware that she was something a bit special, the eldest of seven children to whom she was really a second mother. Her father was away in the Marines, and her mother worked in the evenings, which left Jacqueline in charge of her siblings, making the meals, doing the housework, etc. One thing I quickly discovered about Jacqueline was her great sense of humour, absolutely essential if someone was going to have to put up with

me, so we agreed to 'go a-courting', as they say.

18 March has been an important date in our lives: it was the day I passed my firing exam, and also the day we married four years later in 1967. Jacqueline has always supported me and has joined in with all things railway, going back to my days at the shed when she waited in the foreman's office until I had finished duty, attending model railway exhibitions, visiting preserved railways – even to the extent of working with me on the NYMR. I am a lucky boy indeed!

A few months after being passed fit for firing duties I passed my car driving test first time, in my instructor's Triumph Herald. Mind you, I wasn't entirely without experience of driving a vehicle. While still at school and working with the local milkman he let me do most of the driving of the electric milk float. I had actually been riding a moped to and from work for the previous few months until I was old enough to take my driving test, but it was not a very reliable machine. I would often call at Jacqueline's home on my way to work or if I had finished a late turn, and she would make me my favourite omelette, then off I would go out to the moped, and many times the temperamental thing would not start. This would then involve both Jacqueline and her mother pushing me round the block in an attempt to get the thing to burst into life. Later we had some better luck when Jacqueline entered a sales competition at work and won the first prize, a brand new Raleigh Wisp moped, rendering her and her mother redundant from the task of pushing me about.

These really were exciting times in our lives: Jacqueline also passed her driving test first time – same car, same instructor, Brian Swallow – and we wanted to buy our first car and get around a bit. We didn't really fancy a modern car, which we probably couldn't afford, and anyway the pair of us

A 'Wisp' of good fortune: Jacqueline's prize for selling more Super Plenamins than any other chemist's assistant in the North West! *Author's collection*

loved the look of older vehicles, particularly anything with running boards and a long bonnet, similar to the Riley 1½-litre owned by Jacqueline's favourite uncle who lived in Wales. This was before the term 'classic cars' came into vogue. The cars that interested us were just termed old cars, unless they came into the 'vintage' category. By pure coincidence my driver at the time was Len Parkin, who told me that he knew of a 1939 Rover 10, parked in a private garage near his home. Len actually sorted the deal for us with the owner, and for £10 we became the proud owners of this 25- year -old beauty. So began our love affair with cars from this period, including a couple more Rovers, one of them being the exceedingly rare Rover 14 Drop Head Coupe from 1939, registration FNE 524.

Over the years we must have owned 20 or more of what are now termed classic cars, including a 1953 Triumph Renown that we used for wedding hire. I only wish we had the space and finance to have kept some of them. For instance, what would be the present-day value of our 1930 Alvis 12/50 Saloon, GK 4033? It does still exist, now

fitted with a boat-tailed body. A popular TV series at the time was *The Untouchables*, and it was not long before I was being called 'Eliot Ness' after the main character, who was an American crime-buster famous for his tussles with Al Capone – not that I knew Al. The connection with me was, of course, the cars that Mr Ness drove in the 1930s-based series; they looked very similar to the British ones that we drove, with their long bonnets and running boards We still have an interest in these types of car and until recently our mode of transport was a 1953 3-litre Lagonda, alongside an almost unique Mitsuoka Le-Seyde, an abbreviation of 'Life's Second Dream'. I had this 17-foot-long rare beast imported for me from northern Japan, and only a few of them exist outside that country. It was the nearest thing to owning your very own Cruella de Vil limousine, ideal for someone like me who is a bit shy, and not wanting to draw attention to myself! It is not every day that you see one of these on the road, or our present vehicle, a Crossfire Roadster.

We ran our first car until the early summer, when we spotted for sale in

Above: A rare beast: our 1939 Rover 14 Drop Head Coupe, registration number FNE 524. *Author's collection*

Right: Our 1953 Triumph Renown, which we restored and used for wedding hire complete with chauffeuse Jacqueline. *Author's collection*

This 1930 Alvis 12/50 Saloon, GK 4033, had real Al Capone style, earning me the nickname of 'Eliot Ness' from the TV series *The Untouchables*. *Author's collection*

The 1953 Lagonda 2.6-litre was the last model to use the Bentley-designed straight-six engine, many of which survive in the parent company's Aston Martin cars. *Author's collection*

The Mitsuoka Le-Seyde was not a kit car, but only 500 were built, all of them sold within a few hours of coming off the production line. I had this one imported from northern Japan. *Author's collection*

Exchange and Mart (pre-eBay days) a 1951 MG Y-type saloon. We fancied one of these, being a good deal faster than the Rover, the only similarity between the two being the same colour – black, of course. The Alvis we kept for a good while, eventually selling it to a car dealer friend in Preston; he and his partner had set up the business having been made redundant following the cancellation by the Government of the TSR2 bomber, which was being constructed locally. Our local area was the hub of military aircraft construction, with factories and airfields at both Warton and Samlesbury, where I witnessed the test-flying of the cream of British-designed military aircraft of the 1950s and '60s. My all-time favourite was the delta-wing Vulcan bomber; there can be no finer sight or thrill than watching one of these take to the skies. I have been a member of the Vulcan to the Sky society since its inception, helping to keep airborne XH558 as the only flying example. When she attended an air show, regardless of what else was flying, and appeared at the end of the runway ready for take-off, she was the only aircraft that would empty the beer tent! I vividly recall the real tension that existed in 1962 with the threat of a nuclear war, the Vulcan being part of the V-force. And just a few miles from my present home here in downtown Grosmont is the RAF early warning station at Fylingdales, which would have played such a vital role in any possible conflict, for it would have been from here that any nuclear activity would first be monitored. This is still the case, but living so close to the place gives Jacqueline and me the added comfort of knowing of the existence of a nuclear attack just before most other folk in the country, which should give us just about enough time to make sure that we unplug the telly and bring the cat indoors.

Right, Fletch, you are rambling on a bit! Let's get back to 1964 and, with summer approaching, it was holiday time at last, and we had arranged to stay with Jacqueline's relatives in her home town of Aberystwyth.

These were still very much pre-motorway days in a lot of areas, but not Preston, where the first motorway in the country, the Preston bypass, was opened in 1958. I suppose it was because everybody wanted to avoid Preston! Our journey to Wales took us via Queensferry, Mold, Ruthin, Corwen and Machynlleth, where Jacqueline's uncles and their families lived, then finally to Aberystwyth, arriving late on the Saturday afternoon, but not too late for a quick visit to the engine shed coded 89C. This was GWR 'Manor' territory, the 'Cambrian Coast Express' being the principal train on the line. We stayed with Jacqueline's aunt and uncle who lived a short distance from the railway station overlooking the still-intact Aberystwyth to Carmarthen line. But Sunday morning saw us travelling behind steam on another British Railways line, the narrow-gauge line up to Devils Bridge. The Vale of Rheidol Railway has 12 miles of glorious scenery and the engine works its little heart out. After a visit to the falls and some lunch, it was back down to Aberystwyth. Jacqueline's late grandad (or Dadcau in Welsh), Bill Putt, had been a steam-raiser in his time at the shed and, as he was very well known in the town, a

mention of his name at the shed ensured me the freedom of the depot and access to footplates, including a firing turn on the Rheidol.

It was now day three of our seven-day holiday, and as we had spent the first two days around railways, it seemed such a shame to break the habit and go anywhere else. So Tuesday morning saw us standing on the Carmarthen departure platform at Aberystwyth station for a ride on this soon-to-be-closed line. The engine on our three-coach train was a Collett 0-6-0, which would take us via Strata Florida, Aberayron and Lampeter to Carmarthen. This really was a rural backwater of a line, and it took us the best part of a day to achieve a round trip, but we did it, which was just as well, because the line had gone when we next visited Wales two years later.

On Friday we said our farewells to our hosts in Aberystwyth and drove the 18 miles to Machynlleth, to stay there for two nights with Jacqueline's Uncle George and Aunt Sheila – George with the 1952 Riley 1½ litre. He was well-known for being the town's goalkeeper (also for Luton Town), following the tradition of the Putt family's footballing skills. His father (Jacqueline's Dadcau) also played goalie for Aberystwyth, and her mother, Nancy, played for Aberystwyth ladies.

After unloading cases on the Friday evening we went for a spin with the Riley and MG, visiting the magnificent Ponterwydd dam nearby. Now, just where do you think I was early on the Saturday morning. Yes, right first time, down at Machynlleth loco shed. Unfortunately the 4-4-0 'Dukedogs' had gone by this time, the shed now housing BR Standard class locos, including No 80135, now preserved on the NYMR.

George and Sheila lived about four doors away from the White Lion pub in Machynlleth. This was their local, and

BR Standard Class 4 tank No 80135 departs from Machynlleth with the 4.00pm Shrewsbury-Aberystwyth service. This loco is now preserved on the NYMR. *David Idle*

early Saturday night Jacqueline and I ventured in for a drink, George and Sheila planning to join us there in about half an hour. About a dozen locals were talking around the bar, but when I ordered our drinks they started talking in Welsh, ignoring the pair of us.

'Probably they don't like the English,' I said to Jacqueline.

Anyhow, half an hour later in came George and Sheila, and the locals made a great fuss of them, then George turned around and asked if we wanted a drink.

'Who are they, George?' asked one of the locals.

'This is my niece, our Nancy's daughter, Jacqueline, and her boyfriend John, visiting us from Lancashire,' George told them.

'Oh! We are sorry – we thought you were Brummies!' exclaimed one of the locals. The Welsh in that area were not very fond of Birmingham folk, because at that time they were buying up a lot of property for use as second homes. Anyway, once they knew who we were, we didn't buy another drink all night. Ironically, some 50 years later the White Lion Hotel became the accommodation address for West Coast Railways when working the Cambrian steam service from Machynlleth to Pwllheli. Jacqueline and I stayed the night there before travelling on the journey with myself being roped in for firing duties on loco No 76079, which I thoroughly enjoyed after some helpful tutoring of the route from

regular fireman Chris Birmingham. Sad to say, I could not enjoy the company of George and Sheila again, both of them having passed away by this time.

Reporting back for work coincided with the posting of the summer workings at the depot. These were the additional trains laid on to cover the demands of the main holiday period. They were eagerly awaited, mainly by the passed firemen and passed cleaners, who would be ensured of some regular driving and firing during the 12 weeks. There was much studying of the new diagrams, scrutinising the timings, and the gaps allowed between outward and return workings. The main reason for all this brainwork had no real connection to the working of the trains, but to suss out where it might be possible to get a pint during the shift! It would be fair to say that not all crews were intent on fitting this into their working day, but it should be pointed out that the combined effects of shift working and the tough environment of the steam footplate meant that the opportunity to escape from it for a short time and sink a couple of pints was very welcome. The after-effects could be a tendency by some men to over-fire the engine, with the back boxes seemingly knocking on both engine and crew.

In those days there was a Railway Hotel

or a Station Hotel within easy reach of most stations and engine sheds, which would be frequented by station staff, guards, shunters, locomen and, at the larger stations, postal workers and parcel delivery people. In fact, it wasn't that unusual for the running shift foreman to give the pub a ring if he required you for a job. To say the railways ran on beer in those days is a little extreme; indeed, many men were teetotal, but would visit the pub just for the social side to pass an hour or two, joining in a game of dominoes, darts or cards. I used to think the ideal job must surely have been that of a porter in steam days, at some wayside country station; just imagine it, growing your own flowers and vegetables in the station's garden, issuing a few tickets, keeping the fires going in the waiting rooms, no night work, and enjoying a pint in the adjacent Railway Hotel between the 2-hourly train service. I keep looking for that vacancy! Worlds away from these days of unstaffed halts with bus shelters.

It was around this time of new rosters that the foreman called me into his office one day. I was a bit suspicious, because usually it was not the place you went unless there was trouble afoot, but in this case it was quite an unusual request. He explained that Control had informed him that some crews had been trying to fail their steam engine because the mechanical coal-pusher wasn't working, hoping that they would be given a diesel replacement. Others had been issued with their new diesel uniform, only to find that a diesel was not available, and had been given a steam loco, and had then refused to go into the tender to pull down the coal. So would I be prepared to go down to Preston station each day, taking a shovel, until a solution was sorted out, reporting to Control and awaiting orders from them?

'Well, yes', I said. 'That sounds like something of interest to pass the day.'

So that's what happened. He asked me to cover a 2-10pm shift, as that was when it was occurring, so I duly reported to Control on Preston station, who told me to wait in the porters' room below their office on No 5 platform and they would contact me there.

Nothing at all happened for the first few hours, which was not all that surprising, I suppose, because although there was plenty of steam about at this busy junction station, with trains heading all over the place north and south, very few engines had tenders fitted with a coal-pusher – the 'Lizzies' and some 'Britannias', and that was it. It was now 8.00pm and the shovel and I had seen no action, so I rang the office.

'Are you getting a bit fed up, son?' asked one of the Control officers. 'We actually have had two requests for a fresh engine, but when they are told that staff will meet them and pull coal down during the station stop, or that you will actually go forward with them, they seem to lose interest and carry on. We feel that its just a small number of crews at one particular depot. Anyway, off you go home, and come back same time tomorrow.'

On the Tuesday I duly reported for duty at 2.00pm, having left my underworked shovel hidden overnight in the porters' room.

'Nothing to report yet,' Control told me. 'What we have decided to do, to avoid you spending all your time waiting about, is to leave you free to find something yourself, but do not leave the station and we will broadcast on the tannoy if we need you.'

With that I cleared off, taking the shovel with me just in case. Not long afterwards I was standing on the end of Platform 5 when a 'Clan' 'Pacific' coasted in at the head of a special for Edinburgh and came to a stand with the tender opposite the water column. The fireman climbed up and put the bag in, the driver turning on the water. I thought for a minute, then asked the driver, 'Would you like me to jump up and pull you some coal forward?'

'If you have nothing else to do, son, then get on with it!'

So, action at last! I was glad to be doing something. I only had about 5 minutes but I worked as fast as I could, then jumped off just as they started to move, not forgetting to keep hold of my shovel. The crew shouted their thanks, the fireman threw me a fag and away they went. After they had gone I sat on a parcel truck enjoying a smoke. It wasn't long before the next express ground to a halt next to me hauled by a Fowler tendered 5XP.

'Want a bit of coal bringing forward, mate?' I asked of them, so I joined the fireman in the tender as they did not need to take water. It was a bit awkward with the two of us working in there, so he told me to get on the footplate and put him a fire on, ready for the 1 in 90 pull northbound out of Preston, followed by the 6 miles of heavy digging to Barton & Broughton. I managed to fill up the back end of the firebox before they got the 'right away', then they left me behind on the platform clutching another freebie fag from the fireman. I was beginning to enjoy all this, so I varied my approach a little and instead of asking if they would like some coal pulling forward, I asked instead if they would like me to put a fire on for them, to which most of them agreed. I did get some quite humorous replies as some of the crews found it incredulous that someone was actually offering to assist them in their labours.

'Are you on day release, kid?'

'Will you be here all week?'

'Has God sent you?'

So that was how I spent the rest of my shift. After visiting the north end of the station I moved down to the south end to help out the crews, during which time I still hadn't been called by my superiors in Control. They had a few words with me at 10.00pm before I went home and seemed to think that the crisis might be over as they hadn't received any more relevant complaints. With that, I think they sensed my disappointment and said, 'But we can't say that for sure, so keep coming until the end of the week.'

And that is what I did. I was kept busy all over the station, either pulling coal forward or putting a fire on for the crews on so many different types of engines. In fact, by the end of the week I reckon that I must have fired all of the former LMS passenger types and every class of the large BR Standard locomotives, and never left Preston station!

The following week I signed on at 3.00am, prepared the loco then ran light down to Preston to work the 4.30am parcels train to Blackpool. My mate was old Billy, who owned a small shop near the shed selling a wide range of goods including tobacco, neckerchiefs, hankies, vests, underpants, condoms, tea and sugar, toffees, kids toys, all at discount prices and carried in a large leather shopping bag that went everywhere with him. The mess room was his first port of call after booking on duty, having instructing his fireman to make a start without him, and to splash a bit of oil around the engine. 'I will be out with you shortly.' This usually meant about 5 minutes before we were due off shed.

Our engine for the day was Stanier 'Mogul' No 42963, or 'Crab' to us. It was not often that we got one of these; they were certainly gutsy little things, and the preserved member of the class, No 42968, gave some real eye-opening displays of power during its all too brief return to main-line running. However, I am wandering off the tale, and on this early morning the weather was wet, and I was wet after lugging eight buckets of sand, then climbing up on the frames to fill the sanders, spreading the fire, testing all the equipment, then round the engine with the oil feeder, grateful that she had outside Walschaerts gear rather than an inside Stephenson's. Billy's appearance was beautifully timed, just as I had completed these dual duties; we passed each other like ships in the dark, with me off to the mess room to mash and he for a quick wash. He was waiting on his perch when I climbed back on board, the handbrake was off, he had created the brake vacuum, and the engine was in forward gear. A toot on the Caledonian hooter, the regulator was opened, and No 42963 was off on another revenue-earning trip for its owner, good old British Railways.

Billy had done a bit of early-morning trade prior to leaving the shed; his next customers would be the Preston station staff, and as we ran in his swag-bag was passed off the footplate to a couple of porters waiting on Platform 2. Our four parcel vans were put behind us by the 3F station pilot engine, my old friend No 47472, and Billy left the footplate to collect his shopping orders, but not before telling me to carry out a brake test. Then, with a cheeky wide grin, he told me not to touch any other of the driver's controls – he had some brilliant one-liners. He always had a bag full of his favourite Uncle Joe's mint balls in his pocket, but getting one off him could be hard work. I would be given one for oiling round the engine, 'but don't ask me for another one, fireman, because I have only got 37 left.' He once told me that Santos, which made his favourite mints in Wigan, briefly used an advertising slogan declaring 'Uncle Joe's Mint Balls – Britain's Most Sucked Balls', but it didn't last long, just like our sojourn at Preston.

We headed out and swung left at Maudland Junction, taking the Blackpool line past the lofty steeple of St Walburge's, Preston's equivalent of the Blackpool Tower. It was still dark as we passed through Kirkham, then Poulton-le-Fylde, a bit early yet for any life on these stations, but our 5.15am arrival under the huge station roof of the now demolished terminus at Blackpool North attracted some attention from the night-shift porters, as they came across to unload our train. Now, can you guess what got unloaded first? Yes, you're right first time, Billy's swag-bag. The station staff knew that he was on this job every eight weeks, and the bag would be left with them until later in the morning, allowing the day shift to have a nibble at what was left. But before that we would be kept busy all morning acting as the shunt engine in the extensive Blackpool North carriage sidings. Well, let me just rephrase that: I would be busy shunting the carriage sidings, while my mate paid a visit to one of his wholesale suppliers nearby, then by the time he had walked back to the station for debt-collection duties, he would be getting a bit thirsty, which meant that he had to call in for a glass or two of his favourite bitter, brewed in Blackpool by the now long-demised Catterall & Swarbrick C&S ales.

Meanwhile, back in Dodge, the fireman/shunter and I will have been busy for the last 3 hours in the North carriage sidings putting all the coaching stock into numerical order. We didn't really mind Billy going walkabout, as we could do the job a lot quicker without him on the engine. Our Stanier 'Crab' was an easy engine to manoeuvre back and forth around the extensive sidings, much nippier than one of his 'Black 5s', the usual engine to be seen on this turn. The 'Mogul' had smaller driving wheels, making it quick off the mark; it also needed fewer turns on the reverser. By the way, our shunter would be rewarded for combining his duties as fireman for the morning with a special discount being offered on any purchases made from Billy's mobile store.

During the morning's shunting I had noticed the presence of a young lady sitting by the trackside with a sketch-pad and pen. The shunter told me that she was often to be seen making drawings of the steam engines; nobody told her she was trespassing because her father was a driver at the shed!

Now, being the nosy devil that I am, this interested me enough to wander across to meet this budding female Cuneo. She was quite friendly, asking me if I wanted to have a look at myself leaning out of the cab while driving No 42963. When she showed me the drawing I was very impressed with her work, modestly telling her that it was a good portrait of the engine! She asked if I would be on the same turn the day after, because if the weather was fine the drawing would be finished and I could have it. So all was agreed and we parted, although the thoughts of possibly courting a female railway artist, and featuring in every one of her locomotive scenes, did occupy my youthful brain for a while.

With all shunting now complete, Billy was approaching, having walked up from the station accompanied by our relief crew from Wyre Dock shed, who would take the engine to Fleetwood and work a fish train from there, leaving us two to make our way home 'on the cushions' to Lostock Hall .On our return journey home I was reading a well-known book, *The Lancashire & Yorkshire Railway in the Twentieth Century* by Eric Mason. A chap leaned across from the seat opposite and asked me if I was enjoying the read.

'Very much so,' I replied.

'Good, I am pleased, because I am the author,' he said, and he promptly signed his book for me.

One other thing I recall from that week was that the nation had been gripped by a bakers' strike, and shops were struggling for supplies of any type of bread, but fortunately our family remained unaffected; well, with Billy as your mate, you were not going to be on the breadline! It's worth mentioning that on the second day that week we had a 'Black 5' on the job, which caused a little confusion for our artist lady when finishing off her drawing of the loco. She explained that at first both engines looked alike to her, until

she noticed that Tuesday's engine had gained an extra set of wheels, and the drawing was modified accordingly before it was presented to me.

I remained as Billy's mate for a while, during which time he really took me under his wing, after discovering that I was related to one of his best mates at the shed, my Uncle Bob. They both had a passion for betting on the gee-gees and would not go off shed on early mornings until they had picked out their horses. The next time that we both worked a Blackpool job we were standing at the buffers with one of Bank Hall's 5XPs, No 45717 *Dauntless* (the others being Nos 45719 *Glorious* and 45698 *Mars*, all of them kept in good nick by the Scouse fitters) when some union delegates got off our train and walked past the engine led by TUC Secretary Mr George Woodcock, who looked at Billy and said, 'Thank you, driver, good trip,' to which Billy replied, 'It's a pleasure George.'

Now, I must admit that Billy's reply did set me back a wagon length or two. 'You sounded as though you knew him,' I said.

'Well, as a matter of fact he comes from the same village as me,' Billy proudly told me.

'If you know him, why didn't you offer him your swag-bag to peruse?' I jokingly asked him.

I was given the Billy look, which told me to shut up!

One thing that I always remember about Mr Woodcock was the amount of hair that he had in his eyebrows; he actually had more hair in his eyebrows than Billy had on the top of his head.

Our return work was an early evening stopper to Manchester Exchange, with relief for us at Preston by a Newton Heath crew. We shunted our train, turned the loco, and had an hour to spare standing with our return stock before departing from Platform 3. Billy was a good knowledgeable driver, and we would often discuss loco matters, paying particular attention to tutoring me in the role of budding driver. He would often stand behind me asking me to talk the road and my actions accordingly, as he knew every sleeper end wherever we went. The good thing about being on the footplate was that once away from the engine shed you were your own boss, and we were an established team.

He would often put me on the regulator on some easy-paced main-line turns, such as this evening, then would ask me questions, such as what was going through my mind as I sat in the driver's seat before departing with our train. I answered that my main worry was whether we would have enough steam and water to keep *Dauntless* on the move. This bit of cheek got me no Brownie points, with Billy threatening to cut off my already meagre supply of Uncle Joe's mint balls. But seriously, I would tell him things like, 'I am thinking of our departure time, the weight and length of our train, what stops we have, and where to stop in each station. I am thinking of the road ahead, what signals I need getting away from the Blackpool area, and what signals are mine on the run to Preston, what is the line speed, the speed around certain curves, the speed entering stations, temporary speed restrictions, emergency speed restrictions, where I need to use the whistle, the water troughs at Lea Road, check my running times, watching the steam and water levels, listening to the engine front end, looking for any steam blows or leaks, and how much coal and water we have.'

I would think that I had given him every answer there was, but he would always catch me out with something, which was exactly what it was all about, furthering my knowledge. After that particular session I remember he got me when he asked, 'What should you be thinking about before you open that regulator?' I gave him much of what had already been said, and more besides, but still he was adamant that I

had not given him the answer that he was looking for, and that as the driver I should be able to tell him. In the end, as we were getting near to departure time, I gave up, and said to him, 'Go on then – tell me what I have missed.'

'You're too late,' he said, just as the guard blew his whistle and gave Billy the green flag. 'Right away!' he shouted. 'And don't let her slip.' When he said that, it came to me in a flash – the answer he wanted was 'rail condition'. 'Rail condition!' I repeatedly shouted across the cab to him. He was right, of course, in reminding me of this important factor in the handling of a steam locomotive, for any excessive slipping would see me out of the seat and back on the blade!

As we climbed away from Blackpool North with our nine-coach train, I was taking great care in keeping this less-than-sure-footed breed of locomotive from going into a slip, but all was well as we surmounted the slight incline and begin to draw away from our seaside terminus. Billy was in action with the shovel, adopting the little-and-often technique while building up a nice sloping thin fire to which these 5XPs responded – you didn't fire these engines as you would a 'Black 5'. Over on my side I cracked second valve, which brought *Dauntless* into life, and for the first time we heard that lovely three-cylinder beat that I so loved about these engines. We were well on the move now and passed through the quiet Layton station, with a clear road ahead over Carleton crossing before shutting off for the Poulton curve and the junction with the Fleetwood line before coming to a stand at the end of the long platform at Poulton-le-Fylde.

Glancing around the footplate, everything was how it should be; it had been swept and watered, no pieces of coal anywhere, all spanners and detonators stowed away in the bucket hanging from the lamp bracket on the tender, fire irons and coal pick stored away correctly, the cab and controls clean. My mate said that he was quite happy with my driving up to now, then advised me of another method he sometimes used for getting a train on the move from a difficult spot, which was to start with the engine in mid-gear, then open the regulator just enough and slowly wind the gear down the rack to the point of admission.

'Try it now when we get the right away from here,' he said.

I always did what the driver told me (well, nearly always), and sure enough our 5XP responded and made an effortless departure. As a reward for my new-found driving technique I was given one of Billy's prized possessions, a much sought-after Uncle Joe's mint ball. Now, with plenty of straight and level track in front of us to Kirkham, we could let Dauntless have her head, so we gathered up some speed and soon began to hear that familiar 5X roar once we were around the 40mph mark. Billy was keeping her on the mark firing over the flap, I had my head out of the cab and, by watching the exhaust darken, I could tell just where he was putting each shovelful of coal in the firebox. No 45717 was in pretty good health, as we had found out on the run into Blackpool – she did ride well, had good injectors and a free-steaming boiler. What more could you ask?

I shut off at Bradkirk and began braking for our next stop at Kirkham & Wesham. Waiting there, we briefly reflected on the good run that we just had from Poulton, having now blown the cobwebs off our trusty steed. With station duties quickly completed, we pulled away and joined the four-track main line taking us all the way to Preston. Our 5XP was nicely picking up speed and just beginning to get into her stride when suddenly I very nearly jumped out of the driver's seat, for on the next -but-one track to us a returning holiday excursion for Yorkshire came roaring past on the fast line

headed by 'B1' No 61002 Impala with the whistle shrieking, having had a non-stop run through Kirkham. The fireman was patting the side of the cab just like a jockey on a racehorse, teasing us into challenging them for speed to the winning post at Preston. I looked across at my mate for his reaction.

'Get after them!' he said, and immediately began to feed our steed to supply the extra steam that would be needed.

As the last coach of our rival drifted past us, I dropped Dauntless down to 60 per cent cut-off with full regulator. I did feel a little guilty driving the engine this hard, and asked 64-year-old Billy whether he wanted me to have a go on the shovel. The glare that he gave me in return made me instantly sorry for asking, maybe belittling his almost 50 years of footplate experience.

'Just you concentrate on catching those ruddy Yorkshiremen ahead of us,' I was suitably told!

We were gradually beginning to reduce the gap between us – our 5X could certainly out do the North Eastern engine for speed if we caught him, but he would be quicker off the blocks with his smaller 6ft 2in driving wheels. As we approached Salwick station we had drawn level with the end of the ten-coach train. The signalman was leaning out of the box laughing and urging on yet another set of mad footplatemen as we roared past him, enjoying this Saturday evening duel on this traditional Fylde coast racing stretch. We had also attracted the attention of the passengers travelling in the excursion, who were encouraging us on as we gained ground on them coach by coach, with some leaning out of the windows holding fivers and mimicking bets.

Impala was living up to her name, and it took us 5 miles to catch up with the train, during which time I had been gradually reducing the cut-off, but a look across at the clock and the glass revealed that all was well on the fireman's side, as veteran Billy

Here's a scene at Salwick similar to our duel between 5XP *Dauntless* and 'B1' *Impala*, although these two are heading towards Blackpool. *Peter Fitton*

still had her on the mark. *Dauntless* had responded well to being worked this hard and, with the advantage of her long legs, had got us nicely striding out at just over 70mph, with Stanier gaining ground on Thompson. Approaching Lea Road and the water troughs, I turned round to release the chain securing the water scoop handle, but Billy promptly came across and stopped me.

'No, no, don't dip, we can manage to the Lostock troughs at Bolton – he will have to dip as he has no troughs for 45 miles, until Luddendenfoot.'

We drew level with each other on the troughs, cab to cab. I leaned out, wanting to give the cocky fireman a bit of abuse, but he couldn't hear due to the racket from both engines. I settled instead for a traditional Churchill salute but, with the 'B1' tender overflowing with water, he was too busy strenuously trying to wind up the scoop before the entire footplate became awash. With him committed to taking on water and the subsequent slight drag, *Dauntless* edged past the flying *Impala* and, with the job done, Billy and I exchanged a quick handshake

as he broke into a short victory dance on the footplate. The only time I had seen him looking so pleased was when he had sold up the entire contents of his swag-bag!

We briefly touched 75mph before shutting off, as we were rapidly approaching the Preston suburbs. We then ran alongside each other for a while before passing Ashton box, bringing our speed down for the curves at Maudland, with both of us being given a clear run into Preston station and the parting of the ways, but not before exchanging a friendly whistle and a thumbs-up with the Tyke crew as we passed the former 24K engine shed on our right. We then gave *Impala*'s passengers a final wave as their train headed away and over to the 'Lanky' side of the station, both trains passing under the huge gantry that controlled all movements into and out of Preston. They would travel non-stop through Preston station via Platform 13, then go via Rose Grove and Copy Pit back home into Yorkshire. We veered off to the right, entering the station down Platform 2 and drifting to a stand at the water column at the platform end. As we were 5 minutes early there was time to take on water here.

A set of dour Newton Heath men awaited our arrival and stepped aboard the clean and tidy footplate. Billy had put a nice back end on for the old-hand fireman, who must have been 30 years my senior, and gave me an envious look, mumbling something about boy drivers, which I chose to ignore. I jumped up and put the bag in, then we left the two miserable beggars to get on with it. Nothing was going Lostock Hall way on this fine Saturday evening, so we caught a Fishwick bus for the 4-mile journey back to the shed. The conductors rarely charged railwaymen on duty and we arrived back home, still 1½ hours short of a day. Now, some foremen would give you the 'right away' home, particularly on a Saturday night, but the man on duty had come from another depot and could be unpredictable and moody, especially if his favourite football team had lost that afternoon. Guess what, they had, so we were told to go and sit in the mess room until our 8-hour day was up. I am not going to reveal his identity, but I will tell you that the team he supported was Manchester United, and what depot do you think he had transferred from – ruddy Newton Heath!

Just as an aside, I should mention that it is no longer possible to have a bit of fun on the Blackpool line; the fast lines have all been ripped up, and part of the trackbed now forms a new road out of Preston, with a strict 40mph speed limit on it, somewhat slower than when we occupied that stretch of land, running steam trains to and from the seaside. Happy days!

Ten miles north of Preston was the former privately owned Garstang & Knott End Railway, which was still open for freight traffic as far as Pilling. The one train a day was affectionately known as the 'Pilling Pig'. I was the fireman during one of the last weeks of operation on the branch. There was no rushing about on this job, and at Nateby I had time to have a good look around, as well as at Garstang Town station. There, while rummaging through the derelict goods

yard building, I came across a leather-bound ledger used for entering all goods received in the yard, dating back to the early 1880s. I showed this to the inspector who said I could keep it for posterity. I still visit this area, as one of our grandsons lives at Preesall, and we sometimes visit the former railway station at Knott End, which is now an excellent café. Parts of the trackbed near to here have been incorporated into the grounds of the local golf club, my eldest son having played in competitions here.

Another line that lost its passenger service at about the same time as the Knott End branch was the 7-mile-long Preston to Longridge railway, closed to passengers in 1930. We covered the daily freight work on this line, which is described later, and also had a night turn that spent a couple of hours between 2.00 and 4.00am shunting the yard at the Preston end of the line at Maudland. This involved the loco being inside the tunnels when drawing out the wagons and shunting, not a very pleasant environment. It was difficult to see the guard's hand signals due to the exhaust from the engine – usually an 'Austerity' 2-8-0. Tom was one of my regular mates on this job; he was a Navy veteran from the First World War and had taken part in the Battle of Jutland. I can still see him now as the three of us sat around the fire in the guard's brake van at 3.00am having our tea break and Tom entertaining us with wartime stories. He was about 63 then, but he looked a lot older with a very wrinkly face; if Botox had been around then he would have been a regular customer! I often used to think about all the residents who lived adjacent to the goods yard, as it must have been difficult sleeping, listening to the noise of our engine and the wagons being shunted. Mind you, I suppose that it was a sound that was quite familiar to a lot of folk who lived close to the railways in those days.

Incidentally, when you were Tom's fireman you did both jobs. He didn't like driving but would put a bit of coal on the fire – the operative word being 'bit' – and putting the injector on occasionally. That was about the extent of his exertions. He had come off main-line work due to a nervous complaint and was in the 'trip and shunt link', and I was his mate on many occasions, but I cannot recall him ever driving the engine. That suited me and I soon became adept at driving on the shunts; the ground staff liked to get the job done as quickly as possible in the busy goods yards.

Some of the trip jobs were quite interesting, travelling the few miles from yard to yard on the main line. Motive power was invariably a freight engine, but one early morning when we booked on duty and looked at the engine arrangement board, marked up for our No 66 Target job was 5XP No 45596 *Bahamas*. Tom's craggy face dropped a little on seeing this, for he had not been on one before, and as we made our way across the shed to No 7 road his first words upon clapping eyes on the 5XP were, 'Has this got an extra set of rods? If it has you will have to go underneath and splash some oil around her.' So, an hour later, having oiled up every moving part and done the fireman's duties, we were ready for leaving the shed. Tom told me to do the driving and he would fire the engine, but I wasn't to expect him to reach the front end of the box as it was too ruddy long!

Mid-morning saw us shunting in Leyland yard. Tom had cleared off over an hour ago to visit one of his retired mates living in the town centre, and now our guard told me that shunting was over and we had put all the wagons seemingly in alphabetical order. So, as previously arranged I whistled up for Tom to return because we were ready to depart for Oxheys cattle yard and abattoir north of Preston, 7 miles down the West Coast Main Line. I had just finished giving *Bahamas* a good charge of coal when Tom climbed on board and pushed a packet of ten fags into

my hand, saying that he had bought them for his mate who had packed up smoking. This was quite funny because Tom never had any fags and was always scrounging off his fireman. Sure enough, he then asked me to open the packet and give him a couple!

Anyway, we eventually set sail for Oxheys, and on the pull out of Preston the exhaust from our double chimney sounded nice with our load of just seven cattle trucks trailing behind. Tom was 'firing' and after about five shovelsful he paused to ask me to ease her back a bit.

'What do you think we are – the ruddy "Mid Day Scot"? You're going to cripple me at this rate.'

We soon arrived in the cattle sidings at Oxheys, but this was not the best of places to carry out shunting, particularly for the guard, as the sidings always had a coating of dung, manure and urine, which was not very nice should you lose your footing. However, all went well and our shunting was soon completed. It was now time for breakfast. Tom took out his fry-up of sausage, egg and bacon and put the items in his metal dish with a knob of lard, then on to the shovel, which he held in the firehole door, and breakfast cooking began. My breakfast was sandwiches, which were in the tender locker.

I had just opened the locker door when I heard the unmistakable sound of escaping steam behind me, and when I looked round I saw that it was coming from the right-hand gauge frame above Tom's head. But before I could get to it the glass burst with a tremendous bang and with it came scalding steam and water, filling the footplate. I instinctively grabbed my thick serge coat from the locker, put it over my head, felt my way across to the gauge frame and managed to shut it off. Looking around after the steam had cleared I saw the empty shovel on the cab floor, but, hey up, just a minute, where was our Tom? It was then I heard this faint cry, 'I'm down here.' Looking out of the cab at the fireman's side I could see him about 10 feet away over the boundary fence in the compound among the sheep.

'Have you shut it off ? It was the war that did it – all these years later I am still not right with sudden explosions,' he says, so I told him that it would be safer up here than among all that lot, which will be going for the chop shortly!

Ten minutes later, after giving him his third fag, he had calmed down, his fry-up and tin having long since melted away in the fire box. But he rallied, fortified by the consumption of half my sarnies and cake. He had my respect for being honest with himself for what the men of his generation had lived through; he stopped on the railway after reaching 65 and took on the job of knocking-up. He used his own pushbike delivering the messages to locomen living within a few miles radius of the shed, but if he saw me booking off duty just as he was about to set off with a handful of addresses to visit, it was, 'Come on, Snibber' – that was his name for me – 'Take me in that fine motor car of yours, and I'll get thee a pint or two.' That fine motor was my vintage Alvis that he so admired, but with a top speed of only 55mph we were usually away for quite a while. We always finished up with a drink and a game of dominoes in his local, the ancient Hob Inn in Bamber Bridge. He once had to give me a few tips on playing, when I lost a game still holding the double blank after the other three players had chipped out.

Tom was very good to Jacqueline and me, on occasions inviting us to tea at home with his lovely wife. His start date for seniority was 1919. He had some fascinating stories from those days, and when I think back I have actually fired for guys who had fired for guys who had featured in the Race to the North in the 1890s, working on engines such as that little 2-4-0 LNWR 'Jumbo' *Hardwicke*, which night after night averaged 67mph between Crewe and Carlisle. Now

anyone with even a scant knowledge of this part of the West Coast Main Line knows of the hill-climbing involved, so what speed were they actually doing downhill or on the level? In conversation with these old boys who worked on former LNWR passenger engines including the 'Claughton', 'Prince of Wales', 'George the Fifth' and 'Jumbo' classes, I think that it was generally accepted that these engines were all thrashed to their limits in order to keep time when working these Premier Line express trains. In a recent discussion I had with some trainee footplate crews, it was suggested that we need to have a more up-to-date approach to the working of a steam locomotive, but I disagreed with them. I said that the basic principles still exist today, in that what I was taught 50 years ago by my superiors was just the same for them going back another 50 years in time, and if you went back another 50 years to the real pioneers of steam working, little has changed, and how could you possibly challenge the basic methods of the working of a steam locomotive that has stood the test of time?

The Fylde ballast job was a turn enjoyed by crews. It was a nice 8.00am start, a steady little job transferring ballast vehicles from yard to yard on the Fylde coast. Our engine was usually nothing much bigger than a Class 2, or a rattling and vibrating Ivatt 'Doodlebug'. One of ours is still about – No 43106 – earning its keep on the busy Severn Valley Railway. Jack was the regular guard on this job; he was a friendly if slightly eccentric sort with a penchant for referring to the ballast vehicles by their telegraphic code names. For instance, when giving the driver train details before leaving it was, 'You have three Guillemots, four Sturgeons, two Salmon, one Dogfish and a Plough,' which did not make much sense to the driver, whose usual reply was, 'Just tell me the weight, please, Jack, and then we can get on our way?' He also had a habit, when walking around ballast sidings, of talking to the wagons. 'Mmmm, I thought I took you away last week – you can't stay here for ever,' or 'You are soon back here. No, you are going tomorrow so you will have to wait, I'm sorry.'

We caught him out one day. He had just finished shunting his prized possessions into name order when we told him that we had a message for him from Control.

'We have to go and pick up two Sealions,' we said.

'Where are they? I haven't seen any of those about,' said Jack.

'They're at Blackpool according to Control,' we told him.

'Well, where in Blackpool are they?' he asked.

'The bloody zoo!' we both replied. (Sealions were of course another type of ballast vehicle.)

There were originally at least two stations in Preston, the smaller of them being the terminus of the West Lancashire line at Fishergate Hill, about half a mile from the main station. I happened to live near the former until 1962. It had opened for traffic in the same year as Lostock Hall engine shed, 1882. It had a short life, closing in 1902, with services transferring to the jointly owned L&Y and LNWR station. It remained open, virtually intact, for freight only until 1965. It was always a little ambition of mine to work the solitary freight turn over the line before total closure. Access to the line and station was via Penwortham Junction, about half a mile from my home station at Penwortham Cop Lane on the Southport line, which closed in 1964, the year before the West Lancs goods line. I did work the Southport line on a number of occasions in 1963-64; it was a very rural line that fell foul of the good Doctor. The line attracted a wide variety of motive power, particularly during the summer months, working excursion traffic.

A little cameo from those days is worth recalling. I was the fireman on the pick-up goods one late summer afternoon engaged in shunting a couple of vans at New Longton, the next station after Cop Lane. With shunting completed, we made our way to the box for a booked appointment with the signalman/barber for the guard and driver to have their 2s 6d haircut. With only one style on offer, I politely refused him permission to give my expensive 'duck's arse' haircut a trimming. All this has long gone, and I try to visualise walking into a present-day ultra-modern power signal box, sitting down and asking the 'signaller' whether he has time to give me a short back and sides while we are standing outside at his signal!

With only a few weeks to go before final closure, I still hadn't worked a train down the West Lancs branch, so something had to be done. I found who the rostered fireman was on the Saturday turn and offered to swap turns with him, dangling him the carrot of my Class 1 passenger turn to Barrow, which he jumped at. So I booked on at 5.45am that Saturday morning. Our engine was Stanier tank No 42547 with veteran driver Billy Moss at the helm. We picked up our wagons in Lostock Hall yard, then off we went via the Whitehouse Curve and Penwortham Junction to Fishergate Hill station, or the 'West Lanky' as it was referred to. We spent a few hours shunting, then away to Bamber Bridge yard and back to Lostock Hall, finally arriving back on shed at 12.30pm with my ambition achieved. The station and yard were cleared shortly after closure, and housing now occupies the site.

On 22 September 1962 an RCTS railtour visited Preston WLR station. 'Super D' No 49451 hauled the first passenger train to call since September 1902 and the last ever to do so. Lostock Hall men worked the job, driver Jimmy Burke and passed fireman Jack Brady (who features later as my driver in the slight altercation I had with a signalman on the Horwich branch). The tour was organised by a railway enthusiast friend of mine, Bill Ashcroft, and it was Bill who helped organise 'The Scottish Lowlander' special in September 1964, the last run of 'Lizzie' No 46256 *Sir William A. Stanier F.R.S.* Bill travelled on the footplate with Preston driver Jack Johnson (Jonty) and fireman Roy (Chalky) White to Carlisle.

Wigan is not very far away from Preston as the crow flies, but listening to their dialect leaves me perplexed, or so it did when I was much younger. These days Wiganers are affectionately referred to as 'Pie Eaters', and the steam depot that we used at Wigan was

At Penwortham Junction passed fireman Jack Brady poses for cameraman Peter Fitton with an RCTS railtour on 22 September 1962, which visited the original West Lancashire Railway terminal in Fishergate, Preston, hauled by 'Super D' No 49451. Jack was my driver when I had a slight altercation with the signalman on the Horwich branch! *Peter Fitton*

Springs Branch, a good 2-mile walk from the station. We had quite a few jobs that involved working to and from the depot and I remember my first ever visit to the shed and baptism in the dialect. This day we dropped on with a 'Black 5', left it on the

pit and reported to the drivers' lobby busy with Wiganers. My mate was booking in our engine and I was watching and listening to a set of Wiganers looking at an engine diagram.

'Wat do morrow?' said one.

'Bound fot gu Notlob arsefost evry ole,' he replied.

I looked across at my driver, but he said, 'Shh, I'll tell you when we're outside.'

Once outside, I asked Jerry, my mate, who had been coming here for years, to decipher this alien talk. He explained that one was asking the other, 'What are you doing tomorrow?' receiving the reply, 'I am working to Bolton bunker first, stopping at all stations.'

'But he didn't say Bolton.' I then realised that he had reversed the name to Notlob.

'Yes,' said Jerry. 'Some Wiganers have a dislike of anybody from Bolton, so to be derogatory towards them they refer to it as Notlob.'

My sincerest apologies if I have offended anyone from that lovely township of Wigan. What I really mean to say is that there are some bloody big rugby-playing lads in Wigan and I don't fancy a visit from any of them!

I will always remember one visit we made to the shed when an ambulance was just leaving for the hospital taking a young fireman who had suffered a most unusual and painful accident while clambering back down from the tender into the cab of a 'Black 5'. He had lost his grip on the cab roof and slipped down on to the straight part of the handbrake handle, which had been pointing upwards; it penetrated his anus and although he was in terrible pain nobody dared lift him off it until the ambulance arrived. He was away from work for a long spell. But his misfortune taught me a lesson, and I never left the handbrake with the point upwards!

8 Be prepared

As I have described, the introduction of the Summer timetable meant plenty of rest-day working and overtime. I was sent down on loan to Preston quite often around this time, usually to cover one of the station shunts. But one particular day when I reported for duty and asked which of the station pilots I was on, I was pleasantly surprised when they told me to get along to the end of Platform 6.

'Your driver is there waiting and you are going to Crewe.'

Off I went, and sure enough, standing there waiting for me was this old-hand driver, who must have been nearly 20 stone in weight. His greeting was, 'Are you my mate? Have you been to Crewe before?'

'I have, yes, a few times,' I told him.

'Aye, well I hope that you can do the job, because I can't do it for you,' was his curt reply. 'This is ours coming in now.'

I turned around to see what I first thought was a 'Britannia' approaching, but as it came nearer I was pleasantly surprised to see that we had a 'Clan' on the front of our ten-coach train, No 72006 *Clan Mackenzie*. It had obviously been running hard and fast, for on this warm summer's evening almost the entire front of the locomotive was covered in deceased midges and flies. The Carlisle crew put the bag in and my driver and I mounted our steed.

No 72007 *Clan Mackintosh*, sister engine to No 72006 *Clan Mackenzie*, has a clear road on the up fast at Leyland with a Fleetwood-London fish train. *Stan Withers*

Just as I was putting my bag away in the locker, the driver turned to me and asked, 'By the way, were you ever in the Scouts, son?'

Puzzled by his question I replied, 'Well, no, I wasn't, but I was in the Boys Brigade.'

'Well, can you tell me the Scout's motto?' he asked.

'Yes, I know that – it is "Be Prepared".'

'Right first time,' he said. 'Now get your jacket off, pick that shovel up and fill them back corners of the firebox, get the boiler full and the steam right, and then you're prepared for the climb in front of us.'

While I was doing all this he continued with the lecture. 'Just remember, whether it's night or day, uphill or downhill, freight train or passenger train, stopper or express, engine

first or tender first, light
engine or double-headed,
always "Be Prepared". Now
you remember that all of
your firing career!'

Then off we went with
ten coaches behind us and
first stop Crewe. Let me
tell you something: how
many times over the years
did I put into practice what
that old boy told me that
day! It was the best advice
you could ever have as a
fireman.

We had a nice trouble-
free run to Crewe. My mate
was full of encouragement
and giving advice aplenty, and informing me
of the road ahead. No 72006 proved to be
a very free-steaming loco, and following an
on-time arrival, we hooked off and took the
engine to the shed. The 'Clan' Class locos
were considered by some crews to be little
more than a 'Black 5' with a wide firebox,
but I think that assessment a little unfair, for
how often did you see them manfully hauling
trains that were diagrammed for some
unavailable 'Britannia'? The Scottish crews
in particular were very fond of the 'Clans'
and got some good work out of them. So it
was with a sad heart that we said goodbye to
our 'Clan', leaving her on South shed.

We were given a 5XP for our return,
working a Carlisle parcels train to Preston.
No 45697 *Achilles* presented no problems,
and rode well with the front end giving a
typical 5X roar once we got past 40mph, and
it was with some reluctance that we handed
her over to the set of Carnforth men who
relieved us at Preston. Here my old-hand
driver delivered his parting shot saying,
'I have my regular fireman back with me
tomorrow, but if I hadn't I would have taken
you with me again.' And that meant a lot to
me at the time. Some years later I owned a

5-inch-gauge 5XP No 45697 *Achilles* and driver wait patiently for
the off at a club gala day at Gilling. *Author's collection*

5-inch-gauge 5XP and I named it No 45697
Achilles.

I have a little bit more to tell you about
No 72006 *Clan Mackenzie* and my Lostock
Hall and NYMR colleague driver Brian
Snape, when he was working this engine on
our Carlisle-Manchester Red Bank van train.
Having passed Oxenholme at 45mph he
noticed a gang of platelayers ahead involved
in some jacking and packing work. They
had left it too late to get the jacks out in
time before the 'Clan' reached them, and
dived out of the way, escaping injury. No
72006 went up in the air and bounced down
again, miraculously staying on the rails,
unlike some of the newspaper vans, which
became derailed. Fortunately the signalman
witnessed everything and managed to stop
a down train labouring up the hill behind
a Type 4 diesel. The outcome of it all was
the ganger being reduced in rank and the
platelayers suspended for failing to comply
with the warning from the lookout man.

My next week's work was with driver
Sid Alty, working overnight coal empties
to Healey Mills over Copy Pit with relief
at Sowerby Bridge, then returning with the
ubiquitous coal train. Booking on for the job,

I noticed that a collection tin had been put out to contribute for a wreath for a senior driver who had been ill for a while and had passed away suddenly. Now, how could there be anything humorous about this, you might ask? Well, just after we had donated a few bob in the tin, another driver was booking on and, without even looking at the deceased's name, pointed to the collection tin and enquired, 'Did he have a locker?' We had an acute shortage of lockers at the depot, probably only about half the staff having one, so a locker was a prized possession.

'You're about the third mercenary git to ask me that in the last ten minutes,' the foreman brusquely replied.

Anyway, Sid and I had a chuckle, but had no time to hang about, for the engine had been prepared for us, allowing only 15 minutes to book on and depart from the shed to pick up our train of 60 empty coal wagons at the nearby Bamber Bridge yard. Our engine was no stranger to us, as we had one of our own – 'Austerity' Class 2-8-0 No 90720. Promptly at 9.45pm yard foreman Ronnie Finch got us the road and we began to pull out of the yard heading eastbound into the night with our maximum-length train. I of course remembered the 'Be Prepared' tuition from my veteran Preston driver, so I was ready for the 5-mile, 1 in 100 Hoghton Bank. I have said it before, and nothing will alter my opinion, that the driving of these loose-coupled trains required men of the highest calibre, and Sid was no exception. Our train would be on variable gradients right through to Sowerby Bridge; in fact, in my experience there was very little lengthy level railway on the entire former Lancashire & Yorkshire system.

Once past Rose Grove shed we had our regular water stop at Gannow Junction, and while I was up on the tender top I could hear the shovel going as Sid put on a good fire for me, before tackling another 5-mile climb up to Copy Pit summit. We soon had the road

and No 90720 got into her stride as only an 'Austerity' could do. They were certainly not built for speed. They did have some good attributes: they would steam no matter the quality of the coal, the injectors were of the best, they had excellent braking qualities, and they would still pull if a bit low on steam, unlike the Stanier '8s', where the guts went out of them if steam pressure dropped below the 200lb mark when hauling a heavy load up a bank. You had to keep them right up on the mark, particularly once you were over the top of an incline and needed the steam for braking power; some of the 8Fs had a separate steam brake fitted, and you had to keep hold of these loose-coupled trains, otherwise you were away, the train being in charge of you. This happened to me a couple of times when descending from Copy Pit summit. Despite the steam brake and tender brake being hard on, and the engine in back gear with just a breath of steam, we were often whistling for the road and level crossing gates at Portsmouth or Cornholme, hoping that we were not catching up with another train in front (which did happen once on this line with tragic circumstances).

Anyway, all was well and we had a dip on Luddendenfoot troughs. I have always wondered how this place, situated in the middle of Yorkshire, has a name that makes you think that you could be somewhere in deepest Wales. The next place was Sowerby Bridge, relief at 12.40am and sandwich time, before relieving a Leeds-Lostock Hall coal train as our return work. There was no time tonight for our hand of cribbage, the usual pastime when in between workings. Sid had previously taught me the game in Moss Lane Junction signal box over a few nights while waiting to relieve an Aintree-Copley Hill freight.

Tonight we relieved another trusty 'Austerity', No 90715, which I was glad to see on the front of our 38 wagons of Yorkshire coal. We topped up with water and entered Sowerby Bridge Tunnel after passing the engine sheds on the right. Sid expertly took up the slack on the 'Instanter' wagon couplings holding together our 600-ton train. I actually have a little time to take in the night scenery for a short while until the real work started from Stansfield Hall, for the assault on Copy Pit incline. But on this return work we would have the benefit of what the Yanks refer to as a helper engine from Stansfield Hall, as we were well over the loadings for a single loco. Guess what class of engine was waiting for us. Sorry boys, but you are wrong – it was not another 'Austerity'. As we whistled up it was by now 2.30am, and a Stanier 8F buffered up behind our 38 wagons and began to push us. I was therefore going to be kept quite busy on the shovel for a while until we topped the hill and came to a stand in the goods loop at Copy Pit.

Here we lost the 8F banker and it was time for me to climb down from the footplate, taking our wooden brakestick with me, to assist the guard in pinning down enough wagon brakes to prevent the possibility of our 600-ton load getting the better of our available brake force. Heavy rain started to fall as Stefan, our Polish guard – fondly known as 'Stefan the Shunting Pole' – climbed aboard his brake van with the task complete, and from the back of the train gave me a green light from his paraffin lamp. This I relayed to Sid, who gave a toot on the whistle, then released the steam brake. After giving No 90715 a breath of steam, our train slowly drifted out and away from this remote and rugged railway landmark. It was now time for Sid to really earn his corn, in keeping this load from getting the better of us down the incline to Rose Grove. I looked across at him – he had his Sherlock Holmes pipe on the go, smoking his favourite Condor brown twist, the aroma of which drifted across the cab. Ho took a quick look at the clock and the glass, and gave me a nod and a

wink as he concentrated on the job ahead.

I had it just that bit easier now and, having wedged the brake stick to form a foot rest between the cabside and firebox, I was sitting comfortably in the padded fireman's seat, enjoying a fag and a cup of stewed tea from my can on the warmer plate. Soon it became a battle to keep awake; the rhythm and clanking from the motion of the old 'Austerity' began to lull me into a light slumber, and my mind drifted off. I seemed to be dreaming of sitting somewhere like the Royal Opera House listening to an aria. That's when I woke up with a jolt and realised that it was Sid in full flow with a driving rendition of Mario Lanza's *Because You're Mine*. I had forgotten that Sid liked a singsong at times like this, serenading the fireman, and his semi-operatic voice had the desired effect of keeping both of us from falling asleep. Once I jokingly told Sid that I thought he could have made it as a singer, but it was just his voice that let him down.

Arriving at Rose Grove it was always interesting to listen to the shunters working in the down grid yard signalling to each other, as all communication between them was done using a whistle code. It was here that a little remarshalling of our train took place, resulting in us leaving at about 6.30am with a somewhat reduced load, before finally arriving back at our home base at 8.00am. Here we shunted our train in Lostock Hall yard, then took No 90715 to the shed, leaving it to the disposal crew. It was 8.30am when we signed off. This was the first of five nights on this turn. Ideally you needed to complete your shift in less than 12 hours, as exceeding this could mean that you missed the job the following night, as the regulations stated that you could not book on duty again unless you had had at least a 12-hour rest period.

Some months later, with Christmas nearly upon us – in fact, it was my birthday – I was marked up to work a Barrow-Euston special from Preston to Crewe, with Preston driver Arnold. We had 'Britannia' No 70036 *Boadicea* rostered for the job, which we prepared on shed, then visited the mess room to wash up and fill my tea can. We are due off the shed at 10.20am to run light to Preston. We climbed aboard and were ready to leave when two platelayers informed us that we couldn't go anywhere yet, as they were replacing four sleepers on the track in front of us! Apparently they had been told that we were due off shed at 11.20am. Right – action stations! The running shift foreman was quick off the mark in finding us another chariot (Arnold's terminology for the steam locomotive). So after a quick dash across to the ashpit road with our traps, we climbed aboard freshly disposed 'Black 5' No 44761. Another set of men were busily splashing some oil around her, and checking the lubricators.

Fortunately the engine was the right way round and had been coaled, so after topping up with water we are just 20 minutes late off shed. There followed a quick dash to Preston just as our train rolled into Platform 9 behind a Type 4 diesel. Both crews wasted no time with the changing of locomotives, and true to practice I was prepared for departure with our ten-coach load, the fire, steam and water all to my satisfaction. Incidentally, you may be wondering why we didn't just reman on the diesel and work through with it. The reason was that not many drivers at that time had been trained and passed on diesel traction. But we had the pleasure of working on one of the later-built 'Black 5s' fitted with Timken roller bearings and equipped with self-cleaning smokebox and a rocking grate. These usually performed well, and she proved to be in fine fettle as we got into our stride up the bank to Coppull. There was a covering of snow on the ground and bright sunshine, making it a pleasure to be out, a

'Black 5' No 44761, seen here at Preston, was a more than ample replacement for No 70036 *Boadicea* on my birthday run to Crewe with the Barrow-Euston special, including getting a little bit lost on our return journey! *Dawlish Warren Railway Museum*

real birthday treat for me! Everything was going well on such a good machine – she rode well and was a fine example of this outstanding class of locomotive. We had no booked stops, being right away from Preston to Crewe, and once we were over the Ship Canal bridge, south of Warrington, it was downhill to the troughs at Moore, then she was given her head, managing to attain a brief 80mph at Winsford, before coasting along nicely on our final stretch, and arriving a couple of minutes early at the Premier Line station at Crewe. A healthy crowd of Christmas shoppers greeted our arrival on Platform 1. Here the train was to be electric-hauled to Euston, all three forms of available motive power thus having been utilised.

We left No 44761 in the hands of the fire-droppers on Crewe North and reported to the running foreman, as we had no booked return work.

'Have a cuppa, Preston – I'll find you something to work back,' he told us.

So we followed his instructions, giving us a tea break in Crewe North's cosmopolitan mess room, which was crowded with men from depots far and wide, the noisiest among them being Crewe men, wanting to be heard above all the others. Listening to them gave you the impression that they all worked in the Perth and the London links, prompting an Edge Hill driver to ask of them in his best Scouse accent, 'Who shunts Crewe station then, mate?'

The reply came, 'Ah, we have Stoke men doing that!'

We hadn't been in there long when the foreman's runner came in, telling us to take No 44761 back light engine to Lostock Hall as it was needed for a Glasgow job at teatime. 'We will have it ready for you to go off shed in about an hour's time,' he told us.

Now, what happened next caused a lot of hassle and confusion later, for at the 'giving-off hut' I think the engine arranger must have misheard what I told him, and

for the first few minutes when we left the shed I was busy with the shovel covering the grate and making up the newly formed fire, and not really noticing where the signalman had turned us, until Arnold asked, 'Where is he putting us? We are heading towards Manchester instead of Preston!'

'Do you know the road?' I asked him.

'Well, only as far as Sandbach.'

Upon arrival there, we stopped, and I phoned the signalman and told him we were light engine for Lostock Hall. The signaller replied, 'I have you light engine for Longsight – the engine arranger at Crewe must have misheard you. Does your mate know the road if we put you via Middlewich and Northwich, then back onto the West Coast at Hartford?'

I said I would go and ask him. Arnold's reply came as a bit of a shock. 'I've never been over the line. I know it's a goods-only route, but we can't stop here much longer – trains will be piling up behind us. Tell him I'm all right for Hartford.'

So the signaller reset the route, gave us a green and away we went off to the left at the junction, feeling our way over this strange route. Fortunately we were only a light engine and it was still daylight, so between us and a couple of very helpful and understanding signalmen we eventually found our way to Hartford Junction, and it was with some relief that Arnold exclaimed, 'I don't think that I've ever been as glad in my life to see those overhead wires,' as we rejoined our home territory on the West Coast Main Line.

Back at Lostock Hall depot, our engine was remanned for an evening trip over the border into Scotland. Incidentally, the 'Black 5s' numbered in the 446xx and 447xx series were popular among footplate crews, as they always seemed to be very free-steaming and better-riding engines, the roller bearings making such an obvious difference, just as they did on the last two of the 'Duchess'

Class. This is where we definitely lagged behind American steam policy; they decreed that all large freight and passenger locos should be fitted with roller bearings, and they would freewheel for miles on level track.

Having said goodbye to No 44761, we signed off duty on what had been a memorable birthday for me, with just time to join Arnold for an early evening birthday pint in the local Railway Hotel before heading off home. The landlord at the pub for many years was Harry Ward, the shed being situated just across the road; the goods yard and wagon shops were equally handy, as were the carriage sidings, with the signal box and main line less than 20 feet away, just over the sleeper-built fence at the side of the pub. Add to this the pub's own bowling green, where many crown green competitions were held, and you can imagine that the place was always pretty busy, with Harry as mine host to all grades of railwaymen, particularly in the vault. The only downside to calling in for one quick pint was trying to make sense of someone who latched on to you, wanting to talk but already five pints ahead of you! Harry himself would have to listen to all the gossip and stories from behind the bar and, as you can imagine, he became quite knowledgeable about railway operation and footplate workings. In fact, one night he paused from pulling me a pint as a freight slowly rumbled passed and, looking at the pub clock, remarked, 'The Edge Hill-Carlisle is running a bit late tonight.' Alas, the pub closed a few years ago, by coincidence on the same date, 11 August, as the shed had closed to steam decades earlier.

As I have said, just 20 feet away from the pub and behind the railway sleeper fence existed another interesting establishment, Lostock Hall Carriage Sidings signal box.

Ged's Lostock Hall Carriage Sidings Signal Box has Stanier 'Pacific' No 46238 *City of Carlisle* for company with the empty coaching stock of a Carlisle-Preston football excursion, 1Z13, in February 1964. *Peter Fitton*

Well, it was interesting when my signalman mate Ged was on duty. He was a big, outgoing lad, with a big voice to match, full of fun and humour, particularly after a few pints when accompanied by his sidekick, Alan. I tended to try and keep away if the pair got together, but we were all young and foolish back then. Away from railways, Rugby League was Ged's sporting interest, supporting the almost unbeatable Wigan team. Whenever I passed the box with a train he would be gesticulating with his arms rugby-style, bellowing out to 'keep the ball moving', encouraging us to get a move on. The box had only about 20 levers so I soon became competent enough to give him a break from the strenuous task on his permanent 12-hour shift.

His elderly oppo was a former Class 1 signalman, who had transferred to this Class 3 box. Ged told me that his name was Shakespeare. One evening I joined Ged in the box just as his relief arrived and came up the steps to commence his duty.

'Hello, Mr Shakespeare,' I politely addressed him.

He looked a little puzzled before replying, 'That's not my name – who told you to call me that?'

Ged jumped in, saving the day by telling him that everything had been all right that day, there was nothing to report, see you tomorrow – and he quickly ushered me out of the box and down the steps. Of course, I immediately looked at him and asked what all that was about. He had a look of embarrassment on his face, which was unusual for him, as he blurted out that his oppo had downgraded from a main-line Class 1 signal box because of his nerves, and that Shakespeare was not his real name – he called him that because he had the shakes! With that I felt I needed a drink; unfortunately we could not patronise the adjacent Railway Hotel as Ged had been barred from there following his reaction to the landlord's refusal to serve him and Alan another drink in the best room at just gone closing time of 10.30. After turning on his heels he had headed back into the best room and decided to leave, but not before banking up the open fire with a couple of the pub's best wooden stools to keep the remaining clientele in the comfort they deserved, since they paid a penny a pint more for the privilege of sitting in the best side.

Another pub in the village that had given Ged a red card was the Pleasant Retreat. But it was not living up to its name for Ged and his mate Alan one Friday night, due to the guest pianist refusing to play any popular music for the youthful audience. During the 20-minute interval, when the maestro took a break from boring everybody stupid, Ged thought that the old Joanna might benefit from a little lubrication to liven it up so, as he was passing, he opened its lid and gave it a pint of Boddington's best bitter, spread evenly over its inners. Liberace returned and was halfway through a driving rendition of a modern First World War crowd-pleaser entitled 'There is no need to go down the mines, son, you have plenty of slack in your pants' when the second half had to be hastily abandoned due to the piano keys gumming up and transforming the budding Liberace into a Les Dawson sound-alike.

9 More visits to the pub, and a missing giraffe!

There were still two pubs in the village that we could visit on a Friday night without, hopefully, getting into any bother. At about 9 o'clock we were in the Tardy Gate, having been joined by Alan, and the place was heaving. We were approached by a white-coated travelling salesman who visited all the pubs in the area at weekends, offering a fine array of seafood delights from his basket Alan was straight in with an order, asking him: 'Have you any crabs on you cock?'

The poor bloke must have heard that same joke every night, followed by Ged's one-liner asking him if he had any muscles with him. However, he was always polite, replying that he had.

So Ged told him, 'That's good – now use them to pick up your basket and piss off, as we don't want owt.'

I carried on visiting Ged until the box closed. He was a well-known collector of all makes of cigarette coupons and would do a swop for those that you needed, but I lost touch with him when he transferred to the Class 1 signal box at Euxton Junction (pronounced Exton). Another character and big fella that I worked with was driver Alec, a rough diamond who on the surface seemingly did not give a toss for his fireman. When booking on duty you were allowed 10 minutes to read the latest notices, but Alec looked upon this as his time, only appearing at the last minute, exasperating the foreman with his usual excuse that it was the earliest he'd been late that week. He was heavy-

handed, and his main objective when driving an engine was to get to the destination as quickly as possible, and it was the fireman's job to provide him with enough steam to get him into the pub before closing time.

Once in there, however, he would change completely and spoil you with as much beer as you could drink – and he could sup! I never tried to keep up with him – it was as though he had a 4,000-gallon tender coupled up to him. After being thrown out of the pub, and despite my objections, he would offer me a lift home in his car, but when I suggested we walk he would insist that he was too pissed to walk. He would join in on anybody's conversation – I couldn't get a word in, which was highly unusual for me. He would tell me to stop butting in while he was interrupting.

You couldn't really call him a driver – he just operated the right controls in the wrong way – but he was a likeable rogue and I actually enjoyed working with him. He had some good one-liners, such as, 'Listen, kid, just when you think that you've got a good fire on, start bloody shovelling,' or when getting an engine ready on the shed he would kid me and say, 'Go on, mate, you drive today – take her up to the water column.'

He was the enemy of all goods guards, particularly when we had an English Electric Type 4 diesel on the front of an unfitted goods train with only the straight air brake available for braking. These diesels were a dead weight on wheels, weighing 133 tons, and drivers had to attend a course and prove themselves competent to an inspector before being let out on the road. Alec was the only bloke I knew that had to go on the course three times after complaints from the guards that he was trying to put them through the brake van window, as he only had two positions with the brake – either full on or full release. He told guards to tie themselves in and check their personal injury insurance!

Alec was always in some sort of trouble with the management, and we used to joke that he'd had more suspensions than the hangman, Albert Pierrepoint. We were once standing in Platform 3 at Preston station with a 'Black 5' on the 2.40 afternoon stopper to Barrow-in-Furness. A down afternoon express was about due to pass through the adjacent Platform 4, so we decided to have a look at No 46254 *City of Stoke-on-Trent* as it drifted past us at the regulation 20mph through the station. We saw the top-link Camden fireman leaning out of the cab looking across at us; in one hand he was holding a flat sheet of newspaper and in the other he was shaking the detonator tin up and down, while grinning from ear to ear.

He shouted across to us, 'Bit more vinegar, mate – are they ready yet?'

I looked at Alec and asked him what that was all about. He laughed, and said that the cheeky sod was insinuating that our 'Black 5', compared to his 'Lizzie', was nothing better than a mobile fish and chip cart!

Alec's regular fireman had been brought up in Somerset and was a complete teetotaller. Alec regularly informed him that, when he got up in the morning, that would be the best that he would feel all day! He was a bit of a wazzock, who once offered to help me with some landscaping, telling me that he was experienced. I asked him if he had a driving licence, to which he replied, 'No I can't drive, but I knows the gears.' I tried to visualise him sitting next to me changing the gears while I steered the van, which incidentally had a column change!

Living near me was a chap called Malcolm Leach, who was a well-known local amateur boxer. Malcolm worked for the railways and represented the London Midland Region pugilists; his elder brother Dennis was a driver. One day I was the fireman to Dennis with double-chimney 9F No 92118 on a late-running freight job to Crewe Basford Hall; we had no return work, and the Crewe North foreman could only offer us a partially fitted freight to work back, which Dennis quietly refused; the pair of us had already been on duty for nearly 7 hours, and we didn't fancy more hours stuck in goods loops working one of these jobs back to Preston. So we went home 'on the cushions', during which time we had a discussion regarding the forthcoming 1964

'Baby Scot' No 45550 stands on No 1 road at 24C Lostock Hall with driver Dennis Leach, one of my companions to Villa Park for the FA Cup semi-final clash between Preston North End and Swansea City in 1964. *Tony Gillette*

FA Cup semi-final match, between our beloved Preston North End and Swansea City, taking place at Villa Park, Birmingham, in a few weeks time.

Once back at the shed and signing off, we put in our leave applications to Vinny Hughes, the foreman's assistant. He looked at them and told us that he was travelling down to the match in his car and would we fancy going with him if we could get match tickets? That is what happened. So at 8.00am on that Saturday morning the three of us left Preston, tickets in hand, riding in Vinny's green Austin A40 car. The game was played to a capacity crowd in atrocious conditions. It rained solid for most of the day and with the score level at 1-1 and time running out, Preston's centre half, Tony Singleton, hammered the ball from just inside the Swansea half and it rocketed into the net. There were great celebrations among the mud-splattered and drenched players, for this proved to be the winning goal and our 2nd Division team was through to Wembley, to play 1st Division West Ham United. On Cup Final day we were actually beating them 2-1, but the game swung in their favour, and eventually we lost 3-2. This was no disgrace to us, as West Ham had some top-class players in their team, including the England Captain Bobby Moore and Geoff Hurst, while our claim to fame was having in our side the youngest ever player to take part in an FA Cup Final at that time, 16-year-old Howard Kendall.

A few weeks after the disappointment of Wembley I was heading to Carnforth, another place that we never seem to be away from, working a fitted goods with bearded Preston driver, and ace car mechanic, Tommy Williams. The very first time I saw Tommy was when he drove Caledonian Railway No 123 heading south light engine to a railway exhibition. He was leaving Preston station and leaned out of the cab – if ever a driver looked the part it was

Tommy, sporting his period full beard. He and I always had plenty of mechanical conversations, and at the time I was having a bit of prolonged trouble with the Wilson pre-selector gearbox on my Lanchester 14. Anyway, on the approach to Lancaster the signaller put us into Oubeck loop to allow a few expresses to pass. So it is out with the chalk on the locker door with Tommy educating me on the complications of the Wilson box, accompanied by an almost scale workshop manual drawing, outlining the possible faults.

When I worked for the railways I found that, no matter what problem you had – be it railways, washing machines, vehicles, women, finances, animals, motorbikes – there was always somebody just bursting with knowledge to help you out with the problem.

It was also around this time that I very nearly missed a real plum job due to car problems. Luckily for me, my next-door neighbour was leaving for work at the same time, and gave me a lift on the back of his powerful Vincent Comet motorbike. I might just tell you that Fred offered to sell me this machine for £100 when he retired, but having no real interest in motorbikes I didn't take him up on his offer. I recently saw a Comet auctioned for £52,000 – ah, well, at least I can say that I have actually ridden on one.

Anyway, back to the story. That morning I had been due to sign on at 8.00am, engine prepared, 8.15 off shed, light to Preston, and work an officers' special to Carlisle on the 'bottom road' via Whitehaven and Workington. It was 8.20am when I arrived; Vinny was the foreman, and he told me to dash across to No 4 road and see if the engine had left the shed with the replacement fireman. My driver was jovial Paddy Doyle, and fortunately he had only just whistled up to move off shed as I climbed aboard, so I asked the fireman to tell Vinny to sign me on duty when he went back to the office. Incidentally, Vinny was also a roster clerk, and one of the best; his motto was 'Always look after them that look after you'. If certain other roster clerks that I have worked with had heeded Vinny's philosophy, they would have enjoyed a better working relationship with the footplate staff!

That morning I was lucky, unlike the flock of pigeons that we splattered at Oxheys, just after leaving Preston on our 'Black 5' with an ex-LMS Directors' saloon. I am relating this story to highlight just how regulations have changed regarding train working in the 1960s compared to the present-day 'health and stupidity' regime. I have worked a number of these officers' specials, but this one was unusual in that no propelling movements were involved. It was just a straightforward case of stopping as requested at various stations along the route for a quick inspection, after which the officers met up with staff until we reached Whitehaven Bransty, where a stop for lunch was scheduled. The loco crew also had a lunch provided by the on-board catering staff and – wait for it – we were usually offered a beer apiece to wash down the excellent lunch. I'm afraid that wouldn't be on the menu these days!

After lunch we ambled along, eventually arriving into the border city of Carlisle and, after turning on the triangle and taking water there, the railway officers asked Control to give us an uninterrupted 90-mile run over Shap back to Preston, and this we actually achieved. Our 'Class 5' was in pretty decent nick, so it was more or less 75mph all the way, arriving in Preston some 20 minutes ahead of schedule, pleasing the management to such an extent that before they left us we were given two bottles of beer apiece. Mind you, they were managers in those days and worthy of some respect.

I always used to enjoy working to Barrow-in-Furness, particularly after leaving Carnforth where we could enjoy the lovely coastal views from Arnside, then on to Grange-over-Sands and through the island platform at Ulverston serving the Lakeside branch. We did have some work to Lakeside, mostly on Sundays during the summer, and these were all short rest jobs, meaning that you booked off at Lakeside at lunchtime, then signed on again in the evening for the return work. It was common practice for the loco crew to take their families and spend the afternoon with them, having a sail on Lake Windermere or visiting Bowness. To my regret I was never lucky enough to have sampled one of these idyllic Sundays. I have visited the truncated preserved section from Haverthwaite to Lakeside, travelling behind the former Preston dock tank *Princess*, and *Victor*, my former West Somerset Railway loco, before enjoying a sail and a visit to the museum. I left with the impression of a neat, compact and well-run business, with just a handful of staff, one loco in steam hauling five crowded coaches doing six round trips a day, with a smashing restaurant/café at Haverthwaite, demonstrating how to run a preserved railway and make a decent profit.

Motive power on our jobs to Barrow was usually a 5XP with between seven and nine coaches hanging behind the tender. Speaking of which, I think I must have been a little unlucky when on these jobs, invariably being lumbered with a Fowler-tendered 5XP. They were dirty, draughty things, with less coal and water capacity than their Stanier counterparts. The fire irons were a nuisance; being placed lengthways across the tender top, they got in the way when bringing coal forward, and were usually damaged or bent due to some crews being too lazy to move them when under the coal hopper. I didn't really mind them as much when working freight trains. Some of the 8Fs had these tenders and so of course did the Midland 4Fs and the Horwich 'Crabs'.

The 5XPs could be temperamental engines. For example, during one week's work to Barrow we had four different members of the class, and I used the same method of firing on them all, but with differing results. On two of them I just showed them the shovel, and we had steam a plenty, while another one seemed to like a big back end, which was rare for a member of this class, having a light beat. The fourth one was No 45703 *Thunderer*, which is just what it didn't do and it hadn't done so for the fireman I had relieved at Preston. Its only saving grace was that it didn't have a Fowler tender. If you excuse the pun, the train of thought among the senior men was that this class of engine was too big in the wheel; had they had 6ft 2in drivers instead of 6ft 9in, and a slightly different cylinder size, they would have been a better all-round loco. Undoubtedly when they were hill-climbing a good 'Black 5' could see them off; in fact, the '5s' were the most versatile of all steam locomotives, whatever called upon to do – fast heavy freights, slow coal-hauling, long-distance express passenger, local stopping trains, shunting jobs. A truly great design. The 5XPs seemed to be more at home on a flat, fast railway with eight or nine coaches, such as the Midland main line into St Pancras, although if you got a good one they could perform; I have had personal experience of an excellent unassisted assault on Beattock with No 45690 *Leander* topping the 10 miles of 1 in 60 at just under 25mph with a ten-coach train – but I must admit that I didn't get much chance to take in any of the scenery!

When I started at 24C, the depot had lost all the old Lancashire & Yorkshire engines including the famous 2-4-2 tank locos. They were popular engines in their day, for the limited water capacity was more than made up for by the vacuum-operated bi-directional water scoops, which helped to overcome the myth that a 'Lanky' man could never pass a water column. Some vintage machines that still had some life in them were the Midland 4Fs. I think I had a soft spot for them, but they were not everybody's favourite loco, and it was a standing joke that there was no problem in making them steam – until you put the injector on! They were a fixture on a certain few jobs at the shed, including the 1.10am Accrington goods, usually made up to a full load, a good deal of which was wood pulp. We had this job in the link that I was in, together with another tiresome turn, signing on at 2.40am for the Southport goods. Some of the 4Fs had a tender cab, which was handy during the winter months, but it made disposing of the fire a bit awkward due to the length of the fire irons. But the real secret of having a good or a bad day on these engines depended on who the driver was; if he was used to handling them, then you were OK. I have previously described the universally accepted firing technique with these engines so, unlike Mike on his Class 2 engine, be careful that you do not lose it, as we cannot keep searching the line!

Seasoned drivers of these machines will all tell you the same – just crack open the second valve, pull her back 1½ turns and leave her to find her own way up a bank, then just perch yourself on the driver's wooden seat atop of the reverser, where you can observe your fireman in action, doing his utmost to keep this mobile kettle with enough steam and water to reach your destination. If it was a passenger train that you were working, and it was the carriage heating season, no doubt that would be sacrificed until you got to the top of the bank. An old trick that would sometimes assist with steaming was to fire a few shovelfuls of sand over the arch to give the tubes a clean. Oh, how I do miss those challenges – just how the hell can a diesel locomotive get the adrenalin going the same!

Occasionally we had a footplate inspector riding with us for assessment purposes. Our local inspector was Wilf Marsden, or Mr Marsden to us. It was best behaviour time when he was about – none of my usual cheek and jokes. If you visualised in your mind just what a footplate inspector would look like, then he was your role model – always smartly dressed in a three-piece suit, collar and tie, and the obligatory bowler hat. He was a well-respected figure, and actually struck fear into some men. One day when I was on the south-end station pilot at Preston with loco No 47319, we were standing in No 7 platform near the footbridge when a train came in on the adjacent No 8 platform. Inspector Marsden got off and walked over the footbridge, stopping to look down on our engine, so I put my head in the cab, only to hear him call for me from atop:

'Fireman, are you there?'

'Yes, sir,' I replied, looking out.

'You have some coal on the cab roof – are you that bad with your shovel?' he said, and thankfully away he went, leaving my driver chuckling to himself as he passed the brush up to me on the cab roof.

Some time later I was on a morning freight train to Carnforth. We went light engine from the shed down to our starting point at Ribble Sidings to be met by Mr Marsden, who had with him a fireman on his driving exam. My driver, Ken McKivor, left the footplate and travelled with our guard in the brake van. The Preston fireman, Dick Calvert, was actually a good friend of mine, and we played football together for the railway team.

I had chance to have a quick word with Dick when we were on our own, and we agreed that he would keep a dialogue going with me, about the road and signals, management of the engine, etc. We got away on time with a full load of freight behind our Class 5 locomotive, and Dick's handling of the train was exemplary. The only slight blip occurred when the signalman at Garstang turned us into the loop. Dick

had his head out watching the train into the loop when an overhanging branch clipped his grease-top cap and it fell onto the ballast; obviously he continued on until our train was inside clear, then, with the Inspector's permission, I walked back the 46 wagon lengths and retrieved it. There then followed an interesting chat among the three of us, discussing of all things the pop charts from the 1950s, Dick having been a distant relation of trumpeter Eddie Calvert from Preston, who had a string of hit recordings including a No 1 with *Oh, Mein Papa*. Dick also proved to be a hit on the day and was successful in becoming a passed fireman.

Other footplate inspectors based in our area at that time were Bert Moore, Dougie Cullen and George Hesketh. I and my driver that week, Ken McKivor, shared a passion for the 'Black 5' locomotive, and for three days that week we had Springs Branch loco No 45449, and they didn't come much better than that. It wasn't ex-works by any means, and we had a full load behind her each day. In fact, the second day on our return south we were checked at the bottom of Lancaster Bank, despite Ken having instructed Carnforth to give us a run or a banker, but No 45449 took it all, and lifted the near 500-ton load up that nasty incline from Lancaster in true 'Black 5' fashion. It was a pleasure to be on board that machine. As a sequel to this, my neighbour, who is a retired engineer and was born in Wigan, is building a 5-inch-gauge 'Black 5', and when he asked me of a memorable loco of the class, I related to him about No 45449 from his home-town shed, so he has decided to number it as such, and No 45449 will live on and steam again one day.

The Saturday of that week was one of those days when I wished we could have had an inspector with us, as we relieved a Windermere-Manchester express when it ran into Preston behind 5XP No 45642 *Boscawen*. I anticipated some slackness with the crew when I noticed that the front coupling had not been secured on its bracket – little things like this would annoy me. We climbed on board and the footplate was far from glorious and in a shocking state, as were the crew; no attempt had been made to clean up prior to being relieved. The whole cab was filthy, including the gauge frames. I could only just about see that the water in the glass was 'just bobbin'. We had less than 150lb of steam and the coal was way back in the tender – none had been brought forward.

I asked one of the indifferent pair, 'Have you had a rough trip, mate?'

'No, she's been all right,' replied the old-hand Preston fireman as he stepped down from the footplate.

When they had gone Ken and I looked at each other, shrugged our shoulders and looked round at the mess, which led us to assume that this must be their usual standard of workmanship. It was totally alien to my belief in always leaving an engine in the condition in which you would like to find it. With departure time almost upon us, we both got stuck in to provide the essential ingredients, i.e. fire, steam and water. The station inspector had given us a couple more minutes to bring her round, then away we went, first stop Manchester Victoria, bypassing Bolton and travelling via Hilton House Junction and Dobbs Brow to Pendleton. Leaving Preston it would be uphill for about 15 miles to Adlington – a good test to see what No 5642 was made of. Lo and behold, there was nothing wrong with the engine – it pulled and it steamed, it was a good 'un, like all Bank Hall 5XPs – proving to us that the previous crew could have done with a visit from Inspector Marsden to tighten up on their footplate etiquette.

A similar train, which ran during the summer months from Windermere, formed the 5.12pm Preston to Liverpool Exchange, then back with the 7.40pm to Preston. At other times of the year the train started from Preston, usually with a 'Black 5', but during the summer a larger engine could be seen on the job.

When on this job, Driver Jack ('Heapey') Howard and I had the pleasure of a round trip with double-chimney rebuilt 5XP No 45735 *Comet*, and my memory of it was that it had been a worthwhile rebuild, with a power output identical to the rebuilt 'Baby Scots'. Then on the following day a 'Scot' turned up on the job. 'Heapey' thoroughly enjoyed himself driving this powerhouse, No 46145; it also meant something to me, for it was the last 'Scot' I had copped during my trainspotting days. Now here I was in the fireman's seat with a ten-coach express, but it wasn't that comfortable in the cab of a 'Scot' – no side window, of course, and with no trailing truck, combined with worn back boxes, they could be a lively ride.

My last turn on a 'Scot', ironically, was on what was later to become part of the fleet of West Coast Railways, No 46115 *Scots Guardsman*. It was then seeing out its final days on freight work, and Colin Shaw and I had what I thought then would be my final fling with the locomotive, working the 6.00pm Preston North Union-Warrington Arpley partially fitted freight (this being the same job on which I had No 45543 *Home Guard* a few years previously). Pleasingly I have, of course, renewed my acquaintance with No 46115, working with her on numerous occasions in my capacity as a fireman for West Coast Railways.

A few weeks later it was Bonfire Night and I was working an evening stopping train from Preston to Fleetwood with a young passed fireman, Joe Unsworth; we had Caprotti 'Black 5' No 44746. The weather was absolutely foul, with torrential rain sweeping in off the Irish Sea. It always surprises me the amount of folk who assume that you must be warm and dry in the cab of a steam locomotive! I wish they could have seen us that night – water was coming in from every crevice, leaving us soaking wet, but what amazed me was the large number of bonfires we passed on our journey. I honestly imagined that the rain would have made them difficult to light, or even extinguish them, but no, the hundreds of hardy souls were not going to let a bit of bad weather dampen their spirits. I made good use of the engine whistle when passing a bonfire, which was acknowledged with a friendly wave from all.

The terminus at Fleetwood was a busy place at that time with ferry services to Ireland and the Isle of Man. Freight was plentiful and all this contributed to making plenty of comings and goings at the nearby loco sheds at Wyre Dock. This included ourselves, dropping in and servicing No 44746. While Joe was oiling the motion I climbed up onto the running plate to check the lubricator levels for him, and he told me an amusing story concerning loco preparation. He was the fireman preparing a three-cylinder 5XP with an old-hand driver, who was somewhat overweight but would not trust his fireman to oil up the inside motion, insisting upon doing it himself. It was a tight squeeze for a man of his size fitting between the big ends and balance weights, and sure enough the day came when he did get stuck between the front of the firebox and the balance weight. He shouted for Joe, who was on the footplate, to help get him out. Joe decided to teach him a lesson and jokingly shouted back to him, 'Just stop there, mate, and I'll set her back a bit to release you!'

Now, this brought an instant response and a few seconds later Joe heard the crashing of a pair of hobnail boots, attached to the driver's 19-stone bulk, landing heavily in the pit amid much cussing and swearing. After this Joe was always given the oil feeder on inside-motion engines!

Keeping with the theme of overweight drivers leads to another little ditty, told to me by former Southport driver and friend Ronnie Clough from his firing days. It occurred on one very foggy winter's morning about 5.00am as they were going off Southport shed, chimney-first with a 2-8-0 'Austerity'. They were going at a crawl when they came into contact with an ex-L&Y 0-8-0 goods engine. Ronnie's driver sent him to check that everything was all right on the other engine. No damage had been done, so Ronnie went to look on the footplate. The driver's seat on these engines was situated quite high up from footplate level, and it took a bit of effort to get yourself up there, particularly if you happened to come under the category of obese. When Ronnie climbed into the cab he found this big old driver lying full length on the floor of the footplate.

Upon enquiring if he had been hurt, he was told, 'I'm alreet but tha's gone and knocked me off me perch!'

The fireman complained that 'he would have to help the old bugger back up there', because, for some of these old boys, climbing up onto their seat was the full extent of any physical activity, and once they got up there that was it for the day!

One wet and windswept Monday morning we were ready to go off the shed at 5.30am on board 8F No 48618 to work No 63 Target. My driver for the day was Harry. We reached Preston Ribble Sidings, having travelled light engine, just as the night shunting staff were going off duty, having battled through a horrendous night of bad weather at this exposed hill-top goods yard, which was busy 24 hours a day. Its location offered little shelter for those hardy souls. They had my admiration working the long 12-hour shifts. Sometimes, when I lay awake at night unable to sleep, I thought of them unhooking wagon after wagon with their shunt poles, and chasing wagons with the brake sticks, pulling hand points, all of this performed under dim lighting conditions with only the added relief of their own paraffin lamps exchanging hand signals with one another. It did make you appreciate the comfort of being in a warm bed – and sleep soon followed.

Amongst all this toil there was always humour somewhere. One of the staff was a real company man who would do anything to please his superiors – he was known to have more faces than the Town Hall clock. He also had charge of all traffic to and from Preston Dock and the North Union yard, together with Preston East Lancs yard. He would travel about visiting each yard and all the relevant staff, but much of his time was spent conversing on the telephone with numerous other members of staff, not only discussing railway matters, but usually falsely enquiring of their well-being, for as soon as he put the phone down he would always utter two words: 'The prick.' And that was what all the staff called him, behind his back, of course.

But revenge is sweet, and it came to pass one April day that he received an urgent phone call, supposedly from Control. He was told that the Blackpool Tower Circus train was approaching Preston from the north, and that he was to travel with the train, acting as a conductor for the 6 miles round the loop via Lostock Hall and Todd Lane Junction, then back into Preston riding in the giraffe van, in order to warn the keeper of the overbridges en route, enabling him to lower the giraffe's head in time. Now, being the good company servant that he was, he dutifully made his way down to the station to await the arrival of this semi-regular circus train. After a couple of hours sitting waiting, he rang Control, who of course had never heard of it. But it was suggested that he had a look on his calendar, as the day before had been the last day of March!

Returning to No 63 Target, this took us up the old Longridge branch with a mixed load of vans, produce and coal. Maudland Yard was shunted first, then off up to

Deepdale through the tunnels and past the station that used to serve the football ground. Arriving at the goods yard, we had plenty of coal wagons to shunt, so Harry had a breather and I was in the driver's seat. I remember looking across at him, sitting on the fireman's seat, and cheekily asking him, 'Can you manage at that side?'

I loved his reply: 'More importantly, Fingers, are you sure you can you manage at that side?'

Upon leaving the busy coal yard at Deepdale, having seemingly shunted every wagon into numerical order, we headed off tender-first for a couple of miles to our next port of call, the 'Banana Shop'. This was just a single siding, controlled by a ground frame, so we propelled our two banana vans towards the warehouse, leaving the rest of our train secured on the single-line branch. It was here that our guard had to perform the most important task of his day: he had to meet up with the warehouse foreman and use all his charm on him to procure at least three bundles of Fyffe's finest. He soon proved his worth, returning to the engine clutching them under his arm and, after storing our West Indian contraband in the locker, we pieced up the train and headed for Grimsargh.

It was here that another single-line branch went off, leading to the mental hospital at Whittingham. It sported its own rolling stock and locos, the service was free, and it existed until 1957, long after the passenger service on the Longridge branch had closed in 1930. Visitors for the hospital had to catch a bus to Grimsargh, then travel from there on the private railway.

We had no traffic for Grimsargh that day so it was on with our journey to the line's terminus at Longridge. Here we were met by old Jack, who was employed as the shunter and assisted our guard for a couple of hours until we had exchanged all the empty wagons for the loaded ones and the goods yard looked tidy again. So we took water, and it so happened that we were thirsty too, so the four of us took ourselves into the adjacent Towneley Arms for a lunchtime pie and a pint. Half an hour later, suitably refreshed, we bid goodbye to old Jack, who due to his penguin-like gait was better known in Longridge as 'Penguin the Shunter'.

On our return journey we passed the large Courtaulds factory and sidings, and exchanged a friendly whistle with the crew on the works shunter, a Peckett 0-4-0 saddle tank, awaiting their next delivery of coal. (This engine later worked at Steamtown, Carnforth.) Courtaulds employed hundreds of staff in its heyday, allowing them to have their own sports field and a football team. The Lostock Hall shed team played them once in a pre-season friendly before we became members of the league – they beat us 7-1, which might seem like a whitewash, but they had two or three ex-pros in their team, while playing for us at outside right was none other than Peter Norris (aka Peter Stuyvesant – explanation later), and it was he who scored our solitary goal. A few nights later our local paper had a match report with the headlines 'Norris Scores for Rail from an Acute Angle'. However, he actually had the ball on the right wing, and it was meant as a centre, but the wind got hold of it and it swerved into the top corner. Then the match was held up for 5 minutes until Peter had stopped running around the pitch and shaking hands with everyone to celebrate the only goal of his career! After seeing the *Lancashire Evening Post* report, he came to work the following day having purchased about 17 copies, and began dishing them out to everyone in the mess room. He even gave a copy to a set of Carlisle men who were working a job back home. Goodness knows what they made of Peter's 15 minutes of fame!

Arriving back with our train at the North Union goods yard at Preston we re-marshalled and took some coal empties to Farington yard, where we were relieved and walked back to the shed past the Lostock Hall carriage sidings. We decided to nip into Harry Ward's Railway Hotel for a quick one before booking off. It was busy in the vault, with footplate staff who had been on early mornings, and who must have been on the doorstep waiting for opening time at 11.00am. Some of them were playing darts, so Harry and I took them on, and some others, and beat them, so, never having paid for any beer, we staggered out at 3.30pm, made our way across to the shed, and booked off, making an hour's overtime while playing darts in the pub!

I was with Harry again the following day on the Hoghton pilot. This was a bit of a misnomer, for it no longer went to Hoghton because the station and yard had closed a few years previously. We actually spent most of the time shunting and tripping between the local yards, including Bamber Bridge. It was only a 5-hour job because when you booked on you spent the first 3 hours preparing engines before going off the shed, usually with a 2-6-4 tank, which is what we had on this day. Harry was doing the shovelling and we were travelling from Lostock Hall to Bamber Bridge with about 25 permanent-way wagons loaded with spoil from some weekend track replacement. They were heavy and none were fitted, so we only had the loco brake. As we approached Bamber Bridge Junction we had a red signal, so I started braking in good time. However, those 2-6-4 tanks were not the ideal loco for stopping a loose-coupled freight, and we begin to slide. I took the brake off, quickly applied the front sanders and put the brake on again, but to no avail, and the wagons pushed us an engine length past the red signal.

We got on the phone to the 'bobby' who told us to set back behind the signal, then come to the cabin. So Harry jumped off and went to the signal box to have a word, as they say. He was back after a few minutes, telling me that he had squared things up with Fred the signalman, who was going to say nowt about it. Harry told me that Fred was actually a neighbour of his, and as no harm had been done we could just forget about it; moreover, nobody wanted all the paperwork involved if we had reported it. That's how things were in those days – the railway was run by railwaymen. Unfortunately many of those professionals have left the job or retired early with the onset of privatisation, so many of today's managers lack responsibility and the ability to make decisions. I do have some sympathy, as they are embroiled in all this 'health and stupidity' regime, which used to be called common sense in my day, but now it's a case of 'where there is blame, there is a claim'. I do accept that it is a different world today, including the recording of conversations, which does mean the reporting of all incidents, however minor.

Having mentioned the 2-6-4 tank engines, our depot always had an allocation of the Fairburn and Stanier machines, although not the three-cylinder ones being built for the LT&S section. It always seemed a little strange to me that these had slightly less power but perhaps better acceleration than the two-cylinder engines. I cannot recall us having any Fowler tanks on our books; we often worked on these excellent locomotives, although most of the class suffered from the usual Fowler trait of not having any side windows in the cab.

A regular job worked by one of our tank locos was the morning passenger to Rochdale, on the now closed route via Bolton, Bury and Castleton. These engines excelled themselves on local passenger work – they were quick off the mark, rode well and were speedy, 80mph if needed, just as easy working bunker-first, and with plenty of water and coal capacity. We passed Bolton Wanderers' former ground at Burnden Park when working this job; the signalman at Burnden Junction box had the best view of a match, and never held a ticket. If ever you see the film *The Love Match* starring Arthur Askey as the engine driver, the football ground and Bolton shed feature prominently. Some of this route still exists today, forming a section of the East Lancashire Railway.

If we had a tender engine on this job, after shunting our coaches into the bay we travelled back light engine from Rochdale to Castleton to turn on the triangle. We had an amusing incident one Monday morning during the school holidays when travelling bunker-first down 'Bomb Alley' between Bolton and Bradley Fold. Some little brat threw a cowpat off a bridge and it hit my mate smack in the face. I couldn't see him for cow muck – he wasn't hurt, but it took us 10 minutes to clean him up in the porters' room at Bury station.

These tank engines would be ideal for working trains on heritage railways, and it is such a shame that only a couple of them actually made it into preservation; they can be seen on the short but scenic Lakeside line. Fortunately a three-cylinder version resides in the National Railway Museum; how we would love to see that machine in action again!

The BR Standard 2-6-4 tanks were derived from the LMS two-cylinder versions, and benefited from that design in being slightly superior performers. Like the Fairburns, they had labour-saving firebox rocking grates and self-cleaning smokeboxes.

10 The diesels start to appear

It was at about this time that a few diesel locomotives began to infiltrate the atmosphere at Lostock Hall, and before long management decided that firemen should have training on how to work the train-heating boilers on the Type 2 and Type 4 machines, which later became Classes 24 and 25 and Class 40. The course was spread over two days and was held at Morecambe in the station yard. Our instructor was Billy Wilson; this was a new role for him, promoted from his passed fireman grade. He was very knowledgeable, not just about the boilers, but also the workings of the diesel locomotive and its ancillaries.

The four of us on the course were all firemen from Lostock Hall and travelled by train each day, hauled by the Class 40 we used for the training. Some of us travelled in the cab with the driver, Tom 'Cock' Riley. The second man was Peter Dolan, who shared my interest in model railways, a subject we discussed for most of the journey, during which I could not help but notice that our 64-year-old driver was eavesdropping.

I asked him, 'Are you interested, and do you have a model railway, Tom?'

'Well, no – don't you think I have seen enough of railways at my age?' he replied.

On the second day travelling with them both, Tom was in the second man's seat with Peter, who I did not want to disturb, doing the driving, but when Tom started questioning me about my model railway, Peter butted in and said to Tom, 'Put the lad out of his misery, and tell him about that

huge Hornby Dublo model railway in your attic, which you play with when you're not at work here.'

With that, Tom spluttered a bit before admitting to being slightly interested in the hobby, then when I confessed to having some Hornby Dublo myself, that was it – model railway talk all day long! So here we had our Tom, who was a top-link driver with nearly 50 years' service, whose hobby when away from the big railway was model railways, and over the many years that I have worked with railwaymen, of all grades, it will come as no surprise to learn just how many of them had an interest in model railways!

A few years later, when steam had ended, I transferred to Preston depot and formed a model railway club with premises on the station for just a peppercorn rent. We built up a large layout and membership was open to all grades, including some staff from other depots, who would drop in on club night while awaiting their return work. My belated thanks to senior clerk Bill Johnson at Preston, for it was he who arranged for us to use the club room on the second floor above Platform 6.

Anyhow, back to the boiler training. All the candidates passed the course thanks to Billy's expert tuition. The problem was that our depot really did not have that much diesel work, so it was a case of carrying the instruction book for the Stones and Clayton boilers in our bag at all times. I actually still have mine and use it occasionally when working on heritage diesels.

One of the lads who trained on the

boilers with me nearly came to grief one day while trying to get a Stones boiler on the go, with English Electric Type 4 No D343, standing under the glass canopy of No 4 platform in Preston station at the head of a Barrow express. Things were not going too well. He had gone through all the start-up procedure, but still could not get it to flame after repeating everything. So he decided to put a lighted taper inside. This had the desired effect all right, in spectacular fashion, with a huge explosion out of the top of the boiler, which blasted a hole through the glass canopy roof. He certainly didn't need the use of the soot blower to clear the passages – the explosion was heard all over the station. Fortunately there were no casualties apart from a black-faced and rather embarrassed second man.

We also trained on the Spanner boilers fitted to the troublesome Metrovick diesels. These were not popular with crews, being

the only main-line diesel constructed with just one cab door; moreover, the flat-fronted design was a far cry from having the assurance of a steam locomotive boiler in front of you. A single Metrovick still exists, and although they were not my favourite diesel locomotive, I am firmly convinced that, should this machine ever be restored to working order, it will become the highlight of any diesel gala. I suggested to the diesel group that owns it that, should they launch an appeal for separate funding to bring this unique diesel back to working order, count me in for a contribution. The Spanner boiler fitted to these locos was also temperamental; it would seemingly knock off at any bad dip in a rail joint, and on some days it would not function at all, which meant calling upon a steam locomotive to be attached between the diesel and the train to provide carriage heating. Looking at it from an operational exercise, these were actually good jobs for

Metrovick No D5709 appears to be going quite well at Leyland with a Manchester-Barrow service – mind you, it is on a 1 in 110 downhill gradient here.

the crew of the steam loco, as you let the diesel do all the pulling, just keeping a breath of steam on for lubrication and to take up motion wear and vibration at speeds up to 75 mph, the Metrovick's maximum.

Occasionally there was a down side to these steam heating jobs, which is exactly what happened to me and my driver, who went by the illustrious nickname of 'Just Bobbin'; this was a throwback to his firing days, for whenever he was asked by his driver where the water level was in the boiler, his reply was invariably 'just bobbin', meaning that it was quite low in the glass – but he was actually a good driver and mate. On this day we were hanging about as a spare set of men on the shed when the foreman summoned us out of the mess room and gave us a job to provide steam heat from Preston to Carlisle behind Type 4 diesel No D284, whose boiler had packed up on this very cold winter's afternoon. So off down to Preston we went with our 'Black 5' and hooked up between No D284 and the train. Away we went, soon realising that we were in for a rough old ride. The Class 5 must have been overdue for a visit to the shops as it was a case of shake, rattle, bang, crash, knock, which of course got worse the faster we went. The diesel crew were 'foreigners', with no particular concern for all the discomfort that we were enduring; in fact, I think they were actually enjoying themselves, winding up the Type 4. We had no speedometer, but I know what 80mph feels like on a steam loco and we were doing that before shutting off for the Lancaster stop. They, of course, in front of us, were enjoying the smooth and comfortable riding qualities of the Type 4 diesel.

Now, some of you might be thinking, why didn't we just go up to them at Lancaster and ask them to ease back a bit on the speed as the Class 5 was a dog, but no way were we going to approach the Carlisle crew with that request. You can just imagine the response, as they would have delightedly gone at maximum speed just to put the wind up us, and we didn't fancy 90mph coming down the other side of Shap. Had they been our own men up front, we would have asked, but the Carlisle crew knew that a 'Black 5' at 90mph was going to be a bit lively regardless of its condition.

After leaving Lancaster we were Carlisle next stop, and it was a case of just wedging ourselves in and hanging on between firing duties, but to their credit the Cumbrian crew kept speed around 75mph for most of the way. Nevertheless, I think my mate and I were glad to see Carlisle No 13 box coming into view and giving us a straight run into the station. When I jumped down from the footplate of this bucking bronco, my legs felt like jelly, but the feeling of the terra firma of Citadel's No 1 platform was a blessed relief.

With the engine now hooked off, we exchanged a smiling thumbs-up 'everything all right' with the Carlisle driver, who was leaning out of the cab of No D284. I wasn't going to let him know how we really felt! So off we went with both locos onto Upperby shed, followed by a good wash and a visit to the canteen.

My mate said, 'We're not reporting to Control, and we're not working anything back – sod the extra mileage payment.'

So we said nothing and came home 'on the cushions', having seen enough for that day.

11 More trips to Carlisle

Carlisle became a regular destination from our depot, either working over the West Coast route with passenger trains, or via the ex-Midland Railway Settle & Carlisle line with freights. Some of the jobs involved lodging, in particular those that went over the Midland, the mileage being 112 as against 90 via the West Coast. All the jobs we had were steam-worked, including a non-passenger train that actually required steam heating; this was the banana train, all the vans being piped for heating to help the bananas ripen.

It was a busy time at Preston Docks when one of these boats arrived from the West Indies. Preston Dock, incidentally, was the biggest single dock in Europe when it was constructed in 1898, and was the pioneer of roll-on-roll-off container facilities. The service was operated from Preston to Larne by Northern Ireland Trailers, or NITS as everybody called them. The dock also had its own fleet of steam engines working 24 hours around the clock. We did not actually start the banana trains from Preston Dock; we would wait in the North Union yard with the train engines for the arrival of the 'Super Ds' or a pair of 350hp shunters topping and tailing the train up the 1 in 29 gradient from the docks. There followed a quick examination by the Carriage & Wagon Department while the loco change took place. After coupling up, we heated the vans throughout the journey to Carlisle, or on other occasions we worked these jobs to Ashton Moss, Manchester.

The Midland route to Carlisle was always considered to be the tougher of the two, particularly if the driver was a bit heavy-handed, which didn't help when most of the freight trains we worked were made up to maximum load for the loco. One of my regular drivers with these freights over the S&C was Peter Norris, who was better known by his pet name of 'Peter Stuyvesant'. He was given the name by the lads at the shed because of his extensive route knowledge; at the time, the mid-1960s, there was a well-known brand of cigarettes that constantly featured in TV advertising, with the promotional slogan 'Peter Stuyvesant – the international cigarette – London, Paris or Rome'. So Peter became Peter Stuyvesant – not that we had that many jobs to Paris or Rome! But I am sure he could have found his way there if asked.

Peter certainly did his best to live up to his nickname, although in his defence I always felt confident of his route knowledge when firing for him, and he was one of those drivers who would pick up the shovel himself, or pull down coal to assist his fireman – he was an all-round 'good egg'. Perhaps the pinnacle of his footplate career was on Sunday 19 March 1967 when, with fireman Lawrence Charnley, he drove 'Britannia' No 70015 *Apollo* on the 'Lancastrian Rail Tour'. The following October he was also the driver of No 7029 *Clun Castle* with his fireman, the late John Roach, which they worked from Preston to Carlisle over Shap. I enjoyed working

The author with Peter Norris (aka 'Peter Stuyvesant') at Grosmont. There is never a dull moment when he is about. Here we are aboard No 60163 *Tornado* about to depart for Pickering with Peter (aged 78) doing the firing. *Author's collection*

Pictured here on the up slow line at Skew Bridge, Preston, is ex-Crosti boiler 9F No 92021. Peter Norris and myself had this engine on an overnight freight to Carlisle. *Stan Withers*

men who carved out this iron road, built at a cost of £47,500 per mile. Some crews held the belief that the ex-Crosti engines did not have the same power output as the standard 9Fs; maybe it was because they did not look as powerful, but in my experience they were equal in strength.

After lodging overnight at Kingmoor barracks, the following day was a Saturday, and we got up at about 12.30pm and rang the shed to enquire if they had any return work for us. When we booked on later there wasn't anything, so they instructed us to make our way home 'on the cushions'. We decided to catch the bus back into Carlisle, but we couldn't pass the Redfern pub at Kingmoor without sinking a couple, then later, when getting off the bus at Citadel, we bumped into a load of football supporters on their way to watch Carlisle United at Brunton Park, so we decided to go along and watch the match. The opposition was Huddersfield Town, so we fell in with that lot at one end of the ground, but then got into an argument with some of them when they discovered that we were Preston North End fans, and Preston had given them a

with him, and I recently took him for a pleasurable trip on board No 60163 *Tornado* as my fireman on the NYMR. He is nearly 80 now, but still quite a fit lad.

We reminisced about one of the trips that we had with a 9F-hauled freight. This engine had worked the train from Crewe Basford Hall to Lostock Hall, where we remanned it, went onto the shed and topped the tender up with coal and water, leaving for Carlisle New Yard at 11.00pm with a full load behind us. The engine was ex-Crosti boiler No 92021, which, like us, worked its guts out all through the night over the Settle & Carlisle, the highest main line in England. I often marvelled at the Herculean labours of the good beating a few weeks earlier! Fortunately Peter is a big lad and things calmed down a bit after he threatened to thump the lot of them. At half-time we went and joined the less hostile Carlisle fans. Looking back on that day leads me to think what could actually have happened to us if we had got into a scrap and had maybe been arrested. This incident reminded me of some of the football scenes briefly mentioned previously in the hilarious Arthur Askey film *The Love Match*, where Arthur plays an engine driver, and he and his fireman get into trouble with the referee and other supporters when they go to watch a Bolton Wanderers v Cardiff City match.

We did eventually jump on a train back home to Preston, and I remember looking at one of the carriage prints in our compartment. It was a recruiting advert for employment on the railways, the heading proclaiming that it was 'A Job On The Right Lines'. I thought to myself, yes, we certainly have that! I first saw this carriage print when I was a youngster travelling in a non-corridor coach with my parents, on the way to visit relatives at Banks near Southport; it featured a steam driver urging you to come along and apply for a job in the footplate department, and it did actually inspire me at the time, so I never forgot its message.

A few weeks later it was Carlisle again, this time with an 8F and a full load from Warrington Arpley. My driver was John Burnett, who was a devout Christian and almost teetotal, but would accompany you to the pub where his piano-playing skills made him a popular chap. More importantly, he was a darn good driver. His skills would be needed on this night with an 8F that we remanned at Lostock Hall, the departing crew giving us the good news that, 'You'll struggle with this lot – that's your load!' The fireman pointed to the figures he had chalked on the locker door of the tender: '41 - 45 - 17F. 621'. This meant 41 wagons equal to 45 in wagon lengths – it was important to know this figure with regard to the wagon capacity of the different goods loops), 17 wagons fitted with continuous brakes, and 621 tons maximum tonnage (which varied dependent on the class of locomotive). The guard had been told that a 9F was booked for the job and had made up the train weight accordingly.

John decided to hook off and drop onto the shed for coal, so we positioned the tender under the hopper and filled up to capacity, also giving the tender a drink of water before backing onto our train. We then hooked on, blew up the vacuum for the 17 fitted wagons, whistled up, and got a green light

Some ten years into his retirement, my former driver John Burnett rejoined me on the footplate of a 'Black 5' at Blackburn when travelling from Preston to Hellifield courtesy of West Coast Railways. *Author's collection*

from the guard. It was now 11.20pm and away we went on board No 48054, our place of work for the next 7 hours on this 112-mile journey into the night over the bleak Settle & Carlisle line. I was in action immediately with the shovel, to be prepared for when we attacked the 5 miles of Hoghton Bank at 1 in 100, which lay just ahead. We are soon approaching the bottom of the bank at Bamber Bridge and I was ready for it, the engine was ready for it, and once we were over the level crossing John shoved the regulator into the roof and gave her 50% cut-off.

'Right, let's see what she's made of,' he said to me.

I stuck my head out of the cab and listened to the front end; no problems there, she had four good even strong beats, and was steam-tight in both cylinders, so I left things alone and let the engine warm through for the initial part of the climb.

I never relied on the paraffin-filled gauge lamp and always carried a small torch with me, to illuminate the steam pressure gauge, which as I expected had dropped back to just over 205lb. I had filled the back end of the firebox, the flap was up, the doors were nearly closed, a piece of coal wedged between them to keep them open a couple of inches, the back damper was wide open, the front one was open on the first notch, and the blower was left cracked open a little in case we shut off steam, as I didn't want the fire coming back at me. Furthermore the blower would be hard on before entering any of the many tunnels on this route. We had been pulling for about half a mile at little more than walking pace, but the engine should be warming up now and what I was about to do now would tell me if I was in for a rough trip or not with this engine. It was out with the torch and on to the pressure gauge. Every fireman wants to see that gauge moving the right way after setting off with a newly formed fire – and bingo, she had come

round to just short of the red mark of 225lb and was about to lift the safety valves. Just what I wanted to see. So it was on with the live steam injector, which would have to stay on all the way up the bank with the engine working this hard – I would have to fire against the injector.

John looked across and it was thumbs-up, so he dropped her down a turn to 60% and, before opening the firehole doors, I had the coal ready on the shovel – in with it, over the flap and around the box, before filling up under the door, then close up. There was no need to look at the chimney – I could smell the smoky exhaust. She was steaming well, keeping more or less on the mark with John keeping his eye on the live steam injector singing away merrily at his side. We were now more than halfway up the bank, all was well on the footplate, the water was up and steady at three-quarters of a glass, and steam rigid at 220. We hadn't to allow the steam to drop below 200lb on these Stanier engines, or the guts would go out of them, and we would only labour along up the bank, which to be honest is actually what we were doing, our speed little more than 10mph. The engine was working so hard that it was trying to blow the smokebox door off its hinges, which is not surprising as we were pulling the equivalent of an 18-coach train.

After what seemed an age – and it probably was – we surmounted Hoghton Bank. The engine would pull, it would steam and I had plenty of water in the boiler. The exhaust injector I put on to top-up the boiler just before John shut off, but it had been an all-out effort and it was then that we both made the decision that we would have to reduce this load at Blackburn. John stated that we would stop the railway if we attempted to climb the 'Long Drag' up to Ais Gill with this weight behind us.

We were now approaching Blackburn at Mill Hill and were about to whistle up, to have us put into the goods loop instead of through the station. However, as we drifted around the corner in sight of the bracket signals we found the right-hand signal already 'off', turning us up the goods loop. This wasn't surprising really as they just wanted us out of the way of all other traffic, considering that we had been travelling at little more then a funeral pace since departing Lostock Hall. So as we passed the goods yard shunters' cabin at Blackburn we shouted across that we needed to reduce the load and, 'Would you tell the guard to come up to the engine?'

After coming to a stand we waited for the guard to join us on the footplate. He had the loading slip with him, and suggested we take off six of the 16-tonners; this would reduce us by approximately 100 tons to about 530 tons. 'Will you take them?' That was more or less a full load for this engine, he informed us.

John turned to me and asked me what I thought. With 95 miles still in front of us, I could only answer that the engine seemed to be steaming OK, the fire was in good condition, both the injectors were working fine, so let's go for it. So, with that the goods yard pilot came behind us, took off six of the unfitted 16-ton wagons and pieced us up again.

We whistled for the road, the peg came off and away we went again, through Blackburn Tunnel. We had the left-hand peg at Daisyfield Junction, so we thought let's see how we fare up Wilpshire Bank, 96 tons lighter and now equal to just a 14-coach train. Our 8F responded well to having nearly 100 tons less on its tail, although it was still heavy digging until over the top, then on to the easier grades through Clitheroe and Chatburn, and with a final pull we reached the great metropolis of Hellifield, and into the station loop. It was then tea for us and water for the tender at this isolated oasis.

Some typical S&C weather had now descended upon us; looking through the mist I could hardly see the engine shed, which was later to become a storage place for a host of preserved steam locomotives, waiting for new homes. A couple of fully-fitted night freights hurtled north as we waited in the loop. Then it was our turn to tackle the 'Long Drag'. The usual format was, once out of the loop, get cracking with the fire, be prepared for the road ahead, then, if the Distant is 'off' for Settle Junction, give it the bloody lot for a run at the bank. If you've done it right, before you know it you are passing through Settle station and digging in nicely on the climb, and so we were – but it's not called the 'Long Drag' for nothing.

Soon it was beginning to pull us back. Despite No 48054's valiant efforts, we were down to a slow steady climb. We cleared Taitlands Tunnel, then it was a steady plod, and it didn't come as much of a surprise to find the Distant 'on' for Horton-in-Ribblesdale. As we approached, the Home signal slowly came off, indicating to us that the signalman wanted our attention, and as we slowly passed the box he gestured to us with his arms crossed, meaning that he wanted us to set back through the crossover with the train onto the up road. We whistled acknowledgement that we had seen him and, with the guard's cooperation, that was what we did – no doubt we must have been delaying some faster-moving freights behind us.

When we came to a stand John asked me to walk back to the brake van to ensure that our guard had altered his side lamp, to display a white light to the down road. It can be a little nerve-racking for the crew of a following train to come up the bank and see three red tail lights in front of them, particularly so on a foggy night like this. Twenty minutes went by, during which two more fitted freights made their way up to Ribblehead and beyond, then it was our turn. The ground signal came off and John made his way back to the footplate, having had a chat with the signalman, who was probably glad of a bit of company in the middle of the night at this isolated outpost.

'The bobby told me that we will be going inside at Blea Moor,' said John as he lifted the regulator on No 48054 after whistling an acknowledgement to our guard's green hand signal.

We set off once again into the misty night. It was heavy going all the way, but our 8F kept its feet, did not slip once and was able to get its breath back when we came to a stand in Blea Moor loop. Here I put the bag in the tender and took water while John pulled the coal forward. Afterwards it was tea time and I was off to the signal box to fill our can and to ask how long we were likely to be there before getting the road.

Now, as every loco man should know, you do not just open the door and walk straight into a signal box without first knocking and awaiting an invitation to enter. Many signalmen would keep you standing outside and bring the kettle to you, or, if you had gone to the box to sign Rule 55, they would bring the register to the door rather than permit you to walk over their clean floor with your mucky boots. But at Blea Moor we were fortunate that all the signalmen appreciated the rigours that all staff faced in the daily operation of this unique railway line, so a friendly welcome was the norm at this remote, windswept place, known affectionately to locomen as Bleak Moor. At night this road is as black as pitch, and even with the stars to help it is difficult to distinguish between the hilltops and the sky. On a clear night the light of a lonely telephone kiosk casts a glow that can be seen for miles and, unlike the present day, I do not recall seeing many railway photographers about the lineside during daylight hours.

Our signalman explained to me that if he gave us the road now, we would be put inside again at Ais Gill summit, but if we went back

and enjoyed a cup of tea on the footplate for about 30 minutes, Ais Gill would give us a clear run. This went to plan, and once past Ais Gill summit the hard work was behind us. We settled down for a steady run through the foggy night with both of us scanning ahead, working as a team to read the signals, many of which just came into sight when we were less than an engine length from them, such was the denseness of the fog. It did clear slightly as we came to a stand for water at Appleby, where it was a pleasant surprise to meet up with a set of our own men from the freight link at this Cumbrian outpost, who were waiting to relieve the 1.20am Carlisle-Crewe train, having worked up with the 7.35pm Edge Hill-Carlisle, with booked relief at Appleby. Everything was running late, of course, due to the fog.

After enjoying a quick smoke together, and with our tank now full and a fresh can of tea on board, we whistled up and, with a quick cheerio, we headed on and away through the foggy night. Two hours later, arriving at Bog Junction at Carlisle, we were relieved by a set of Carlisle men at about 5.30am. We both fancied a hot meal, so we made our way to the station canteen and enjoyed a well-earned breakfast. Then, instead of lodging, we decided to get the first service back to Preston and home to bed after a hard day's night. Lodging was never very popular with crews, most of the barracks being situated next to goods yards or engine sheds and not conducive to a well-earned rest; our preference at Carlisle would be Upperby barracks as opposed to the less salubrious and distant offerings at Kingmoor. Your cubicle would comprise a bed (hopefully the sheets would have been changed), two chairs, a small chest of drawers, an occasional table and a Bible. Food was reasonable as long as you avoided the sponge pudding if facing a heavy firing stint shortly after! By contrast, overnight accommodation provided by present-day rail companies has to be a three- or four-star hotel.

Continuing with the theme of heavy trains over the Midland to Carlisle reminds me of the time when we worked trains conveying long welded rails originating from the Fazackerly p.w. depot near Liverpool, which we would re-man at Lostock Hall. These trains usually ran at night or on a Sunday, due to their slow speed and train weight, and were always double-headed, with a mixture of 9Fs, 8Fs and 'Austerities' providing the power. My baptism on these jobs was one hot summer Sunday with Dick Tomlinson, the other crew made up of driver Alan Green and fireman Jimmy Sergeant. It was a 6.00am start and we relieved the Scouse crews on the station platform at Lostock Hall at 6.30. We manned the train engine, a 'WD' 'Austerity', the assistant loco being a 9F, and we dropped down to the junction water column and filled both tenders.

These rail trains were an absolute dead weight of almost 1,000 tons, so we needed a couple of good free-steaming machines for the 112-mile journey, and we are strictly limited to a maximum of 25mph. At 7.00am we were given the road and immediately faced the 5 miles of 1 in 100 up to the summit of Hoghton; this would be a good test for the locos, and would certainly give their tubes a cleaning. Now, if I may quote an undertaker's favourite saying, 'That it is not unusual, for one to make arrangements prior…' This we did before departure, and agreed that the 9F would do most of the heavy digging with us pushing him, but avoiding climbing over the top of its tender. We also agreed to exchange footplates to ease the workload, and to have a break from the rough-riding, knocking, banging and clanking of the 'Austerity' to enjoy the smoothness and luxury of the eight-year-old 9F.

The climb to Hoghton was going very

well as Jimmy leaned out of the 9F cab and we exchanged an 'all is well' thumbs-up as we mounted the hill and drifted down past Cherry Tree Junction, where the line from Brinscall joined us, then once through Mill Hill station steam was required again for the 5 miles through Blackburn to the next summit at Wilpshire, having taken the Hellifield route at Daisyfield Junction. It had been a steady slog all the way from Lostock Hall, but once we were through the tunnel at Wilpshire it was reasonably level after Clitheroe, and we arrived in the goods loop at Hellifield, where water was taken by men and machines. The crews shared an appraisal of the journey so far and the general consensus was one of complete satisfaction. We were joined by our guard and the travelling loading inspector charged with the safety of this mammoth load, and, following an examination of all the vehicles, they were both happy. Alan returned from the signal box with the news that once the bobby pulled off for us we were guaranteed a clear road to Blea Moor.

A few minutes later the road was ours, so let battle commence! Ahead of us was a real 'head down and arse up' time for any fireman – the downhill stretch to Settle Junction was not any advantage to us with the train speed limit of 25mph. As we attacked the climb with both engines feathering at the safety valves and regulators in the roof, we blasted through Settle station, which fortunately does not have an overall roof or an awning otherwise I am sure that we would have lifted them off their brackets. Our 'Austerity' was going well, my mate had the cut-off down the rack at 60%, using full regulator, of course; one definite good point about these engines was the efficiency and reliability of the injectors, being able to pump water into the boiler at a steady rate. With the engine working at near its full capacity, there was no possibility of being able to turn off the injectors, faced with another 10 miles of climbing the1 in 100 to the safety of Blea Moor loop.

The 9F was obviously being driven likewise, judging by the lovely double-chimney exhaust that was echoing back to us as we passed through the cutting and entered into the short but wet confines of Stainforth Tunnel. This was one place on the climb where we did not want our engines to lose their footing, both drivers taking the precaution of applying the leading sanders to counteract any slipping. We passed through with no problems on this sunny Sunday morning and, do you know, I cannot think of anywhere else in the world that I would rather have been except on the footplate of that steam locomotive earning its keep, pounding its way up one of the toughest and most scenic railway lines in the British Isles. Thank you, God! If anyone living in the quiet village of Horton-in-Ribblesdale had planned on having a Sunday morning lie-in, that idea was rudely shattered by the combined sound effects of 74,000lb of tractive effort from the two British Railways steam giants, which just happened to be passing at that time – but we did refrain from blowing the whistles!

There were 2 more miles of slogging before Ingleborough came into view over on our left; this is one of the Three Peaks of Yorkshire, the others being Whernside and Pen-y-Ghent, so there was not much further to go now before Blea Moor, and I reckoned that we had enough fire in the box to reach there, so after we passed the remote outpost of Ribblehead station and over the majestic double-track viaduct, it would be cigarette-and-sandwich time in the loop for train examination, as well as tender topping-up time. Arriving there, Jimmy offered to walk across to the box with the two tea cans, and while he was away we discussed the swopping of footplates, the three of us agreeing upon it, so as that was the majority vote the swop took place.

After our break all four of us got stuck in with the task of bringing the coal forward in both tenders. The tender of the 'Austerity' constantly oscillated against the engine when on the move, which did help to bring the coal within reach of the fireman's shovel, this action leading driver Bill Bamber to once remark, 'What you have with an "Austerity" is a 25mph engine coupled to a 60mph tender!'

The morning local to Carlisle went by, and we followed it. We were now manning the 9F, and the depth of fire you have in its firebox can be a bit deceiving owing to the box being wide but not very deep. With the bulk of the hill-climbing now behind us, it was just a matter of firing to the road ahead; we would need to keep her warm until we surmounted the summit at Ais Gill, so I fed some coal into the back corners and under the door. I put nothing down the front to avoid any smoke in the confines of Blea Moor Tunnel just ahead of us; this is the longest of all the tunnels on the line, at 2,629 yards. It is part way through here that the gradient changes from 1 in 100 up to 1 in 440 down, and approaching Dent we soon begin to appreciate the difference in riding quality of this modern machine, with all the controls that I needed in front of me, and all that the driver required within easy reach. There was no real need to leave the seat unless engaged in firing the loco, or to carry out the one task that I could not fulfil at the fireman's side on the loco, taking water from the troughs, as the handle that operated the scoop was situated behind the driver on the tender.

We were soon approaching Garsdale water troughs, the highest in Britain, but as we had only travelled 10 miles since our last water stop, we had more than sufficient to reach Carlisle, 55 miles ahead. Jimmy would also be taking things a little easier on the 'Austerity'. There was not much point in him leaving his seat, as the 'Austerities' did not have a water scoop; to make up for this, they had a tender with a large water capacity. Garsdale station was devoid of any life as we rattled through. This was the only junction on the line, and was, and still is, often referred to by railwaymen as Hawes Junction.

Continuing on our journey north, and after passing through two more tunnels, Ais Gill's Distant signal was sighted and was showing clear. From there just a breath of steam was all that was required to keep us on the move, and passing the box we exchanged a friendly wave with the signalman, whose border collie was lying on the top step enjoying the sunshine, no doubt providing some welcome company for its master at this noted spot. I had now swept up and swilled down our footplate and given the coal a good soaking through the open tender doors, so all was well with the world. I looked back to see if Jimmy was as relaxed as I was and enjoying this break while running down hill towards Kirby Stephen West. I caught sight of him leaning out the cab, which was swaying from side to side; he was looking ever so clean and tidy in his white shirt and tie, reminiscent of our mentor Lostock Hall master fireman and Mr Clean himself Jack (Digby) Hesketh.

Jimmy was younger than Digby and me, but he was a class act in the art of firing a steam locomotive. He was also a very good amateur footballer and the leading goal-scorer for year after year in our local side. We all thought that he could have made it as a pro footballer, but he loved the steam locomotive too much, never more so than when he was chosen to be the fireman when *Flying Scotsman* visited the North West and

worked a number of specials. Never having set foot on an 'A3' 'Pacific' before, Jimmy immediately mastered the machine and much praise was rightly bestowed upon him. He left the railways at the end of steam but did occasionally visit me at the NYMR, and we would share the footplate. Needless to say, he had lost none of his firing skills, showing my fireman how best to fire a Bulleid 'Pacific', after having just completed his own maiden trip on the machine. It came as a cruel blow to lose him at barely 50 years of age, leaving a wife and children.

Ace fireman Jimmy Sergeant leans out of the cab window of Bulleid 'Pacific' No 34072 *257 Squadron* at Goathland when he visited me on the NYMR. *Author's collection*

Our long welded rail train was following along nicely behind us in an orderly fashion. We had a booked stop at Appleby for train examination, after which no time was lost and we were on the go again for the final 30-mile leg of our journey. While this is probably the least scenic section of the route, it is a nice steady plod more or less downhill all the way. Approaching Culgaith we passed over one of only two level crossings between Settle and Carlisle. Another place of interest coming up was Long Meg, the mines there producing gypsum and anhydrite, carried away by trains being worked to Widnes almost exclusively by one of our class of locomotive.

The line now runs through well-wooded parts of the Eden Valley, now and again allowing a glimpse of the river down to the right. We had three tunnels coming up in the next mile or so – the two Baron Wood tunnels before entering Armathwaite, then the viaduct of the same name. Eventually the welcoming sidings of Durran Hill came into view and we drifted into them and came to a nice gentle stop in the late-afternoon sunshine. Within a few minutes two sets of relief footplate crew were making their way towards us from the shunters' cabin, a few pleasantries were exchanged and we decided to walk to the station rather than ride part of the way, as the train would be standing a while for examination.

At the station we were a bit disappointed to discover that we had just missed a service back home to Preston so, with nothing for another 2 hours, what do you think we decided upon? Right first time – off we went to the Caledonian pub, just a few minutes walk from the station. We all bought a round in the vault side of the pub (women being barred from it in those days), and got chatting to a station inspector who had just come in for a drink. He told us that a parcel and mail train was due to leave for the south in about 10 minutes, so we all hot-footed back to the station. The guard said it was alright for us to travel in the BG among all the parcels and mail bags, and by the time we passed through Penrith slumber had overtaken us all after a long hot day on the footplate.

Back in Preston we found that the last train for Liverpool had gone, Lostock Hall being the second station on the line, but the last service for Colne had not yet left, and we hopped on that to Todd Lane Junction, walked the mile or so to the shed and booked off, having been on duty for more than 16 hours.

We did have a few double trip jobs to Carlisle with passenger work, but the majority of freight jobs were single trips due to the long hours on duty, often necessitating lodging at Kingmoor or Upperby depots.

My next visit to Carlisle was with a young passed fireman on his first driving turn, Tony Gillette. We knew each other very well and I have already mentioned him, having shared the footplate with him on numerous occasions when I was a trainee fireman. Our train was another of those heavy salt trains of 'HGs' (high goods) from Winsford to Carlisle. We picked up the job at Lostock Hall if we were going over the Midland, or at Preston if going via the West Coast. We signed on that Friday lunchtime to be informed that the train had not yet left Winsford, so into the mess room we went to await further orders. Four o'clock came and the foreman had changed shifts, and about 10 minutes later driver and deputy foreman Peter Stuyvesant came into the mess room. He told us to go with him, as our train was standing on the up through line at Preston station awaiting relief, and Control had only just informed him that we would be going West Coast to Carlisle. 'The quickest way to get you to Preston is in my car, so come on with me.'

There wasn't a lot of room in Peter's minivan, and he didn't hang about with the driving, just like he drove steam engines, with full regulator, and we reached Preston in record time, leaving him to return to Lostock Hall and his foreman duties. We made our way across to the ramp at the end of Platform 1, then over to the down through line, where the bright evening sunshine was highlighting the handsome outlines of 'Britannia' 'Pacific' No 70001 *Lord Hurcomb* standing at the head of our freight. It was no surprise to find an empty footplate, the Crewe men having abandoned ship to catch their train back home. We had only missed them by a couple of minutes, and as was usual practice they had left our train loading of 485 tons written in chalk on the locker door.

Around this time I had completed more than a thousand firing turns and was being entrusted to do more of the driving. I did have the seniority to take the exam, but was not quite at the required age of 23; this was a bit frustrating as men junior to me had been passed for driving. So the footplate arrangement for this trip was that if we had gone via the Midland to Carlisle, I would have driven to Hellifield, but since we were going West Coast, I would drive to Carnforth.

I rang the signalman in Preston No 4 to ask him for the road, and a few minutes later he pulled off the Starter and the Distant and we set sail on to the 1 in 90 pull out of Preston, needing full regulator and a long cut-off. These salt trains were heavy, but the 'Brit' responded well and we were given a clear road out of Preston, with the former motive power depot on our left. In steam days it was possible to witness from the shed every train arriving at or departing from Preston, and of course a show would be put on by some of the engine crews, with exaggerated bursts of unnecessary power, sending a vast array of sparks and cinders almost into orbit, trying to impress any mates who might be watching from the shed yard. But once out of sight normal service would soon be resumed – it doesn't have quite the same effect with a diesel or electric loco!

We got a good road to Lancaster, missing out the loops at Barton & Broughton and Garstang. Also, surprisingly for this time of night, a visit to Oubeck loop was avoided, but shortly after passing there we got two yellows. We had been coasting for the last couple of miles in anticipation of being put inside at Oubeck, so it was only now that I started braking for the first time since leaving Preston. The initial braking had little effect on our speed, so I dropped the lot to feel just what our brake force was like on this partially fitted train. It did have some effect, but we now had one yellow in front of us and the signal after that wasn't that far ahead at the top of Lancaster Bank, adjacent to No 1 signal box.

Realising that the train was now in charge of us, it was time for some drastic action if we were to avoid passing Lancaster No 1's signals and dropping down the 1 in 98 beyond there, so it was on with the steam brake. Then my mate screwed on the handbrake as I put No 70001 into back gear, opened the drain cocks, then opened the regulator a couple of notches and gave a series of short blasts on my pride and joy, that lovely chime whistle, only this time I wasn't playing. I then looked at the speedometer and thankfully found that our train had responded to our all-out braking efforts, and we came to a stand just at the right side of Lancaster No 1's signal. It was 'off', and as we drew forward the signalman came to the window displaying a red flag, so we stopped opposite him.

He shouted that he could not pull off the signal for the section ahead. 'That's why I checked you – I thought you were going to pass it! Are you having braking trouble? I can see the glow and the smoke coming off the blocks!'

We told him to inform the Carriage & Wagon examiner at Carnforth to meet us, as we obviously did not have enough fitted vehicles for the train weight. The signalman agreed with our request, then gave us a green flag with instructions to pass the section signal at danger, then obey all other signals. It was our opinion that the crew we relieved at Preston must have experienced some braking problems with the train. No wonder they had abandoned ship prior to relief!

We were put into the goods loop at Carnforth to be met by the C&W examiner.

I screwed the engine down while the three of us examined the train, the guard meeting us as we went along. We were surprised to see that he was wearing a passenger guard's uniform, and was reluctant to help out and maybe get his hands dirty. He told us that no goods guards had been available for the job, which is why the train was late away; he had volunteered to cover the job provided the train was prepared for him.

'So don't try putting the blame on me if there isn't enough fitted head brake force,' he said. 'I'm a passenger guard – you can't expect me to know all the loadings for freight – I've been swinging on the brake in the van.'

The C&W examiner discovered that not all the wagons had been piped up. He corrected this and we then became a fully fitted freight, so I altered the headlamp code to middle and right-hand. The C&W examiner carried out a satisfactory brake test, and after this we rang the signaller for a road out of Carnforth, informing him of our upgrade and that we would require banking assistance at Tebay. He told us that two expresses had to go, then he would have us on our way. So we set about preparing Lord Hurcomb for the hard bit of his day's work, facing the 30-mile climb ahead of us to Shap Summit.

Tony was on the throttle now, and we were both busy in the tender pulling down the fuel, as this 'Brit' did not have the luxury of a coal-pusher. I began to transfer the coal into the back corners using the infallible method passed on to me by fireman 'Digby' Hesketh (nickname to be explained later). We soon had No 70001 with steam, water and fire, and a few minutes later we got the road and the hill-climbing began. I always found the 'Britannias' to be very much a fireman's friend and cannot recall ever having had a rough trip with any of them. They steamed well with good injectors, and rode very well. Perhaps the only complaint

about them was the draughts that got into the cab at speed if the side sheets between engine and tender had become torn, but on today's run we would not be exceeding our maximum 45mph when working this short-wheelbased freight.

We had a good run up to Oxenholme, managed to avoid Grayrigg loop, and settled down for a steady run through the lovely Lune Gorge on this bright summer evening, just about gaining enough speed for a quick dip on the troughs at Dillicar. Then Tony gave me the pleasure of whistling up for the banker at Tebay, the melodious sound from Lord Hurcomb's chime whistle echoing across the Westmoreland Fells. Our banker was alerted to its task ahead, and the 2-6-4 tank engine buffered up to our brake van, so I again had the pleasure of exchanging the whistle codes with him to start the climb up Shap, reminiscent of the Argo Transacord LP recording of the same scenario that I once had as a background sound to my answerphone messages!

Despite the standing start, our 'Pacific' soon got into its stride, and passing Scout Green box I gave the signalman the customary three or four shovelsful of coal at this remote location. The 5-mile climb at 1 in 75 went well – the Tebay boys at the back always did their share of the work and we blasted past the famous Shap Summit board and exchanged a friendly wave with the signaller in the box, signifying that all was well. Then followed a pleasant dash down to Penrith, now with the confidence of having sufficient brake force available. We managed to avoid being put inside any loops and before long came the welcome sight of Carlisle No 13 signal box, putting us on the goods route to the New Yard, avoiding the station.

Maybe because it was a Friday night, traffic was light and we were able to dispose of our train in quick time and drop the engine onto Kingmoor shed, quickly booking it in and sorting out our lodge, followed by a final dash up to the Redfern pub, just in time for a couple of pints before last orders.

The next day we booked on at lunchtime after having breakfasted, to be given a real plum return working. The foreman asked us, 'Do you fancy taking a light engine for Edge Hill to Preston? It's one of theirs and we're sending it back home because of leaking tubes.'

'Yes, that we will do for you,' Tony told him.

So out into the shed yard and, following a quick preparation of our 'Black 5', we were off the shed and away in less than 45 minutes. We told the signalman that if he gave us the road he wouldn't see us – we wouldn't stop anything. So away we went with greens all the way until Thrimby Grange, where we paid a quick visit to the loop. I have to say that I have never worked as hard in keeping a light engine on the move – water was pouring out of the tube ends! When we left Thrimby Grange we had a clear run right through to Preston, after topping up the tender on Brock troughs. Our relief crew stepped aboard on the up through road at Preston. I told the fireman that I had managed to keep her going by not firing to the front of the grate; the tubes were leaking so badly that the fire would not burn. So Tony's first driving turn was one to remember and, by working back from Carlisle, we qualified for mileage payment. When we arrived back at the shed we had only actually been on duty for 5 hours, but the foreman was our good mate Barney Campbell, who knew we had been away from home on a

lodging turn, so he allowed us to sign off and go home, and be paid for 8 hours work.

Mentioning deputy foreman and driver Barney, his party piece was to walk into the mess room, take off his cap and throw it 20 feet onto his own hook on the wall, bringing a spontaneous round of applause. I personally

At a Lostock Hall reunion, your author, on the mic, introduces Barney Campbell, with drivers Freddy Wells, Harold Dixon and Paddy Johnson listening in. *Author's collection*

never saw him miss. He started a little business adjacent to the shed, selling and erecting garages on a site formerly occupied by tennis courts; later he diversified into becoming an outlet for caravan sales. This really took off and is now run as a family business occupying large areas of land in Lostock Hall and its surroundings.

I did briefly mention the goods loops at Carlisle that enabled some trains to bypass the busy station, and it was on these lines that a couple of incidents occurred. One of them involved a set of our own men who were working a Carlisle-Morecambe twenty coach empty stock train with 'Britannia' 'Pacific' No 70017 *Arrow*. These loops were worked by Permissive Block, allowing more than one train in the section at the same time, which led to a mistake on a summer Saturday afternoon when the empty train collided with the rear end of a stationary freight. Fortunately no one was hurt; the freight guard had heard the approaching locomotive and bailed out just before *Arrow* demolished his brake van-and a nearby platelayers hut! Regretfully this was the end of the road for the 'Brit', being deemed too badly damaged to repair. The other incident involved a runaway Freightliner train, and it was not long afterwards that BR closed the route.

Anyway, why don't we have another trip to Carlisle, but this time with a passenger train instead of a freight? As well as the *Arrow* crash, a momentous event also took place on this day, Saturday 30 July 1966 – the World Cup Final between England and West Germany. I had watched all the earlier rounds, two of the games having been viewed on a flickering black and white telly that Barney and Vinny had fixed

'Britannia' 'Pacific' No 70017 *Arrow* has made a good job of demolishing the platelayers hut and half of a freight train on the former up goods loop at Carlisle with a Morecambe-bound empty stock working. There were no injuries, but the engine was written off. *Cumberland News*

up in the foreman's office, but I was not to see anything of the final until the day after. The offer of a firing turn on a 'Britannia'-hauled special to Carlisle proved to much of a lure. My signing-on time was 12.30pm, and I had to travel to Preston and link up with one of their drivers. Following the disastrous fire at the shed and its subsequent closure, most train crews now signed on duty at the station. I knew some of the drivers and firemen based there, as many of them came up to Lostock Hall for a period of time depending on seniority before they gradually

returned to their own depot, then at the end of steam all staff transferred to Preston.

My driver for the day was Les Rampling, or 'Ramps' for short. He was one of the drivers in the London link mentioned previously. I had fired for him before and I also knew his brother Dennis, who was a fitter at the shed. Les was a big handsome fellow, who loved telling a tale or two while straddled over a mess room chair, usually smoking a hand-rolled fag wrapped around with his favourite liquorice paper, but his pride and joy was his rare-breed basenji nonbarking dog. I remember him telling me once that his mate also had an unusual dog, called a 'Sooner'.

'Why is that?' I innocently asked of him.

'Because it would sooner piss in his house than in the garden!'

On this day we were working one of two specials coming from Liverpool to Glasgow. The station inspector told us that the passengers on both trains were returning from visiting Lourdes, and that one train was running directly behind the other, ours being the first one in, on No 5 platform with No 70022; the other special would come in on the adjacent No 4 platform with No 70002. Both would take water on arrival. So Les and I made our way along Platform 5 and relieved the Edge Hill crew on No 70022 *Tornado*.

'She's a good 'un,' the Edge Hill fireman told me just as No 70002 pulled in and stopped alongside us to take water. I wonder if anybody photographed the front ends of the two 'Brits' standing side-by-side ready to head north, on this momentous day of the World Cup Final. The other relieving driver, Gordon Etherington, was also from Preston, and we exchanged a bit of banter with him about us being Carlisle next stop, whereas he called at Lancaster. We told him that he should alter his headcode from express to a stopper, then, with a whistle and a flag from the guard, we were off.

I had prepared the fire while the Scouse crew were watering the tender, so all was well, but only for a couple of minutes, as someone 'dropped the brake' 300 yards out of the station opposite No 4 signal box. One of the signalmen opened the window to tell us that the station inspector had told the guard to drop the brake as we were on the wrong engine, and that we should be on the other train in Platform 4.

Les said to him, 'What's the difference? We're both working to Carlisle.'

The signalman told us to wait and he would contact the station inspector. Just then the cab door opened and on to our footplate came Gordon and his fireman, to tell us that our guard had dropped the brake because the inspector had told him to, as he had made a mistake with the loco crew rosters. So with that, Les and I gathered our belongings and walked back the 300 yards to Preston station, to be met by the hapless inspector, apologising to us that he had confused the engine numbers.

So, now on board No 70002 *Geoffrey Chaucer* I was busy with the fire, which hadn't been touched due to the mix-up. Then the guard came up to tell us we were late, and were we ready to go? Les politely told him to bugger off and that we were only going when his fireman said that he was ready. So when I was prepared we whistled up, the inspector pressed the 'ready to start' button to the signal box, and we got a yellow aspect then a green from the guard. Then the yellow signal changed to green, and No 70002 was away to visit the cities of Lancaster and Carlisle.

We had a pretty routine trip, but I do recall a bit of priming leaving Lancaster, and as we only had three-quarters of a glass showing this was a timely reminder to avoid over-filling the boiler on the gradients ahead. We had a nice handy ten-coach train, so no bankers were required, and No 70002 climbed Grayrigg and Shap without any undue effort. It was decent weather, with the added bonus of a little sunshine, which pleased the photographers out on the lineside during our climb from Carnforth to the summit of Shap.

I might just digress a little here and fast forward to 1982, when I was firing on the West Somerset Railway and my driver was Ian Wright from the Bluebell Railway. We were chatting about steam days on BR, then about World Cup Final day, and he happened to mention that he had been photographing on Shap that day, so I told him that I had worked over there with No 70002. He said, 'I think I photographed you – I will check my collection.' And sure enough, Ian had snapped us, the photo showing driver L. J. Rampling leaning out of the cab of No 70002 as we climbed the hill – many thanks to Ian!

We ran into Carlisle down Platform 1, and put the bag in. There was no sign of our relief, so the inspector asked Les if he was prepared to work through to Glasgow with the train, and I hoped that he would agree, but I was in for a disappointment when Les told us that he had 'crossed the road off' to Glasgow a few months previously due to signalling alterations around Motherwell.

The inspector said, 'That's fair enough – I will try and find out where your relief have got to.'

Les and I looked knowingly at each other, for we knew exactly where they would be – the World Cup Final had gone into extra time. Some passengers, leaning out of the window of the first coach, were listening to the match on a portable radio, so we joined them until our relief appeared from the pub a few minutes after the full-time whistle. They jumped aboard No 70002, created the brake, blew the whistle, had a green from the guard and away they went, 20 minutes late, without ever saying a word to Les and me as we stood on the platform watching it all.

As our train disappeared into the distance heading towards the Scottish border, Les jokingly remarked, 'Well, we must assume that they were actually a driver and a fireman from some depot – they were dressed like footplatemen, and seemed to know how to work the controls.'

Ideally I would have liked to have gone through with it, as that proved to be my last opportunity, for not long afterwards steam finished into Glasgow Central.

Les and I went for a wash and brush-up

It's the afternoon of World Cup Final day, 30 July 1966, and we are climbing Shap on board 'Britannia' 'Pacific' No 70002 *Geoffrey Chaucer* on a Liverpool-Glasgow special with driver L. J. Rampling at the controls. *Ian Wright*

into the mess room on the platform. He rang Control, but they had no back work for us. Shortly afterwards another inspector came in and asked, 'What men are you?'

We said, 'Preston.'

'Aye – I was hoping to hear some Scottish voices. But I have an empty stock for Law Junction – will you lads work it forward?'

I looked at Les in the hope he might take a chance and work forward with a much less important train for the 80 miles to Law Junction, but he said to us both, 'I'm sorry, I've just refused the other inspector to work forward due to the signal alterations around Motherwell, which encompasses Law Junction.'

So that was that, and we made our way across to Platform 5. Waiting there was the other Preston crew who had come up with No 70022, so we all boarded a Glasgow-Euston express back to Preston. Ironically we passed the northbound empty stock train just after leaving Carlisle, headed by one of the versatile and popular BR Standard Class 5 locos. We all agreed that it would have been a doddle of a job with one of those at the head, including the pull up Beattock. The four of us managed to find seats in an almost empty compartment towards the back of the crowded train, which we shared with two young female Chinese students who had to put up with listening to Tales of the Rails from their travelling companions. It transpired that Gordon and his fireman had had to wait for more than 20 minutes for their relief to appear, and had also been asked to work to Law Junction with the ECS train, but Gordon did not sign the road beyond Carlisle.

Arriving back at Preston some 2 hours later, we said goodbye to the two Chinese students, having involuntarily educated them in the everyday workings of the entire British Railways system – I think they were glad to see the back of us! I said cheerio to Les, and never actually worked with him again before he retired after a splendid 50-year career on the footplate. I wish I had been able to tell him that some 45 years later I would actually work from Preston to Glasgow with steam on a number of occasions, overcoming my disappointment on that World Cup Final day in 1966. England won, of course.

Just as a matter of interest regarding the England football team, a few years later, in about 1969, I went on a coach trip from Preston to London, which included a guided tour of the old Wembley Stadium. It was all very interesting and they even allowed us onto the pitch; the tour finished with a glimpse of the silverware awarded over the years to the England team, including the almost meaningless home international championships, runners-up in Europe, etc, but on closer inspection the only real success in the entire history of the England football team is the solitary 1966 World Cup win – and, lest we forget, we played all the games on our home pitch. Now, the point I am making is, why is there always such high expectancy of success by the media whenever the team play, considering our dismal lack of achievement over the years? Likewise, if a club team is struggling they sack the manager, but on the CV of most of the new applicants for the job I guarantee it will state that the reason for leaving their previous club is that they were sacked for lack of success. 'These are the ideal credentials, just what we are looking for – can you start Monday as our new manager…?'

12 Disposal, and excited schoolgirls

I have previously mentioned the difference in the workings at various depots regarding the disposal duties of steam locos. At Lostock Hall we had a disposal link comprising eight weeks' work, signing on at different times throughout the 24 hours. The disposal link was rather cruelly referred to as 'the not to go' or 'the can't piss link', because the majority of drivers in the link were there for health reasons and confined to shed limits. Firemen moved into the link by progression, which is what happened to me. However, due to a shortage I was not paired up with one of the regular old boys, so one of the younger passed firemen was covering the vacancy and I dropped in as his mate.

The real bonus of promotion to this link was the actual hours worked and the duties performed. For instance, the agreed working day consisted of the disposal and shedding of six locomotives – then your day's work was complete. But it was the luck of the draw – when you booked on duty there might be six engines or more waiting on the pit roads, or there might be none. Sometimes it came about that the previous crew had not been able to complete their full allocation, which meant that you had to wait about for them to finish before you could make a start yourselves. But as it was summertime when I went into the link, there were engines aplenty for Jack, my 30-year-old mate, and me.

We were fit lads, and a box full of fire meant little to us. In fact, some days we could be back at home after just 4 hours

of hard work, particularly if some of the engines had rocking grates and self-cleaning smokeboxes. Our routine was to dispose of one engine apiece, which included the fire, ashpan and smokebox, shedding the engine, taking water and maybe turning the loco. We loved seeing the BR Standards on the pits when we booked on; we didn't really have the same love for 5XPs or 'Scots', or the occasional 'Duchess', which, amazingly, apart from the last two of the class, did not have rocking grates, so it was a case of lifting out four fire bars with the tongs then manually raking or paddling the fire into the ashpan. After this you were underneath raking the ash out, and it would all be blowing back into your face. Oh, how labour intensive and unpleasant! You had to be a dab hand at manipulating the metal tongs, which were used to take out and replace the fire bars – no mean feat on engines like the Horwich 'Crabs', which had those extra-long fire bars, so just one slip and they were in the firebox, leading to much swearing while getting them back onto the footplate.

We kept our own fire irons hidden away after each shift. The handiest tool we had was a 2-inch-diameter, 7-foot-long heavy metal crowbar, which we used for breaking up the clinker, bearing in mind that some of these engines had worked in from Birmingham, Glasgow or London, not to mention all the overnight freights. Sometimes they could up to 6 inches deep in clinker over the entire grate. God, I must have been fit in those days!

Jack and I were a really good partnership. We had a laugh one day because next to the disposal pits was one of the platforms of Lostock Hall station, and trains that stopped there came to a stand with the engine opposite the ash pit. One morning I was disposing 'Royal Scot' No 46128 using the 2-inch-diameter bar and sweating profusely when a Liverpool-bound train drew to a stand opposite me with a real character at the controls, old-hand Bank Hall driver 'Chalky' White driving No 75048, a Standard Class 4. We gave each other a friendly nod and away they went. Now by sheer coincidence I was doing the same thing the day after with the same loco and sweating away with the heavy 2-inch bar trying to break up the clinker when the same 'Standard 4' came to a stand again with 'Chalky' in charge.

Well, he couldn't resist it, could he, shouting across to me in his Scouse accent,

'Jesus, our kid, that's a rough one – have you been at it since yesterday?'

Some weeks we only actually worked about 20 hours, but of course the railway paid us for 42 hours. I have to say that some of the disposal crews were a bit crafty at times; if the engines fitted with rocking grates were at the back of the long queue, they would shunt them about to the front, leaving the non-rockers to be dealt with by the next unsuspecting crew when they booked on duty – not that we ever did that, of course! There was also the vexed question of emptying the smokebox of ash. We always checked each engine (unless it was self-cleaning, signified with an 'SC' plate fitted to the smokebox door), and if it really needed cleaning out then it was done, particularly so if the engine was being stopped for a boiler washout.

However, not all disposal crews were as diligent. Some of them, like old-hand driver

'Black 5' No 44731 calls at Lostock Hall station with a Preston to Liverpool stopper. This was the scene of some banter between myself and Bank Hall driver 'Chalky' White on 'Standard 4' No 75048, while I was disposing of 'Scot' No 46128 on the adjacent ash pit road. *T. Lewis*

George and his mate, disposed of the fire and ashpan and, before shedding an engine, would sometimes throw a bit of ash under the smokebox door to give the impression that the smokebox had been opened and emptied of ash. George was the laid-back type – he was the one who had the sweet shop near my home. At the opposite extreme was another old boy, Joe, a very excitable character who would not dream of putting an engine away without emptying every last bit of ash (or 'stuff', as he called it) from the smokebox, and as you might have guessed the pair of them would clash on numerous occasions.

A typical scenario would see Joe, the conscientious one, sitting in the mess room on a winter's night with his fireman, waiting for his arch-enemy George and his mate to complete the last of their allotted six locos so that they could make a start. Then the door would be flung open and standing there in the doorway would be George, seemingly looking completely exhausted, with smokebox ash in his hair and muck all over his face and neck, sweating profusely from a soaking brow – all staged of course, his fireman having previously applied all his 'make-up'.

He would then glare at Joe and, while mopping his brow, would say to him, 'That last one was a rough blighter! I was very nearly knocked off the engine frames into the pit when I opened the smokebox door – it was full of stuff right up to the chimney! Was it one that you missed emptying last night, Joe?'

Well, that would be it. Joe would bite every time, jumping up out of his chair and pointing at George shouting, 'Thee, thee, tha's never done a bloody smokebox in thee life. I gonna report thee t' gaffer – I'll get thee sacked yet!'

The gaffer or running shift foreman on nights was all-round good egg Barney. He knew of everything that went on and had a soft spot for Joe and would help him if he

could, never more so than one night when Joe went to see him in the office to complain about one of the 'Austerity' engines that came on shed at about 02.00 each day after working in with a freight from Wakefield to Lostock Hall. His complaint was that the engine's smokebox was always full of 'stuff' and that he thought the Wakefield men were 'flonking' (neglecting) loco preparation duties by not opening and examining the smokebox for 'stuff' prior to leaving their shed. Barney told him to leave it with him for a while and he would ring Wakefield shed himself.

A little later on he instructed his foreman assistant Vinny to go into the fitting shop and, when he rang him, he had to reply, 'Hello, Wakefield shed, foreman speaking.'

So, when Joe returned to the office Barney was on the phone laying it on quite thick, threatening to have the crew suspended from duty and the locomotive impounded at Lostock Hall (not that we wanted any more 'Austerities'). With that, a very irate Joe asked to be put on the phone and told the 'Wakefield foreman' (Vinny in the fitting shop next door) that every night that week the smokebox had been full up with stuff.

Vinny then asked him, 'What exactly do you mean by stuff?'

With that Joe gave him both barrels. 'That's just what I'm saying – if you bloody lot up there in Yorkshire don't know what stuff looks like, then it's no wonder that the bloody smokeboxes are full of it!' slamming the phone down.

Poor Joe was restricted to shed turns on medical grounds; he had come off main-line duties after a few nasty experiences, one being a collision with a parcels train due to a signalman's error, which resulted in Joe's engine being knocked completely over on to its side; following a couple of suicides he eventually came off main-line duties.

The effect of this sort of thing varied a lot; some drivers could shrug it off and just

Lostock Hall 'Austerity' No 90277 lies on its side in Preston station after a signalman's error caused a collision with a stationary parcels train in foggy conditions on 16 January 1958. Fortunately there were no injuries, although the driver elected to come off main-line duties afterwards. *Bill Ashcroft*

put the event at the back of their mind. One such driver whom I knew very well – I was the best man at his wedding – had three suicides during his career, but he would often say to me, 'John, I have never killed anybody – it was all their own doing.'

Speaking for myself, I think that I was pretty fortunate to get away with just one sad happening. This occurred in the early hours when working a freight from Preston to Carlisle. Approaching Scorton we saw a body in the cess that had obviously been struck by a previous northbound train. We stopped and reported the sighting on the nearest telephone, located at Bay Horse. We were later informed that it was the body of a young public schoolboy, worried about his exam results.

On a brighter note, at that time there was plenty of rest-day working, which brought us additional payment, but entailed a six-day working week for most crews. In the disposing link we felt as though we were private contractors, just appearing for a few hours a day. But we didn't make the rules – we were just abiding by the local agreements.

Jack also had a pretty good route card, so the roster clerk duly gave us some decent jobs on our supposed rest day. One job he gave us I will never forget. We went as passengers to Crewe 'on the cushions', prepared a loco on the South shed and worked a return schoolgirl hockey special from Crewe to Blackpool, the train originating from Wembley of course. This was in the days when the stadium would be full of screaming schoolgirls cheering on the England ladies hockey team. We were given a decent loco for the job, 5XP No 45666 *Cornwallis*. On the day all went well at first; we got the engine ready and, still with a couple of hours to spare, Jack and I left the engine and the shed to visit the Crewe Arms Hotel just down the road. Once inside we managed to fight our way past all the thirsty railwaymen of Crewe and elsewhere to reach the bar, where we stayed wedged in for an hour.

After enjoying a couple of pints of Cheshire bitter, we took a brisk walk back to the shed to be met with a huge disappointment, for *Cornwallis* was nowhere to be seen. We searched all over the shed in case it had been moved onto another road, before reporting to the foreman's office. He piped up with, 'Sorry, Lostock – we had a failure and used yours to replace it, but we have another for you and it's all prepared. Your traps are here in the office, and the engine is on 5 road – it's a Black 'un, 4912.'

This is a blow as we knew *Cornwallis* to be one of the better 5XPs. Anyway, we would have to make do with the Class 5, so went off down to the station with No 44912 and into the bay platform to await the arrival of our special. This came in electric-hauled from Euston. The loco change took only a few minutes, then the Preston guard came up with our load: 'Eleven on, 388 tons, Warrington, Wigan, Preston, then right away Blackpool,' and off he went to the back of the train to carry out the brake test. Meanwhile I was preparing everything for departure. Jack had been talking to a few people on the platform and told them they could have a quick look on the footplate before we left. Suddenly I was surrounded by five giggling schoolgirls wanting to know if this was actually a real steam train.

'Gosh, it is hot on here!' one said.

'That's probably something to do with that fire!' I told her.

'How fast will it go? Can we blow the whistle?'

'Yes, you can blow the whistle, then get yourselves back into the train as we will be leaving in a minute.'

The platform clock moved to 21.10 as we departed from Crewe. My usual preparation was complete, but it was going to be heavy digging with 11 on, so I hoped that No 44912 would respond accordingly. I didn't touch anything for the first couple of miles, giving the Class 5 time to warm through, then, as the water began to come into sight in the glass, I shone the trusty torch onto the steam gauge expecting near full pressure, but the ruddy thing had hardly moved off 200. Right then, let's try a bit more air, so up a notch with the front damper and a quick look at the fire, up with the flap, followed by a quick charge of coal around the box and

under the door, with the doors partially shut, blower on slightly. Check the chimney, leave things alone for another couple of minutes, then check the gauge again.

Now, usually a 'Black 5' is every locoman's best friend, but this one was a 'Bad 5'. The stubborn sod had moved a little to 215lb, so it was on with the live steam injector, which would have to stay on as we were down to half a glass. A quick burst with the exhaust injector brought us back to three-quarters of a glass, but at the cost of the steam, which was back to 180lb. Now, any experienced footplateman reading this will know that we now had a tussle ahead of us, mortgaging the steam and water to keep her on the move.

Above the rattling, shaking and knocking from the back boxes I give Jack a shout, 'She's a stubborn cow!' as we passed through my favourite place on the Crewe road at Hartford. We were still just about keeping time, having reached about 70mph and it was still slightly downhill. The steam pressure had dropped back to 150lb, but the water was steady at half a glass. I wanted to run a fire iron over the grate to try and liven things up, but there was no way I was going to risk doing that until we passed Weaver Junction and away from the 'chicken mesh' (the overhead electrification wires). After that we had a slight hump to Birdwood, then one more to Acton Grange, so it was in with the bent dart to give the fire a good rousting. Now let's see what the chimney was saying. Yep, she was smoking, so I'd done it some good, The needle made 10lb, then Jack came over and bellowed in my ear that he would dip the troughs at Moore. Shortly afterwards we shut off for the Warrington stop, then it was on with the exhaust injector to give us a couple of inches in the glass for the downhill approach and subsequent braking for the station.

We had a few minutes at Warrington, so I left on both injectors and put an iron through the fire; the grate felt clinker-free, so it was a quick burst of 20 shovelsful around the box, fill up the back end and off with both feeds. We pulled away a bit healthier now, with a full glass and 200lb of steam. The scented aroma from the adjacent soap works contrasted with the smell of our burning coal as we left Warrington behind and Jack decided to give No 44912 a good thumping. The engine briefly responded, so it was back on with the live steam injector – there would be no chance of turning this off again.

The road ahead climbed for 7 miles up to Golborne, and halfway up this climb it became pretty clear that she did not like the heavy digging. I was trying every trick in the book, but she was not really responding and, crucially, the water level was beginning to drop. Had the engine been fitted with a rocking grate, I could have lifted up the outer securing clamps and given the grates a rocking to liven up the fire.

Then Jack said, 'Get over here, and watch the road.'

As he picked up the shovel I worked the doors for him, closing them after each charge as we topped Golborne summit, but the water was now 'just bobbin', to quote a well-known phrase, and it was Jack who shut off steam, as we were down to 140lb.

'We'll have a few minutes here,' he said as we let No 44912 drift to a stand. I was working hard trying to keep some life in the fire, then a few minutes later our Preston guard, Paul Dowthwaite, came up to ask us how long we would be and should he go back and protect the train.

'No,' said Jack. 'By the time you walk back we'll be on the move. We can have a few minutes in Wigan station.'

So, after about 5 or 6 minutes we got on the move again. Luckily, our arrival in Wigan North Western was actually only 6 minutes behind schedule due to the recovery time built into our workings. I had both injectors singing away as the station

inspector enquired if we wanted another few minutes for a 'blow-up'. Jack agreed to this because in front of us was a 5-mile pull up to Coppull, some of it a 1 in 104.

Eventually we left Wigan about 10 minutes late, but we did have steam, water and something resembling a burning fire, which should and did get us over the top at Coppull. From there it was downhill to Preston, enabling us to blow some of the cobwebs off No 44912 with an 80mph final thrash with our 11 coaches. She didn't like it at that speed and threw us about a bit, with almost every moving part objecting to it, but we had picked up about 5 minutes of the delay as we made our rapid entrance into No 5 platform, which was crowded with parents waiting for their darling daughters to return from a long and exhausting day in London. Some of the cheeky devils came up to the engine and asked us why had we stopped between Warrington and Wigan. So I told them that I had to go into the train to use the toilet as we do not have one on a steam engine!

'Well, it took you long enough,' one of them said, and up the platform they all went, still giggling to themselves. (They must all be grandmas by now – I wonder if they still giggle at each other!) I honestly felt like joining them, but we still had the last leg of our journey to complete to Blackpool.

We got the 'right away' and Jack told me to take the regulator as he wanted to have a go on the shovel to Blackpool. That was fine by me as I did know the road. So off we went past the old Preston shed, forking left past St Walburge's church, then onto the four-track racing stretch to Kirkham, only tonight we had nothing to race, nor did we have an engine capable of breaking the lap record, so no heroics, just a nice steady run to Blackpool North. Jack managed to just about keep enough steam and water in the boiler on this listless machine over the reasonably flat road, and I brought her to a nice gentle stop in one of the excursion platforms at the North terminus. We were a bit late, but there were no complaints, although there could have been had it been a commuter train.

Anyway, no time was wasted in pushing back our stock into the carriage sidings, where the shunter informed us of more 'good news' in that the turntable was out of order on the North shed, so that meant a tender-first run back to Lostock Hall. We did ask to go round the triangle at Poulton-le-Fylde, but one of the signal boxes controlling it was closed at night. Incidentally, the turntable that was at Blackpool Central was almost unique in being electrically operated, and during the very busy summer months a shedman was employed to work it; he would not allow foreign loco crews to work it in case they broke it, and then it would be a visit to the foreman's office for you, where, years ago, you might have been confronted by a Mr Maunsell or a Mr Gresley, both of whom spent part of their railway careers at Blackpool Central shed.

Arriving back at Lostock Hall shed following our tender-first run, during which it had rained heavily and given us a soaking, we were in the driver's lobby booking the engine on shed and Jack was filling out a repair card for No 44912. This was noticed by another driver standing next to him, who remarked, 'Surely you haven't had that old cow. We wired it off last week at Crewe, reporting it shy for steam.'

'Well, it's just as bad,' Jack told him. 'Those crafty sods at Crewe said nothing to us.'

Our foreman heard what was said, and told us that it would not be going back into traffic until it was examined, and if necessary would be sent back light engine to its home shed.

Hearing this made me feel a little better as no fireman likes to think that he has let the side down by having to stop for steam and having a blow-up, but this was the only time that it happened to me. Engines in

poor condition were nothing new to us at that time; many were overdue for shopping, only the basic repairs being carried out – you were lucky to have two good working injectors. Crews had a lot to put up with, and it was quite demoralising to see the usually clean and tidy old-hand drivers going home filthy dirty after a shift on some run-down machine. It was understandable that many were glad to see the end of steam working, with paraffin lamps and paraffin signals, and welcomed the new diesel age. I was involved in the sad demise of one 'Black 5', No 45436, which we reported as not being fit for traffic, mainly due to rough riding and knocking boxes. The foreman told me to throw the fire out and put the engine in the back road out of the way, and that was the end of No 45436.

While I was with Jack we had so much time to ourselves working the short hours that I obtained a part-time job working for an agricultural contractor who owned an oil-fired mobile steam boiler, which he hired out to market gardeners to steam-sterilise their greenhouses. It was an easy 10-shillings-an-hour job. I would set up the boiler, which was on the back of an old Albion wagon, which I loved driving between sites; it had no power steering and the art of double-declutching was essential with the crash gearbox. The boiler used was identical to that on a small shunting engine. It had originally been coal-fired, then coke and finally oil, and once steam was up it was a case of working the injector and helping to bury the pipes in the soil around the greenhouses, covering the pipes with tarpaulins to retain the heat. After 20 minutes or so in one place the pipes were moved along, and the operation repeated. These days all greenhouses are sprayed and fumigated to kill off disease and bugs.

About this time I bought myself a little Standard 8 van to get about from job to job. I also used the van to travel to work, and it was on one of these journeys that I was innocently involved in a motor accident at the entrance to Lostock Hall shed, which was awkwardly situated on the main Preston to Leyland road between two hump-back bridges. While waiting at this entrance one night to let the oncoming traffic clear before I could safely turn right into the shed, I was suddenly hit from behind by a car, which sent me across the road into a hedge. Fortunately I was only shaken up a bit and had a slight whiplash injury. The car that hit me had five pensioners inside, who were on their way home from the pictures. The noise from the crash was heard in the shed, and two first-aiders looked after us until the ambulance arrived. Luckily none of us needed hospital attention – in fact, I was able to book on for work. I was on the 22.00 engine disposal turn, but Jack very kindly did all the six fires, leaving me to shed the engines.

A few days later my insurance company declared my little van a write-off, so they claimed off the other motorist's insurance, but unfortunately he was insured by a company called Fire Auto & Marine, headed by the fraudster Emil Savundra. This company went bust, leaving an estimated 400,000 people without insurance. I didn't get paid anything, which forced me to scrap the little van. It was quite a rare vehicle in the 1960s and, according to the Standard register, fewer than ten are in existence today. (Just as a matter of interest, the Lostock Hall site remains undeveloped because of the restricted access off the busy Watkin Lane.)

While Jack and I were good friends both on and off duty, the same cannot be said for some of the drivers with whom I worked. It was during the summer workings that I found myself marked up for a couple of weeks with one particular driver who was known for not liking any change to his regular routine or swapping firemen, but he had no choice as his own fireman had gone on the sick, and I soon began to see why. Nothing that you

did suited him and his mood could change for no apparent reason. I was warned of this by other firemen, which did at least give me some solace. I suffered the first week in silence, letting his chiding go over my head, making the week just about tolerable. The second week we signed on at 07.05 and walked to Todd Lane Junction station to catch a train down to Preston, then relieve the 07.38 from Wigan to Windermere, departing at 08.15.

The day started badly when the driver (I shall call him Jim) booked on with me but then set off on his own to walk the three-quarters of a mile to the station. When I caught up with him he told me to keep behind him, and on the train to Preston he went and sat by himself. We relieved the crew of a 'Black 5' and I was then given another list of instructions from him on how he wanted things doing. These started with fully opening the back damper and keeping the front one shut, not using the blower – that was his responsibility – and no black smoke.

'Keep the footplate clean, and do not read back any signals to me. I will tell you when to dip on the troughs as I don't want the tender overflowing.'

I thought he was going to put down the proverbial chalk mark dividing the footplate into his side and mine. Now, bear in mind this was my second week of blunt instructions. I could understand some of it, had I been a complete novice of a fireman – no one minds being put right if a driver is not happy – but I was one of the senior firemen at the depot. Anyway, I tried not to let his attitude bother me. I would have had a bit more respect for him if he could actually drive the engine in a professional manner. For instance, on the 1 in 90 climb out of Preston station our engine, No 45154 *Lanarkshire Yeomanry*, was not responding to his full-regulator, 20%-cut-off driving style, and it began to buck to and fro. The change-over valve would not operate for the exhaust injector due to the short cut-off being used, so it was off with that and on with the live steam injector. The loco was trying its best to go back into Preston station instead of heading for the Lake District.

Our first stop with this lightly loaded six-coach train was Garstang & Catterall. There was more trouble here, for he shut off without putting on the blower and the footplate was shrouded in smoke and, luckily, just a few flames. I cracked the blower open with the shovel and, guess what, I got the blame for failing to anticipate when he was going to shut off! Well, I did happen to know where the shut-off point was for this station, and it wasn't where he had closed the regulator, because we would have stopped short of the platform had he not been forced into opening it again to give her a bit more steam to reach the platform. The mere fact that one of his demands had been for me not to touch the blower had slipped his warped mind.

Away we went from our first stop, and I had more problems with the exhaust injector wasting, so rather than risk a confrontation by asking him to drop the cut-off down, I went across to his side and put on the live steam injector, shutting off the more economical exhaust injector. Away we went, our speed gradually building up. The loco was a bit rough-riding and, passing Oubeck loops, 4 miles from our next stop at Lancaster, Jim shouted across to me, pointing underneath his seat, to tell me that the live steam injector is wasting. I had checked it a few minutes before and it was all right. Now, I was always brought up with the belief that the working of a steam locomotive required a joint effort from driver and fireman, but no way was he going to do anything to assist me. As he would not have adjusted that water valve under his seat to correct the wastage I went across and dealt with it myself, asking him to move his legs out of the way to enable me to do so.

All this time I was getting verbals from him regarding my competency as a fireman and wishing he had his regular mate back with him. With this I just thought to myself, sod it, I'm not putting up with this for another week, but I wasn't going to argue with him. I told him that if I wasn't good enough for him then he had better get someone else from Carnforth, because I was getting off there. I had no reply from him, so as we came to a stand at Lancaster I jumped down from the footplate and asked the station inspector to ring Carnforth shed to send a fireman across to the station to relieve the fireman on the 8.15am Preston-Windermere job. He said that he would pass on the message. So I climbed back on board and away we went, Jim not the least bit interested in why I had been in conversation with the inspector.

Before Carnforth we had a couple of more stops at the wayside stations of Bolton-le-Sands and Hest Bank, with a dip for water on the troughs under his instructions. As we came to a stand at the down main platform at Carnforth, I was ready with my traps to leave the footplate to my volatile mate, but there was no sign of a fireman to work the train forward. I was then confronted by the station inspector, who informed me that the shed did not have a spare fireman. He asked me just what the problem was and, after listening and voicing his sympathies regarding my situation, he proffered an experienced railwayman's point of view.

'Look son,' he said, 'you have made a stand but give a thought to the passengers. They need to be on their way. Your train has been stood here over 10 minutes. Get back on board and sort it out when you get back to your own depot.'

He was right, of course, so I reluctantly climbed back on board No 45154. My driver did not say a word to me or even give me a look; he just took the brake off, then with a green from the guard he shoved the regulator into the roof before I had taken my coat off. I knew exactly what his intentions were, because I hadn't prepared the fire for the climb up to Oxenholme. He wanted to catch me out and flatten me, but I got the shovel going pretty rapidly and *Lanarkshire Yeomanry* was a reasonable steamer and had plenty of guts even at 150lb, which was the lowest the pressure dropped before I got the better of things and on top of the job, so not another word was exchanged between us until we arrived at Windermere.

There the shunter climbed aboard and asked me if I would hook off for him when we pushed the stock back over the crossover as he would be in the guard's van controlling the brake.

'He's not doing that – it's your job to do that!' Jim told him.

The shunter looked a bit shocked, because the fireman usually did hook off, then the engine would draw forward over the crossover and stand clear, the shunter releasing the guard's brake and controlling the stock down the gradient back into the platform.

'Well, if that's how we are going to work,' he told Jim, 'you can stop here and wait for me to have my breakfast, which I had put off to deal with you!'

This meant that we would not have much of a break, being in at 09.40 and away at 11 o'clock. When the shunter came back everything was rushed, and departure time saw me with a sandwich in one hand and the shovel in the other.

The shunting arrangements at Windermere were, I always thought, a bit risky, with responsibility being with the guard or shunter to control the train purely with the handbrake(s) when descending the gradient into the station. It was around this time that the inevitable happened during such a shunting move, when braking control was lost, resulting in the coaches crashing through the buffer stops and finishing up in the street next to the bus stop. Fortunately the bus for Bowness had just departed! Miraculously there were no casualties, but the W. H. Smith kiosk was badly damaged. The Lostock Hall steam crane had to be in attendance for a few days clearing the mess under the guidance of shedmaster Harold Sedgebeer and crane driver Harold Martin.

So, on this morning when we left Windermere I expected some heavy-handed driving from my mate and he certainly laid into them on the way back to Preston. I have never worked as hard on a six-coach train; it was all done deliberately, of course, but stopping at the principal stations allowed the loco and me to recover, resulting in us being 4 minutes early into Preston, where it was my job to hook the engine off the train. Incidentally, you may think that I should have voiced my opinion of his driving, but that has never been my style, and I would never dream of telling a driver how to do his job! I have heard some firemen talking sarcastically about their mate, that he does not actually drive the engine, he just operates the controls.

The signalman in Preston No 1 box set the road for us and off we went light engine on the up slow line via Farington Curve to the shed. Once we were on the depot and had coaled the engine I ring the foreman's office (after first checking the telephone earpiece!) and reported the engine on shed, then dropped onto the ashpit road for disposal. Jim was straight off the engine and into the shedmaster's office, leaving me to deal with the fire, ashpan and smokebox. When he reappeared, after unburdening his troubles to Mr Sedgebeer, I had done my duties and we duly put *Lanarkshire Yeomanry* into the shed for a well-earned rest after having had the guts knocked out of her by my 'driver'. As for me, I give the foreman a verbal explanation of the day's events, and was requested to put it all in writing to our shedmaster. I duly acceded to his request, signing off my explanation form as you did in those days: 'Your obedient servant, J. T. Fletcher, Fireman 193'.

The following day saw me standing to attention with cap in hand facing our shedmaster in his office, giving me a dressing down.

'Right, Fletcher, I have looked through your report and your driver's, and I will admit that you are not the first fireman to have had an altercation with this driver. I have looked back through your records, which are blemish-free to date. I also note that senior driver Robert Fletcher is an uncle of yours with 44 years service, all trouble-free. I want you to remember this, that the driver is the captain of the ship; he is not always right and possibly he was a bit out of order in this instance, but you must respect his command. Now get yourself out of here, and back to your duties.'

So with that I went down to the office to sign on duty for the day. The foreman called me in to have a word.

'I've been told to put you back on the roster,' he said, 'but I have a problem with the roster this week. I am struggling for firemen – how do you fancy putting behind

what has happened and firing for Jim again? And before you reply, I can tell you he has said that what is in the past remains in the past and does regret you having to see the shedmaster. Some of his problems stem from losing his regular fireman of the last two years.'

When he had finished telling me all this, I thought about it for a minute, then told him that, yes, I would go back with him and hopefully prove my worth as his fireman. So the following day I was back on the footplate with Jim. We shook hands and I have to say there was never really a wrong word between us again, All right, I did have to adapt the firing to his particular driving technique, but let's not forget that he was the 'captain of the ship'!

Some time later I was told that Jim had been involved in a frightening incident when he was younger which may well have affected his character. It was wartime and he was the fireman on a heavy ammunition train from the Euxton ROF (Royal Ordnance Factory) to Carlisle via the Midland. The engine was an ex-L&Y 0-8-0, and coming down Wilpshire Bank the weight of the train got the better of them, and they became a runaway. The train was proven to have been travelling at an unbelievable 90mph when it passed over Whalley Viaduct, eventually coming to a stand a few miles further on, the rising gradient enabling the crew to bring it to a stand. Both had remained at their posts, which must have been a very frightening ordeal for them on this old freight engine, which usually trundled around at a more sedate 25mph.

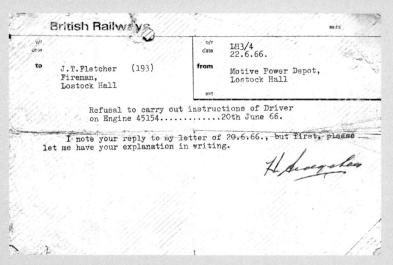

A request from our shedmaster for an explanation regarding the incident with 'Black 5' No 45154 *Lanarkshire Yeomanry* on 20 June 1966. *Author's collection*

It was a miracle that no derailment occurred with this ammunition train, otherwise the consequences would have been unthinkable. The line remained closed for three days until bridge engineers had completed a full structural examination of the huge Whalley Viaduct, for it was feared that the combination of the train speed and weight may have disturbed this monument to the railway age.

Mention of the ROF works leads me to mention the shed's association with this now defunct organisation. In its heyday thousands of staff were employed in armament production, many of them travelling to the factory in the special works trains, the ROF having a railway station of its own between Euxton Junction and Chorley on the Manchester line. Our depot had the majority of work hauling these trains. We had two afternoon jobs, one to Blackpool Central and the other to Wigan North Western. Motive power for the seaside job was invariably a 2-6-4T, with the train home for the 'pie-eaters' usually attracting one of their own machines; among the regulars were 'Baby Scot' No 45521 *Rhyl*, or 'fully grown' 'Scot' No 46168 *The Girl Guide*. I loved these engines and liked nothing more than leaning out of the cab watching parts of the inside motion rocking to and fro to the beat of the engine. The routes taken by both these trains took them over some long-since-closed sections of line. The Blackpool job had a Preston stop, then from Kirkham it took the little-used so-called 'new line' via Marton, bringing it to Blackpool South station. The run to Wigan was via Chorley, then at Adlington Junction we veered right, and took the line to Boars Head Junction, passing through the disused station at White Bear, then over the rickety wooden bridge at Red Rock, which always seemed too fragile to support a big passenger engine. When the factory closed, most of the land at Euxton was taken up with housing, and Buckshaw Village was born, a new station being built to serve this new community.

Somewhere around this time I took up playing football again with a local team. No, not Preston North End, as I was never anywhere near that good, although I used to dream of playing alongside my hero Tom Finney. Once it got around that I was playing, some of the staff asked me if I fancied the idea of starting up our own football team at the shed. So it was left to me to call a meeting, then to approach the railway welfare committee for some finance; everything then came together pretty quickly and without a hitch. We played a few pre-season friendlies, then kicked off our first season in the Preston & District League. Having a good quota of players to select from made team selection a lot easier, helping to overcome the problem of most of us working on shifts. Not all of us were young fellas in the team. Eric Edge, Peter Norris, Jimmy Clayton and Brian Parker were all in their mid-30s.

One of the opposing teams in our league was Kirkham Open Prison, who for obvious reasons played all their games at home. The match would attract a reasonably sized crowd because the convicts did not have that much else to do on a Saturday afternoon, so they might as well go along to the match for a bit of fun. Such was the case on the day we played them. They quickly took to me, after hearing my team mates calling me by my nickname, 'Fingers'.

'Give it to Fingers – he must be one of us with a name like that! You're kicking the wrong way, mate!'

They kept up the humour throughout the game, and carried me off at the final whistle, having disastrously scored an own goal, which gave us a 3-3 draw.

13 North Eastern engines

Although our depot was situated right in the heart of Lancashire, not all of our work was on regional motive power. Indeed, it was possible to see a variety of locomotives from the North Eastern Region, and we occasionally got to operate these machines, including examples of the 'B1', 'K3' and 'J39' classes, although I personally never worked the latter two. However, I did enough on the 'B1s' to be able to make comparisons with our own 'Black 5s'. The ex-LNER 'B1' 4-6-0s were supposed to be more economical than Stanier's Class 5s, but they were not popular with the ex-LMS men. They were very dirty, with dust blowing around the footplate from the ashpan. There was only a front damper, which, when open at speed, caused air to rush through towards the footplate, whereas the 'Black 5s' had front and back dampers and would steam efficiently with only the back damper open. I found the footplate awkward to work on, and the tender had only a small aperture from which to shovel the coal, whereas the 'Black 5' had a large shovelling plate and large doors that could be opened to gain access when the coal became out of reach.

My first acquaintance with one of these machines was not long after passing for firing, on loan to Preston on a summer Saturday. I signed on at 08.00 and waited for Control orders with a Preston driver in the guards' room on Platform 1. We had just made a can of tea when sure enough the phone rang and we were given a job to Blackpool, our train being quite handily

routed down Platform 1, so it was a case of stepping out and stepping on board and relieving a Bradford-Blackpool North special with North Eastern 'B1' No 61020 *Gemsbok*. The Yorkshire fireman that I relieved had left it prepared with a full glass and plenty of steam and a good back end of fire, and as this was a special there was nobody to get on or off and we were soon pulling away up the 1 in 90 gradient with 11 LNER coaches, which weighed more than ex-LMS stock.

After being given a quick lesson by Clifford, my Preston driver, I did my best to try and master the shovelling through the strange North Eastern 'oven door'. He advised me to bend my back a little more than I would normally when firing an LMS engine so that I could be more direct and actually see where the coal was landing. (This was not the same Clifford who became my regular mate in later years.) Shortly after passing on his expert tuition, Clifford amused me by taking out his false teeth, wrapping them up in his handkerchief and putting them away in his jacket pocket. He waved me across to his side and, blurting and spitting into my left ear, said, 'You'll soon see why I've done that.'

So I went back across to my side just as we are approaching Lea Road troughs, and it was time for a dip. My mate having just given me a wetting, I didn't fancy another, so it was important that I judged correctly the lowering and raising of the water scoop. Once over the troughs our speed increased to about 60mph at Salwick and, as we were running on the fast line, we missed out the station. Now, with every chance of a clear run through Kirkham it was then that I noticed the vibration and the solid riding of our 'B1' locomotive. As we have already seen, the four-track main line from Preston to Kirkham could be the place for a bit of fun if there were simultaneous departures, but we were on our own that day.

No wonder these 'B1' machines were fitted with padded seats. Cliff hung onto the whistle lever and gave me a toothless grin as we roared through Kirkham and on to Bradkirk, then Singleton and on towards Blackpool North. He glanced across at the steam and water and we exchanged thumbs-up, so he was happy with the situation and *Gemsbok* managed a brief 70mph on the level before shutting off for the Poulton curve. The 'B1' certainly let us know that it was doing 70mph by the heavy vibration characteristic of this class of loco, and with which I was later to become familiar.

My mate demonstrated his versatility as we approached the buffer stops at Blackpool North by being able to skilfully judge the braking of the train and slip his false teeth back in at the same time. When we came to a stand he said, this time without spitting all over me, 'What did I tell you, kid? Rough as a dog, these things. Any engine that starts with a number 6 shouldn't bloody well be on our region, and think yourself lucky we didn't have one of those "K3s", which make a "B1" feel like a Rolls Royce! They do pull better, having an extra set of rods underneath them, but no padded seats, just a bloody piano stool to rest your bum on. I used to stand on the tender, which rode better than the engine! Thank God they have all been turned into razor blades and scrapped!'

Cliff was interrupted halfway through his appraisal of anything North Eastern by the sudden presence of two pretty young ladies at his cab window, praising him for his on-time arrival at Blackpool. Now, Clifford was well known for fancying anything in a skirt, so he leaned out and, giving them his best toothy grin while patting the side of the cab, he told them, 'Ah! Yes, girls, but its all down to having such a good engine and fireman!'

Do you know something? They don't make them like Cliff any more – I think the mould must have been broken after his generation!

My next encounter with one of the class was to Blackpool again with driver Ronnie Hall, afterwards working a shuttle to Fleetwood and back. It was the summer of 1964, and we did this twice. On the second trip, while taking water at Fleetwood station, I remember that our guard came up and gave us the distressing news that American Country & Western singer Jim Reeves had been killed in a plane crash. It might just be me, but I can remember news items like that. I can tell you where I was when Kennedy was assassinated, or the time Buddy Holly and Eddie Cochran perished.

I had numerous trips on the 'B1s' working coal empties back into Yorkshire, and as I became more experienced on these machines I might just concede a couple of useful items fitted to them that I would have liked on a 'Black 5'. One was the separate steam brake, making the working of a loose-coupled train that bit easier, with less chance of snatching the couplings and giving more controllable braking. The LMS equivalent of this was the primitive wrapping and pulling on a cloth attached to the steam spindle on the LMS Deeley brake, the Achilles heel of the Stanier locomotives. Additionally, I thought the design of the pull-out injector steam valves on some of the 'B1s' were easier to operate than the conventional wheel type on other locomotives. The 'B1' was also known as the 'Antelope' Class, although the only named ones that I can personally recall working on were Nos 61036 *Ralph Assheton*, 61020 *Gemsbok* and 61215 *William*

Henton Carver. My driver on the latter was Paddy Doyle, and we worked a lunchtime coal empties to Sowerby Bridge. Paddy had a conductor from Rose Grove and he was good enough to let me ride with the guard in the brake van while he did the firing. Some of the brake van interiors were adorned with many poetic verses, rhymes, riddles and puzzles whose authors were a wasted talent in just guarding trains, when they could have earned a living scriptwriting for comics. For instance, one little gem that I recall in a brake van that must have been allocated to an area with overhead wires, and written above the brake van coal stove, was this piece of useful advice: 'If you want an electric fire, just raise the stove pipe two feet higher.'

Another 'B1' turn I recall was when I was with driver John Burnett, who was just as enthusiastic about steam as I was; he also liked having a go on the shovel, leaving me to widen my driving experience. We were together on a couple of trips with a 'B1'. The first, one Bank Holiday Monday, wasn't overtaxing; when it seemed that everybody else was working specials to the seaside, we were shunting Chorley and Horwich yard. The 'B1' was not really ideal as a yard pilot, the bucket seats making life awkward when shunting tender-first. A few weeks later we had another 'B1', working coal empties back to Yorkshire with relief at Gannow Junction, Burnley. We had a problem with greasy rail conditions after being put into the rarely used goods loop at Huncoat. John had to be at his best with the braking after the 'B1' went into a slide approaching the trap points, but all went well, mainly due to the controllability of the engine's steam brake, which I have previously praised.

One of the more interesting jobs that we worked from Rose Grove to Preston was the late-evening Wakefield-Preston stopper, where literally anything could be seen on the front, such as a 'B1', 5XP, 'Black 5', 'Crab' or 8F, the train being the return working of our Liverpool-Skipton diagram. The first time I had the job one of my favourite 5XPs, No 45705 *Seahorse*, rolled up and my driver was speed king George Whalley. It is not a very fast railway back to Preston, but he managed a very creditable 78mph down Hoghton Bank before braking heavily for the restriction through Bamber Bridge. But the rarest machine to turn up on this job must have been Low Moor's 'J39' 0-6-0 No 64801 one Friday night; John Burnett was again the driver, but regretfully I wasn't his fireman that week. I was on an 05.00 disposing turn and spotted the 'J39' in the shed the next morning. It was marked up to work the 12.10 Saturdays-only stopping train from Preston to Bolton, so I duly turned out at Skew Bridge, south of Preston, with my trusty Halina Pet camera to witness this possibly unique occasion, but I was in for a disappointment when a Fairburn 2-6-4 tank came past. It transpired that the 'J39' had failed on the Saturday morning and I never did find out how it got back to its own depot. Perhaps it didn't, and is still there languishing somewhere on Lostock Hall shed!

Continuing with the theme of North Eastern machinery, I readily admit that at the time I couldn't get enough when it came to enthusiasm for the steam locomotive – the only thing I looked forward to when signing off duty was the thought of going back to work again the following day. I even used to go down to the shed on my day off, and on one such occasion my diligence was rewarded, for standing there on No 9 road was North Eastern 'Pacific' No 60131 *Osprey*. Upon enquiring of the shed foreman, I was told that it had worked a 20-coach empty stock train from Law Junction, Motherwell, to Lostock Hall carriage sidings. In fact, the reporting number, 3X04, still adorned the front of the loco. When I climbed aboard this stranger, it immediately felt a

'A1' 'Pacific' No 60131 *Osprey* drifts through Platform 2 at Preston station with 3X04, a 20-coach ECS working from Law Junction to Lostock Hall carriage sidings on 31 July 1964. *Arthur Haymes*

little claustrophobic; the cab was almost totally enclosed, and even the gap between the engine and tender roof was covered, certainly a hot environment on a summer's day. I then went to pester the shed foreman about when it would be going off shed, what would it be working, at what time, and who would be on it.

'Oh! Clear off, "Fingers",' said the foreman. 'Go and have a look on the shed board – I'm too busy to answer your questions.'

It came as a bit of a shock when I looked at the engine arrangement board to see No 60131 marked up to work the 9.45pm Bamber Bridge-Laisterdyke coal empties, the crew being driver Dick Thomas and fireman Joseph Booth (who is still involved with steam as a driver on the Ribble Railway at Preston). So when I came to work the following day I did not expect to see *Osprey* still on shed. But according to Joseph, when they arrived at Bamber Bridge yard, having

travelled the 2 miles light engine from the shed, the yard foreman turned them back to the shed, stating that Control was unsure of the engine's route availability for going over the Calder Valley. Control later insisted that it must go back over the same route it had come on, that being the West Coast Main Line. So on the following day, Tuesday 4 August 1964, it didn't work just any old train – No 60131, a North Eastern 'A1' 'Pacific', was diagrammed to work one of the principal London Midland trains, 'The Lakes Express', and this it duly did. To quote the editor of one railway journal, 'This was the only occasion that a North Eastern "Pacific" had ever worked a West Coast named train, and I state named train.'

The rostered driver, who had obviously never handled one of these engines before, reportedly told Control that, as he was unfamiliar with the locomotive but was expected to work a Class 1 train to time, if he incurred any delays while working it Control would have to take the blame. And what do you think happened? Well, *Osprey* flew just like its namesake, arriving well before its booked time at Penrith, with a beaming and satisfied Midland man at

On 4 August 1964 No 60131 *Osprey* heads north through Lancaster with the front portion of 'The Lakes Express'; the second coach has a carriage board attached. *Bill Ashcroft*

the controls of this 'foreign' machine, and moreover having had a far more comfortable footplate ride than with a 'Scot', the usual motive power for this job.

Another day when I booked on duty our engine for the day was No 44767, which was standing on No 6 road. This was the unique 'Black 5' fitted with the Stephenson Link Motion (more of this later) and, unbelievably, standing on the next road to us was 'A4' 'Pacific' No 60010 *Dominion of Canada*, minus its chimney. It was on its way to Crewe and being towed there by a grimy Springs Branch 'Black 5', on the first stage of its journey to eventual preservation in Montreal, having been presented by British Railways to the Canadian Government. It was due to have a cosmetic restoration at Crewe before being shipped out, but why the missing chimney? Again I believe this was at the behest of that fountain of knowledge,

the Control boys; apparently they had no record of an 'A4' on the Calder Valley route, and insisted on the chimney being removed due to bridge restrictions. They obviously had some sort of memory lapse, for just a few short years previously an 'A4' had traversed that same route when No 60022 *Mallard* worked a Northern Rubber special to Blackpool North, and double-headed the midnight return train with ex-MR Compound No 1000. I photographed the train on the outward journey at Preston, then cycled to Blackpool North shed, where scores of enthusiasts were allowed to wander and roam to their heart's content, remaining at the trackside to witness the midnight departure. Of course, that was in the days when Health & Safety used to come under the heading of 'common sense'.

Just to finish off this particular tale, years later I was reliably informed that the driver of *Mallard* for part of the run to Blackpool was from the predominantly freight depot at Sowerby Bridge. Therefore this would have been the first time that he had ever set

'Black 5' No 44824 reverses through Lostock Hall station on 16 August 1966 propelling dead 'A4' No 60010 *Dominion of Canada* en route to Crewe Works for renovation before shipment to Canada. *Bill Ashcroft*

foot on a 'A4' 'Pacific', which would have been totally alien to him, but such was the versatility of many drivers from the steam era that he would have probably looked upon it as just another steam engine. He thoroughly enjoyed himself according to reports – and let's not forget the lad on the shovel, for without his skills we go nowhere.

I will finish off the *Dominion of Canada* story by telling you about a visit that one of my friends made to see the engine years later in the museum at Montreal. Kevin Gould was a driver on the North Yorkshire Moors Railway and the museum staff therefore gave him permission to look all around the engine and take whatever photos he wanted, the engine being virtually untouched since leaving these shores, so he duly spent nearly two hours photographing and giving the engine his attention. The final place

he checked was the driver's locker on the footplate, which, when opened, revealed in a dark corner a small package. He pulled it out to reveal an empty packet of Woodbines, which must have been in there at the time it left Britain, and probably would have belonged to some driver or fireman from the steam age.

Another North Eastern engine with which I have connections is No 60007 *Sir Nigel Gresley*. This goes back to 1967 when the engine had been overhauled at Crewe and was having running-in trials between Crewe and Preston, with a visit to Lostock Hall for disposal and examination. It was around this time that I first met Crewe driver Bert Stewart, and during a conversation he told me that he had transferred from Lostock Hall to Crewe, and that his brother Horace, whom I knew, was a guard at Lostock Hall. He then went on to explain just how he became the regular driver on No 60007. He had witnessed the gradual restoration of the engine at Crewe, and simply had a chat with the shed boss, saying that he would like to be considered as the driver once restoration was completed. He was told that his application would be considered, bearing in mind that at this time many drivers and firemen had finished with steam operation, and had been issued with the smart new uniforms for diesel and electric traction, so I don't think Bert had much opposition. This proved to be the case and, after a successful period of running-in, the day came for its first operational run following restoration.

Bert told me that not long after leaving Crewe, and at just over 90mph, he had a tap on the shoulder from the footplate inspector to ease her back a bit. Also, during the run the footplate was visited by some invited dignitaries, a Mayor and his Mayoress together with others; at one time there were six people in the cab sampling some of this high-speed run, most of them having gained access to the footplate via the corridor tender. This maiden voyage has been well documented, and proved to be a resounding success on such strange metals. Certainly Shap was taken in fine style, and there later followed some further creditable runs with Bert at the regulator of No 60007. I think it would be safe to say that the only regular driver in preservation of this ex-LNER 'A4' was this former Lostock Hall man. Soon after retirement Bert took a pub in Chorley, The Sebastopol, which soon became a regular drinking hole for a great number of railwaymen. After sinking a few pints of best bitter, they would take to the floor with an abundance of steam stories.

I kept in touch with Bert, who was of great help when we held our very first Lostock Hall reunion in 1994, alongside Barney Campbell and myself together with Bob Gregson, the author of the two recent books, *The Lancashire & Yorkshire Railway around Preston* and its companion *The London & North Western Railway around Preston*, both highly recommended and packed with historical facts and photographs.

Bert also wrote an enjoyable book about his exploits throughout his railway life entitled *On The Right Lines*. He visited me a few times at the NYMR, and we would ride the rails; he was able to renew his acquaintance with the 'A4' when I took him on a trip to Pickering and back. Sadly he is no longer with us, but I hope that I have kept up the traditions of a Lostock Hall man working on *Sir Nigel Gresley*, not only on the NYMR but all over the country on the main line. This included one memorable Scarborough-King's Cross special, which we worked throughout with No 60007. We 'flattened' the formidable Stoke Bank, attaining 73mph before entering the tunnel near the summit with our 12-coach train; Bert would have been proud of that, and of the dedicated team of volunteers who look after this magnificent machine.

My penultimate story relating to North Eastern engines came about when I had left the railways in the 1970s and was working with my father and staff in our landscape gardening business. We took on extra staff during the season, and one of these was a good friend of mine who had worked on the footplate at Preston. One day during a break for dinner I happened to ask him if he had passed for driving on steam, and he then began to relate this interesting experience. I should first remind you that not all footplate staff shared my enthusiasm for the job. Now, my mate was always safe and conscientious, but to him one steam engine was like any other. On the day of his practical exam in 1967 he and the inspector had to travel to Carnforth, due to the scarcity of steam-hauled trains at that late date. The inspector told him that he had arranged to assess him on a parcels train coming in from Barrow-in-Furness and steam-hauled to Crewe. At this point I asked my friend what engine they had on the job, and this was his reply.

'At first I didn't know what it was – when it ran in at Carnforth I had never seen one like it. The frames were curved and it was painted blue. After getting on board, I had to ask the driver we relieved how to work the controls, but once under way I soon got used to it, and the comfy cab with padded seats. It had a great whistle, and we just flew along. I had to shut off at 75mph, this being our max with the parcels train, otherwise I am sure I could have got a ton out of it.'

I interrupted him and told him that what he had driven on his exam was a famous steam locomotive, and I asked if he had passed.

'Yes I did,' he proudly told me, 'and I will never forget the name of that engine as long as I live – it was *Sir Nigel Stanier*. Funny how you never forget important things in your life.'

I didn't have the heart to correct him; he would have no doubt related the same story to his children and grandchildren.

A short final comment regarding North Eastern engines relates to the 1980s when I was driving for the NYMR. We had an apprentice fireman on board our engine, No 60532 *Blue Peter*, and during a conversation with him he informed me that his father had been a driver on the railway working on similar engines to ours; in fact, he was the driver on the unique occasion when the 'A1' 'Pacific' No 60114 *W. P. Allen* worked a Gainsborough Model Railway special train right through to Blackpool. We had heard that this machine would be heading the train, and went to Preston station to witness what we believed to be the first 'A1' to work a train into Blackpool, our own 'Lizzies' and 'Princesses' all being barred due to weight restrictions.

'A1' 'Pacific' No 60114 *W. P. Allen* heads 1X22, a Gainsborough Model Railway Society special at Ashton on its way to Blackpool. *Author's collection*

14 One that got away – and some that didn't

Late one Friday afternoon – pay day for everybody – I was heading home through the shed, having just booked off from another firing duty, when I was accosted by a group of footplate staff mingling around No 46248 *City of Leeds*, one of the last of the class still in operation. They asked me if I fancied giving them a hand to clean her before she left the shed.

'Yes, I'm up for that,' I told them.

They had already made a start, most of them concentrating on the boiler, cab and tender, the motion being the least popular, of course, but a couple more lads and I made a start. After a while someone remarked that BR had started to sell off some of its steam locos and he wondered how much they would want for *City of Leeds*. Some 10 minutes later I had been appointed as the one to approach our chief clerk, Jim Walmsley, going to the office and asking him if he would enquire about a purchase price for the loco. He gave me an incredulous look, and asked if I had been sent to him as a wind-up. He eventually believed that I was serious, and made a call, but as it was late Friday afternoon most of the staff at Rail House at Crewe had gone home. However, they promised to ring him back, so I returned to my cleaning duties and told everybody that we were awaiting a reply.

Then someone said, 'I think we've got one.'

I turned around, and standing there was Jim next to the engine. He said to us, 'Right, are you all ready for this? The price is £4,000, less 10% because you are railway staff, but the engine has to be moved to its new location within six weeks of purchasing,' and off he went back to the office, probably chuckling to himself.

Now it was nitty-gritty time. We had all just been paid, so we had a look at what we could put on the table, not forgetting of course to keep 30 bob back to give to our Mums for our keep. As far as I can remember we managed to scrape up £108 between us. Well, it was a start I suppose, but we couldn't persuade Jim to take it as a deposit on No 46248, then to pay off the rest at so much per week out of our wages. Even if some agreement could have been reached with British Railways, there was still the small problem to overcome of where could we keep the loco! I could just imagine my Dad coming home from work and asking me what was that standing in the driveway – and telling him that Pickfords had just dropped it off there, but it would only be temporary until we found a suitable railway line to put it on! Looking back, £4,000 was a lot of money in 1964; a semi-detached house in Lostock Hall would have been £1,700, and you could certainly have bought yourself a fine desirable detached residence for £2,500. But we had tried, and it was a sad day when No 46248 went for scrap not that much later.

I do know for a fact that some of the would-be benefactors of the engine became involved and contributed towards saving some of the numerous ex-Lostock Hall locomotives that are now in preservation.

One of those preserved 'Black 5s', with which I have been associated, is No 44767; although it was never allocated to our depot, it spent a good number of years at the next shed down the line, at Liverpool Bank Hall, therefore it was regularly crewed by Lostock Hall men. Some of the jobs that the engine worked hardly taxed its capabilities. The local passenger services in particular just comprised five or six coaches. So it was only when you put some real weight behind it that the loco was able to demonstrate the widely held belief that it was the strongest of all the 842 'Black 5s'. Later in its BR days it was transferred to Carlisle Kingmoor, and had little chance of an easy life at that depot, with Beattock to the north and Shap and Ais Gill to the south, and maybe a day out over the Waverley route! The engine was easily recognisable by its unique Stephenson outside valve gear, which gave it a much stronger exhaust beat in comparison with other members of the class.

As is now the case with steam locos, many have spent a longer period of time working in preservation than they actually did earning their keep on British Railways, and thanks to Mr Ian Storey No 44767 is one of them. For a long time it was based on the NYMR, working trains over the years alongside a number of other 'Black 5s'. Comparisons were obviously made between the Walschaerts engines and the Stephenson-driven No 44767. Back in BR days the loading on the 1 in 49 sections of the NYMR for a Class 5 engine was six coaches, but since those days this line has become the busiest heritage railway in the country, with subsequent loadings increased due to the demand, so now it is quite common to witness a Class 5 loco tackling the 1 in 49 grades hauling the maximum load of eight coaches. The only exception to this was when No 44767 was available for traffic, then the loading could be increased to nine coaches. The 1 in 49 is a stern test

for the crew and the locomotive, certainly when you compare this with the gradients of Shap at 1 in 75, or for that matter Beattock's 1 in 60, although I do accept the difference in the length of the gradients.

Not all the 'Black 5s' shared the success of the Stephenson and Walschaerts engines. You certainly could not enthuse the same about the engines fitted with the Caprotti valve gear. Downhill there wasn't much that could catch them – they would coast for miles. The problem was going up the hills! They did not possess the power of their classmates, to the extent that our shed foreman was reluctant to roster them on Class 5 work, as in his opinion they were nearer to being in the Class 4 power range. You certainly do not see many photos of them from BR days dragging heavy trains unassisted up some of the more recognised gradients.

Over the years I did keep some notes, and turning to these I am able to refer to events that I recorded from those days. On one particular Monday I was the fireman on No 45000 and my driver was new to me, having transferred from Kirkby Stephen shed when the line over Stainmore closed. I met him in the drivers' lobby when we booked on at 8.00am and he introduced himself as Bob Barker. My immediate impression was that I had better behave myself today as Bob was a big lad, but as is often the case with someone his size he was actually the proverbial gentle giant. Our job for the day was the Horwich tripper, which comprised engine preparation, then to Lostock Hall goods yard, local freight to Chorley and, after shunting the yard, away to the former loco works at Horwich for more shunting. By that time this once proud symbol of the Lancashire & Yorkshire Railway had been reduced to wagon building and repairing.

As we began to prepare No 45000 Bob called me down from the footplate to join him in the pit underneath. I was immediately met with a gut-wrenching stench. No, it wasn't coming from Bob, but when he shone the flare lamp up to the frames and under the boiler we could see just what was causing the smell. There were lumps of flesh and fur stuck to the underneath of the boiler and frames, so Bob hot-footed it back to the office and returned with the shed foreman and foreman fitter. The latter said that he was under the impression that the loco had been steam-cleaned and prepared for traffic having collided with some young bullocks a few days previously. Bob told him that he was not taking the loco while it was in that state and, with the foreman's agreement, we were given an 'Austerity' 2-8-0 to replace the 'Black 5'. (I've just had a horrible thought – I do hope that No 45000 has rid itself of the animal bits, as I believe it is now on public display at the National Railway Museum!)

We dashed about and got our replacement engine ready, Bob asking me if I wanted to do the driving. So away we went with me on the regulator of one of our home-based 'Iron Lungs', No 90258, which by the way was almost ex-works with a very stiff reverser making shunting ruddy hard work. This therefore almost guaranteed that the fireman would be given a driving turn, although in fairness to Bob he did not know beforehand! By mid-morning we had arrived at Horwich, and after about an hour's shunting it was break time, so I decided to have a look around the birthplace of many former Lostock Hall locomotives. The works could boast its fair share of gifted apprentices who later in life became CMEs of other railways, including Nigel Gresley, Oliver Bulleid, Richard Maunsell and Henry Fowler.

I could just imagine a gifted young Nigel Gresley looking around the place and, upon sighting an L&Y 'A' Class 0-6-0 goods engine with the spartan open cab, which offered little or no protection, the non-superheated boiler and gravity sanders, thinking to himself that if he ever got into any position of authority in the world of locomotives there would be no way on earth that he would consider building a machine like that! I can always remember Uncle Bob telling me that after cycling for 5 miles from his home to the shed in pouring rain at 3 o'clock on a winter's morning to find waiting for him one of those 0-6-0s, he used to say that he had more protection from the weather on his pushbike than he would have on that footplate. Horwich Works is now but a shadow of its former self; what hasn't been demolished has been divided into units, although some of the original L&Y offices remain. There are rumours of impending demolition of what remains, to become housing land. What still does remain from my day is the football team and the ground. I played there on a number of occasions, and the team is still known as Horwich RMI (Railway Mechanics Institute).

The local branch line to Horwich, from Blackrod, closed to passengers in 1965, and I worked on one of the last trains. I will tell you about that shortly, but going back to the week I had with Bob, I questioned him about the work they had at his previous depot of Kirkby Stephen. At first I was confused in thinking that he was referring to a shed on the Settle & Carlisle line until he pointed out that his station was situated about a mile away and near to the town itself. He drew for me a diagram of his railway, which branched off to the right at Tebay. I had seen it, but we never went down there, of course – usually it was just a glimpse of it when passing through Tebay station. He then described the two large metal viaducts on the line, and I could not possibly forget the name of one of them, Deepdale, the name of Preston North End's ground. They were not allowed to double-head trains over these structures.

I also recall him telling me about a film that was made about the line in the 1950s called *Snowdrift at Bleath Gill*, which highlighted the harshness of winter over the isolated Stainmore route. In later years, after I moved to North Yorkshire, I would sometimes travel by car over the route along the A66, much of which ran parallel to the line. It was only then that I began to appreciate just how tough it must have been to operate a train service over this wild, rugged railway. I still use the A66, although it can be subject to closures during the winter months, and frequently call in at the preservation site at Bob's former station of Kirkby Stephen East, where enthusiasts are working hard to transform the site into an operating railway again.

As an aside, shortly before he left the railway Bob drove the penultimate BR steam train on Saturday night, 3 August 1968, with loco No 45212 working the Euston-Blackpool service forward from Preston.

I had an interesting four days with Bob, at the end of which I felt confident enough to have signed the route from Kirkby Stephen to Darlington via Stainmore. It was just a pity that they had closed the line in 1961! Bob took Friday off and my mate for the day was Jack Brady, otherwise known as the 'Cleaner's Lawyer' when he was younger. I had shared the footplate with Jack on a number of occasions; he was a sharp lad, well up on union agreements, and if you took him on you had to make sure you knew your stuff. I had many a light-hearted set-to with him, and he usually finished up by telling me that I was a cheeky sod, and to come back when I had some service in, as I knew nowt! Jack actually lived next door to an aunt of mine in Preston. When he was first married I used to kid him that my aunt was always complaining about that noisy couple who lived next door to her.

He was also a bit soft-hearted and I was always scrounging fags off him, but he got his own back on me the day he stood in for Bob. All week, when on the return run from Horwich, the signalman at Blackrod Junction would not give us a road until the stopping passenger train had gone, meaning that we were behind it all the way to Leyland and finished up working overtime. But this was Friday, and lads' night out, the most important night of the week for me. However, just as he had done all week, the signalman was holding us at his Home signal on the Horwich branch. We stood for 20 minutes or more and I remarked to Jack that if he had given us the road there is no way that we would have delayed his passenger train, and that signalmen like him should not be put in charge of busy junction boxes, they were incompetent and they should be kept on a single-line branch, with just one train a day to deal with. Moreover, he should also be reported to a signalling inspector – in fact, the next time I saw one I would tell him about this useless prat!

We watched the stopper leave Blackrod station on the main line, and when it had cleared Adlington Junction it was our turn. I estimated that he had held us for nearly half an hour, during which time we could easily have reached Euxton Junction, with absolutely no chance of delaying anybody. So as we drew down with our 8F I was hoping to see the signalman to give him a nasty look as we went past, but as we got nearer the signal box Jack started to put the brake on, then stopped with the engine right alongside.

He shouted to the signalman, 'Have you a minute, bobby? My fireman is a bit annoyed with you, and he wants to have a word.'

The signalman slid open the window, his huge bulk filling the frame. He was giving me the evils all right, and said to me, 'Right, son, what words of wisdom are you about to impart to me that you think might improve on my 36 years of signalling experience?'

It is not often that I am stuck for words, but I must admit that his comment did set me back a wagon length or two. I had to think of something and quick, so I meekly asked, 'Do you think it would be beneficial to have a telephone installed at that branch signal, in order to communicate with you?'

I didn't really hear his reply due to him slamming shut the signal box window. End of story!

Just as an aside to all this, as we got nearer to Adlington Junction there in the goods yard, or Fairclough's yard, stood an ex-Lancashire & Yorkshire Railway Barton Wright 3F 0-6-0; it was there for years after withdrawal and was eventually purchased from Fairclough's for preservation, and is at present on the East Lancashire Railway.

We had a few other jobs to Horwich, including the first passenger train of the day. We came off shed about 5.00am to Lostock Hall carriage sidings, then empty stock to Leyland for all stations to Horwich. It could be a bit tricky on a Monday morning when climbing up from Blackrod, as it was a steep branch line, and nothing had been up there over the weekend. It was always a wise move to ensure that you filled the sanders on the allotted loco, usually a 2-6-4 tank belonging to 24C. The next part of the turn was to work a stopping train to Bolton, then back to Horwich with the 8.40am. At this time we had quite a number of drivers who, as young men, had been called upon to serve in the First World War, and others who served their country in the 1939-45 conflict. I looked upon them as heroes, although not all of them would mention the part they had played. One of them was my driver for the week on the Horwich job. Wilf was ex-RAF, having been a rear gunner, and still retained the moustache and mannerisms from those days. Before he took an engine off the shed he always gave it a thorough examination, or as he referred to it a pre-flight check. He enjoyed nothing better than a few drinks in a slightly upmarket pub near where he lived and always drank in the best room, where a pint of beer in those days cost 1s 6d.

By pure chance we found ourselves working during what was to be the last week before closure of the Horwich branch

to passengers. Regular travellers included three managers from a local mill, who always travelled on the 8.40am from Bolton to Horwich, alighting at our first stop, Lostock Junction. On the Monday morning they came up to the engine and told us that they had been using this train for years, and as Thursday would be their last day, would it be possible for them to have a ride on the footplate with us for the 5 miles to Lostock Junction. Wilf readily agreed to their request, so Thursday came and, before departure with our 2-6-4 tank, I prepared the fire, water, etc, as I wouldn't be able to do much shovelling with five of us on board. I positioned our guests around the footplate, with one of them in the fireman's seat. Wilf told him to blow the whistle, and away we went with our three-coach train to Lostock Junction station, where photographs were taken and the men thanked us, saying that it had been their boyhood dream to ride on the footplate.

As they got off, one of them gave me half a crown (2s 6d) saying, 'You and your driver have a pint apiece on us,' and off he went.

Wilf asked me, 'What has he given you?' so I told him 2s 6d.

'That won't buy us two pints – I don't drink in the vault,' he cheekily replied. 'Go off and tell him that, and ask for another sixpence.'

So that's what I did, running off down the platform, and when I told them what Wilf had said, they actually apologised before readily giving me another coin! I think I should explain here to our younger readers that in those days pubs had separate rooms, and people dressed to go to the pub and sit in the plusher confines of the best room, paying a little extra for the drinks, whereas the vault was the place where you went if in working clothes, or maybe to play cards, darts or dominoes, with the drinks being a little cheaper.

I enjoyed working with most of the drivers, whether they were 23 or 63 years old. We did have some who were actually booked drivers at 27 years of age. On one occasion my mate was a passed fireman aged 25, and I was aged about 20 but looked older than him; you could have mistaken him for an 18-year-old, and he was often referred to as 'the boy driver'. I was with him one Saturday night; we had worked an express to Manchester Victoria, then taken our 'Black 5' up to Newton Heath for servicing After that we were rostered to work a relief Belfast boat express to Heysham, formerly worked by Newton Heath men. With a couple of hours to spare we are in The Railway Hotel just outside the shed playing darts, our opposition being a set of Newton Heath men, a driver and fireman, both in their 50s. The dartboards in Manchester are quite small, with hardly enough space to get a dart into the bull. It was the decider of the three games, and I managed to hit the bullseye with a lucky dart.

Andy, my driver, said to me, 'Right, that's it, we'd better be going. We don't want to be late off the shed.'

'Yes, your driver will be looking for you two,' the Newton Heath fireman said sarcastically.

'Sorry, mate, but he is the driver,' I said, pointing to Andy

This really upset the fireman, who was older than both of us put together. 'You must be bloody kidding!' he ranted. 'Yes, you'd better be off, or his mother will be wondering where he is at this time of night. You're a couple of cheeky young bastards, coming here taking beer off us and pinching one of our best jobs!'

And with that ringing in our ears, we made a hasty exit from the pub back across the road to the shed and the safety of our engine!

There was a lot of jealousy among some footplate staff who had been less fortunate than others, finding themselves working at a depot where promotion was slow, known as a 'dead man's shoes' depots. I have always considered myself to have been fortunate in my footplate career. For instance, I could have lived in the area around Norwich or Ipswich, where steam had ceased when I started my career, but when I started at Lostock Hall depot we had just seen the amalgamation with the former LNWR shed at Preston, turning Lostock Hall into a sizeable main-line steam depot. Before that most of the work at 24C had been local passenger and freight jobs, utilising tank engines, 'Austerities' and so on, and a 'Black 5' was considered a sizeable loco. As previously mentioned, all that changed on the day when sparks from 'Super D' No 49104, standing in Preston shed, set the wooden roof on fire. The building was deemed unworthy of repair, resulting in the transfer of some men and machines to Lostock Hall.

As a young fireman that suited me down to the ground, as these men had vast route knowledge along the West Coast Main Line and experience with larger steam locomotives. It wasn't long before we began to enjoy regular work to Carlisle, Barrow, Windermere, Crewe, etc, manning 9Fs, 'Britannias', 'Scots', 5XPs, 'Clans', and the odd 'Duchess' job. Also – just for the record – we did have plenty of shunting and trip jobs! All this work led to rapid promotion for everyone, the original Lostock Hall men soon proving themselves adaptable to working these new routes and motive power. I became a booked fireman in just over two years, working with booked drivers, some only in their mid-20s, which was unheard of at depots outside the big cities, and in contrast to my uncle, who had been in his mid-50s before he became a booked driver, after 35 years' service. It is my belief that the combining of the two depots did lead to the longevity of Lostock Hall, establishing its place in railway history as the very last operational steam depot on British Railways, when the final working steam locomotive, No 70013 *Oliver Cromwell*, left our shed on Sunday 11 August 1968.

From 1963 to 1966 inclusive, the depot had a summer London link, comprising four sets of men covering the 400-mile round trip from Preston with the up 'Lakes Express,' lodging in London, and returning with a Blackpool express. Motive power varied from the occasional 'Duchess' to 'Scots' and, in the final year, 'Britannias', with just the occasional diesel. These jobs could well have been the swansong of long-distance steam haulage, and from memory the crews involved were former Preston drivers L. J. Rampling (Ramps), Fred Roberts, Albert Goodwin and Len Parkin, and firemen Bill Catterall, Jim Clayton, Colin Potter and Jack (Digby) Hesketh.

Jack was my firing mentor and was given the name Digby due to him always looking dapper, clean and smart. It was top-link fireman Jack who demonstrated to me his own unique method with the shovel, showing me how a right-handed fireman got the coal to reach the back left corner of a wide-firebox engine without resorting to the energy-sapping method of putting the entire shovel blade into the firebox and having to manually flick the coal off in that direction. Using Digby's method to achieve the same results, the shovel blade only partially entered the firebox at a 180-degree angle, the back of the blade making contact with the right-hand corner of the firehole door – with a dextrous flick the coal sailed off the shovel and hit the back left corner of the box! I have demonstrated this technique to many a budding fireman and, once perfected, they quickly realise just how less strenuous the firing becomes when working on these locomotives, particularly over long distances.

Another thing Jack passed on to me – and which I have always followed – was the importance of footplate cleanliness. I can just see him now, stepping off the footplate of a 'Pacific' at Preston station, looking almost immaculate in white shirt and tie after a 200-mile stint on the shovel from Euston. His footplate was kept meticulously clean: all coal was kept off the floor, which was swept after each firing stint, and he always made the point of saying that the engine footplate is your place of work and you should take pride in it. I often wondered what he was like at home, and if it was him who did all the chores around the house for his missus! His choice of firing shovel was very interesting, being a hybrid between a Southern and a Western variety. I did manage to obtain one of these for myself, as they are suitable for all types of passenger engines apart from North Eastern machines, on which I use a lightweight Lucas – and I emphasise lightweight. With the heavier make of Lucas you should do what we did with them on BR, which was to keep them in the back of the stores out of use. I have seen lads using them on some preserved railways, but they are not really suitable for main-line use, when you could be shovelling tons of coal every day to earn yourself a living.

Another driver I worked with at the top end of the seniority scale was George Whalley, who used to frequent my local pub, the Plough Inn at Penwortham, where I would often join him for a hand of crib. He knew my father quite well so I was careful not to swear too much in case it got back to him. Silly, really – I don't suppose it ever entered George's thoughts, but they were things that used to occupy my young mind. I fired and drove for him on many occasions. He was a fit chap who enjoyed a stint with the blade. One memorable week I was George's fireman due to his regular mate in the top link being on sick leave. Now, one thing about George was that he liked to drive a steam engine as fast as he could make it go without breaking any speed restrictions, and the job we were on that week was ideal for a bit of fast running from Crewe to

Preston. We had a 'Britannia' every night of the week and George warned me that he wasn't going to hang about.

After loco preparation on Crewe South shed, we waited in the bay platform then, once we had taken over from the electric loco, we were soon away. With No 70033 *Charles Dickens* on the first night, we were all prepared for a mad dash with our 11-coach train over the 25 miles to Warrington. Actually, the first 20 miles is slightly downhill to the troughs at Moore, his aim being to hit 90mph before having to shut off for the Warrington stop.

Once under way with our train, George would turn his grease-top cap back to front, then stick his head out of the cab to capture the feel of some high-speed running. At Hartford, 13 miles out from Crewe, No 70033 was going well with George managing to punch 80mph out of it, but it would take more effort from us and the engine for the next 10 miles if we were going to push her up to 90mph. I had had the injector pumping away and the shovel going since a few miles out of Crewe, the only slight problem being that the coal dust swirling about due to tears in the side sheets between engine and tender. I couldn't use the slacker pipe until Weaver Junction, when we would be away from the overhead wires. Then, passing Preston Brook I went across and briefly stood behind George; looking over his shoulder I could see the speedo registering just short of 90mph as we approached Moore troughs on the last downhill bit. I then had to turn around and judge when to dip the water scoop without overfilling our tender. About two-thirds of the way over the troughs I dipped for 1,500 gallons, then out with the scoop and task completed. I again looked over George's shoulder, and he pointed down to the speedometer, which was hovering around the 90mph mark. We both let out a yell before shutting off shortly afterwards for the run down to the Bank Quay stop.

Once stationary I gave the footplate a brushing and watering down, built up the fire and had both injectors on to top up the boiler before we were away again to our next stop at Wigan North Western. Before leaving there I was again busy with the shovel, making sure of a well-covered fire grate ready for the climb up to Coppull, and the possibility of a speedy dash downhill from there to Preston. We topped Coppull in good shape and George gave her the gun down to Euxton Junction. We rattle over it at the permitted 80mph, but *Charles Dickens* couldn't rest just yet, as we wanted 90mph out of him before the enforced shut-off point at Farington, 2½ miles short of Preston. Luckily we had greens all the way; Leyland station was just a blur as we flashed through, the engine full out and unable to give us any more, so now it was all eyes on the speedometer as we rapidly approached Farington. Just as George finally shut off, we attained a further brief 90mph. But there was no time for plaudits yet as the heavy braking kicked in, the blower was hard on, dampers partially closed, and both injectors on, as I wanted the steam pressure knocked back to avoid any blowing off when we arrived under the majestic overall roof of Preston station.

George had judged his braking to perfection, bringing our 'Britannia' to a stand at the end of the main northbound No 5 platform. On arrival we looked at each other, the adrenalin having put satisfied grins on our faces. We were both a bit mucky, but were savouring the excitement of having had a fast run in the unique environment of the footplate of a steam locomotive. Naturally we were a few minutes ahead of time, which allowed our guard to come up to the engine for a brief chat. He asked if we were on this job all week.

George told him, 'Yes we are, so you'd better tie yourself in, because we'll be motoring.'

'That's good,' replied the guard. 'I really

enjoyed that run and I'm looking forward to the rest of the week.'

A few minutes later he gave us the 'right away', and we had a nice steady run forward from Preston, with no heroics needed for a punctual arrival at Blackpool.

The rest of the week was a bit of a disappointment speed-wise. We had a different 'Britannia' each night, but could not better *Charles Dickens*'s 90mph. Our hopes were raised on the last night, the Friday, when we were given the aptly named *Flying Dutchman*, No 70018, but one thing it wouldn't do was to fly along. We had a real job to punch 85mph out of it, although in fairness we did have an extra coach that night.

A sequel to this story was when George retired a few years later. He would always refer to me as 'Charles Dickens' whenever I partnered him playing crib in the local pub, and he would often regale folks reliving that trip, which was the highest speed either of us had ever attained with a steam locomotive.

Another ex-RAF man with whom I had the pleasure of working was Frank Fletcher, one of six Fletchers at Lostock Hall. Four of us were related – my Uncle Bob was a senior driver, my cousin Raymond a fireman, and my brother-in-law Kelvin Woodburne a passed cleaner. I have mentioned the quite extensive route knowledge of some of the drivers, and my first week firing to Frank was a true example of this. After booking on duty at 5.30pm at Lostock Hall, we travelled as passengers to Preston, then changed trains and on to Lancaster, changed there, Lancaster Castle to Morecambe, changed again, then, after a quick pint in the 1930s art deco Midland Hotel, caught yet another train to our eventual destination of Hellifield, or 'Hell of a Field', as we often called the place.

It was when we finally arrived there, after three changes of train, that we work forward with a Carlisle-Ordsall Lane van train, usually with an 8F on the front. If you are not familiar with the railways that existed at that time in the North West of England, you could follow our route using a railway map from the period. The first stretch was from Hellifield to Daisyfield Junction, then through Blackburn, onto the Preston line to Cherry Tree Junction, where we branched left taking the line to Brinscall, eventually joining the Preston to Bolton line at Chorley, on to Adlington Junction, taking the line to Boars Head Junction via White Bear and Red Rock, bypassing Wigan to Haigh Junction and over the 'Whelley' line, then Hindley, Dobbs Brow Junction, Walkden, Swinton, Pendleton and Salford. Finally, after 4 hours running, we arrived in Ordsall Lane yard. Leaving our van train there, it was light engine via Miles Platting to Newton Heath loco for servicing and turning, then back light engine to Lostock Hall depot via Queens Road, Cheetham Hill Junction, Manchester Victoria, Bolton, Euxton Junction and Farington Junction. As none of the run was in daylight, every credit must go to Frank's excellent route knowledge, considering that a large part of the journey was made over little-used track, entailing long sections and few signal boxes. Speaking as a fireman, I cannot think of a worse scenario than hurtling along in the dark and not being confident that your driver knew exactly where you were throughout the journey.

I was with Frank one summer evening preparing our loco, 'Black 5' No 44672, on Crewe South shed to work forward with one of the Blackpools mentioned previously. Our engine was one of the final modifications of these great locomotives; it had roller bearings and a rocking grate, while much of the motion lubrication was grease instead of corks. It also had a self-cleaning smokebox, making it an easy loco to prepare – 30 minutes max – giving us time for a quick pint before our night's work. On the next road to us was parked Great Western 'Hall' Class No 6908 *Downham Hall*, which my mate said reminded him of a local beer-drinking contest! It was being prepared by a set of Salop men prior to working a stopper back to Shrewsbury.

We could hear the driver telling his fireman to stand clear, and he would just set the loco for oiling, following which he disappeared underneath with a flare lamp, oil bottle and feeder, and squeezed himself up into the cramped confines of the inside motion to begin the lengthy process of oiling up No 6908. We were watching all this activity and my mate just couldn't resist saying something:

'You shouldn't need to have to go underneath and oil up a two-cylinder passenger engine these days,' then, pointing to our 'Black 5', he told Taffy the fireman, 'You want to get yourselves one of these fine machines – half an hour prep time, and everything's done! Anyhow, our drinking time is going while I'm trying to convince you what a proper engine should be like!'

But no way would they have swopped engines with us – they loved those old-fashioned antiquated machines, which took up a full hour of preparation time. The GWR 'Castles' had 120 oiling points, taking up to 1½ hours to prepare one of them for the road.

15 Fire! And football hooligans!

Keeping to the theme of working with drivers who were ex-forces personnel, this next fella served part of the war manning the armoured train that was based on the Romney, Hythe & Dymchurch Railway. I hadn't known of its existence and must admit to doubting Tom's claim that a train such as this would be based on a miniature railway. He then produced a couple of photos as proof and told me that one of the reasons for its location was to protect the vulnerable Kent coast. He had seen fighting in France and was among those brave lads evacuated from Dunkirk. I was told by one of his mates that Tom had ridden through France to Dunkirk on the back of a white horse that he had commandeered! So, as you can imagine he was quite a character who rarely wore his full railway uniform, preferring a flat cap and a dark sports jacket; I enjoyed working with him and it was with Tom that I possibly had the most interesting day's work of my career as a fireman.

It was certainly different. We had signed on for a night run to Hellifield and back, working down with an Ellesmere Port-Moss End tank train, which we relieved at Lostock Hall, the motive power being a Class 47 diesel. Our return work was a Carlisle New Yard-Crewe Basford Hall freight, with relief at Lostock Hall. At first all went well on this Friday night/Saturday morning job. When we arrived at Hellifield we were relieved and sat in the station mess room having supper, awaiting our return job.

It was about 5.00am when in came the inspector to tell us that our train will be the next one into the goods loop, with engine No 70014. 'He has dipped on the troughs, but tell me if you want a top-up at the column.'

We duly went out and relieved the Carlisle crew.

'She's a good 'un, mate,' the fireman told me as he climbed down from the cab, and as always when relieving these Cumbrian boys coal had been brought forward in the tender; and the footplate was tidy, with a clean glass on the lighted gauge lamp, giving me a true reading of the boiler water level.

It was not long before the inspector reappeared on the platform across from us, and asked, 'Do we want the road now? Otherwise you could be waiting about until a football special passes us by in about 30 minutes.'

Tom told him that we were ready to go. So I whistled up in true 'Britannia' style, from the back of our lengthy train the guard responded with a green light from his brake van, so we headed off just as dawn was beginning to break. Our route back to Lostock Hall had only one gradient of any note, but it was severe, climbing from Whalley up through Langho to the summit just beyond Wilpshire Tunnel. We had a steady run to Clitheroe, then it was 'be prepared' time, as I began to feed *Iron Duke's* firebox. It was not possible to have a good run at this bank because of the speed restriction imposed on Whalley Viaduct at the bottom of the climb, but No 70014 was ready for it when we hit the hill, Tom giving it full regulator and using 60% cut-off as we began the assault on the 5 miles of 1 in 87 ahead of us.

One thing I will say about the 'Britannias': when working like this you could certainly hear them coming, and as we approach Langho we are just nicely getting into our stride when Tom turned round to look back along the train, then suddenly slammed shut the regulator, telling me to look back as the train was on fire! Sure enough, the tarpaulins covering the first five wagons were well ablaze, with the risk of spreading further.

We came to a stand just short of Langho road bridge – this was before they built the present station here. Our first reaction was to spray water from the slacker pipe and we also threw a few buckets of water gathered from the injector overflow, hoping it might burn itself out, but the fire was beginning to spread to the next vehicle. We decided to split the train, and were then joined by the guard; fortunately we did have a good 'fitted head' of brake power, so our guard secured the train, and with Tom watching from the footplate I dodged between the fifth and sixth vehicles, split the vacuum pipes and was able to lift the 'Instanter' wagon coupling without having to ease up on the buffers. I then replaced the vac pipe and we drew forward with the blazing vehicles and stopped with the engine on the bridge.

It was now daylight, and we had stopped in the middle of a long section, almost devoid of signals and lineside telephones. We made a quick decision that I would go down the embankment onto the road in search of a telephone box, or knock someone up who may have a phone in their home, bearing in mind this was very much a rural area at that time. The guard went back to protect the train. Tom said he would look after the engine. Down on the road I decided to head uphill towards what looked like civilisation.

I had not gone very far when I heard the sound of a wagon labouring up the hill on this quiet Saturday morning. The driver, realising that I was from the train, stopped, and I asked if he knew of a telephone box in the area.

'I think there is one in the village up ahead – jump in. I'm on my way to Blackburn market.'

Sure enough, after a few minutes' travelling up the road we came across a telephone box and, after thanking my saviour, I quickly dialled 999. When I had been put through to the fire service, they told me that the fire had already been reported by a local farmer who had seen the blaze, and that the fire engine should be there any minute. After thanking them, I set off back down the road, then I heard the fire engine approaching and stepped out into the road to wave them down. I told them that I was from the train that was on fire, but the driver cut me short, and just told me to get into the fire engine. However, it was all a bit cramped and awkward, as three of the firemen were still getting ready, putting their gear on, and I felt that I was getting in the way.

When we stopped at the bridge we all jumped out and they began to unravel the hoses. It was then that I had the presence of mind to warn them not to go near the other line next to our train, and certainly not to put their hoses across the rails! Also, by this time the police had arrived and I was met by a burly sergeant and told him who I was; he immediately asked me to go with him to help him identify someone. I suddenly became quite worried as to what might have happened while I had been away. We walked over the bridge and on to the grass embankment, where he stopped me. He said, 'Can you identify this man?'

I looked down, and sitting there in the long grass in his flat cap and old sports jacket smoking a fag was Tom. So I told the sergeant, 'Yes, I know who it is – this is my driver off the engine,' to which the sergeant just shook his head and walked away, whispering to me as he passed that he thought he had found a vagrant!

A short time later, with the fire now under control and both of us back on the footplate after inspecting the wagons, which had been loaded with steel cabling, our guard had decided that they were fit to travel provided there were no vacuum problems with the brakes. So we set back onto the train and, while the guard was hooking on, the fire officer in charge asked to come aboard the engine. He had also inspected the vehicles, which fortunately were metal-bodied, and he agreed with our guard that as far as he was concerned they were fit to travel. So I was getting ready for the off and piling coal on the fire, when the officer stopped me for a second and delivered this amusing observation.

'I have just been watching you – you're a fireman and I work as a fireman, but we appear to have two distinctly different aims in life, me to put the fires out, and you to keep the fires burning!'

So with that we said our goodbyes, with one problem sorted but another big test still to overcome. We were at a dead stand on this ruddy big hill, on board a large-wheeled passenger engine that is somehow going to have to find enough power to get us on the move again. This is going to be a test of man and machine. Now Tom may not have always worn a driver's uniform, but he could handle a steam engine, and one thing in our favour was having a separate steam brake, as fitted to all the BR Standard Class locos, which would enable us to ease the loco up against the tender, a recognised practice to give the engine momentum to gain that short forward movement without the weight of the train.

For those not familiar with this practice, let me explain the routine. First you create full vacuum on loco and train, then apply the steam brake, screw on the tender handbrake, put the engine in full back gear, release the steam brake and squeeze the loco up to the tender. You then apply the steam brake again, put the loco in full forward gear, put on the front sanders, open the regulator wide and release the steam brake, the fireman releasing the tender handbrake at the same time. Believe me, it works – ask *Iron Duke*!

When we did this to him, and during the 5 seconds that it took to release that first long exhaust beat, the whole cab shuddered and shook with seemingly every nut and bolt gripping each other, then crucially forward momentum was gained, and the next three beats seemed to come from deep within the innards of the locomotive – but crucially we were on the move again.

To get us moving, the exertion and power output that was required can only be appreciated by those familiar with the location and starting position of our near-500-ton train on Wilpshire Bank. Needless to say our exhaust was almost a single beat for the early part of the climb until we approached the tunnel. Still with the sanders on, we had by then accelerated to a heady 10mph! But the 'Brit' was into its stride, and they could dig in on a heavy pull. Then we were on through the tunnel and over the summit at Wilpshire; the hard work was now over and we are given a clear road down the 4 miles to Blackburn, where we were turned onto the goods loop opposite the station.

Just as we came to a stand the station inspector came out of his office, and unbelievably asked us where we had been. We had delayed the football special by nearly an hour, and all he seemed concerned about was that and the large police presence awaiting the arrival of the latter, which was carrying Scotland supporters up to Wembley for an international with England. This arrived a few minutes later and the police waded in, as apparently there had been an argument leading to a supporter receiving a stab wound. A police inspector remarked to us that they must have supped too much Irn Bru! So it was going to be a while before that got sorted.

Tom's reaction to all this was a total lack of interest. He looked across at me and said, 'Best go and put the bag in – we might as well top the tank up while we're waiting.'

It wasn't that long before the police had dragged a couple of suspects out of the train. The guard told us that their mates had grassed on them when the police had threatened to terminate the train at Blackburn, meaning they wouldn't get to see the match. He said they had pulled the communication cord between Carlisle and Hellifield, so it wasn't only us that had delayed them.

Anyway, we followed the special down to Lostock Hall, where the crew relieving us did know about the fire, and they couldn't really miss the scorched vehicles next to the engine. So we made our way back across to the shed to sign off duty, Tom filled in his report of the incident, and as he lived near me I offered him a lift home in my 'new' car, a 1953 Rover 90, but he decided that the walk home would probably do him good. Incidentally, Scotland won the match 3-2, inflicting the first defeat on England since they had won the World Cup.

I cannot finish this account about Tom without divulging one of his pet hates – working with passenger guards! He had no problem with the goods guards, whom he looked upon as part of a three-man team – driver, fireman, guard. They had to have the same knowledge of the route and gradients as the driver – it was essential when working loose-coupled freights that they applied or released their hand brakes at the right time. They had to be adept at shunting and the use of sprags and the shunt pole; for all this they received less payment than the passenger guards, who also received mileage

payment for some work. So there you have it – when we had occasion to transport a passenger guard on our footplate, perhaps at the beginning or end of a shift with no alternative transport back to his home depot, Tom would take great delight in some fast light engine running – the rougher the ride, the more it pleased him to see the smartly attired passenger guard hanging on to the cabside, or the water scoop handle, his face as white as his neatly pressed shirt. I was under strict instructions not to offer up the fireman's seat to allow him a modicum of comfort.

Tom took a particular dislike to any reference to the passenger guard 'working' a train, for in his opinion the driver and fireman worked the train, and the guard followed on behind, a viewpoint shared by many footplate crews. There was no malice attached to Tom's viewpoint; in fact, he and I shared a similar sense of humour, none more so than when it came to giving the passenger guard your name and depot, etc. This would only work, of course, when the guard was from another depot and didn't know Tom. For example, when backing on to a passenger train and before departure, it was the guard's duty to come to the engine and give the driver the timings, the load and the stops, etc. He would then enquire of the driver his name, also his home depot, to which Tom usually had some real gems. His favourite fictitious replies included Harold Edward Thistlethorpethwaite, home depot Walton-on-the-Hill, Lower Level. The poor guard only had about an inch width in his journal for the driver's name and about the same space to enter his depot. So when he had finished writing all these lengthy details, the journal was full and occasionally we would be late away. Another of his favourite pseudonyms was Percy Thomas Heckmondwhitealgh, and he would spell out every letter of the surname to the astonished guard. I only ever remember him being quizzed by one guard, who said that he couldn't quite make out how Tom could be based at the 'Lower Level' when the depot was actually situated on a hill!

Another of Tom's traits was his inability to keep time when working a Class 1 passenger train. He was quite happy just ambling along at his own speed. We would run into Preston station well behind time with a so-called 'flyer', and the irate inspector would come striding up to the loco to demand an explanation. However, upon seeing Tom in the driver's seat, it was a case of an incredulous shaking of his head, and storming back into his office to take his venom out on the office door!

Tom also had very little time for railway enthusiasts. If any of them approached our loco he would sometimes close the cab window and ignore them. A classic case of this happened one morning at Windermere, prior to departing with the 11.00am express to London with 'Britannia' No 70037 *Hereward the Wake*. This guy came up to the cab just prior to departure and asked Tom in a broad American accent, 'Hey, Mac, just what is her top speed'?

'Sixty miles an hour,' came Tom's curt reply.

'Gee, is that the very top speed of this mighty fine locomotive?' the Yank persisted, to which Tom replied: 'No, that's the top speed of this bloody driver; now piss off and get into the train or you'll get left behind!' Turning to me, he said, 'Bloody Yanks – I had enough of them during the war, all of them wanting to be an Audie Murphy.'

Anyway, if I might just elaborate a little about the 'Britannia' Class locomotives,

they were a very popular engine not only on the Midland but also particularly on the Eastern Region, working the Liverpool Street to Norwich jobs. I have been told that some crews were actually in love with their machines, and were reluctant to give them up even when electrification came along. In fact, the 'Britannias' proved to be popular everywhere, apart from the Western Region, where seemingly hardly a day went by without some Welsh farmer waking up to find another one in one of his fields, the crews complaining they couldn't see where they were going due to the handrails on the smoke deflectors obscuring their view of the road ahead. They had reason to complain, I suppose, with most of the signals on the Western being positioned for a right-hand-drive engine, whereas the 'Brits' had a nice padded driver's seat on the left. But we all used to reckon that the real reason for the unpopularity of the 'Brits' on the Western was quite simple – none of them had been built at Swindon!

I hope it doesn't come across that I might be anti-Welsh. Goodness gracious, Dai, I would be in serious trouble with my Welsh wife and all my Welsh relatives! In fact, in the 1950s, when I was in my teens, we would stay on holiday with an aunt and cousins in Cardiff, and where do you think I spent most of my time? Well, I wasn't that hard to find – I would be either on Cardiff station, or at Ely, where I copped most of the Western 'Britannias'. I vividly remember the first one that I ever saw, No 70018 *Flying Dutchman*, on Canton depot. I think that is where I fell in love with the 'Brits', particularly the whistle, of course.

16 A little filming, and guards and passengers

People often ask me to show them any photographs taken from the days of steam with myself and workmates, but the truth is that very few people owned a decent camera, or in fact any camera, in those times. The order of the day seemed to be Box Brownies or Kodak 127s – OK if you weren't moving about, and the print sizes and reproduction were often disappointing. My own camera was a Halina Pet, which I still have; it was able to reproduce some reasonably decent shots, but like most things in life you only got what you paid for. I nearly forgot to mention the stigma attached to actually taking photographs of your workplace. Many of your colleagues could not see your interest and disliked having their photo taken, and would refer to you as a railway billy, or a bloody trainspotter. If I am being honest, they were probably right in thinking about some of us in that way, but on the other hand I do not recall any of them refusing to accept any of the photographs taken of them. It is difficult to estimate how many of us might have been looked upon as a railway billy. I suppose present-day terminology would be railway enthusiasts, and there are plenty of those who are train crews on today's railways, judging by the camera interest when we pass them with steam specials.

I had even more difficulty a short time later with the coming of the Kodak Super 8 movie camera, which my wife was able to purchase at a discounted price. Since she was in the trade, it came with projector, tripod and screen, although there was no sound.

Now, if you thought that getting someone to pose for a photo was difficult, just try asking them to cooperate when filming them with the movie camera, especially on the footplate, where for instance they would ask me if it was all right to move about when I was filming them, and whether it would spoil the film if they did. Getting them to look at the camera was almost impossible, some of them displaying the petulance reminiscent of some Hollywood film actors.

Eventually word got around that I had this camera, so I decided to put on a showing of some footage that I had taken around the shed and out on the footplate. I pinned a note up in the drivers' lobby inviting anybody to the viewing one night in the room normally used by the ambulance class. We arranged chairs around the screen, and about 15 staff had assembled by the time I put the lights out and the films on, for I had spliced them into a 20-minute roll. For the first couple of minutes they kept telling each other to be quiet, and this amused me because the films had no sound! Then when they saw themselves or their mates on screen some of their comments were hilarious, for let's not forget that very few of them had ever seen themselves on a moving film.

Some of the more printable outbursts included:

'Hellfire, Joe, you're even uglier on screen than in real life!'

'Just look where Fred has the regulator and cut-off! What a rough bugger – wouldn't like to have been his fireman that day.'

'Bloody hell, Alf, I think you are younger-looking on screen – mind you, I am due for my eyesight test next week!'

'"Fingers", that can't be you firing – there's 220lb of steam on the clock. You never have that much when you're firing for me!'

And so on and so forth. They would not let me go home until I had rewound the film three times, but showing it had the desired effect and I had no more problems with them in front of the camera. What a great shame that the video camera was not around in the 1960s – think what we could have done with that! I could have actually recorded their voices and opinions – and the true sounds of the locomotives. The Super 8 films, lest we forget, were not cheap to purchase, costing me £3 plus processing for a 4-minute film, when my fireman's weekly wage was about £13. I probably took quite a few hours of film before the end of steam traction, and my only regret is that I did not take enough film of the personnel at the shed! Much of the film was footplate-based and regrettably, of course, you cannot go back and film it all again.

I did actually continue to film at Lostock Hall engine sheds after 1968. I paid a visit there in the 1970s, when it was in use as a diesel refuelling and maintenance depot, then later as a carriage and wagon repair yard; my final visit was to cover the demolition in 1990. The great majority of my filming can be seen on the DVD *Memories of Lancashire Steam*, available from the Grosmont Shed Shop, or *Summer of 68* issued by Kingfisher Films. These also feature rare footage taken by two of my Lostock Hall footplate colleagues, Tony Gillette and David Greig.

'Now there's a famous seaside place called Blackpool, that's noted for fresh air and fun, and Mr & Mrs Ramsbottom went there with young Albert their son.' So went the famous Stanley Holloway monologue about their Albert's visit to the zoo, just one of the many attractions that drew millions of visitors each year to Blackpool, including hundreds of train crews and locomotives bringing special trains throughout the season. A good deal of these originated from north of the border, being particularly busy on the Glasgow Fair holiday weekends, when we would pick them up from Carlisle or Preston and work them forward to either Blackpool North or Central, travelling via one of the three routes from Kirkham: the coast run via Lytham St Annes, the direct route via Marton to Blackpool South, or to the terminus at Blackpool North.

Many of these were overnight trains, which arrived in Blackpool in the early hours, where just a few years previously they would have been met by barrow boys who for a few shillings would carry or transport their luggage to their bed and breakfast accommodation. Pubs opened earlier during the holiday season to deal with the thirsty Scottish visitors, many of whom would already be well oiled on the journey down from Glasgow. Some confusion of the mind would doubtless set in after departure from Preston, as these trains went via Todd Lane Junction and Lostock Hall, then back through Preston station and on towards Blackpool, there being no direct north-to-west route. Things became easier with diesel haulage, when the locomotive would run round the train at Preston, and the same happened later when the Todd Lane route closed, but we are talking about steam-hauled trains, and it was not unknown to have the communication cord pulled by some inebriated Scotsman who had lost all sense of direction after the train had passed through Preston station twice within 20 minutes!

More trouble would occur if one of these trains made an unscheduled stop on returning to Preston station, as there would follow an immediate evacuation for the toilets, cafes and bars! No end of time was spent in rounding up the passengers and getting away again, so Control would instruct signalmen to hold these trains outside the station, or route them on the through lines, but this was not always possible, much to the annoyance of the station staff and inspectors who had to deal with it all. I recall arriving at Preston from Carlisle on one of these jobs with driver Arthur Chesters and No 70025 *Western Star*. It was just before 6.00am on Saturday, and George, the senior inspector, was ready to go off duty after another hectic Friday night/Saturday morning shift dealing with these overnight specials. So as we passed him standing on Platform 6 I leaned out of the cab and enquired of him, 'Have you had a rough night, George?'

'Not too bad, fireman – just three fights and a miscarriage!'

George was quite an imposing figure with a bellowing voice to match, which was often put to good use issuing passenger information from some distance, none more so than one busy afternoon when he was supervising the departure of the 4.30pm London express, with Crewe its first stop. At the last minute a businessman came running down the station slope, George warning him not to attempt to board the already departing express. However, running along, the man drew level with a coach door and, managing to open it, threw in his briefcase and brolly and was able to clamber in just as the train was passing George.

The flustered passenger asked him, 'This is for Carlisle isn't it?'

'Yes, sir – change at Crewe!' George gleefully informed him.

Another incident with one of these trains occurred as it was leaving Carlisle for the south after a station stop and the usual ticket check. A porter noticed that a bloke was standing up outside on a buffer between the fifth and sixth coaches, gripping the corridor connection and water drainpipe. The train was non-stop for the 90-mile run to Preston, so he immediately got on the phone to the signalman, and the train was brought to a stand a few miles down the line at Wreay.

There the fireman walked back down the side of the train and met the guard coming the other way, who told him, 'We've been stopped because of a report of a passenger riding outside on a buffer, between two coaches.'

Upon investigation, the guard shone his light on to this upright figure who was wedged with his back to the coach end. The over-officious guard asked him what he was doing up there, and whether he had a ticket.

The reply came in a best Glaswegian accent: 'Do you think I would be riding up here if I had a f–ing ticket, you daft pillock?'

They managed to coax him down and locked him in the brake van until they arrived at Preston, by which time he had somewhat sobered up.

Jumping on a train at the last minute reminds me of the day when Ronny, my driver, and I were booked to go passenger to Carlisle for a job back to Crewe. We literally just managed to jump on board the Glasgow express from Preston at the last minute, having spent too much time yapping in the mess room. No sooner had we piled into the empty compartment when the train started to move. Suddenly Ronny saw a leather briefcase up on the luggage rack, so he grabbed it, dashed to the carriage door and thrust the briefcase through the open window into the arms of a startled porter, hurriedly telling him to hand it in to Lost Property as it had been left on the train by someone.

Ronny then came back and sat opposite me in the compartment and said that it was lucky he had spotted the case. 'Somebody will be grateful for its return.'

'Yes, that's your good deed for the day,' I told him.

We hadn't been going long before the compartment door slid open and in came this smartly dressed chap, who sat down opposite us. We exchanged a friendly good morning with him, then he looked up to the luggage rack, and then at us, and with a hint of panic in his voice asked, 'Have either of you seen a brown leather briefcase? I left it on the luggage rack while I went to the toilet just before we left the station.'

I think I should just explain at this point that nature had given Ronny a bad stammer, particularly when he became a little excited, so it was left to me to explain to the chap, as after all I was a fellow culprit. The crisis was resolved by informing the guard, who in turn informed the station inspector at our Lancaster stop, where the unfortunate chap alighted from the train to await the next northbound departure to arrive from Preston with his briefcase hopefully now secured to the guard's wrist!

Later that same week saw us going as passengers to Glasgow on consecutive days, to work back south with some holiday specials. It coincided with a training programme for guards to become 'super guards', or conductor guards to give them the posh title. Prior to this, passenger guards had little to do with the issuing of tickets, or making passenger announcements and so on. But with the introduction of more modern rolling stock and public address systems throughout the train, the role of the guard altered significantly over the years. The description 'Train Manager' seems to have been adopted by some operating companies, but back in the early days of this new role in the 1960s and '70s many goods guards had passenger work thrust upon them by the changing face of the railways, and subsequent reduction of local freight work and the closure of yards. What you have to bear in mind is that the majority of these blokes had spent most of their working lives in solitude riding about in four-wheel brake vans, and having no real contact with the public. As you can imagine it was a difficult task converting them to the role of conductor guard in daily contact with the travelling public, checking and issuing tickets, and making announcements on the train's public address system, and it was performing this

task that would flummox most of them. Initially they were told to use their own descriptions and words, but this soon had to be altered when management realised that some of the terminology they used was causing confusion and embarrassment among passengers.

An example is the train announcement made by Tommy, our 60-year-old former goods guard, delivered in his best Lancashire accent as we approached the terminus at Glasgow Central. It started with him giving a few taps on the microphone, then asking of his fellow trainee, 'Is this bloody thing switched on?' followed by, 'Now then, listen here, we are getting near t' end o' t' run at Glasgee Central. I haven't gettan a watch, but I think we are about someweer to time. If any on ya is thinking of going a bit further north, then see one o' Jock lads on t' platform for further info – he'll put thee reet, and when tha does get off train, for God's sake durt forget thee traps. If tha's had a good trip, do come with us agen sum time. Tarrah!'

This caused much confusion and shaking of heads among the departing public, but what they did not know was that Tommy was actually one of the better ones, and it got worse as the week went on. Now, being a Lancastrian I suppose it is only good manners to translate Tommy's announcement into modern terminology: 'This train is now approaching our last stop on your journey, at Glasgow Central. We are arriving on time at 11.33. Any passengers travelling further north are advised to proceed to the main concourse where full timetable information is available, and do please take a moment to ensure that you have all your belongings with you when leaving the train. Have a good day, and thank you for travelling with us.' I think I prefer Tommy's home-made version – what a shame it didn't last the second week, by which time the guards had been given prepared scripts to read from, but it was good fun while it lasted.

17 More filming, and injector problems

I have briefly mentioned that master of the monologue and veteran Ealing Comedy actor Stanley Holloway – he has always been a favourite of mine, particularly in the two railway films in which he starred. One, *The Titfield Thunderbolt*, was filmed on the closed Hallatrow-Limpley Stoke line. In the opening sequence, a Bulleid 'Pacific' is shown going over Midford Viaduct on its way to Bath, via the beautiful Somerset & Dorset line. I have seen some of the out-takes from this film, when some members of the cast, including Sid James, had a bit of fun. When filming had finished for the day, they became unofficial footplatemen and took the GWR 0-4-2 tank engine up and down the branch line in the evening, under supervision, of course – that's if live-wire Sid could ever be supervised. Originally the producers were going to use actors to portray the loco crews, but the BR men from Westbury depot proved to be naturals and played the role themselves.

Stanley Holloway also appeared in many of the railway scenes in *Brief Encounter*, some of these being filmed at Carnforth station, where there now exists a replica of the station buffet seen in the film. There is also a splendid museum, tracing the history of the station and surrounding railways, all put together by volunteers in the restored station buildings.

Another of my favourite black and white railway films from the steam age is Ealing Studios' *Train of Events*, with Jack Warner of *Dixon of Dock Green* fame playing the main role of the engine driver, whose train collides with a petrol tanker on a level crossing, the engine being a member of the 'Royal Scot' Class. I was reliably told by a former Willesden driver that Jack Warner did actually drive the engine during filming, again under supervision, of course, and he proved to be a bit of a natural. He is seen on Willesden shed preparing the loco and walking down the steps of the pit to go underneath to oil up the engine – but he had an accident, slipping on the steps and injuring his back, apparently suffering from back pain for years afterwards. This brings to mind the present-day Health & Safety culture of 'where there's blame, there's a claim', which did not exist then – you just picked yourself up and got on with it.

I think Stanley Holloway might have appreciated the railway humour when two of the versatile 'Standard 4' tanks, Nos 80125 and 80129, appeared on Lostock Hall shed having been towed from their home on the Scottish Region, hopeful of finding some useful work to perform as replacements for our ageing Fairburn 2-6-4 tanks. They had been standing for a couple of days on one of the outside roads when the foreman instructed a steam-raiser to go and light them up, prior to having a mechanical exam. He hadn't been away that long when he reported back to the foreman that it was going to be a little bit awkward raising steam in them both, inviting the foreman to come and have a look at them. The slight problem that had arisen was that, before leaving Scotland for the journey south, some of the motion had been dismantled and placed in the firebox, with rods sticking out of the firebox door. After some consultation, a decision was taken to send them off on another journey, this time to the scrapman, leaving many of us hugely disappointed in missing the opportunity to work on these excellent BR machines.

Another of the versatile BR Standard designs was the 9F 2-10-0. Much of the work we had with these was freight, although they

have been different. They were prone to dropping sparks and cinders from the ashpan side doors and, when working tanker trains, we always had a few box vans acting as barrier wagons.

This was the case one day when we entered the private sidings at Heysham Moss with one of these trains. I was looking out of the cab of No 92199, watching out for the shunter to stop us when we were inside clear of all roads, when from out of the cabin came a member of the security staff, remonstrating

'Bill', No 47293, pilots 'Ben', No 47008, back to Lostock Hall shed at Preston East Lancs side, having completed shunting duties. They travelled together as the short wheelbase on the 0-4-0ST did not register on the track circuit. *I. Vaughan*

were equally at home working passenger trains, with some outstanding performances over steeply graded lines like the 1 in 50 gradients on the Somerset & Dorset. I firmly believe that had they been allocated to the line when introduced in 1954, the future of that important cross-country route might

with me to put out the fag I was smoking as it was a fire risk. I thought to myself, now here we are with this damn big 9F dropping sparks, ashes and cinders all over the place, and he's rollocking me for having a smoke in the cab! Anyway, I did as I was told, but when I looked across the cab to my mate, he was smoking his pipe, and said with a grin, 'Adolf will be happy now that he has given you an earful, and he won't be bothering about me!'

I always enjoyed the variety of footplate work that we had at the depot, from shunting and freight work through to the top passenger links, enabling me to gain experience on engines small, medium and large – and they didn't come much smaller on BR than the 0-4-0 Kitson saddle tanks. We had two of these – No 47002 and the later version, No 47008, with extended side tanks and coal space. One of our firemen suffered a nasty blowback when preparing No 47002, receiving severe burns to his midriff as he was unable to get away from the flames due to the confines of the narrow cab; he remained off work for more than a year.

The only duties we had for these engines were in the tightly curved yard at Greenbank, a mile north of Preston station, which they shared dependent on availability. Each always travelled to and from the shed to the yard coupled to the engine used on the nearby Dock Street shunting turn, this being one of the 3F 'Jinty' class. One of the reasons for running about together was that the saddle tank's short wheelbase rendered them unable to register on the track circuits. The pair became affectionately known as 'Bill and Ben'.

The Kitson engine had a regular driver, Norman, and he looked after it as though it was his own, often speaking to it and praising it for its shunting capabilities. He always gave it a thorough oiling prior to leaving the shed, and again when they reached the yard after travelling all of 3 miles! Also, at any break in the shunting the oil can was out, and bearings and lubricator checked. The fireman was expected to polish the cab, the brass and the pipework, and keep the engine clean throughout the day. The windows, floorboards and exterior were not allowed to be neglected, the whole engine being looked after as though it were a top-link express passenger locomotive; in fact, more time was spent on spoiling the engine than shunting the goods yard! That is, until Norman went on his holidays, or 'on the sick'. Then, I am ashamed to say, the little engine got

somewhat neglected, and was certainly not given the same treatment by the stand-in crews. It wasn't unknown for Norman to come down to the goods yard during his time off, on a surprise visit, and give them all a rollocking for neglecting his pride and joy.

Around this time diesel shunting locos gradually began to replace their steam equivalents in the Preston area; they became known as the '350s', then later in life the '08s'. They really were popular with crews and shunting staff alike, making the job a lot cleaner and safer, and eliminating many of the risks from shunting with a steam loco, particularly in the hours of darkness, with gland packings blowing and other steam leaks creating difficulties in sighting staff. The Preston Dock branch benefited from their usage, although many footplate staff had doubted that anything could suitably replace the ageing ex-LNWR 'Super Ds' for power and brake force on that steeply graded line. Speed did not matter, but tractive effort did, and these little diesel machines could produce 35,000lb compared to the 28,000lb output from the steam engine. The difference in brake force was made up by an extra 'fitted head' of vehicles, or by the guard pinning down more wagon brakes. No comparison could be made with the superior footplate conditions on the diesel, so the changeover took place within months of the trials beginning, and the 'Super Ds' were quickly forgotten.

The only problem with the '350s' that I can remember was the lack of fuelling facilities at Lostock Hall, so initially we had to take them the 26 miles to Rose Grove depot. We booked on in the evening for this job, and coupled two of the locos together, usually being diverted via the little-used Padiham branch to Rose Grove, due to the slow speed on this 50-mile round trip. It was a boring night's work, but tolerable if you had a mate who liked a chat or a laugh, and hopefully not someone who could talk a glass eye to sleep, as 20mph in the dark seemed a long way, particularly when you finally returned to Lostock Hall, having used up some 25 miles of fuel on the return journey! Some time later we gained our own fuelling facilities and the shed continued as a diesel maintenance depot after the end of steam in 1968.

Mention of the Padiham branch brings back some memories of this now-closed line that ran from the outskirts of Blackburn to Rose Grove. In my day it was mainly used as a diversionary route, and towards the end of its life it was truncated from Rose Grove to Padiham Power Station. An incident on this line involved another of the Fletcher family employed at the shed, my fireman and late cousin Ray. Together with a very portly old-hand driver, he was working an Aintree-Copley Hill night freight diverted from its regular booked route through Accrington, to travel via the Padiham line and rejoin the main line at Rose Grove, then over Copy Pit, with relief booked as usual at Sowerby Bridge. The diversion through Padiham took them over a route that had lost its regular passenger service in 1957, but soldiered on with seasonal and excursion trains until 1963, seeing very little use after that. The gradients on the line were not that severe until the final stretch from Padiham up to Rose Grove Junction.

Things had not been going well with the injectors on their 'Black 5' since they had relieved the Aintree crew at Lostock Hall; they had reported having trouble with one of them, but had managed quite well on the reasonably level railway from Aintree. With hindsight, the engine should possibly have been replaced at Lostock Hall, but in those days it was nothing uncommon to experience injector problems with steam locomotives; indeed, it was a privilege to have an engine with a couple of good working injectors! On this cold winter's night the train had a clear road through Blackburn station and

the tunnel, and climbed past Daisyfield Junction before swinging left onto the Padiham branch at Great Harwood Junction. The engine's exhaust injector had given up completely at this point, but the live steam injector was singing away and pumping the water in, being closely watched by driver Billy in case it should knock off – and that was just what happened as they neared Padiham, and no amount of persuasion by the driver and fireman could get it to pick up again.

The engine soon began to blow off and the train was brought to a stand to assess the situation. The water level in the boiler was dropping gradually as the two men battled to get either injector to work. In front of them, beyond Padiham, was a very stiff climb, and there was no way that they could attempt this without a working injector. The situation they were in that night was a footplateman's worst nightmare; the water level had now got dangerously low, and there was the possibility of the firebox fusible plugs melting, or the frightening possibility of damage to the firebox crown. They were also miles away from any help, on an engine with no rocking grate to drop the fire, so it was out with the fire irons in an attempt to paddle out as much of the fire as possible, shut the dampers, and turn down the blower.

One thing in their favour was that cousin Ray was a big strapping lad who had served in the Scots Guards, so he was able to handle the long heavy paddle just as if it was a firing shovel; it was up to him to save the situation, because Billy was not physically capable of this arduous task, but to his credit he did continue attempting to coax an injector into life. But a saviour did appear when the train guard climbed onto the footplate, on the opposite side to where Ray was throwing the fire out, and asked what help he could give. He pointed out to them a ballast bin, full of stone, adjacent to the engine, and asked whether that would be of any use in helping to extinguish the fire. By this time the paddle that Ray was using was bending with the heat, although he kept on cooling it down by placing it next to the injector overflow pipe and turning on the water.

When Billy suggested trying to throw some stone ballast on the fire, the helpful guard climbed down with the engine bucket and firing shovel and there began a bucket convoy of ballast, with Billy able to throw this into the firebox in between the increasingly tiring efforts of fireman Ray, still toiling with what was left of a bent and twisted paddle. The boiler water level had now disappeared from the gauge glass, but much of the fire had been dealt with, and they decided to finish the job by using the ballast to quell what was left. The end of all this strenuous work saw three men listening anxiously for the tell-tale sound of any escaping steam from the fusible plugs, followed by a visual inspection using the guard's handlamp. By the grace of God all seemed well.

A quick decision was then taken in regard to train protection, and to inform authority what had happened to the train, stranded in this rural location. So, following the Rule Book, the guard went back to protect the rear of the train while our exhausted fireman set off to protect the front. Eventually contact was made with the outside world and rescue came. Pleasingly, later on that week our dutiful crew were informed by letter that thanks to their efforts no damage was sustained by the locomotive.

I personally had experience of not one but two instances involving firebox lead plugs, but both of these involved locomotives that had been left for too long waiting in the queue on the ashpit for disposal duties. One was a Horwich 'Crab' that must have been standing unattended for hours, and when climbing up the steps I could hear the sound of escaping steam from the firebox, so I immediately put on

both injectors. Fortunately, the fire had gone out and we dragged the engine into the shed where, after an examination by the boilersmith a few days later, the plugs were replaced and it was passed fit for traffic. The other time was when Paddy, one of the steam-raisers, came bursting into the mess room saying that a Midland 4F on the ashpits was low on water and he was sure that the plugs had melted. I do have to admit that there was no immediate rush to deal with the urgent situation, possibly due to the class of engine involved! However, again the fire was out, and the melted plugs had knocked the steam out of the boiler, so we paddled out the remains of the fire, then put this masterpiece of Midland engineering to bed. Unfortunately it was able to return to traffic later that week…

One regular job we had over the Padiham branch was a late-afternoon light engine that we prepared and worked off Rose Grove shed to Blackburn, then started out of the bay platform there with a Southport stopping train. On one particular week with driver Jack Howard, better known as 'Heapey' after his birthplace, we had Horwich 'Crab' No 42942. We were always glad to get one of these – an engineman's friend, with nothing fancy about them, capable of slogging all day long, free-steaming with a good pair of injectors, they were one of the better products to emerge from my local works at Horwich. The only complaint was the draughts in the cab when running tender-first, due to the narrow-bodied Derby-designed tenders. One of our stops before Southport was at Banks, where one of my aunts lived in Bonds Lane. We would visit quite often and on one memorable occasion I remember that we travelled by another form of traction when my father and I cycled from Preston to Banks on a tandem, which my father had borrowed from his mate.

There was a level crossing just before the station on a side road, but the actual crossing keeper's cottage was occupied by the Harrisons; he was a platelayer, his wife manned the crossing, and two of his sons were firemen at the shed, one of them being my good mate Donald, who I have mentioned earlier. Donald still resides near Southport, and no train ever passed this crossing without paying the traditional toll charge of a few lumps of coal kicked off the footplate for their house fire. This happened on many branch lines throughout the region; you did your best to help your fellow railwaymen, particularly during a harsh winter.

A problem with the onset of the diesel age was maintaining a supply of coal in this way to all the stations, signal boxes, crossing keeper's houses, platelayers huts, retired railwaymen's houses, water trough cabins, fogman's huts and so on. I certainly do not recall anyone asking us for some diesel fuel, or standing on a level crossing swinging an empty fuel can in the hope of attracting our attention for a gallon of diesel!

Southport was another popular destination with loco crews, especially during the summer season – not as hectic as Blackpool, much more sedate, oozing an old-fashioned atmosphere in those days. It came as a sad blow when the Preston-Southport line closed on 7 September 1964; our depot lost an entire link's work, and my local station closed. On that day I went to photograph Standard Class 2 No 78041 working a Southport-Preston service crewed by 24C men, driver Alan Green and fireman Norman Callaghan. The very last departure was behind Lostock Hall's 2-6-4T No 42296, driven by Harry Moulding with Raymond Scard as his fireman, and the guard being the dapper Ronnie Gillibrand. I do own the smokebox number plate and shed plate from the loco, and I was given the BR Board official enquiry document that proposed the line's closure, part of which outlines the 1964 passenger census, this sham being carried out

when all the schoolchildren who used the line were on holiday! What do we have these days as a replacement for this important route? An outdated road congested with traffic throughout the summer.

I recently tried getting to Southport to view the Vulcan bomber display at the air show, but gave up after travelling just 7 miles in 4 hours; neither was there room on the occasional Wigan to Southport train. What it really needs is the curve reinstating at Burscough Junction, linking up again the Preston to Ormskirk line with the Southport to Wigan service, enabling through trains from Preston to Southport, cutting out the present-day lengthy Preston-Wigan-Southport journey. How short-sighted we have been in closing these local lines. Although I am not 'anti-Beeching', he was mandated to do a job, and to be honest a lot of the lines had become little-used due to the motor car becoming affordable to the working man. We saw a big downturn in passengers at this time, to the extent that many services that had once warranted eight-coach trains were reduced to running about with three or four vehicles, and these could be less than half full at off-peak times.

Our railways needed updating and in many ways this has been achieved, but at a cost of vast sums of public money swallowed by privatisation, which I am totally against. In fact, I am a member of the action group 'Bring back British Rail', which you can find on t' internet! It is my belief that the British Government spent years looking for any harebrained scheme that looked half credible to rid themselves of the running of our railways, and privatising them was the cop-out. I do visit Ireland on occasions – yes, they have closed lines over there, but they have not ripped them up to the extent that we have, some of them having been reopened to passenger services in recent years.

Speaking of closures, as the years drifted

by more and more steam locomotives were being withdrawn and depots closed. For instance, when I started in early 1962 there were more than 400 steam depots and 10,000 steam locos. As 1968 dawned many areas of the country were steamless. We kept hearing rumours of when steam would be totally eliminated, yet at the beginning of that year the majority of our jobs at Lostock Hall did not involve diesel haulage, but it was certainly a time of sadness. Consequently the place became a Mecca for the steam enthusiast, particularly at weekends, when there were fewer management staff on duty, making it easier to gain admission to the depot. Although a few of the visitors did have valid passes, a lot of them did not, but in my opinion our depot staff were very tolerant and sympathetic. I think it would be fair to say that Lostock Hall was an easy cop!

Furthermore, I do recall certain loco crews cashing in on an enterprising scheme to provide visiting enthusiasts with a little bit of footplate experience. This involved taking up to four of them at a time on an engine up the shed yard and back for 2s 6d each; if they looked sensible they were allowed to drive it under supervision or, failing that, they could blow the whistle, or put some coal on the fire. Unfortunately, after a few prosperous weekends of operation somebody at the shed, envious of them making a few bob, did blow the whistle on this beer-money scheme, resulting in the whole lot being shunted into the sidings.

We became involved with the working of a wide variety of steam specials during the spring and summer of 1968, right up to the last day of regular steam operation and depot closure on 4 August 1968, together with Carnforth and Rose Grove depots. It was a hectic last few months prior to this, and some main-line passenger workings were still steam-hauled, including the 17.05 from Euston, which formed the 20.50 to Blackpool South, and the 17.25 from Glasgow Central,

which formed the 21.25 to Liverpool Exchange. There was also the 12.44 Preston to Blackpool, which was the rear portion of the 09.05 from Euston. Carnforth depot and men still worked the 'Belfast Boat Express' from Heysham to Manchester Victoria and return.

This was to be steam's final fling working Class 1 express trains. In the previous year, 1967, the loco crews on the Southern had 'done steam proud' and gone out with some glory – now it was our turn to rewrite the record books. Many unprecedented timings were achieved by some crews working these machines to the absolute maximum of their capabilities. The workings of these final steam-hauled BR passenger trains have been well documented over the years, and are unlikely to be repeated, particularly while a maximum of 75mph is in force for present-day steam traction on the rail network.

Most of the engines involved later went for scrap, but some have survived, including some former 10D engines – Nos 43106, 44806, 44871, 45110, 45212, 45305, 45407, 48773, 78022 and others – many of which I have worked on since. But somehow or other our best 'Black 5', No 44888, failed to reach the preservation world; I do know that it was inspected by a society, and the rumour was that it had a slight crack in the frames but, as one of our fitting staff remarked, 'Which "Black 5" didn't have a crack in its frames?' The last time I fired No 44888 was only a couple of weeks before its withdrawal, when we had it on an evening freight from Preston to Carnforth, and luckily I captured it all on film, sharing the driving with one of my regular mates, John Burnett.

By this time in 1968 I had become one of the senior firemen at the depot and progressed into the No 1 link. Unfortunately I was just under the age limit to go for my exam to become a passed fireman; in fact, junior hands to me who met the age criteria had passed for driving and my final week's work before the end of steam was with my regular driver, Clifford Nelson, working the 10.50 freight from Preston Ribble Sidings to Heysham with 'Black 5' No 45407. I had taken my movie camera the first day and filmed the job from start to finish.

Later in the week, on Thursday 1 August, when we signed on duty the foreman's assistant told us that a reporter and photographer from the *Sunday Times* would like to travel with us, as the paper was covering the story about the end of steam here in the North West. The reporter would meet up with us once we arrived at Ribble Sidings, and travel in the guard's brake van, then when convenient we would be interviewed and a few photos taken. It was pure good fortune that I had decided to put on a clean pair of overalls that day, and when preparing a loco I always spent time on polishing and cleaning the cab, so today was no exception. No 45407 had been our steed all week and did clean up pretty well using the traditional method of a small brush to daub the back head with a three-to-one mixture of paraffin and steam oil before wetting it all using the slacker pipe, then a final wipe down. The shine would last all day and was guaranteed to please the most fastidious of footplate inspectors!

We went light engine to Ribble Sidings and backed up on our train. The Preston guard appeared at the engine with our two travelling companions, and much to my surprise the reporter was a slim, attractive young woman wearing a rather short mini-skirt. Following introductions all round, it was decided that Steve, the photographer, would join us on the footplate, with Anne the reporter travelling with our guard in the brake van until we arrive at Heysham Harbour, then we could all have a chat. Now, as often happens on the railway things do not always go to plan, and sure enough this was one of those days. We departed from Preston hopeful of a good run to Lancaster,

but with the Distant against us approaching Oubeck loop, the inevitable happened and we were 'put inside', some 4 miles short of Lancaster. The signalman informed us of a derailment at Morecambe, involving some 100-ton tank wagons; nobody was hurt, but long delays were expected.

Upon hearing this our guard escorted the lady reporter down to our locomotive. I climbed down from the cab and I swear to this day that it was her idea to visit the footplate to interview us. As you can imagine, gaining access to the footplate while clad in a tight mini-skirt was going to be a little difficult but, being a gentleman, I let her go up first. Now, I know what you're thinking, but honestly, I just kept my eyes on her feet, in case she lost her footing on the loco steps – Scout's honour!

During the interview Clifford and I were asked for our opinions regarding the ending of steam on British Railways. We differed a little here; I was unhappy that many steam locos that still had years of working life left in them, a lot being less that ten years old, were being scrapped, to be replaced by some classes of diesel locomotives that were simply not up to the job and constantly failing in traffic. The diesel training for footplate crews left a lot to be desired, amounting to just a couple of weeks in some cases, after a lifetime working with steam. Equally the fitting staff had their problems; for instance, in outside industry it was a five-year course to become a qualified diesel fitter, while BR expected seasoned steam fitters to become competent with diesel traction in months. Furthermore the tools and equipment used on steam maintenance became obsolete, the fitters then having to equip themselves with an entirely new range of suitable tools for use on diesel traction, a coal pick not being of much use on a two-stroke Metrovick! Some may disagree, and argue that a coal pick would have come in very handy when working on one of those awful machines.

To sum up, I have always thought that we should have run steam until a programme of electrification had been completed on our main lines, similar to what happened on the railways in France.

Clifford was also a little sad to see the ending of steam, but understandably, of course, after his 32 years working with them he was looking forward to the cleaner and easier working environment with diesel traction, although he would miss the variety and challenges required when operating steam locomotives.

I worked with Clifford for longer than any other driver. I loved working with him as he was very tolerant of my cheeky youthful ways, but he was more than just a driver – he was a true engineman, and I like to think that I learned a lot from him. Sadly we lost him to cancer aged just 56, but his family do have a copy of all the film footage taken on our many happy journeys together, when we shared the footplate of the old steam locomotive.

Continuing with our 15 minutes of fame, Anne the reporter was quite happy with our responses, and then it was time for the

Driver Clifford Nelson and fireman Fletcher relaxing at Oubeck loop, Lancaster, while being interviewed by *Sunday Times* reporter Ann Robinson on 1 April 1968. *Sunday Times*

photographs. We were asked to pose at the front of No 45407, sitting on the rails at the end of Oubeck loop, and this was the photo used by the newspaper article in the 4 August 1968 edition of the *Sunday Times*. Clifford's words got into print. I don't suppose they had room for all I said, and the article was really about the end of steam

Cliff and I pose in front of our steed being held in the loop here due to a tanker train derailment at Morecambe barring our passage to Heysham Harbour. *Sunday Times*

The *Sunday Times* reporter and later TV personality on the footplate of our 'Black 5'. You would be the 'weakest link' if you did not recognise her! *Author's collection*

and the impact on railwaymen's lives in general.

When we had finished the interview and the photographs, Clifford rang the signalman only to be told that we could be waiting for quite some time. So it was decided to send for a taxi to transport our two guests to Lancaster to get a train back to London in time to put the article together before going to print. So as we said our goodbyes, I asked Anne to give me an address where I could send her the photos I had taken of herself and the photographer. They hadn't been gone very long when we were advised that our train was to be diverted to Carnforth

My letter printed in *Steam Railway* in 2008 commemorating the last day's events and a brief resumé of my footplate career. *Steam Railway*

'Anne' end-of-steam story The Weakest 'Top Link'?

As a fireman at Lostock Hall in the 1960s, I have many fond memories. I worked on steam right to the very end and in the last month there was a lot of media interest. On Thursday August 1 1968, my driver, Clifford Nelson, and I booked on to work the 9.50am Preston-Heysham freight with 'Black Five' No. 45407. The shed foreman asked if we wouldn't mind taking a footplate passenger, a reporter from *The Sunday Times*.

We had a clear road until being

John (left) and Clifford with No. 45407. SUNDAY TIMES

put inside at Oubeck Loop south of Lancaster. It was here that a good-looking young lady (who had been travelling in the brakevan) was escorted up to the engine by the guard. She was hardly attired for the footplate! She interviewed us and asked about our views on the end of steam. Eventually she and the photographer took a taxi back to Lancaster for the train to London.

The following Sunday - August 4 - a lengthy article appeared in *The*

Sunday Times. And the female reporter? Well, you would have to be 'the Weakest Link' not to recognise her! It is, of course, TV personality Anne Robinson.

On the day it came out, Lostock Hall men had the majority of turns on steam. The roster clerk ignored all the usual agreements and offered the known steam diehards all the steam jobs. I was with Clifford again. He wasn't just a driver, he was an engineman (and only footplatemen will know what that really means). Cliff died shortly after the end of steam at only 58, and what I learned from him helped guide me through my railway career.

It was with some pride when we stepped off the footplates of those engines some 40 years ago, knowing that we had played a part in the last 'official' day. Unbelievably, 40 years on, I am lucky enough to be still working on ex-Lostock Hall 'Black Fives' - No. 45407 for West Coast Railway's Company on the main line and Nos. 45212 and 45110 (as a guest) on the North Yorkshire Moors Railway.

After more than 47 years' involvement with steam, and

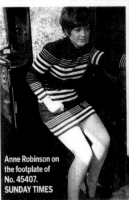

Anne Robinson on the footplate of No. 45407. SUNDAY TIMES

thousands of hours of footplate turns, I still consider it an absolute privilege to be able to do the job and work with some of the finest people I have ever met. I would like to wish everyone connected with the good old steam locomotive the very best for the next 40 years!
John Fletcher, Grosmont, North Yorkshire.

because the derailment at Morecambe was going to take quite some time to clear up.

Some 20 minutes later we pulled out of the loop with our train and onto the main line. We got a clear run through Lancaster, so Clifford let her roll down the bank through the station. There I noticed a couple standing on the up platform waving to us, and they turned out to be Anne and Steve, awaiting their London train home.

Upon arrival at Carnforth we left our freight train in the loop to be worked to Heysham later in the day, when the Morecambe derailment had been cleared up, and it was due to this that our return freight working from Heysham was cancelled, so after a visit to Carnforth's turntable with No

45407 we returned light engine to Lostock Hall. There I cleaned the fire and ashpan, emptied the smokebox, then placed the 'Black 5' in the shed. I thought at the time that I would never again work with No 45407, as it was to be withdrawn from traffic some three days later, but over the years since then I have renewed my acquaintance with this fine locomotive on numerous occasions thanks mainly to my footplate colleague and loco-owner Ian Riley.

By the way, Anne later became quite well known in the media, presenting many radio and television programmes, and you would be the 'weakest link' if you did not know of Anne Robinson.

18 4 August 1968, and a few diesels

Soon came the dreaded day of 4 August 1968, which saw my last steam footplate turn for British Railways and the end for the remaining steam depots, Rose Grove, Carnforth and ourselves, all closing to steam on that day.

Six 'Farewell to Steam' specials had been organised to commemorate the event and fortunately, by its geographical position, Lostock Hall shed and men featured almost exclusively in the workings of these special trains. Obviously we knew in advance that it was going to require a commitment from quite a number of drivers and firemen to work on the final Sunday. I was personally hopeful of being chosen and actually put in an application to be considered as the fireman on any one of the specials. I received back a standard reply stating that BR was unable to consider my application, citing the usual local agreements regarding Sunday duty and availability. I didn't really expect a

PH69
P12

LM/P.File
22.7.68

Fireman J.T.Fletcher,No.193,   Motive Power,

LOSTOCK HALL M.P.D.   LOSTOCK HALL.

APPLICATION TO BE CONSIDERED FOR DUTY AS FIREMAN ON STEAM SPECIALS
SUNDAY, 4TH AUGUST.

With reference to your application of the 19th July to be considered
as a Fireman for any steam special on the above date, please note
that I regret I am unable to give consideration to the application.

The firemen utilised on this date will depend on the usual
local agreements regarding Sunday duty and availability.

                         SHEDMASTER

My plea for a last-day firing turn on 4 August 1968 appeared to have been unsuccessful! Author's collection

Climbing beyond Stalybridge to Standedge on 4 August 1968 is 1Z78, double-headed by 'Black 5s' Nos 44871 and 44894 with both crews on view – Cliff and myself leading Ronnie Hall and his fireman 'Tom Jones'. We also had conductor drivers on board from Manchester to Huddersfield. *G. P. Cooper*

positive reply, but at the very least they knew of my interest when compiling the roster.

I have previously stated that not all the men at the depot had enthusiasm for the steam locomotive, and it may well have proved a difficult task for the roster foreman to include the genuine steam men for these jobs, without infringing the strict local agreements.

The eagerly-awaited roster for that Sunday was posted in the locomen's lobby on Friday 2 August, and it was Clifford who told me that we were together on 1Z78, the Stephenson Locomotive Society Special No 1, with loco No 44871. To say I was pleased would be understating things, but closer

scrutiny of the roster gave me a feeling of genuine satisfaction, for when I saw the names of the other crews who had been chosen for these jobs, I realised that local agreements must have been dispensed with for this final day and, without exception, preference had been given to the genuine steam men at the shed.

Saturday 3 August was my rest day, and somehow I resisted my yearnings to visit the shed on its penultimate day. Instead I busied myself with the continuing decoration of our new home, then prepared my kit ready for the big day on the Sunday, including camera and movie camera, followed by preparation of sandwiches, tea, etc, then a final polish

Last-day mayhem at Lostock Hall: 'Britannia' 'Pacific' No 70013 *Oliver Cromwell* attracts attention on the turntable before departing off shed in the charge of driver Frank Herdman and fireman Eric Ashton. *Author's collection*

of my steel-toecapped boots. I was in bed by 10.00pm, but did not sleep too well, and was up early on the Sunday at 6 o'clock and left for my last day on steam at 7. Jacqueline took me in our 1939 Rover Drop Head Coupé, but she needed the car herself, so she dropped me off at the shed at 7.15, in good time to prepare No 44871, and make her presentable externally.

I found her standing outside No 7 road, and was genuinely shocked to discover just how clean the loco was; in fact, when I looked around the shed most of the other engines had also been cleaned. I did spruce up the firebox back head with my recipe of a five-to-one steam oil/paraffin mixture brushed on, then swilled off with hot water from the slacker and wiped over with a cloth, guaranteeing a gleam all day! Clifford also reported early for duty and

we set about getting our 'Black 5' ready for the long day ahead. This involved double-heading throughout with sister loco No 44894, crewed by driver Ronnie Hall and fireman Eric ('Tom') Jones. Our diagram was light engines to Manchester Victoria to await the arrival of our 10-coach train from Birmingham, 1Z78, then away at 10.37 via Stalybridge, Huddersfield, Sowerby Bridge, Copy Pit, Blackburn and Bolton, then relief for us at Wigan Wallgate, where, after taking water, the train was away again to Kirby, Bootle, Stanley, Rainhill, Eccles, Manchester Victoria, Droylsden and Stockport Edgeley. The diagram did not state which was to be the train engine, and which was to be the assistant loco, and the fact that the other crew hadn't yet arrived made up our minds that we would become the leading engine.

With that decided, we turned the engine

And then it was all over for us and our machines! In the late evening of 4 August 1968 'Black 5' No 44871 shares the ashpit roads at Lostock Hall with fellow surplus class members. *David Idle*

and dropped it on top of No 44894 just as the other crew arrived, explaining to them that the tour organisers wanted them in that formation, and as we were the senior crew they accepted it! As you can imagine, the shed yard was very busy, with some 14 engines due off the shed that morning. The occasion had attracted a large gathering of enthusiasts and it was while I was returning from the mess room to our loco with a freshly made can of tea that I was asked by a couple of these lads, 'Is your engine clean enough for you mate?'

There followed a bit of banter between us, until I humbly accepted that not only had they cleaned our engine, but the gang of them had spent the previous night cleaning the grime off all the engines involved with the specials. I gave them our thanks on behalf of all the steam crews at the shed, and I do remember enquiring of them as to why

they did not come and work on the footplate themselves.

'Not damn likely – we're not that keen!' was their reply.

Actually, what they said proved not to be quite true, for some years later I met up with a few of them again, and I have actually worked on the footplate with some of them on preserved and main-line steam locomotives, but time has moved on for myself and Messrs Gould, Hunt, Proud, Bodfish, Castle, etc, and we are now all of pension age or have gone for scrapping.

Looking back on the day, our 1Z78 special seemingly did very well for time-keeping, unlike most of the others that became bogged down with various delays. We had a good run throughout and I was able to capture the journey on film from the footplate. The only down side to my final day occurred as we approached Manchester

Victoria in the morning with the light engines. I was filming No 45156 *Ayrshire Yeomanry* approaching us on its departure from the station, when the engine went into a slip next to us, and a small piece of metal got into my left eye, proving to be extremely uncomfortable for the remainder of the day. Some people have remarked to me that, in the film, I seem to be in tears wiping my eye with a handkerchief after being relieved at Wigan; while admitting to being a little upset on the day, it was actually part of locomotive No 45156 that was giving me grief!

The film depicts both crews involved on the day, and one of the relief firemen is the late Dennis Chatwin, who is shown standing on the back of No 44871's tender while taking water at Wigan Wallgate; I was the best man at his wedding a few weeks later. So, after watching the two 'Black 5s' depart from Wigan, in what was to be the end of steam working for us all, we made our way back to Lostock Hall. I still had some footage left, which I used around the shed, my final piece showing driver Eric Edge and fireman 'Tom' Jones giving a traditional goodbye. As for me, I just signed off duty with a heavy heart. Having completed some 1,500 footplate turns, 90% being on steam traction, I certainly was not looking forward to the following day, when all of us would be transferred to Preston and a life on the dreary diesels.

I have purposely not referred to the special train that ran on 11 August, the '15 Guinea Special'. I had no real interest in going along to see this lone special, laid on by British Railways, although it did involve a couple of ex-Lostock Hall men and of course No 44871, but in my mind, and also to the great majority of railwaymen, the true ending of BR steam had been a week earlier on 4 August.

A whole new chapter in my life began on Monday 5 August 1968 when I signed on duty at Preston, but no longer as a fireman; my grade card said that now I was a 'second man'. On closer inspection of the men's names marked up in the various links, it came as a bit of a shock to realise just how many of my former workmates had left the job rather than transfer to Preston depot and life on the diesels. Historically we were the very last BR steam footplatemen. I was in a slightly different position, as our union ASLEF had negotiated a position of security for some second men. This depended on our seniority date, and a star next to your name identified those who could not be made compulsorily redundant.

We had no actual depot at Preston, but a signing-on point had been established on the second floor of the main building on Platforms 4 and 5, the locomotives being stabled in holding sidings just north of the station in Dock Street and Pitt Street yard. These mainly consisted of Type 2s (Classes 24 and 25) and Type 4s, later Classes 40, 47 and 50. I had no real interest in working the diesels, even driving the things, no doubt because I missed the steamers, having been involved almost exclusively with them until the very end of their working days.

We had been at Preston for about four weeks when BR suddenly offered a voluntary redundancy package of £320; in effect, this was a payment from them to buy our star status and accept redundancy. Obviously I discussed this at home with Jacqueline; we had been married for about 18 months, and had bought a house that required some restoration. We worked it out that the money would probably allow us to complete the rest of the work required, but at the end of the day I would be the one making the decision. Just to explain what £320 was worth in 1968, a semi-detached house could be bought for just over £2,000 and plenty of job opportunities existed outside the rail industry. When added to my general lack of enthusiasm for diesel traction and the offer of employment elsewhere, the decision was really made for me.

My stay at Preston depot lasted for less than three months, my last week of work being with Scouser driver Dick Thomas, who happened to be a near neighbour of mine, so we travelled to work together during that week, relieving a Freightliner train at Preston, working it to Carlisle New Yard and returning with another Freightliner bound for Birmingham, being relieved at Preston. Our motive power all week was Class 47s.

My last day was to be the Thursday. Dick did the driving on Monday and Tuesday, leaving me to finish my railway career as the driver on my final two days. My last act was to sign off duty on Thursday 24 October 1968, passing my clock card to foreman's assistant Vic Drew, followed by a last farewell and handshake from driver Vinny Commons, who happened to be just signing on duty. I emptied my locker and drove home, on the way dropping Dick off at his house – and that was that. Adding just a little anecdote to this, by pure coincidence the man who signed and approved my redundancy was Preston Area Manager R. Oliver – 'Mr Oliver' to us. If we fast forward 15 years, Bob became my railway boss again when he was appointed General Manager of the North Yorkshire Moors Railway, where we enjoyed a little less formality and became quite good friends.

19 A career change, life as a guard and a problem with slippers!

My new job didn't take me very far away, for I gained employment at Lostock Hall but this time at the new gas works, the old water gas plant having recently been demolished and replaced with an up-to-date plant in conjunction with the recently discovered North Sea gas. On my first day it came as a pleasant surprise to discover that two of my new work colleagues were ex-footplatemen, so I felt at home straight away.

My new job involved a training period before going on to shift work and inspecting each of the four plants every 2 hours alongside the other operators, and carrying out maintenance work as required. It also involved working at heights of up to 60 feet, but we had been assessed for it, safety harnesses being worn during high winds and bad weather.

I kept in touch with many of my mates off the railway and we all usually got together at Deepdale on match days, watching Preston North End. I had been doing the new job for about six months when, after a victorious mid-week match, we all dropped into our local for a celebratory couple of pints. The subject of railways soon cropped up and what had been happening at the Preston depot since I had left. I was talking to driver Bill Bamber, and he just happened to mention in our conversation that, due to a shortage, the railway had been recruiting train crews, with some of the vacancies being taken by ex-footplate staff who had recently taken severance payment. Now, I had never really

given any thought to rejoining the railways, but will admit to missing the company of like-minded people. Bill then let it slip that any amount of overtime was available, so, after a few more pints, I had made up my mind that I was going to apply to rejoin the railway.

It was now early summer 1969, and the name J. T. Fletcher reappeared on the list of railway employees. At this time we signed on duty upstairs on Platform 5 using premises vacated by the GPO, which had moved en masse to new premises and sorting offices in West Cliff adjacent to the station. This left a huge empty floor space, which had once been the former LNWR ballroom situated just along the corridor from the staff mess room. It wasn't long before this became an unofficial games room; it was large enough to enjoy five-a-side football or a bit of indoor cricket in between train working.

The only downside to these sporting activities was that in one corner of the room there was a storage compound, protected by an 8-foot-high security cage, and the ruling was that whoever kicked or hit a ball into it had to climb over and retrieve it, which is what happened to me one afternoon when playing cricket. I climbed over and threw the ball out, then noticed that on the shelves inside the compound were folders with names of staff on them who had been at Lostock Hall depot; on closer inspection these turned out to be the personal records of staff no longer employed in the footplate department. I searched and found my own files, including all records of my footplate service. I took them along to the clerk's office, and was told that I could keep them if I wanted to, as they were obsolete, and any relevant details would have been copied. So I have been able to refer to these as a source when researching dates and other details during the writing of these memoirs.

After working for the railway again for about three years as a guard, during which time we had completed the restoration work on our Victorian home in Preston, we now had an addition to the family, so decided upon a move to a larger house and actually settled on a property in Lostock Hall. These almost new houses became a popular choice with other train crews and their families, which quickly led to some of our mates referring to the area as living in 'Taper Boiler Avenue'.

Many of the guarding turns involved just myself and the driver, and of course I knew most of them, and would occasionally share some of the driving. It was around this time that BR started modernising the Preston area and station. This involved the closure and demolition of parts of the station, and we were working almost every weekend, during which time I became quite friendly with some of the men in charge of the project. Most of the former LNWR signal boxes had to be demolished to make way for a new signalling system and power box, to be built on the site of the former steam shed. The contractors had no interest in the historic value of the original signal and telegraph equipment – they just smashed or broke most of the items. It was heartbreaking really, so I asked for, and was given, a few artefacts that I had managed to rescue.

One of these Saturday night demolition

The magnificent Preston No 5 signal box, scene of the leather slippers find, and the adjacent car park facility. *Author's collection*

duties later became part of local railway folklore, for the majestic Preston No 5 signal box was to be closed after the final 2-to-10 shift clocked off. I had been given permission from Steve, the demolition foreman, to rescue an LNWR block instrument before demolition began. So at 10 o'clock we watched the last signalman leave the box and set off to walk to the car park. We were waiting in the guard's brake van of a train positioned near to the box.

Steve said to me, 'Right, you've 5 minutes to go and have a look, then I want you back to move this train into position to get started on the demolition work.'

So off I dashed up the steps and entered this huge Victorian example of LNWR railway signalling, a feeling of utter sadness enveloped me as I looked around. The place was silent for the first time since being built in the 1880s, but my task was to salvage something. I strode swiftly down the full length of the box and found that one LNWR instrument had been disconnected, obviously now redundant, so with this under my arm I began to make my way out. Just as I was passing the fire grate the dying embers illuminated a nice-looking pair of leather slippers, which seemed to be about my own size. The signalman had obviously left these, now having no further use for them. So I slipped them under my coat and rejoined Steve and the demolition gang in the brake van. I gave Steve my signature in his scrap material book and the block instrument was now legally mine. OK, so I forgot to mention the signalman's leather slippers, but Steve only had small feet and they wouldn't have fitted him anyway!

For part two of this story we need to move forward a few months (by the way, the leather slippers fitted me a treat), and I am in the staff mess room at Preston station enjoying a break between jobs. Sitting at a table with their backs to me are four blokes who were on a guards' training course; all

had been signalmen in the Preston area and had been made redundant by the modernisation scheme. I could actually hear all of what they were saying as they were reminiscing about their days as signalmen and incidents that had occurred, when one of them said to his mate, 'Tell them what happened to you Joe, on your very last turn in No 5 box.'

Joe's opening salvo began: 'To my dying day I will never get over what happened to me on that last day. It got to 10 o'clock at night and the three of us signed the train register for the last time. The box was built in 1884 and had been open 24 hours a day, every day since then – it had never been unstaffed or switched out until that night. Then we all said goodbye to each other, and made our way down to the car park and headed off home. Then when I had gone about a mile down the road I suddenly remembered that I had left my leather slippers in the hearth, so I turned the car around and headed straight back. I parked up and dashed up the steps and into the box, and went over to the hearth to pick up my slippers, but unbelievably they were gone! I looked everywhere for them before realising that some bastard must have been in and nicked them in less than the 10 minutes that I'd been away.'

His mates responded with words like, 'That's bloody unbelievable!' 'What an arsehole, lousy git,' etc, etc. I could have turned around and added my own opinions on this heinous crime, but I decided instead to quietly make my way out of the mess room. I came away feeling quite guilty, now that I knew the previous owner, and made it my business to somehow return the slippers to him. A few days later, after much thought, I came up with a simple solution. I discovered that he had a locker and found out which one it was, then I looked up what time he next signed on for duty and simply left his prized possessions in a carrier bag on the top of his locker. I then visited the locker room shortly afterwards to find that the slippers had gone, hopefully taken into custody by Joe. Well, I couldn't really go and ask him, could I? But I did sleep better that night.

I enjoyed my time as a guard, particularly when working the loose-coupled freight trains, as route knowledge from my footplate days came in very handy and I like to think that the driver and I made a good team on these jobs, working over the undulating gradients that existed between the many collieries in the area. Non-BR steam locos were still at work in some of these places, and more than once a versatile 'J94' saddle tank rescued us after we had slipped to a stand with our diesel loco coming out of Bickershaw and other steep colliery exits.

Another benefit to the guarding duties and shift work was that I could spend time earning some extra money working with my father in our landscape gardening business. This certainly helped to keep me fairly fit and, following a college course, I gradually took over some of the garden design work. Over a few years the business became fairly busy to the extent that I was spending more time on the landscaping than the railway, so the inevitable happened – I gave up the security of the railways and joined the ranks of the self-employed.

In the beginning it was tough going and truly lived up to the motto of the self-employed: 'As one door closes, another slams in your face.' During the first winter the weather was too harsh for much of the time to make a living at landscaping, so I joined a driving agency to earn some income. This led to me taking my Class 3 HGV test, finding work with the Co-op delivering fruit and veg in a range of vintage vehicles including a 1965 Karrier Bantam, a Leyland Comet, and an old Albion – none with any power steering. I became quite sentimentally attached to the Bantam – it had less than 20,000 miles on the clock, and the spring after returning to landscaping work I purchased it, although nobody else drove it due to it having no synchromesh and requiring double declutch action to change gears. The staff preferred to drive the more modern BMC, FG wagons we had. Incidentally, for 40 years until 2013 I renewed my HGV licence yearly and, remarkably, due to changes in the law, I was entitled to drive all classes of commercial vehicles excepting an artic, yet I had never taken another HGV test.

I was now living in an entirely different world and over the next five years we took no holidays or any time off sick. Amusingly, one of our main horticultural suppliers had premises near to a pub where the landlord had been a well-known public figure, the executioner Albert Pierrepoint no less. The pub was usually busy, being within just a few miles of the police headquarters at Hutton, with many of the staff knowing Albert personally – but he always denied the existence of a sign in the pub stating 'No Hanging Around The Bar'.

20 Return to Minehead, a visit to Pickering, and another career change

After a few years my father retired, coinciding with some successful tendering for industrial landscape work, which kept our staff fully occupied for a few more years.

We eventually took some holidays and, with three young sons looking to be entertained for a couple of weeks, we decided upon a visit to Butlin's holiday camp at Minehead. This time we would stay for two weeks, unlike my fleeting visit in 1962. One day during the first week we ventured out to sample a ride on the nearby fledgling West Somerset Railway. Our morning train was headed by an 0-6-0 Bagnall saddle tank named *Victor* pulling six coaches. Having previously had some experience of firing on that day in 1962, I was a little pessimistic regarding the ability of our motive power on the steeper sections of this 36-mile round trip. The engine did actually perform reasonably well, the only blip occurring after leaving Williton, where we should have been Crowcombe next stop; we were labouring quite heavily up the long gradient when our driver decided on a Stogumber stop for a quick blow-up.

Overall I was impressed with this lengthy preserved railway. On our return to Minehead I had a brief chat with the driver, who introduced himself as full-time driver/ fitter Don Haines. He told me that the railway was short of volunteers, particularly footplate staff, and after mentioning to him that I was an ex-BR fireman he asked if I

might be interested. So began my few years as a fireman on the railway, after sending Don a copy of my BR firing certificate.

Later that summer we had another holiday in the area, staying in a caravan at Blue Anchor Bay. That week I undertook a successful firing exam with inspector George Yardley, so exactly 20 years after first firing on the line I was back again, but what a contrast in motive power! The only working steam engines were these big Bagnalls, *Victor* and *Vulcan*, the ultimate industrial locomotives, fitted with roller bearings, rocking grates, outside Walschaerts valve gear, chime whistles and very few oiling points. With cylinder sizes similar to a 'Black 5', they were ideal for pulling heavy loads over short distances, as in their former home at Longbridge Works. They were definitely not intended for working six-coach passenger trains on a daily duty involving 60 miles over steep gradients, but that was the challenge and I loved every minute of it.

A typical day for the crew would be a 7.00am start, light up, prepare and clean the loco, coaling being done by hand off the loading ramp, before working the morning train to Bishops Lydeard, followed by a quick turn-round and back to Minehead. There it was onto the shed for fire-cleaning, take water, check round the loco and oil up, fill lubricators, take on more coal then away again at 2.30pm to Williton where, after taking water, we worked a return train to Minehead, shunted the coaches away, then

At Bishops Lydeard on the West Somerset Railway, driver Ian Wright and myself are on board 0-6-0ST outside-cylinder Bagnall *Victor*, with guard Hein Burger looking on. It was Ian who took the photograph of us climbing Shap with No 70002 *Geoffrey Chaucer* on World Cup Final day in 1966. *Author's collection*

onto the shed, dispose of the fire and empty the smokebox. But don't think that was the end of our 11-hour day; the fitter was on his own, and might want an extra pair of hands to carry out any repairs to the loco.

Some mornings, due to a shortage of station staff, I tidied the platform and cleaned the toilet block, then nipped back to the footplate to see how *Victor*'s fire was going. Occasionally, again due to shortage, I would have no driver because he had to work the morning DMU into Minehead; by that time I had oiled up the loco, and we were ready for going off shed. Now, anybody who has worked on these Bagnalls will tell you just how demanding they are to keep them on the move with enough steam and water when working to the limit of their capabilities. Firing was a real art; just a few shovels of coal in the wrong place and they didn't like it. You had to keep them as hot as possible, particularly before leaving Williton for the long climb ahead to Crowcombe. It was definitely a case of 'being prepared', with a white-hot fire and water right up in the glass, then, just as the safety valves simmered, off you went, teamwork being essential on these temperamental engines. With a good mate and calling upon all our

footplate skills, it was possible to get these engines to respond. It must be pleasurable working on the footplate on the present-day West Somerset Railway, operating with true passenger engines doing the job they were designed for and able to handle the loads with some ease. But knowing loco men as I do, I wouldn't mind betting that some of today's crews would relish the challenge of a Bagnall again on the line.

The shortage of volunteers on the railway at that time was reflected by the state of the station gardens, including those at Blue Anchor. It did help, of course, that we had plenty of experience in that department, with our landscape gardening business, and I managed to persuade our landscape foreman to accompany me on one of my 600-mile return voyages to the railway. We used one of our Transit vehicles to transport ourselves and all the necessary tools and equipment, as the railway did not possess much in the way of gardening tools. We spent an enjoyable week with sunny weather on the restoration of the gardens at Blue Anchor and Minehead, leaving behind much of the equipment and tools for use by the newly formed station groups.

The railway was in its infancy in those

days, with little money available, and things were so bad one day that we had to mix wood in with the coal on the afternoon trip to Williton to keep the engine going due to the shortage of coal. I think that must have been one of the lowest points in the history of the railway. But in my mind I always had confidence that things could only improve, and over the years since then the West Somerset Railway has become one of the finest heritage railways in the country, and I am proud to have played just a small role

Seen here at Minehead, Hudswell Clarke 0-6-0 outside-cylinder side tank *Jennifer* was not up to the punishing 60-mile daily steam mileage on the West Somerset Railway. *Author's collection*

in its development. Had the railway been nearer to home I would have become rather more involved, but I was grateful that it had given me the opportunity to work with the steam loco again, and by pure coincidence it opened up my next move to a preserved railway, and this is how it came about.

I arrived one week for footplate duties on the WSR to find that we had an engine from the North Yorkshire Moors Railway, an 0-6-0 side tank named *Jennifer*. Driver Brian Mellors and I had it all of that week. It wasn't in particularly good condition, requiring daily maintenance and repairs to keep it going, and proving so bad that I think it was eventually stuffed and mounted on a plinth outside Minehead station. I do believe these days it is in much better health pulling trains on the Embsay Railway. During that week I got into conversation with the man who had brought it from the NYMR. I learned where the railway was situated and some other facts, which I must admit did interest me, so I decided to pay a visit in the near future. But this wasn't to be my final association with the West Somerset Railway, for I was to return – all will be revealed in a later chapter.

Later that year we duly paid a visit to

Pickering and the North Yorkshire Moors Railway, taking a late summer break with the boys in our own caravan on a site overlooking the bay at Scarborough. During the week we decided to have a day out on the railway, and drove across in the luxury of our recently purchased towing vehicle, a metallic blue Ford Zephyr 6, arriving at Pickering to see a 'Black 5' waiting at the head of our Grosmont train. I was having a look at No 45428 when from out of the cab someone called, 'Is that you, "Fingers"?' I was taken aback, wondering who would know me this far from home, but I realised it must be somebody from my railway past. It turned out to be one of my former drivers from Lostock Hall, Brian Snape. He told me that he worked full time for the railway as a driver and invited me to join him on the footplate. I had a round trip with him and enjoyed it so much that I decided to became involved with the railway, so on Saturday 11 December 1982 I made my first visit as a working volunteer, and I am still there all these years later.

Shortly after arriving in Grosmont that evening I decided to call in at the pub adjacent to the station, suspecting that it would house some thirsty volunteers from the nearby loco sheds. Sure enough, I found the place to be quite busy, and I was soon in conversation with some blokes involved with the restoration of ex-GWR 0-6-2T No 6619. Kevin Gould, Peter Proud and Kevin Hudspith were my first contacts, and I was welcomed to join them on the Sunday morning after they kindly arranged my accommodation in the salubrious confines of the engine shed cottages. I enjoyed working with them, particularly when I discovered that some of these boys were actually part of the team who had cleaned the engines at Lostock Hall on 4 August 1968!

The following spring I wound the clock back 20 years and began my career as an engine cleaner again, having turned down the chance to take a firing exam, as I wanted to know the line and its personnel before progressing further. Each turn involved me in a 300-mile round trip from my home in Preston. We stayed in our caravan on Mick Atkinson's farm site adjacent to the railway at Goathland. I must admit that the NYMR felt a little more like home to me in comparison to the WSR, for at that time many of the footplate staff were ex-BR steam men, and remarkably the General Manager was Bob Oliver, who had been my boss at Preston.

The line is similar in length to the WSR, but with much steeper gradients, engines having to work to their maximum on the 1 in 49 climbs. It is also heavy going for the crews: 112 miles a day involving three round trips, including loco preparation and disposal, or the easier 72 miles on two trips. Operating the railway was not dissimilar to some of the branch line work we had on British Railways. If you were a novice and wanted to gain some footplate experience on a steam locomotive, this was the place for you. From my point of view I have derived much pleasure in working with people from all walks of life, who have the same enthusiasm for steam and over the years have developed into competent footplatemen.

In the early years of my involvement with the NYMR we had our caravan on a small farm site in Goathland each summer, bringing it back to Preston during the winter. Later we were given permission to leave it all the year round at Goathland station. Most of our visits were at weekends, and we soon made lots of new friends who shared a common interest in the operation of this steam railway running through some of Yorkshire's finest scenery. We usually arrived by car on Friday evening about 9 o'clock, having covered the 150 miles from Preston in about 3 hours. We always took our border collie with us, as well as the cat and the three boys! This used to amuse some of the station staff, watching us all pile out of the car, particularly when I told them that we sometimes brought the goldfish and put it in the beck behind the caravan to enjoy a swim; on the Sunday night, just before heading for home, I would catch it in the net and pop it back in its bowl. Now that everybody was in the car, we could set off for home!

It was around this time, after having had

Three former Preston railwaymen working for the NYMR: driver Brian Snape (left), General Manager Bob Oliver, and driver John Fletcher. Brian and myself were at Lostock Hall together, while Bob was our General Manager when we transferred to Preston. *Author's collection*

some footplate rides and feeling
more confident of working the
line, that I asked the shed boss,
Peter Smeaton, to arrange for me
to take a firing exam. This he duly
did over two days with footplate
inspector Roy Cross. The first day
was a rules, regulations and theory
exam, including route knowledge,
followed the day after by a practical
firing exam. This consisted of loco
preparation of 0-6-0ST No 31
Meteor, followed by two return trips
to Pickering hauling the regular six-
coach train. Fortunately I had some
experience of firing this industrial
loco, being tutored in how to get the
best out of it by my ex BR colleague
and Chief Loco Inspector Keith
Gays.

There was no margin for error
working this heavy train up the
hills with a loco that weighed just
a quarter of our train weight, but
Meteor with her 54-inch driving
wheels was no stranger to doing a
hard day's work. The firing technique was
strictly 'little and often' around the box,
closing the doors between each charge and
waiting for the chimney to clear before firing
again, one injector remaining on throughout
the climb. Water was taken at each end of
the line and on shed, five times in total,
and coal taken on twice, followed by engine
disposal, making this a hard day's work for
man and machine. At the end of it I am
pleased to say that I became a registered
fireman again, this time on a preserved
railway, but I am sure that I worked just
as hard that day as I had done 20 years
previously when gaining my BR fireman's
ticket.

The NYMR at that time did not have
a fleet of large locos to call upon. *Meteor*
became my personal pet, followed by its
industrial stablemate *Antwerp*, an 0-6-0

'The Mighty Meteor' at Grosmont MPD. The burnt
smokebox door is evidence of a hard day's work. Footplate
inspector Keith Gays is being watched by fireman Simon
Alcock. *Author's collection*

saddle tank. These two and the 'J27' were
the norm for some months, while a day on
the 'K1' or a 'Black 5' when available made
the working of trains that much easier,
similarly when GWR 0-6-2T No 6619
entered traffic.

Looking back some 30 years to those days
and my time spent on the West Somerset
Railway firing some 60 miles a day on
industrial engines, performing work they
were never built for, it actually stood me in
good stead when I changed for a 72-mile
day on engines with the same pedigree at
the NYMR! The first industrials to arrive
on the line were a pair of former colliery
engines, Nos 5 and 9, formerly owned by
the Lambton Hetton & Joicey Collieries
and sporting 'LHJC' on their side tanks.
When working on one of these engines I
think that I upset more than a few enquiring

enthusiasts when asked what the initials stood for. What else could I say but 'Lostock Hall Junction Company'? So when No 5972 *Olton Hall* first visited the NYMR on loan from West Coast Railways, it arrived without its nameplates, just the backing plates attached to the wheel splasher. Well, it couldn't be seen running about without a name, could it? So what name did we give it, chalked on the back plates? None other than 'Lostock Hall'.

At this point I have obviously moved across the footplate and achieved my ambition at the age of 40 of becoming a steam driver. That may seem to some folks like a long apprenticeship but, looking back to my Uncle Bob's footplate career, he started as an engine cleaner in 1919 and only became a booked driver in 1957 – now, that is indeed a lengthy wait for promotion, but it wasn't unusual in the days of steam. By comparison, how things have changed

on the railways of today. His great-nephew, my youngest son, John-Lloyd, drives on the national network, fully qualified after just a year's training, and rightly so, as lengthy waits for promotion have disappeared with the steam age.

My own promotion to driver in July 1986 came after a lengthy spell swotting up on rules and digesting the 'black book' (*The Handbook for Railway Steam Locomotive Enginemen*), the steam man's Bible. My theory and rules were taken with Chris Cubitt and the following day my practical exam was with Chief Inspector Keith Gays on 'K1' No 62005 – two round trips to Pickering with rostered driver Paul Wilson on the shovel. All went well on the day despite a few nerves on my part, for Keith was your true pro, reminiscent of the old school of BR inspectors from my day. He did remark that my engine trimmings were not quite up to MIC standard, but then again

My Network Rail train driver son samples a different form of traction on the NYMR. *Author's collection*

Kevin Gould (left), myself, unknown and Sean Bowler pose with a Norwegian 2-6-0 locomotive at Bodiam on the Kent & East Sussex Railway. *Author's collection*

oiling-up locomotives has never been one of my strong points!

Mention of Paul Wilson leads me to tell you of another railway with which I became involved, the Kent & East Sussex. Paul was a driver there and during a conversation he let slip that the footplate department was struggling a bit in finding enough crews to keep the job going; in fact, some NYMR staff were already passed for operating KESR trains. I must admit to being keen on the idea but, having just 'got my wings' in Yorkshire, I decided to wait a while. But if we fast-forward ten years I am heading to Rolvenden loco sheds on the KESR accompanied by Kevin Gould and our wives. Kevin was already passed for driving there and I was to act as his fireman for the week. The girls spent most of the week touring

around, even squeezing in a trip to France for the day. This was to be the first of many visits made to the railway with Kevin, and also his cousin Sean Bowler. I was later to pass for driving on this lovely line, which has been extended over the years with the ultimate hope of linking up again with the national network at Robertsbridge.

Another railway with which I became involved, albeit briefly, was the Weardale Railway, which also had difficulty finding qualified crews and steam locos around 2004. They borrowed our 'J27' and later acquired an 0-6-0 saddle tank aptly named *Mardy Monster*. The service usually comprised just one engine in steam hauling a short rake of coaches. The railway was heavily subsidised and grant-aided, which led to it being completely overstaffed for what was on offer, with workers who did not know each other personally identifying each other by numbers!

This led to an amusing incident one

The Weardale Railway's *Mardy Monster* – but which one? *Author's collection*

Sunday morning as I approached Stanhope driving the 'J27'. Two members of staff were stationed at the ground frame when one of them attempted to move a lever as we passed over the point. The other one stopped him from doing so, so I decided to report this after arriving in the station. Upon telling the manager of the incident, he looked at the roster and said that he would go out immediately and have a word with both number 9 and 13 and demand an immediate report from them. I often wondered whether they signed it with their name or number!

Prior to its not unexpected demise the railway became reliant upon the one working steam locomotive to operate the service. *Mardy Monster* was actually Britain's most powerful industrial locomotive, which, despite the tireless efforts of the small group

of skilled fitting staff, began to develop steam leaks and blows at almost every orifice. Thus, when I arrived for duty early one Sunday morning towards the end of the running season and looked out of the shed office window for the engine, I had to ask the fitter where it was.

He said, 'It's there,' pointing across the yard, but the only thing I could see was a cloud of steam, so we walked over and sure enough behind all this steam was the engine.

'Please don't fail it, Fletch – we've nothing else. It's just got to last a few more days.'

So I agreed to take it and, after a harrowing day's graft, my repair card for the engine read: 'Left leading sander steam-tight, everything else blowing or leaking steam'! Fortunately these days the 'Monster' is in better health, and operating trains on the Elsecar Railway.

21 Moving to Yorkshire, and the Shed Shop

Now, I had better be careful what I say as a Lancastrian living here among these grand Yorkshire folk, for I actually managed to sneak into beautiful downtown Grosmont while they were sorting out the asylum-seekers…

Being a long-time member of the RSPB, you might not see me as a lover of cats, but I am actually fond of them and help to look after the two that live at the engine sheds. They came to us as strays and I made the mistake of feeding them, and of course they came back again – we have fed them every day for the last ten years! But they do uphold the tradition of railway cats by keeping down the vermin population. The three of us have actually featured in the media, including the front page of that internationally renowned pet journal *Cat World*. (Well, somebody must have heard of it…)

All our family loved exploring the delights of the North Yorkshire Moors and the quaint fishing port at Whitby – it really was our second home, and we began to make plans to gain a foothold in the area, particularly as our family business was beginning to show a healthy return, two of our three sons becoming partners. So a decision was made to invest in a property in the Grosmont area. After much searching we found an unmodernised country cottage in the hamlet of Esk Valley, within walking distance of Grosmont. It really is an idyllic location, with a field to the front giving uninterrupted views of steam locos climbing the 1 in 49 gradient to Goathland. It had an open aspect to the rear with a large garden, so we set about bringing the place up-to-date, including an extension at the back. Many of the surrounding properties were still in original condition and I think we were looked upon as the pioneers of property restoration in Esk Valley. The work

Myself with Moony, the original engine shed cat, in Grosmont's Shed Shop. It was white at birth but, living around steam locos, it was always filthy and covered in oil, but it was never troubled with any rheumatism! *Author's collection*

took more than two years to complete, but by the end we had a property of which to be proud.

The lovely village of Goathland and surrounding areas were chosen as the location for the hugely successful TV series *Heartbeat*, about the lives of village policemen in the 1950s/'60s. Being a fan of the music and cars of that period, it interested me greatly, and my music hero Buddy Holly wrote and recorded the title song in 1958. Some of the filming involved our railway, including for a while the opening sequences of every episode, and almost overnight Goathland became better known as 'Aidensfield', becoming a tourist hotspot and attracting visitors from all over the world, many of them wanting to sample the scenery by travelling on our period steam trains.

The railway has also featured in many other films, including the railway scenes in the first 'Harry Potter' film, giving us a huge publicity boost. We have had lots of exposure on other TV programmes and documentaries, many of us making appearances in some of them, helping in promoting our railway. I seem to have become typecast as an engine driver in my filming jobs. One of them I did with Julia Bradbury, and we were filming a scene on board No 60007 *Sir Nigel Gresley* when I mistakenly called her Juliet. I immediately apologised, saying that it was just the Romeo in me! The producer said that was a great one-liner, which he would leave in the script, but it finished up on the cutting-room floor. I should have reported him to Equity – not that I was a member, but I am in the RMT!

Some other thespians who have had the misfortune to appear alongside me, or I have met, include Todd Carty, Zoe Salmon, John Craven, David Dimbleby, Fred Dibnah, Pete Waterman and David Shepherd.

Mention of No 60007 reminds me of one

EastEnders actor Todd Carty and his son featured in some publicity filming with myself and fellow driver Gerry Skelton. *Author's collection*

Two visitors to the railway: BBC presenter David Dimbleby joined us on board visiting loco No 3440 *City of Truro* for a footplate ride while filming in the area to promote Yorkshire tourist attractions. *Author's collection*

Some of the staff involved with the restoration of Standard Class 4 No 75029 are seen at the unveiling of the nameplate *The Green Knight*, attended by the loco's then owner, artist David Shepherd. *Author's collection*

Saturday when the then Bishop of York, the Rt Rev and Rt Hon Dr David Hope KCVO, made an official visit to the railway and rode with us on the footplate from Pickering to Grosmont. At the Levisham stop he asked if he could blow the whistle when we were ready to depart. I invited him over onto the driver's seat, and at departure time he blew the whistle. I then told him to open the regulator, which he did, and as No 60007 began to ease away the look of sheer joy on his face brought an impromptu response from me when I said to him that during his sermon the next morning he would be able to inform the congregation that during his lifetime he had moved heaven and earth and *Sir Nigel Gresley*! Luckily for me he wasn't offended and remarked that they would indeed be informed of his brief spell as an engine driver.

One of the rewards of our filming stint with Zoe Salmon, who spent a weekend with us firing and driving Standard Class 4 No 75029 for the *Blue Peter* programme was being given a Blue Peter badge upon completion of the two days of filming. This I innocently pinned to the lapel of my everyday work coat, not realising its significance to the general public. It breaks down any class barriers and is an instant

The Bishop of York, Dr David Hope, at the controls of 'A4' 'Pacific' No 60007 *Sir Nigel Gresley*. *Author's collection*

conversation piece. As an example, when travelling recently on the crowded London Underground, where normally nobody would speak to you, a complete stranger excitedly asked how I came to be wearing a Blue Peter badge. Had I been on the show? Who did I meet? By now I could sense that half the carriage were awaiting my response and they were not disappointed when told that to get the badge I had to spend two days on the footplate getting steamed up with a blonde Belfast beauty!

By contrast, my day with fellow Lancastrian Fred Dibnah was like talking to a long-lost friend; he being from Notlob

the church land; every lunchtime his Land Rover disappeared down the church drive, taking him to the local hostelry for a 2-hour quaffing session and enthralling the locals with his steeplejack exploits. We met the vicar late one afternoon; Fred had not yet returned, but he said it didn't bother him at all because he had given him a price for the whole job, not by the hour.

Pete Waterman is another of my heroes, for it was he who rescued my all-time favourite steam locomotive, the ex-LNWR 0-8-0 'Super D', which for years had been kicked about from pillar to post until his generosity gave it life again under the auspices of the National Railway Museum. When the engine was at York, after receiving some expert maintenance tuition from Peter's mechanical wizard Steve Latham he frightened me by saying that he had actually travelled at 70mph on a 'Super D' – albeit on the back of a low-loader! I later had the pleasure of being its regular driver during its spell on loan to the NYMR and acted as instructor/inspector,

Blue Peter presenter Zoe Salmon proved herself to be a useful fireman on board 'Standard 4' No 75029 during a weekend's filming for the programme on the NYMR. *Author's collection*

(Bolton) and me from Preston, we spoke the same dialect to such an extent that even today folk remark of the similarity of our voices, although I have to admit that he could even out-talk me, which is no mean achievement! I had actually seen Fred in action prior to meeting him at the traction engine rally, where he was entertaining the crowds with his trademark 'de-mon-stration'; it was there at the end of the day that a supposed quick pint with him made me wish I had been teetotal! A few years earlier he had been restoring a church steeple and we were landscaping a garden that backed on to

familiarising crews with the idiosyncrasies of this unique machine. Peter and I shared the footplate occasionally after he had performed the reopening of yet another railway building, structure, shop, station or line extension somewhere around the country. I am pretty sure that by now he must have reopened more than Dr Beeching managed to close! I share is interest in O-gauge modelling and I had the pleasure of operating his extensive layout portraying Leamington Spa, in between discussing his vast knowledge of the pop music industry. And yes, he is a Buddy Holly fan!

'Super D' outing at Levisham: from the left, myself, 'Super D' doctor
Steve Latham, Footplate Inspector Christopher Cubitt, and loco
saviour Pete Waterman. *Author's collection*

riding at speed. This led to them being sent back to their home depots after little more than a couple of weeks on trial and the resumption of the 'Lanky Tanks' on these jobs.

In 2008 I was asked to take up the duties of Footplate Inspector at the NYMR. It was around this time that another of my ambitions was achieved when one of my first tasks was to assist with the training of crews on another loco I had waited some 45 years to handle since first setting eyes on

'Standard 4' No 75029 was previously owned by the artist David Shepherd, and I was involved with the restoration of the loco following its purchase for our railway by Peter Best. During this time we researched its past life on BR, and found that it and other members of the class had been briefly allocated to 27C Southport shed in 1958 to assess their suitability for replacing the aged ex-L&Y 2-4-2 tanks still in use working the tightly timed commuter services to Manchester. Remarkably, the 'Standard 4s', despite being the most up-to-date offering in steam motive power, were unable to keep time with these trains, attracting complaints of poor steaming, not being quick enough away from station stops and rough

one at 82F Bath Green Park – a former Somerset & Dorset 2-8-0, No 53809. Boy, was I like a little lad in a toffee shop with this magnificent machine, testing it to the limit hauling eight coaches on gradients similar to those on its former stamping ground.

I moved on from this to training footplatemen from the Railway Preservation Society of Ireland (RPSI). They were all diesel drivers, visiting us to familiarise themselves on steam traction. A couple of

An ambition achieved: driving a Somerset & Dorset locomotive, 7F 2-8-0 No 53809, which in the right hands mastered the 1 in 49 gradients of the North Yorkshire Moors Railway. *Author's collection*

the men had some steam experience and were known to me from my visits to their headquarters at Whitehead in Northern Ireland. This was the starting point for many of the steam excursions that I had travelled behind in the days when wooden-bodied coaching stock provided the accommodation. Motive power included *Merlin*, the three-cylinder compound, or fellow 4-4-0 *Slieve Gullion*, on which I had the pleasure of a firing turn from Dublin to Enniscorthy. It was during this trip that I noticed the veteran booked fireman constantly working the gauge frame test cock to check the boiler water level, when to me it was plainly on view and reading a safe level. I did eventually have to ask him his reasons for doing that. His reply was a statement of pure Irish logic delivered in his soft southern lilt: 'Aye, well, it's like this you see – 'tis far better to have a glass full of water than a glass full of steam.'

There is still something very unhurried about Irish steam travel – the gorgeous scenery, the hospitality, the fiddle band and, of course, the Guinness, which I can assure you does taste even better in the Emerald Isle. If you do visit I urge you not to miss the Ulster Folk & Transport Museum at Cultra in the north. Housed there among the many examples of transportation is Ireland's largest and most powerful steam locomotive, *Maeve*, a three-cylinder 4-6-0. The only survivor of three locomotives built at Inchicore Works in 1939, their weight of 139 tons usually restricted the trio to the Dublin-Cork main line. In creating this handsome class of locomotive the designer, E. C. Bredin, appears to have embraced the best parts of an LMS 'Royal Scot', a GWR 'King' and a Southern 'Lord Nelson'. Ireland's 5ft 3in track gauge further emphasises the size of this machine, with plenty of space on the footplate for a good old Irish jig!

While in Ireland I explored what was left of the narrow gauge, including my favourite, the Tralee & Dingle Railway, probably the most remote and spectacular railway byway in the British Isles, threading the mountainous Dingle peninsula in the far west of Kerry with 31 miles of track and gradients of 1 in 30 commonplace. How I wish that I had been around when the entire line was open. However, all is not lost because the Tralee & Blennerville Steam Railway Group hopes to reopen some 3 miles of the line, on which the last trains ran in 2006. They do have ex-T&D steam loco No 5T, which I must admit to having a personal interest in as the NYMR restored its boiler, and we did have a spare cabside number plate.

Over the years I have made frequent visits to my former steam depot at Lostock Hall to film any changes, my final visit being in 1990 when I filmed the demolition of this hallowed hall. The demolition contractor was known to me through business dealings for the purchase of traditional Yorkshire stone paving, stone troughs and garden architecture; I was therefore able to purchase some items and incorporate them into our garden at Esk Valley. I was able to rescue the stone window sill and bricks from part of the shed master's office, which we turned into ornamental seating. The beams from the roof of the foreman's office made a lovely pergola. The 'PRIVATE' sign from the foreman's door now resides on another office door at the Shed Shop in Grosmont, complete with my coat hook, which I rescued from the mess room. But my most cherished possession is the 8-foot-long wooden sign 'LOSTOCK HALL ENGINE SHED' from the signal box that controlled movements on and off the shed. Another possession remaining in the garden is the original bell tower from the demolished St Leonard's Church in Penwortham, Preston, where we married in 1967. It didn't look all that big sitting on top of the church, but it took six of us to lift it into place in the garden.

With both Jacqueline and myself then in our 50s, it became mid-life crisis time, necessitating the biggest decision of our lives. A family meeting was held and our accountant was invited as the guest speaker to explain the pros and cons of handing over the running of the business to our two eldest sons, Wayne and Paul. They were both in their 20s and had been in the business of landscape gardening since leaving school. There is no doubt about it being a young man's job, as it is heavy, physical work; I was ready to hand over the reins to them and eventually this is what we did. We sold our home in Preston, which happened to coincide with the cottage next door to our house at Esk Valley coming on the market. So we purchased it, then spent the winter restoring the place for use as a holiday cottage to give us some income, as neither of us had a job, and our youngest son was finishing his schooling in Whitby. The holiday cottage proved popular, helped by the fact that we had restored it with a railway theme to attract the enthusiast market. We even had both front doors on the cottages fitted with stained glass depicting steam locomotives, one a 'Duchess' and the other an 'A4' 'Pacific'. To complete the scene we had wall plaques made, naming one cottage 'Lostock Hall', and next door 'Rose Grove'. I even persuaded the chap next door to that to let me name his house 'Carnforth', thereby commemorating the last three surviving steam depots on British Railways. We decided that a period vehicle was important to complete the scene, so what better than a big 1948 Austin 16, parked outside the

Esk Valley Cottages, idyllic accommodation for the railway enthusiast and family. *Author's collection*

cottages advertising the 'Rose Grove' holiday cottage!

Needing some employment, I started to commute to Preston, staying with either one of my sons in order to help with the business four days a week. But within a few months we both found local jobs. Jacqueline is a qualified practice nurse and began work for the NHS at Whitby. Then a vacancy occurred as the manager of the fund-raising shop at Grosmont engine shed. This shop had been established by some staff working at the MPD, the railway providing the premises. It had been doing a steady little trade making about £5,000 per

Our two older sons, Wayne and Paul, photographed when they took over the family landscape gardening business, which they have expanded over the years. *Author's collection*

Take your pick of the front doors at Esk Valley Cottages – an LMS 'Pacific' at 'Lostock Hall' or an LNER 'Pacific' at 'Rose Grove'. *Author's collection*

Our big 1948 Austin 16 could climb the gradients in the area as well as any steam engine! *Author's collection*

year, management agreeing that any profits would be directed into funding projects and improvements over and above the budget allocated to the depot by the Finance Committee. I presented railway management with my business plan for the shop, including projected turnover and profits. This was accepted and I was offered the job, confident of my ability to make the shop a financial success, but my main concern at the time was that, as I had spent many years being self-employed and making my own way in life, I obviously wanted to continue making a success of any enterprise that came my way. Much of my everyday life had been spent dealing with business people, and I was unsure if that was going to be the format with the NYMR management. With this in mind I offered to take on the job in a self-employed role for the first 12 months, with any profits going into an NYMR Shed Shop account. What this meant was that either of us could pull out should the venture prove unsuccessful.

This was agreed upon, but a good working relationship with the NYMR management was soon established – the only condition being that I only had three months to implement the first stage of the business plan. This involved gutting 50 per cent of the shop, a complete redecoration, additional lighting and sockets, water heater, cold drinks machine, ice-cream freezer, coffee machine and a host of other tasks, including stocking. Fortunately I had business connections with a nationwide supermarket chain, which kindly donated a large range of modern shop fittings, display stands, gondolas, shelving and office furniture, and to finish off we were given a children's ride-on 'steam loco'. Through another business contact I was able to secure one of the remaining purpose-built 'Thomas' model railways that were made exclusively for just a handful of high-end toy shops, both these acquisitions being coin-operated. These two attractions alone have been extremely popular over the years and have given us a healthy financial return.

Grosmont Shed Shop stalwart and accomplished railway photographer David Idle with myself and grandson Alex ready to deal with the daily invasion of visiting bargain-hunters. *Author's collection*

To raise the profile of the fund-raising shop we invested a considerable amount in a whole new range of stock, including model railway items from Hornby, Bachmann and Dapol. We had our own in-house DVDs, and became the sole agent for lucrative nameplate and bridge plate castings, for use as house names or numbers. My own view was that there wasn't much point in stocking the same items as the other three shops on the railway – we had to be exclusive and of interest. I think we have achieved some of that, judging by the often-heard remark that this is not just a shop – more like an emporium! We just about made the deadline for opening, thanks to members of the shed staff who gave much help in their free time, in particular the Naylor brothers, Peter and Phil, as well as Adam Dalgleish and a former business partner of mine, Steve Davies, who travelled across from Preston on a regular basis. Just before opening I recruited a couple of volunteer shop staff, David Idle and Adrian Scales, without whom the shop could not have achieved the first year's profit of a very pleasing £25,000.

That was 18 years ago, and we have bettered that figure in certain years, particularly since I was joined by my right-hand woman, Margaret Beesley, who over the years has become someone who can be relied upon as my knowledgeable shop supervisor, to the extent that since opening it has now raised more than £500,000 for the NYMR, to be spent on projects purely at the MPD. We have also developed our own internet sales site, having introduced the sale of steam-age footplate overalls and supplying most of the preserved railways both here and abroad, with thousands sold over the years. We have also made frequent use of auction houses including Vectis and, of course, eBay, where just about everything is on offer to the extent that I often remark that you now have 'dealers dealing in dealers'.

At about this time – 1998 – many of us real ale lovers had become disgruntled with the only pub in the village, so what did we do about it? We opened up a real ale club! As you can imagine, the logistics involved in realising this ambition were huge. We had no money, no premises, no brewery contacts, no village support and no drinks licence – we were out on our own, but what we did have was bags of enthusiasm and determination, and it was this that drove us forward. By good fortune the Grosmont Co-op was downsizing and splitting part of the building into units, so we applied for one of these that had been in use as a storeroom and garage for a delivery vehicle. Meanwhile we applied for a drinks licence, which entailed a visit to the local magistrates court by the main instigator of our proposal, Keith Rogers, one of the fitting staff at the shed and a little bit unfamiliar with the process and format of the granting of such a licence, including having to raise his arm and swear on the Bible. Now, God must have been listening to us that day for our application was successful, objections from the pub and their allies being overruled.

A committee was formed, the lease was signed and an appeal for funds was launched. Plans for the alterations were accepted and work commenced. Within weeks some £12,000 had been promised from individuals, so it was decided to remain independent of breweries and go it alone. Luckily we did have some skilled and not-so-skilled labour available to us, enabling all the work to be completed in just three months using all-volunteer labour except for plastering work. 'The Crossing Club' was a huge success thanks to the dedication of the volunteer staff, one of my less taxing roles being a regular Sunday night spot

The Bore, after being presented with the 'Boreometer' by Simon Alcock at the Birch Hole Inn, Beck Hole. *Author's collection*

manning the bar. This became a popular attraction, particularly when I introduced the unique theme of 'Live Music from Dead Artists'. The committee rewarded me for my efforts with a 'clock' – well, actually the 'Boreometer' clock, a modified former pressure gauge with the needle working its way round pointing to six different readings varying from 'Interesting' through to 'Comatose'!

Likewise, during my time on the footplate at the NYMR a fellow driver (who thinks that I do not know it was him) cobbled together a rather apt loco headboard 'The Preston Rambler', which accompanied me on many journeys over the line. This was only bettered by the appearance of my former vintage BR Lostock Hall pushbike, which had been used for 'knocking-up' duties

My former Lostock Hall 'knocking-up' bike
has been somewhat incapacitated by unknown
members of the footplate department at
Grosmont shed. *Author's collection*

The aptly named 'Preston Rambler' about to
depart from Grosmont shed with the 'Super D'.
Author's collection

and which somehow found its way tied to
the smokebox door of 'Austerity' locomotive
No 3672 *Dame Vera Lynn* upon arrival at
Pickering station one Sunday morning. I
suppose it made a change from being atop
water columns and the coal hopper. Of
course, no one knew who the culprits were!

The Crossing Club debt was paid back
within 12 months, all £12,000 to the
members. I had the honour of being the
Chairman for the next seven years, during
which time the Club won two awards for its
beers from CAMRA! It continues to thrive
under the present committee, who have
worked tirelessly to continually improve the
viability of this village asset.

I have been involved with footplate
work at the railway since 1982, and over
the course of the years I have become
reacquainted with many of my former
colleagues from Lostock Hall MPD who have
visited the railway. Some visits have been
by prior arrangement, while at other times
it has been by pure chance that we have

met. It was with this in mind that I decided
that a reunion would be most appropriate,
particularly as the advancing years have
taken their toll since we were young men in
the days of steam. So I arranged to hire our
Great Western Saloon for our first gathering,
appropriately in millennium year 2000, and
this has now become an annual event.

I left the Preston arrangements in the
hands of former Footplate Inspector Jimmy
Boyle and fitting supervisor Peter Whelan.
The format consists of a mid-morning arrival
in Grosmont following a journey by coach
from Preston. First on the day's agenda is a
conducted tour of the engine sheds, then a
round trip to Pickering in the GW Saloon
adjacent to the engine, with lunch provided
by the Catering Department. We usually
have an NYMR representative on board to
promote the railway, to discuss and answer
any questions, and supervise the changeover
of footplate passengers. A draw for this
privilege is held on the coach before arrival
at Grosmont. Some of the lucky few are
my former drivers and it delights them to
handle a steam locomotive again for part
of the journey under my supervision as the
footplate inspector. My main duty is being
the route instructor, as it certainly does not

Lostock Hall reunion day on the NYMR, including my fireman Ray Stewart, gathered round our own ex-10D 'Black 5' No 45212 after arrival into Pickering. *Author's collection*

involve instructing them on how to handle a steam locomotive!

Back at Grosmont it is time for photographs before adjourning to the Crossing Club, where we are usually joined by a few members of the NYMR footplate staff for a Saturday afternoon session of steam stories among the many guests. Funny how each year an extra coach seems to be added to some of the trains!

All too soon it's departure time and hopefully we will all meet up again the following year, but as we all know life is not always like that, and since our first reunion in 2000 some of my former colleagues have gone up into the 'Top Link'.

Staying with the theme of reunions, I have mentioned in passing that our youngest son is a train driver. I don't know where he gets his interest! The traction he drives are all units, both diesel and electric, and I try to visualise some time in the future, when he and his mates hold a retirement reunion, what their 'Tales of the Rails' will comprise.

His predecessors, my generation, have no shortage of tales and tale-tellers about the steam locomotive and the steam age. Somehow I cannot envisage the gathered company being spellbound with stories from the diesel age, such as, 'Hey, Jason, do you remember that 158 unit that we always got on the morning CrossCountry 27-stops-to-Tamworth job? Do you know I could never get that right-hand windscreen wiper to work – was it the same with you?' Or, 'Hey, Ahmed, do you remember having to relieve me on that 170 unit when I couldn't get the air-conditioning to work, and they had me working for over 32 hours that week – I was absolutely knackered! Thank goodness Bob Crowe came along, and negotiated a much more manageable 25-hour working week...'

Incidentally, I did remind my son that we had air-conditioning on the old steam locomotives. Well, we did when you managed to prise open the vents on the cab roof with a few deft strikes of the coal pick!

22 A notable visitor on the 'S15', and trips to France and Germany

Another reunion that comes to mind took place one Bank Holiday Monday in the 1980s, when I was the driver on the 13.50 service from Grosmont to Pickering. Our loco was ex-Southern Railway 'S15' Class No 30841. I won't tell you who my fireman was, but he was an experienced hand who was not on the footplate 5 minutes before departure with our eight-coach train. I was just contemplating putting a fire on when a wiry, elderly chap clad in railway overalls approached the cab, telling me that he was a retired steam driver and asked if it would be possible for him to have a footplate ride. Quite by chance our operating manager was on the platform, so I obtained a footplate pass for our guest and welcomed him aboard.

He asked to do the firing, to which I said, 'Be our guest if you think you can still do it,' so he set to with the shovel just as my fireman appeared, to be told that the old boy was on the shovel. He had already got a good back end in the box, and a full pot of water, so away we went, with me keeping an eye on him. Once we passed the shed it was full regulator and 60% cut-off for the next 3 miles up the 1 in 49 gradient to Goathland. I watched the old boy lift up the small flap on the firehole, which severely restricts the gap for shovelling on this Southern engine, demanding experience and accuracy from whoever is firing; this left me to think that, if he could fire over that, then he was definitely a pro. It was a pleasure to see him in action. I marked him down as a Southern

man when he turned on the injector steam valves, knowing that these opened anti-clockwise on our 'S15' as opposed to being clockwise on the 'N15'. He also swept after each firing, leaving no loose coal whatsoever on the footplate, which he washed down a couple of times before Goathland. He had the steam on the mark all the way, adjusting the dampers as required, and the water level remained constant at three-quarters of a glass. I told him I was going to shut off for the station stop, so on with the blower, down went the firehole door flap, then the damper, and on with the other injector – a perfect display of firing. I asked my mate why he couldn't be like that, instead of having just about enough steam to get there, the water 'just bobbin'', the footplate covered in coal and dust, and passengers unable to view the lovely scenery due to the air being polluted with black smoke, reminiscent of the German battleship *Bismarck* leaving port!

I think my words were wasted, but it was time to let my guest have a go on the regulator while I gave him the route. I could tell that he had driven one of these 'S15s', which, like the Horwich 'Crabs', have a small first valve ideal for starting or shunting. But second valve is needed once under way, and the cut-off needs to be wound back to gain this; then open it full, and bring back the regulator handle to mid-position within reach of the driver, the engine remaining in second valve of course. All this our guest driver accomplished without any prompting from me, confirming my belief that he was an ex-Southern man. Considering that he was unfamiliar with the route, he put in a good shift on the regulator and we arrived Pickering on time. He was leaving us here, but we just had time for a photograph and a brief chat. I was right in my assumption of his background when he told me that he was an ex-Nine Elms man who had fired Bulleid 'Pacific' *Yeovil* from Euston to Inverness during the 1948 Locomotive Exchanges. Unfortunately, in all the rush of running round the train with the engine I forgot to ask him his name, but the operating manager had entered it on his footplate pass that he gave me – Bert Hooker.

Afterwards I made it my business to enquire about Bert's railway career. Apparently he was very well known on the Southern and I was pleasantly surprised to hear of some of his high-speed running with steam. He was also the driver on the 'Solway Ranger' in June 1964, when No 35012 *United States Lines* 'flattened' the S&C on its return run from Carlisle – the sparks are still coming down to this day! Much of his railway life is admirably covered in a book he wrote of his days at Nine Elms depot.

My interest in railways also encompassed foreign steam, particularly French motive power, and I made several trips over the Channel to witness the action after the demise of British steam. My favourites were the Chapelon locomotives, which were unbelievably quiet when running, particularly his compounds, added to his enthusiasm for his Kylchap exhaust system. As a footplateman, the different methods of enginemanship adopted by the French crews intrigued me – for instance, the absence of any slacker pipe to keep the dust at bay, the fireman (or *chauffeur*) and the driver (*mecanicien*) usually filthy a short time into the journey, and poor-quality coal, often in the form of briquettes, having to be broken up with the pick, creating more dust. With

a beret on the head and a cheroot hanging out the corner of the mouth, this was the archetypal French steam man.

I managed to blag my way to the granting of a footplate ride from Calais to Lille on board Chapelon 231 'Pacific' No 23E22 after showing the *mecanicien* a few photos of myself on board British steam. It did help of course having the name Fletcher ('Flèche d'Or' being the French name for the 'Golden Arrow') – well, I think it did! Our 'Pacific' had two regulators, cut-off was only ever adjusted by nothing more than 5 per cent each time, and the riding was excellent, although top speed was restricted to about 70mph. I did work the shovel on the easier stretches, punctual running being imperative on the SNCF. From Lille I rode in the train to Paris and was invited to share lunch with them in the depot canteen; this lasted for nearly 2 hours and comprised four courses washed down with a couple of bottles of a fine claret.

During lunch, in broken English, the *chauffeur* explained to me the rudiments of French footplate work; he had opted to remain as a fireman upon joining the railways. Steam drivers came from a different background; with a good standard of education, they served in the workshops for a number of years to gain the mechanical knowledge required before moving to driving. I was taken by surprise when he told me that the retirement age for footplate staff on French railways was 55. We did visit the SNCF again years later in 2007 on a four-day steam-hauled excursion from Paris to Biarritz behind various locomotives, including an American-built '141R' and a Chapelon 'Pacific'. What a difference in exhaust music there was from these two machines, the '141R' typically American, loud and brash – and I mean loud – complete with the blackest smoke display as we approached Toulouse, when the *chauffeur* decided to give the tubes a clean, obliterating the entire station and the large crowd of his fellow citizens who had gathered to observe the passing of the steam special. I doubt any of them actually saw the engine, but they must have been deaf not to have heard this behemoth.

The preserved Chapelon 'Pacific' at Lyon. Now, that's a machine every loco man would like to get to grips with! *Author's collection*

Interestingly, over the entire journey, which involved loco changes, fire cleaning, taking on water and coal, much of this in the confines of busy stations by a team of dedicated support crews, I never saw any of them wearing hi-vis gear. This led me to ask why in Great Britain we seemingly cannot visit the toilet without having to wear a pair of hi-vis underpants, yet in France health & safety is obviously interpreted differently. It was the *mecanicien* who answered my query in typically time-honoured French fashion, saying that 'while you British continue to rigidly comply to every aspect of these rulings, they accept our more relaxed approach and leave us alone.' I said that I had recently read that approximately 50,000 people in the UK are employed by the Health & Safety Executive, and asked him if he knew how many the French employed in the same capacity. He paused to think for a few moments then said approximately no one that he knew of! This was followed by a short tirade of logic about accidents and claims that, in the UK, 'if you trip up and fall down it is your own stupid fault for not looking where you are going!' End of story.

Another country that persevered with steam traction for longer than the UK was Germany. My only visit there was made in 2008 to a 'Plandampf' or steam festival, incorporating a visit to the Hartz mountain railway, our base for three of the days being at Neustadt. The first day was spent watching the arrivals of the locos from all over Germany; approximately 15 took part,

and we attended the photo shoot at the depot in the evening. My first impression of seeing the locos was the uniformity of German steam, all in black livery with red wheels – no petty disputes here regarding what colour or shade they should carry! Neustadt depot was quite extensive, but was able to house only about half the attending fleet under cover, the remainder having to stand outside in the open. As usual I put my foot in it when I asked one of the German stewards why this was.

'Because your RAF bombed it and the bloody signal box!'

This was my first day and I had somehow innocently brought up the war, but the next day I made up for it when I made friends with a German who was firing one of the huge 'Pacifics'. I was allowed onto the footplate at Karlsruhe while the engine was being serviced, and permitted to put a round of coal into the huge firebox before departure, so I thanked her as I climbed off the engine. Yes, that's right, 'her' – she was a fraulein, and a big girl with a mop of purple hair. Definitely not the sort of lass you would want to upset. Here again the absence of any form of hi-vis clothing was noticeable.

No loco livery disputes here at the Neustadt 'Plandampf' – all the locos are painted black with red wheels. *Author's collection*

Now, I may be giving the impression of being anti-health & safety. Far from it – we all want to work in a safe environment and the tightening of some outdated safety measures is welcomed, but I feel that in this country we have gone over the top in enforcing legislation that previously came under the category of plain old common sense.

Having got that off my chest, I want to let you into a secret ambition of mine – to live in an old railway station restored to its former glory as it would have been in the halcyon days of steam, with me as station master and Jacqueline as station porter. Or perhaps the other way round! Such a property rarely comes on the market, the chances being even smaller if you want to live in a certain area. We did look at one years ago at Ribbleton, on the former Preston to Longridge line, but a large

housing estate would eventually surround the area and we lost interest. It wasn't until about ten years ago that interest was revived in the idea, when not one but two properties became known to us in our adopted county of North Yorkshire, the downside being that they would be for rental only. However, we decided to view them, being situated not far away on the former Malton-Driffield line.

The village station at North Grimston had been converted into bungalow-type accommodation on the single platform, but still had plenty of scope to restore some original character, with the bonus of a large piece of land, formerly the trackbed and goods siding, which came with the property. The next station up the line towards Driffield was at Wharram, which was possibly being made available for rent with somewhat larger three-bedroom accommodation and the former booking office on the platform, coal drops, loading dock and water column all still intact. As the station had closed to passengers in 1950, the whole place was like a time warp, and nearby was the mediaeval village of Wharram Percy. The area was much more isolated than North Grimston, and this appealed to me so I decided to go for this second option, but there was a potential problem with the letting, for if an estate employee applied for the property the owners were obliged to give preference to them, and this is what actually happened a few weeks later, so my ambitious plans to eventually reopen the entire line fell by the wayside. I am pleased to add that a preservation society, The Yorkshire Wolds Railway, has established a site near the former Sledmere & Fimber station, were some track has already been laid. I could have given them my wholehearted support had I been the station master at nearby Wharram!

Our grandchildren love the North Yorkshire Moors and riding on the railway when they come to visit us in Grosmont; the youngest, Jaxon, aged 8, is extremely independent and loves to help me in running the shop. We get along fine, both of us being about the same age! My eldest grandson, Alex, has spent some time with me on the footplate as a trainee fireman, and was making good progress despite letting go of the shovel into the firebox at Pickering. This led to my fireman Neil Barker firing the engine on an eight-coach train back to Grosmont with a household shovel, hastily purchased from Cooper's hardware shop across the main road! We mentioned this to no one, yet the day after, when we climbed aboard our engine for the day, GWR 0-6-2T No 6619, there were six firing shovels on the footplate! Neil was a natural engineman, and I was his mentor over the seven years that it took him to rise from cleaner to driver,

Me and my regular fireman Neil Barker with Bulleid 'Pacific' No 34101 *Hartland* enjoying our silly selves at Pickering while awaiting a return working to Grosmont. *Author's collection*

On ex-Southern 'S15' No 30841, this was Neil's enforced substitute firing implement for working an eight-coach return from Pickering, which he mastered completely throughout the 18-mile run. *Author's collection*

achieving probably the fastest promotion by anyone in that department. He would have made an inspector had his life not ended in such a tragic way some 20 years ago – he is still sadly missed on the railway.

Music is the No 1 interest with grandson Alex these days; he has become an accomplished guitarist and briefly played in a group, but made the mistake of asking me if I could think up a novel name for them. One of the group worked in cardiology at the local hospital, but I don't think he was too impressed when I suggested 'Dicky Hart and the Pacemakers'. A few months later I heard that the group had split up, and when I next saw him I told him that it was such a shame, but under the circumstances I had thought of a more appropriate name for them – 'Disbanded'. Anyway, *I* thought it was funny!

In 2016 the NYMR presented long-service awards to those with 30 years' involvement with the railway, and I received mine, although my length of service was 34 years. During this lengthy period I have seen so many changes in operating and staffing levels on the railway, and the extension of our services by a further 6 miles into Whitby, making a 24-mile journey from Pickering, while on certain dates you can

travel another 18 miles from Grosmont to Battersby. Thus 42 miles of steam travel, or a complete round trip of 84 miles, is sometimes possible. It requires a lot of manpower (and womenpower) to operate Britain's busiest heritage railway, and it would be impossible to turn a wheel without the input from a large and dedicated volunteer labour force backed up by about 115 full-time staff at the time of writing.

The present timetable sees most services from Pickering going through to Whitby, but as I write this our railway has come under a new regime and the early signs are of a more business-like approach being developed rather than simply just the running of trains from A to B. After all, we have all the ingredients, having been gifted a landscape of beautiful scenery complete with a steam railway running through the middle of it, and have graduated from the days when all that was required was to light up a steam engine and folk would come flocking from miles around. Not so these days, when we are an established part of the local tourist industry competing with the likes of Flamingo Land, Eden Camp, Sea Life, etc. People expect all the facilities for a day out, and rightly so.

23 'The Jacobite' and *Hogwarts Castle*

When visiting France and Germany and the Kent & East Sussex Railway, my two travelling companions were Kevin Gould and his cousin Sean Bowler. These two boys had travelled extensively in the railway world and it was they who unwittingly became responsible for introducing me to the next and final part of my footplate career. Both of them worked for the North Yorkshire Moors Railway, Kevin as an experienced driver and part-owner of 'Standard 4' No 75014, while Sean was an engineer, having previously served with the RAF. During a conversation with them one spring morning the subject of holidays came up – well, railway holidays to be precise. It came as a surprise to be told that they were off to Scotland as part of the support crew working 'The Jacobite' steam train service from Fort William to Mallaig, which they had done for a number of years – but it was all new to me. So, not having any idea what it involved, I became a little more interested when told that some of the duties entailed being on the footplate as the owner's rep and assisting the fireman if requested to do so. They explained further that the accommodation for the week was not in a four-star hotel, but just a converted Mark 1 coach with bunk beds, or sleeping in the compartments; a kitchen filled the remainder of the available space. It was an early morning start, lighting up and preparing the engine, and a late finish after the 84-mile round trip, followed by engine disposal

duties. Remuneration was nil apart from an allowance for some essential foodstuffs. Was I still interested?

Well, I must have been to have spent some four separate weeks up there that year alone on support crew work. This brought me to the attention of the train operating company, West Coast Railways, and its resident inspector/driver Peter Kirk. The following year I was invited to join the footplate staff subject to a medical, a rules test and a firing exam, which satisfied Inspector Kirk. I passed on engine No 48151 working a Morecambe-Ravenglass special, with booked fireman Kevin Gould keeping an expert eye on proceedings, shortly before his own promotion to driver. Of course such an important day had to have an amusing incident. We turned the engine on the triangle in Sellafield Works where security was tight, all staff being searched beforehand and sniffer dogs checking everybody and everything including our 8F steam loco. I did warn the dog's handler of the hot spots around the loco, his reply was that his dog wasn't bloody stupid and was only doing its job. When it made the mistake of sniffing the cylinder drain cock pipes which were red hot it lept back a wagon length squealing and howling was then removed from duty and taken to the first aid hut to have its nose bandaged and vasalined!

So I became a fireman again after the third exam of my career, but this time I was resuming my duties as a main-line fireman after a 30-year break! Over the next five years I came to know the whole West Highland line and its Mallaig extension, becoming one of the regular firemen on this beautiful line, this time being paid for the work and sharing the duties with being shop manager and a driver on the NYMR. I think it is very fortunate that I do enjoy railways!

Motive power used on the West Highland line varied season to season depending on availability: gutsy 2-6-0 'Mogul' No 62005 and its LNER stablemate 'B1' Class No 61264, ex-LMS 8F No 48151, BR 'Standard 4' No 75014 and 'Black 5' No 44767 were all quite capable machines over this steeply graded line. The wet climate contributed to the locomotives' performance around the tight curves by acting as a lubricant on the wheel flanges. A real bonus for me was the fact that most of the drivers with whom I shared the footplate at West Coast were ex-BR steam men, so we spoke the same language, and of course some of them were still real characters.

One of the first drivers I worked with was Tony Brassington, or 'Brasso' to his mates, who rolled his own cigarettes. At that time I was still learning the road to Mallaig and the exact location of the gradients. As the week went by I became aware of a foible he had, which unwittingly gave me an indication of the road ahead, for whenever he started to roll a fag I noticed that shortly afterwards a gradient would appear in front of us, so whenever I saw the fag tin come out it was time to get shovelling in preparation for the climb, prompting him to remark by midweek that it was unusual for a new fireman to pick up the route so quickly over the 84 miles – so he rolled me a fag in appreciation! Whenever or wherever I went with Tony I always had plenty of steam for him, and he would often remark how uncanny this was, considering that I had never been over many of the routes before. My only real worry when firing for Tony was that if he ever decided to pack up smoking I wouldn't know where we were!

Another good thing about Tony was that he was always prepared for any emergency, and was short of nothing in his bag, the contents of which resembled a mobile shop, with a choice of beverages ranging from tea (four flavours), coffee, decaf coffee, cocoa, drinking chocolate, Horlicks, pop, water, milk (two varieties), cream, brown sugar, white sugar and sweetener, plus small packs of biscuits, packets of salt, pepper, vinegar, sauces, jams, marmalades, a full range of plastic forks, spoons and knives, together with toiletries, soaps, shampoos, hand creams and the obligatory toilet rolls. It was more like a survival kit, but did come in very handy if we were stranded in a loop in the middle of nowhere.

Another good driver

'The Jacobite' with 'K1' No 62005 *Lord of the Isles*, fireman 'Fletch' and driver Tony Brassington ('Brasso') at Fort William station *Author's collection*

mate I had on the line was a legend – or leg end – Frank Santrian, whose footplate career had taken in 5D Stoke, 3D Aston and 5A Crewe. He was a fit lad despite being a good ten years older than me, and was always on the go. 'The Jacobite' had the convenient signing-on time of 08.30, but Frank was up and about well before that at 05.00, urging me to join him on his daily 5-mile constitutional around the streets of Fort William or for a bike ride around Ben Nevis, all this after spending a couple of hours the night before with him in the local swimming baths seemingly rehearsing for a cross-Channel swim!

Our company provided us with a car for travel from the hotel (yes, hotel for paid staff) to the loco depot, stopping off on the way to collect our guard, Florence 'Nightingale'. True to form Frank would always be first in the car with the engine running and already in first gear with the radio tuned to the local Fort William channel blaring out his favourite bagpipe music or some Jock giving advice on how best to cook haggis. There followed a quick burst to Florence's residence and, while we never caught her in her nightie, there were days when the poor lass could have done without the rush inflicted upon her each morning.

About an hour later, having left the depot, we had shunted the train into Fort William station and could sit back and relax for about 45 minutes before departure. Sorry, did I say relax? Not when Frankie was about!

'Come on, Fletch, let's give Florence a lift to water the coaches and to clean the windows,' he would urge me, 'because its ladies' day today,' which to Frank meant that any lady who approached the engine would be told that and invited to climb onto the footplate and inspect the engine. Just to clarify, it was actually ladies' day every day and Frank would be in his element telling them of his 50 years on the railway. If he

forgot any detail he would turn to me to prompt him, as I heard the same stories every day.

'The Jacobite' steam service attracted plenty of foreign visitors, including the Yanks, who were particularly curious about the motive power heading the train. One morning, when our engine was No 62005, I was asked the usual question by an American guy: 'Hey stoker, does this locomotive have a name? Just what class is she?'

I told him it wasn't named and that it was a 'K1' Class.

With that he turned to his wife and laughingly remarked, 'Gee, Martha, I ain't never heard of one of these, but I have seen a K9 – that was the dog in that there Dr Who movie!'

Well, that was it for me. I had become fed up with telling people that it had no name, just a 'K1' 'Mogul', so I wrote a letter that same night to the owners of the engine, the North Eastern Locomotive Preservation Group (NELPG), suggesting that for marketing purposes the loco should carry a name when working 'The Jacobite' train. At the next NELPG meeting I gave a short presentation, after which my suggestion was discussed and received a favourable response. Two names were put forward, both deemed to be suitably connected with the West Highland line and having been formerly carried by Gresley 'K4' Class locomotives built for the line: *Cameron of Locheil* and my personal choice, *Lord of the Isles*. A vote was taken and it was agreed that when working in Scotland the 'K1' locomotive No 62005 would carry the name *Lord of the Isles*. My offer to contribute towards the costs of casting the nameplates was naturally accepted, and it gave me a feeling of great pride to be present at the naming ceremony and to be involved with Frank on the unique occasion of working the inaugural trip to Mallaig with No 62005 sporting its new nameplates.

Driver Frank Santrian, the legend, with 'leg end' trouble after setting his overalls on fire during the 'clinker contest'. *Author's collection*

Upon arrival in Mallaig much favourable comment was expressed by passengers and locals savouring the rarity of the event. It was generally agreed that the name represented the true essence of transport in the Isles and that it was remarkable that it hadn't been thought of sooner. So, after all the backslapping and congratulations followed by shunting the train ready for the return run, it was time for another of Frank's daily rituals involving me, the 'clinker contest'. During the lunchtime break the fire was cleaned and clinker removed – usually the support crew had this on their duty list, but not when Frank was the driver. He insisted on doing the job, and of course his trusty mate – me – helped him. That's what the contest was about – who could withdraw the biggest piece of clinker from the firebox without it breaking up. He usually won, apart from the day when he got too near the red-hot clinker and set fire to his overalls and ruined them, involving him in the expense of buying a new pair of overalls from me, via the Shed Shop.

Whoever lost the 'clinker contest' bought the lunchtime chips from the harbour café, and on that inaugural day it was me. We were sitting on the harbour wall watching people and the boats entering and leaving Mallaig harbour when Frank spotted McBrayne's ferry from the Isle of Skye coming in to dock; as it turned to reverse back to the jetty, its name came into view and our hearts both sank when we saw that our steam engine's nameplate

Our *Lord of the Isles* rival docks at Mallaig harbour – but it was not a coal-fired version like ours! *Author's collection*

Aboard 8F No 48151, with driver John ('Paddy') McCabe at the regulator and his fireman 'Buzby' Fletcher. *Author's collection*

Publicity given to the filming of the 'Hogwarts Express' via my son's Central Trains' staff magazine. *Author's collection*

was not the unique item we thought it to be, as the huge ferry boat docked alongside us boldly displaying the name *Lord of the Isles*!

Another driver with whom I worked on a regular basis was John McCabe, or 'Paddy' to his mates. Like Frank, he was good company, having had a long footplate career at the Carlisle sheds Kingmoor and Upperby. After one memorable trip with him I gained a new nickname, 'Buzby', so do read on.

The fleet of locos owned by West Coast Railways have featured in many films, but the star of the show has to be ex-GWR No 5972 *Olton Hall*, better known of course as the loco that features in the 'Harry Potter' films as *Hogwarts Castle*. The West Highland line's iconic Glenfinnan Viaduct was selected by the producers for some railway scenes to feature in four of the films. Paddy and myself were rostered to work the six-coach empty stock train, with John Dooley as the guard and Brian Caldwell as the travelling fitter on the two-day 300-mile journey to Fort William for the inaugural filming, which would take about a week to complete.

All went well on the first leg of the trip. After leaving Carnforth in the morning, a stop was made at Carlisle for water. We left there on time, briefly reaching the loco's maximum allowed speed of 75mph before a booked visit to the down loop at Quintinshill, witnessed by a bevy of photographers anxious to capture the visit of a steam locomotive briefly at rest where so many soldiers unwittingly came to rest due to a signalman's tragic error on a May morning in 1915.

Our present-day 'signaller' in Carlisle

No 5972 *Olton Hall* assumes its much-changed guise as *Hogwarts Castle* at Carlisle on our journey north to Fort William. Travelling fitter Brian Caldwell is about to complete his exam of the loco. *Author's collection*

power box informed us that, after the passing of two down passenger trains, we would be on our way and that he would give us a run for the 55 miles to our next water stop in the loop at Abington, provided we were on time at Beattock summit thus avoiding being looped there. I was reasonably familiar with the road, knowing that it was exactly 50 miles from Citadel station to the summit of Beattock. The climb begins at milepost 37 just beyond Wamphray for 3 miles at 1 in 202, followed by the brutal 10 miles of 1 in 75 to the top. By comparison with Paddy, my route knowledge to Glasgow was scant. This was his railway, he had been coming over here all his working life, and it was a privilege to share the footplate with him. The real stranger to the route was our motive power, *Hogwarts Castle*, its unique livery and crest attracting the public's attention throughout our journey.

She was a bit lively at our maximum 75mph, which to some may seem a quite satisfactory speed to be travelling with a steam loco, but on the railways of today we were actually the slowest train on this main line. Having quickly adjusted to the engine being right-hand drive by firing it left-handed, and raising the flap after each

charge to retain the heat, the loco was responding to my efforts, ensuring that Paddy has sufficient steam and water as we hit the bottom of the bank at a healthy 70mph. I must apologise, but I won't be able to write much for the next 10 miles or so, being head down and bottom up on the shovel firing this Great Western engine up a damn great hill in Scotland. Ah, the joys of steam preservation! Paddy was handling her like a veteran Swindon man; if he had been wearing a pair of GWR overalls you could have mistaken him for an 82C man. We came over the top of this Caledonian Railway incline at just short of 30mph, a more than respectable effort by the three of us, and, as we were actually a few minutes ahead of time, we avoided sitting in the loop at the top watching the traffic go by.

Paddy let No 5972 have her head on the 7 miles of downhill running before shutting off and entering Abington loop, where all three of us would be having a well-earned drink while ace mechanic Brian Caldwell ensured that all was well with our film star. Everything turned out to be fine as we said goodbye to Abington and the crew of our water tanker. We now had an easy 15-mile downhill run, bringing us to the former grandiose junction station of Carstairs. Oh, how I loved this place in steam days, particularly the vast array of semaphore signalling controlling the wide variety of locomotive and train movements there used to be. It is so much different these days, where just a handful of colour-light signals suffice for the current layout, and it was one of them that signalled us into the down loop for a 20-minute break to allow the passage of two Glasgow-bound flyers.

Leaving there, we had a short 5-mile climb to Craigenhill, then it was downhill for the next 10 miles, passing the site of the former water troughs at Carluke and the array of sidings at Law Junction to just beyond Motherwell. Here we left the West Coast Main Line at Lesmahagow Junction, clear of the early-evening rush that was about to begin. We were now on the Coatbridge line as we passed the site of the former 66B Motherwell steam shed and settled down for a steady plod to our overnight stop in the salubrious surroundings of Moss End Yard.

Arriving there, the yardmaster had kept us an empty road equipped with high-density security lighting and within view of the buildings used by the yard staff, for this place was notorious for theft of anything that was not screwed down or securely locked. As we passed the shunters' cabin, one of them came out and asked us if we had made the engine secure, jokingly offering us the use of his car steering lock. Our support coach was adjacent to the engine and would accommodate the crew overnight, while we had the luxury of a nearby hotel, which in reality barely eclipsed the comforts of the support coach.

After an anxious night our taxi picked us up at 06.00 and whisked us to the yard, where we reported for duty. All appeared to be well: the loco was being coaled, the water tanker arrived and manoeuvred into place adjacent to the tender, and by 08.00 we were ready to depart, leaving the yard via the long goods loop before coming to a stand at the end of it to await our path out onto the main line. Now, Paddy had been quite athletic in his younger days, playing lots of badminton among other sports, but it had left him with a dodgy knee, and I invariably offered to climb down onto the ballast to speak on the phone to the signaller.

Paddy had stopped with the engine about 30 feet from the lineside phone; upon reaching it I opened the door to remove the handset and speak, but there wasn't one. I shut the door and stood back to examine the entire unit, then opened the door again and this time looked more carefully, assuming that the phone had been vandalised. I looked about to see if there was another phone nearby, but with none in view I made my way back to the footplate – but not without opening the door and trying one last time, before having to perform the unenviable task of informing Paddy that the phone must have been vandalised and that I had been unable to contact the signaller. He greeted the news with some dismay, slowly edged his way across the footplate, clambered down the steps and walked with me to the phone. He slowly bent down and opened the door, and to my surprise spoke into the box saying, 'This is the Driver of Five Zulu One Four, standing at Charlie Oscar Two Seven, empty coaching stock for the West Highland line, repeat back if you have received my message.'

I asked Paddy how the signaller could hear when there was no handset? He then told me that these were new vandal-proof phones recently installed in the area; they had an inbuilt speaker concealed in the back, and when you opened the door a bell rang in the signal box, alerting the signaller. Paddy had no sooner finished telling me this when an outburst of loud profanity erupted from the speaker, delivered in a high-pitched Glaswegian tone.

'Are yous tekin the piss – five times a've bin up and doon off ma arse in tha last few minutes! Which prick keeps ringin' ma, an then disna answer?'

Paddy apologised to the signaller on my behalf, telling him that I was a simple Sassenach unfamiliar with the anti-vandal telephones, and from that day on he has always called me 'Buzby', after the talking bird in the TV advert promoting British Telecom, whose catchphrase was 'Make Someone Happy'. This was obviously not the case with our signaller!

Paddy's excellent route knowledge came to the fore during our journey, which took us around the back roads of Glasgow, on to Dumbarton, then coming to a stand at Craigendoran, the junction for Helensburgh at the foot of the West Highland line. Here we took water, and now that we were away from the overhead power lines it was safe to enter the tender and bring coal forward in readiness for some stiff hill-climbing, some of it on gradients steeper than Beattock, on our long journey of 100 miles over this highly scenic route to our destination at the Highland oasis of Fort William. I secretly envy the Scotrail staff who work this line, as you could never tire of travelling along it; it must have been even lovelier when steam ruled the route and burned back the lineside vegetation.

Our former GWR loco was performing well and seemed to be enjoying its working holiday hundreds of miles away from its birthplace. Paddy informed me of the whereabouts of several speed restrictions imposed on the loco as its wider cylinders only just cleared some of the platform edges. We spent some time in the loop at Glen Douglas as the afternoon unit passed us with some incredulous looks from its passengers, all gathered at the right-hand side of the coaches, cameras to hand, to catch a glimpse of the 'Harry Potter' engine. They had obviously been informed of our presence by the train guard, as any news travels pretty quickly around this remote area thanks to the railway's communications system. Near the top of our final climb, before our water stop at Crianlarich, junction for the Oban line, No 5972 was just beginning to drop her head a little, so before tackling the 6 miles of 1 in 60 beyond here to the summit of Corrour we decided to clean the fire and empty the smokebox. I had also been there with steam specials, the route being like most others in this area, rich in steep gradients and curves. The inner man also needs attention, and a visit to the station café here at Crianlarich is to be recommended to sample their home-made flapjack to complement our bacon sarnies and fresh tea.

The weather was keeping fine for us as the newly refreshed ensemble left for the spectacular part of our journey, the next 30 miles of breathtaking scenery incorporating the steep climb to Corrour, the famous Horseshoe curve, and the 'populous' Bridge of Orchy! Followed by the wilds of the incomparable Rannoch Moor, most of the best views are obtained from the driver's side of the cab, but I was fortunate in this being a right-hand-drive locomotive, giving the fireman the best sights between some arduous firing duties on this mountainous road. I have always been in awe of the men who built this railway, and I can slightly relate to some of the problems they must have faced, our own family business of landscape gardening being one of the last professions that demands heavy manual labour undertaken outside in all weathers using traditional hand tools.

We were held at Rannoch for the evening unit for Glasgow to pass, and I must admit to feeling a bit tired at this point, as it had been a long day for us all. Fortunately the hill-climbing was almost coming to an end as we obtained the forward token and entered the next single-line section, having pulled forward yet more coal in the tender, prepared the fire and topped up the boiler in readiness for the final 8 miles of uphill slogging to Corrour. After this we descended for some 20 miles to Spean Bridge, then a short almost unnoticeable rise before coming back down to earth and negotiating the final leg into the great metropolis of Fort William, with less than 1 ton of coal remaining in the tender after our 300-mile adventure to the Highlands.

Our film star would now be in the hands of the support crew for the next day, preparing her for filming. She would be turned, examined, cleaned and serviced ready for the 16-mile run down the West Highland Mallaig extension to Glenfinnan, to take the stage on another icon from the golden age of railways, Glenfinnan Viaduct, built in mass concrete by Robert McAlpine. We also prepared for our important silver screen debut by linking up with the other footplate crew involved in the filming, spending the remainder of the day sightseeing.

The following morning we were all up and about bright and early trying on the uniforms provided by the film's wardrobe department. They were of a boiler-suit type, maroon in colour to match the locomotive, so they really did look the part with a matching cap and 'Harry Potter' logos. These we had to keep clean; they were only to be worn during the actual filming. Our overnight accommodation had been in a hotel just outside the town adjacent to the Caledonian Canal, a quiet and picturesque location. We travelled from there by taxi after a hearty early Scottish breakfast, arriving in good time at Fort William yard to be greeted by the sight of an immaculately presented *Hogwarts Castle* eagerly awaiting its filming debut, the loco support crew proudly standing by and admiring their handiwork. The resident fitter, Lackie McNeil, was using the Chaseside digger to perform the delicate task of coaling the tender, taking great care not to spoil its cleanliness.

Half an hour later, with shunting complete, we headed down the single-line Mallaig branch with guard Florence aboard our five-coach train to begin the day's filming at Glenfinnan, this time with Frank Santrian on the regulator, Paddy being the afternoon relief driver. We passed over the viaduct, coming to a stand in the station to be welcomed by the film's outside location manager and his crew. We changed into our uniforms and were given radios and issued with cans of aerosol spray as used by the SAS to keep the midges at bay; Glenfinnan is recognised as being the midge capital of Scotland!

We were then briefed on the day's proceedings, which required us to reverse across the viaduct, then travel back towards the station before coming to a stand just short of the points indicator, all movements being filmed by a cameraman in a helicopter flying just above the train. We took instructions by radio from the film crew via the location manager, who was on the footplate with us; he asked that we keep our heads inside the cab when on the move as they were filming the train and not us. He also wanted us to make plenty of steam effects from the pipes at the front, and also from the 'front and back hole' on the top of the engine! By the second day of filming Frank had educated him enough to be able to describe the front pipes as the drain cocks, the front hole as the chimney, and the back hole as the safety valves. We also asked him to give us as much time as possible to prepare the fire and steam pressure before making each full-bloodied attack up the steep gradient leading onto the viaduct if they expected us to attain the maximum 25mph allowed.

During the morning session we passed over the viaduct at least four times in between visits back to the station loop or sidings to allow the Scotrail services to pass. Our relief crew arrived in the early afternoon on the back of a quad bike due to the rural location. We accepted such a lift back to the film company's base camp in a field adjacent to the main road; the glamour of film work had made us hungry, so the complimentary lunch and refreshments went down very well despite the interruption of some young female autograph-hunters who, upon seeing our 'Harry Potter' clothing, assumed we were a couple of actors taking a break from the arduous task of filming. Well, weren't we? Anyway, we signed their autograph books and off they went, looking more than a little perplexed as to who we were.

The following day was even more interesting, with the introduction of a cherry-picker adjacent to the viaduct and a radio-controlled miniature helicopter to gain close-up views down the side of the train as we passed, with the compartments now occupied by schoolchildren in period uniform. Frank and I had become used to the routine adopted by the location man and the pilot of the full-size helicopter, and we were nicely prepared each time the helicopter appeared and hovered over us, the pilot calling 'action' down the radio to us veteran showmen, enjoying the surreal experience of the miniature helicopter flying alongside just a few feet from us.

After we completed our shift I was not going to leave the scene without a closer look at the cherry-picker and hopefully have a demonstration flight with the radio-controlled chopper. Both operators recognised me as one of the footplate crew – well, I think I would have been disappointed if they hadn't, considering that they had spent the last 5 hours using up valuable film on us, even though they informed us that a full four days of filming on the viaduct involving more than 20 run-pasts would amount to little more than a minute of actual screen time. I was offered a lift up to the top of the viaduct in the cherry-picker, but chickened out; that structure is a damn site higher when you are standing at ground level! But I was permitted to stand next to and watch the flying skills of the guy with the little chopper (does that sound right?) expertly flying it alongside the train, filming the action at such a height that it was almost out of view.

In the finished film you will see a Ford Anglia car zooming over Glenfinnan Viaduct! Now, I do not want to be a spoilsport, but during all the four days spent filming there I must admit to never having seen a flying Ford Anglia, or for that matter a stationary one. All personnel involved with the film were sworn to secrecy, but I recently decided to come clean and tell my eight-year old grandson that perhaps that bit wasn't for real, to which he sympathetically replied, 'Grandad, don't feel too bad – it's what they call special effects. Look, I'll show you on my I-Pad.' Suitably told!

I have had quite a long association with No 5972 *Olton Hall*, beginning when the engine visited the NYMR in green livery, then came my time spent as the fireman working charters with it for West Coast Railways, the first of these being a return Chester-Carnforth trip with another Lanky man, Albert Seymour, on his first driving turn for the company, having just retired from Newton Heath depot. I had the pleasure of sharing the footplate with Albert on many occasions. This included further work with No 5972, the toughest being the 'Scarborough Spa Express', which entailed two round trips between York and Scarborough, requiring an early- and late-turn driver but with just the one fireman for the 170-mile shift. The 'SSE' could be loaded to 10 or 11 coaches, which was a heavy train for an engine that was then not in the best of nick. The biggest problem was the valve setting being out, meaning that when you put her into second valve all hell broke loose at the chimney with the exhaust beat; its one saving grace was that, if you fired it right, it would steam. The fireman really earned his corn on that job, which included all the hooking on and off, watering, coaling, turning and assisting with disposal. The situation did improve as loco fitter Brian Caldwell got on top of the job when the engine was out of traffic, giving him the opportunity to use his skills to carry out the necessary repairs.

The last job that I did with the loco was a special involving two round trips from York Museum to sister museum Shildon, top-and-tailed with the 'Hall' and 'Black 5' No 45305 and spread over two consecutive weekends. Operations manager Peter Walker offered me the choice of loco.

'Give me the Hall,' I told him.

'Good – that's what I hoped you'd say, because I couldn't get anybody else to go on it!'

The first run on the Saturday had to be diesel-hauled due to the museum staff being unfamiliar with a GWR 'Hall', which should have had a warming fire lit on the Friday; however, all was well for the afternoon steam trip by the time we returned to York with the diesel. This was to be driver Frank Coupland's first voyage on the engine, so we discussed tactics beforehand, both agreeing that as the 'Hall' was the leading loco outwards to Shildon, it must be allowed to do all the work hauling the nine-coach train, and the 'Black 5' likewise with the return.

After we left the museum to time in the early afternoon, it did take a while for No 5972 to get warm, but she soon began to feather at the valves thanks to a joint effort between driver and fireman, making it an enjoyable day. It was a little breezy on the return, travelling at 60mph tender-first, as we were being dragged as part of the coaching stock. It was a little more interesting the

following weekend when we had Britannia 'Pacific' No 70013 *Oliver Cromwell* as a replacement for the 'Black 5' on the back of the train, but again it was my choice to remain on the temperamental one leading the procession. All went well except that on the return trip neither Chris Cubitt, the driver, nor I anticipated the 75mph tender-first sprint up the East Coast Main Line, but it was perfectly legal as we were being dragged and classed as part of the rolling stock, allowing the 'Brit' to stretch its legs a little. But boy, was it just a bit draughty on the footplate of No 5972 with its open-backed tender! Luckily for me Chris has quite a bulky frame, which acted as a suitable draught-excluder when I positioned myself behind him!

It was with Chris that I had my first ever firing turn on the NYMR and also my maiden voyage for West Coast Railways when we took 'K1' No 62005 from the Moors to his former depot at Thornaby. But how things had changed since the heyday of this former ultra-modern depot constructed at the end of the steam age; demolition has left the place almost unrecognisable, as it has with so many once important outposts from that era. It surely would be heartbreaking if it were possible to bring back some of the old boys from those days to witness the mass destruction of their railway; I am sure that they would find it totally unbelievable.

Having just briefly mentioned No 70013 *Oliver Cromwell* and Chris, the three of us regularly worked the morning 'Scarborough Spa Express' from York via the scenic Knaresborough, Harrogate and Leeds route, this being a particular favourite of mine, never tiring of the outward or the return journey. In fact, if it were possible to reinstate this route, I am sure the three of us would be more than happy to resume our roles!

24 An M6 problem, and to Carlisle yet again

The infant West Coast Railways gradually began to spread its wings after I had been with the company for about three years. It employed more ex-BR steam men, who brought with them a wide variety of route and traction knowledge and experience in the handling of 'foreign' steam power with locos from all the 'Big Four' companies and the BR Standards. Among the men with whom I worked was the much-respected former Crewe Traction Inspector Bill Andrew, whom the company had appointed as Operations Manager. Like me he was a former Lanky man, having started his railway career at Bacup shed.

One of our first jobs together very nearly didn't happen due to problems on my way from Preston to Crewe; the M6 was almost at a standstill for about 6 miles with holiday traffic around Warrington on a hot summer Saturday morning, time was running out on me and the thoughts of delaying or cancelling the job gave me some concern – I did not have a mobile phone then, and the loco was stabled on Crewe Heritage Centre prior to us working over the Midland to Carlisle. Drastic measures were called for, so I pulled onto the hard shoulder with my classic Merc and opened the bonnet about 4 inches, clipped it into place and drove down the hard shoulder at about 10mph passing all the stationary traffic. No one was abusive – they just assumed that I was having engine problems – and after passing the lot of them I stopped and shut the bonnet, rejoined the carriageway and shot off in the fast lane, next stop Crewe.

On arrival I parked at the station and with just minutes to go before our booked departure I ran down the steps to the platform and there standing in one of the bays was our engine, having come off the shed with the support crew's Responsible Officer (RO) Brell Ewart standing in as the temporary fireman. All that I had time for was a quick apology as within minutes our electric-hauled 12-coach train arrived in the adjacent platform. Its loco hooked off and ran forward onto the Chester line, allowing Bill to draw forward with our support coach and set back onto the train. As our guard was controlling the movement at the driver's side I was now able to concentrate on building up the fire on the 50-square-foot grate of Stanier 'Pacific' No 6233 *Duchess of Sutherland*.

After piecing up the train and carrying out a brake test, which took about 15 minutes, during which I had built up the fire, we eased our way out of Cheshire's No 1 railway station and headed on to the down fast line on the first part of our journey to Cumberland's capital city of Carlisle.

Previous experience with this big girl told me that she did need time to warm through. I had given her a good breakfast of nearly a ton of coal into the back corners, and sure enough 8 miles down the line, passing Winsford, I could feel the extra heat coming from the fire, the pressure gauge had risen to just 5lb below maximum at 245lb and water was at three-quarters of a glass, so it was on with the exhaust injector. Our speedometer was also just 5 below maximum at 70mph, prompting Bill and I to exchange a quick thumbs-up, indicating that all was well with the three of us. We also got a nod of approval from Brell Ewart, standing behind Bill and watching our handling of the locomotive.

I had hold of the shovel again passing Hartford (the scene of a previous story from 40 years earlier). The railway rises a little here, so a look into the firebox, using the shovel to deflect the glare, told me that the back corners and sides needed feeding, and 20 shovelsful down each side and ten under the door suitably dealt with the situation. It interests me to know whether other firemen count each shovel of coal every time they fire a loco; I have always done this since my youth, finding that it relieves the monotony and can also improve your judgement of just how much coal is required at a particular time. It is important for a fireman to pace himself, particularly on a hot day when feeding a large-firebox engine. I always wear a pair of welder's lightweight gauntlets when firing these engines, reminiscent of post-war firemen wearing ex-services black berets and motorbike gauntlets to protect the arms when firing into the back corners. My bib and brace footplate overalls conform to BR style and the wearing of any hi-vis clothing is strictly forbidden on my footplate.

My 'fuel transfer tool' is a hybrid Southern/Western, the medium-size blade making it not too heavy. Having some knowledge of three factors on the journey can save a lot of wasted energy with the shovel: the road ahead, whether it is level, uphill or downhill, and remembering my motto 'Be prepared', particularly when working on engines of this size, where it can take many minutes of continuous shovelling to make an impression on the grate. Fortunately most of the jobs operated by the company are over my former stamping grounds, but in the case of any uncertainty I always discuss with the driver, remembering that it is a team job we are doing.

Speaking of this, Bill closed the regulator to coast down the hill, leaving just a breath of steam on, and we passed through Warrington at our regulation 75mph. Then it was firing time again, preparing for the next 15 miles on mostly rising gradients to the summit at Coppull. For the first time on our journey we began to hear the 'Duchess' getting into her stride as she attacked the climb to Golborne, the heavy double-chimney beat echoing back off the sides of the deep cutting. Bill was using his customary style of driving this big 'Pacific' with full regulator and controlling the power output by expert use of the cut-off, befitting his years of experience in handling these machines. We surmounted the climb and she leaned over on this canted and curved stretch as the sun highlighted the shining maroon paintwork on her long boiler.

We took advantage of the short change in gradient, and as we approach Bamfurlong, the former stamping ground of the ex-LNWR 'Super Ds', a feeling of sadness came over me, but soon disappeared as we passed Springs Branch depot, where a contingent of 'pie-eaters' had turned out to give us a wave as we passed. I acknowledged with an 'Ilkley Moor' on the engine's Stanier hooter.

A further inspection of the fire after being given a clear run through Wigan prompted me to pick up the shovel again and fill up the back corners, being careful not to overdo it because once we were over the top it is downhill to Farington Junction. I never tired of hearing this engine climbing the hills and doing just what it was built for on its home ground, the West Coast Main Line. It was an absolute credit to those unsung guys who helped maintain her in such tip-top condition that the riding quality was superb: it couldn't have been much more comfortable riding in one of the coaches.

I looked out of the cab as we rushed through Leyland station, knowing that a few of my former footplate mates from Lostock Hall would be gathered on the platform to capture the scene, as they did whenever a steam special was about. I gave a good long blast on the whistle and got a friendly wave in exchange. Then the moment had gone, as Bill cancelled the AWS horn, warning us of the double-yellow aspect for the junction route ahead at Farington, where we swung to the right and joined the Blackburn line, this being my own back yard up to Hellifield. However, the scenery was much changed since my days in the 1960s.

It did not surprise us to be brought to a stand at Lostock Hall for the first time since leaving Crewe, obeying the red aspect of the signal protecting the junction with the line from Preston, joining us to our left. This time I could not blame my old mate Ged in the Carriage Sidings signal box for delaying us, as they were both long gone. The real reason we were waiting there was because we had arrived nearly 10 minutes before our booked time, and there was no chance of leaving early as we had a booked stop for water in a most unusual, if not unique, location at one of the wayside stations between there and Blackburn at Cherry Tree, the erstwhile junction for the line over Brinscall through Heapey, which joined the Preston-Manchester line at Chorley.

Bill returned from speaking on the lineside phone to the signaller in Preston power box, who had told him that we would be leaving to time once the local Colne service passed through and that we had a maximum of 20 minutes to give the tender a drink at Cherry Tree. I had plenty to do in the time available before departure; 5 miles of 1 in 100 lay ahead of us, and as the coal was no longer within reach of the shovel it was time to bring the coal pusher into operation. Brell offered to see to this task while I took the opportunity of a well-earned drink of water mixed with rehydration powders from my trusty enamel heavy-duty flask, my constant companion at all times when working on main-line steam. With

the coal pusher now dormant, I began to transfer its contribution around the firebox, concentrating where the 'Duchess' likes to be fed, in the back corners, then, just as two of the four safety valves began to feather, we got the road. Once clear of the junction, for the first time we were away from the 'chicken mesh' (overhead catenary) and it was safe to use the slacker pipe, so it was on with the exhaust injector and within a couple of minutes we were dust-free on the footplate and tender – it is much more pleasurable working in a cleaner environment!

A quick word here about the connection between the overhead wires and the 'Duchess' 'Pacifics'. After withdrawal from traffic, some of the copper fireboxes from these engines were melted down at Derby Works and converted to copper wire with added silicon, being used in the overhead electrification of the West Coast Main Line, thus enabling a section of obsolete motive power to contribute to the running of modern trains. Just thought I would slip that one in, hopefully keeping you from falling asleep!

We were now passing over Bamber Bridge level crossing at 35mph, 1½ miles from a standing start at Lostock Hall. More importantly for us, this was the bottom of the 5-mile climb to the summit at Hoghton, and as I finished firing I clipped together the firehole doors, leaving a nice 2-inch gap for admission of secondary air. Combined with a fully open back damper and a one- notch opening of the front, this usually meant that, if you had fired it right, a glance at the chimney would indicate good combustion, and the next thing to happen should be an upward movement of the boiler pressure gauge needle. I must have climbed this hill hundreds of times since the early 1960s working on a wide variety of motive power and trains, which gave me an intimate insight into just what effort would be required from each individual locomotive.

I estimated that Bill would use his customary full regulator setting, varying the cut-off between 35 and 45% as we ascended the climb with our 13-coach train. Half way up, passing Mintholme crossing, I leaned out of the cab to check the exhaust. This had now cleared, steam was steady at 225lb against the injector, and this four-cylinder giant of steam was effortlessly gobbling up the gradient with the ground underneath us vibrating to the deep-throated exhaust beat as Bill dropped her down to his benchmark 45%. This brought me into action again, answering with a 35-shovelful burst into the back corners and sides of the firebox, creating a dark exhaust that pleased the gathered throng of photographers at Hoghton level crossing adjacent to the former station and signal box and 1 mile from the summit.

The pub next to the level crossing, 'The Sirloin', is a centuries-old coaching inn just a minute's walk from the medieval castle at Hoghton Towers. It was there that legend has it King James I knighted a loin of beef he had enjoyed, and in remembrance of the event a pub within the parish was renamed accordingly. I wish that I hadn't mentioned that steak, as hunger was beginning to take a grip on me, not having eaten since breakfast, but I revived a little as we surmounted the summit in good order at a steady 40mph and begin the 4-mile downhill dash to Cherry Tree through the picturesque Hoghton Bottoms. I had now brought the live steam injector into life to ensure a full pot of water when we came to a stand. Pleasington station came up before then, but there was actually more life on the adjacent golf course, and the novelty of seeing a steam locomotive taking on water at the next wayside halt ensured a good turnout of curious sightseers as we drew to a stand in Cherry Tree station.

We were quickly united with the road tanker and piped up for the intake of water. The engine's support crew began to mill about, oiling and checking the running gear. One of them asked permission to go underneath the loco at the front end to deal with a sticking inside cylinder drain cock that had been blowing since our last stop. Fortunately one of the members had carried out the most important task of any support crew when he appeared on the footplate with our cups of tea and bacon butties, which looked so good it was a shame to eat them! Stopping there was a break from the usual format, replacing a Hellifield water stop and making us right away to Appleby. The route to Hellifield is not too arduous once you top the climb from Blackburn at Wilpshire, then there are a few more bits of uphill after Clitheroe and a pull into Hellifield, but it would be quite a change to pass through there without stopping.

With the three of us suitably refreshed, it was time to associate myself once more with my trusty 'fuel transfer tool', the coal pusher having been in action again during our break. Thirty times the blade entered the firebox before I was satisfied that it would be enough until we passed through the tunnel just beyond Blackburn station and joined the Hellifield line at Daisyfield Junction.

As we pulled away and said goodbye to Cherry Tree and seemingly its entire populace, Bill closed the cylinder drain cocks and as it was now all quiet from there. He turned and gave a nod of satisfaction to Mick, the support crew wizard now on board with us to Appleby. During the steady pull through the revamped Blackburn station I carefully scrutinised the platform in the faint hope of seeing the return of a popular public attraction from my youth, the beautiful glass-cased model of an Isle of Man steamship, the ultimate marketing item of a once proud company now owned by a Portuguese bank, which has yet to see the potential publicity of the ship's return.

Bill kept her going steadily through the wet tunnel, carefully avoiding the risk of

slipping, then as we emerged we sighted
a green signal with route indicator, and
branched left onto the Hellifield line. The
fire wanted my attention now that we were
clear of the tunnel, to get us over the top
of this short steep climb through the outer
suburbs of Blackburn. However, my firing
needed to be carefully limited as, once we
were over the top, we were faced with a steep
5-mile descent to Whalley (pronounced
'Wall-e'). I had a rare opportunity to relax a
little now as we descended the bank passing
through Langho, and my mind drifted back
to briefly relive the incident with the train
fire there in 1967. The rumbling noise under
the footplate reawakened me to the present
day as we travelled over the lofty Whalley
Viaduct, then through Clitheroe where
my sister Judith lived for many years in the
nearby village of West Bradford.

The tall chimney of the cement works
at Horrocksford is visible for miles around
here, and during the construction of the M6
motorway in the 1960s we had regular jobs
from there hauling the cement trains to Shap
summit. Those block trains were heavy and
from memory the maximum load for a 'Black
5' was about 14 'Presflo' wagons.

Fifteen minutes running time from
Clitheroe brought us to the ornamental
portals of Gisburn Tunnel, which could be
described as a folly, for when the line was
constructed in 1850 the Lister family at
nearby Gisburne Hall (with an 'e') took legal
action to ensure that their estate would not
be affected by the new railway, hence the
short, shallow 156-yard tunnel. Once we
were through, our brief relaxation was over
and it was time to 'be prepared' for what
lay ahead of us beyond Settle Junction, the
starting point of the 25 miles to Ais Gill
summit, including the small matter of the
15-mile continuous climb of 1 in 100 to
Blea Moor. Mick and I discussed tactics; he
would operate the coal pusher on the climb,
enabling me to concentrate on the firing.

Bill and I were a good team, having
worked together for some time. He was a true
professional, and we were on his favourite
engine. I was also familiar with his handling
of the locomotive, and he in turn hopefully
had confidence in me as his fireman. On
the approaches to Hellifield I began to build
up a fire, holding back somewhat in case
we were checked either there or at Settle
Junction. The big 'Duchess' wound her way
off the Clitheroe branch onto the Skipton-
Carlisle line, and as we passed the station
box at Hellifield the signalman slid open the
window and shouted across to us, 'You are
right away Blea Moor!' This was just what
we wanted to hear, so let battle commence!

We had a nice 3-mile drop in gradient
to the junction, giving me the chance to
get an absolute roaster on – 50 shovelsful
matched our 50mph as we hit the bottom,
where the junction signalman was out with
his camera and shouting encouragement,
but his words were drowned as Bill gave Sir
William's finest full second valve and wound
her down to 45% cut-off. Our exhaust acted
as a warning to those people a little too close
to the platform edge as we blasted through
Settle station, with the pressure gauge edging
towards the red mark approaching Taitlands
Tunnel. I chose to use the live steam injector
to steady the pressure and would probably
keep it on for most of the climb, which
should maintain a healthy three-quarters of a
glass on the gauge frame.

What is of importance when working this
locomotive is to absolutely avoid any heavy
blowing off from the safety valves. The boiler
is fitted with four of them, with the working
pressure set at 250lb. With experience you
can work any train and avoid the risk of
lifting the valves by using 230/240lb on the
gauge as your maximum with a locomotive in
this power range.

Our run to Carlisle was going well, the
bright sunshine enhancing some panoramic
views of the magnificent Yorkshire scenery

on this most beautiful of railway lines – it is nearly as nice as my native Lancashire! No 6233 is doing everything we ask of her as she pounds up the hill in charge of us two ex-Lanky men. Mick has kept me supplied with a plentiful amount of coal, my driver is using the steam as economically as possible, each stride bringing us nearer the top, as Ribblehead Viaduct comes into view at my side just as my mate closes the regulator and reopens to first valve, which somewhat quietens our twin-chimney exhaust beat. Unlike the once double-tracked viaduct from our day, it is now single, with a 20mph speed limit, preventing us from a possible 50mph topping of Blea Moor. The signalman gave us a clear run over this magnificent monument to the steam age, and I glanced down at the lucky patrons of the Ribblehead boozer, all of them enjoying a pint outside in the sunshine. I regretted having done so, as it made me feel ever so thirsty; just a few weeks earlier Jacqueline and I had been there on a day's outing in one of the vintage coaches operated three times a week by Cumberland Classic Coaches from Kirkby Stephen.

As is customary when crossing the viaduct, the engine whistle saw plenty of action, which brought to life everybody in the surrounding area, who exchanged our greeting with friendly waves. I often wonder whether people wave if it is one of the regular diesel units traversing the viaduct. Moreover, I have never really been a big fan of the hooter that Sir William fitted to most of his locomotives, which tended to choke themselves and you could hardly describe them as being melodious, but I have written to him at Crewe Works suggesting that the next batch of engines he builds be fitted with the 'Britannia'/'Standard 5' chime whistle!

The present-day double-glazed Blea Moor signal box is a much-modernised version of the one from the steam age. Gone is the 'bucket and chuck it' toilet – it even has electricity and running water. As we passed the box my offer of a few shovels of coal was turned down, as his modern electric fire has no use for it! Our own fire was in good shape, sufficient to see us over the top to Ais Gill as we entered the supposedly haunted Blea Moor Tunnel, the longest on the line at 2,629 yards. Passing through in the pitch blackness, with just the light from the fire illuminating the footplate, I can honestly say that I have never seen anything that would frighten me, and I have fired for some gruesome-looking drivers over the years (present company excepted, of course).

A few miles further on we passed through the highest main-line station in England at Dent. In steam days this landmark was a reminder to the fireman to prepare himself for picking up water on Garsdale troughs not far ahead. Perhaps you could put it down to the years of footplate familiarity drilled into us, but Bill and I both instinctively turned round to check the tender water gauge as we passed over where the troughs had once been. We had a short final burst through the two tunnels that brought us out at the site of Ais Gill signal box and the former up and down loops, the milepost on the up side telling us that we were now 260 miles from St Pancras.

Prior to its closure and removal to Butterley, the signal box at this bleak and isolated spot was usually occupied by a friendly incumbent, one of whom gave me his own version of the weather in that area, telling me that they often had six months of winter followed by six months of bad weather! He was also well versed in the facts surrounding the train crashes that occurred near here in 1910 and 1913, his party piece being to quote the words of the unfortunate Hawes Junction signalman: 'Sir, I beg to inform you that I have wrecked the Scotch express.'

Our train was now on the 15 miles of downhill running to the outskirts of Appleby, followed by a slight knoll of a couple of miles before reaching the station. We were travelling at the line's regulation maximum speed of 60mph for steam, Bill was letting the engine drift with just a breath of steam on, and I was sitting on my perch following a clean-up of the footplate and watering of the coal in the tender to keep the swirling dust to a minimum. I was also keeping a watchful eye on the road ahead, the 'Duchess' riding the curves like the great lady she was. The fire and I were both having a well-earned break, as it had not been touched since before Ribblehead – nor will it be until we are ready for departure after taking water at Appleby.

Our iron horse came to a stand at this town famous for the Appleby horse fair. I keep on meaning to come and visit the place when in full swing each year in early June, as my father worked as a ploughman with horses in the 1920s; but they have never really interested me, being of the opinion that they bite at the front and kick at the back! After enjoying a sandwich and a cold drink I rejoined the footplate, now inhabited by a couple of lads from the support crew busy with the maintenance work. More coal was to hand courtesy of the coal pusher, and we had 15 minutes before departure, giving me just enough time to build up the fire again. Then I was asked by one of the support crew members, a young lad called Simon, if he could have a go on the shovel; in fact, he just happened to have his own Lucas shovel with him, so how could I refuse?

Our guard whistled up the passengers to return to the train following a leg-stretching stroll on the platform to look at or perhaps take a photo of the locomotive. Bill had a look at his watch; we were due away, so he brought the engine whistle into action, our guard responded with a green flag, and we left behind the bustling market town of Appleby. We now had about 30 miles of almost downhill running to Carlisle, my

apprentice had skilfully built up a heavy fire covering the grate on this less than spectacular final leg of our 160-mile journey from Crewe, and the track condition over part of this stretch can be best described as lively. A couple of times the usual smooth-riding 'Pacific' lifted us off our feet and, when passing Howes Siding, the tea can on the warming plate went into orbit, spilling the entire contents over the cab floor. Fortunately the remainder of the footplate equipment was fastened down or stowed away for safety, a lesson that I learned from my very first days on the footplate.

My pet hate is seeing a bucket in the fireman's corner; this must be secured over the lamp bracket on the tender or, better still, left in the support coach. The coal pick should not be left lying on the top of the tender door frame, and all fire irons must be stacked away safely on their securing pin. Believe me, if you should be unfortunate to collide with anything on a steam engine, even at slow speed, it is not a cushioned impact. One of my fireman colleagues related his good fortune when approaching another loco at 15mph; he ducked forward in the fireman's seat just before the impact, which sent the fire irons straight over his head and out through the front cab window. He narrowly missed being decapitated as the fire irons on his 'Black 5' had not been secured properly on the pin.

The scenery had now changed from rural tranquillity to gentle suburbia as we approached Cumbria's capital city of Carlisle. where we had a clear approach, bringing us into the impressive Citadel station. With a final brake application Bill brought our maroon beauty to a stand, completing the 160-mile journey with another punctual arrival. Simon had run the fire right down, which pleased our relief and the support crew boys, including my good mate Malcolm Baker, who would service No 6233 once shunting was complete.

While the driving and firing of steam locomotives is still an arduous task, our job is made a little easier when operating present-day main-line steam with the introduction of the locomotive support crew, who carry out all the maintenance, repairs, preparation and disposal, and one of them acts as the RO, the Responsible Officer. His varied duties include overseeing the fitness-to-run (FTR) exam, the planning and timings, and arranging the coaling and watering facilities; the support coach also comes under his jurisdiction, including its own FTR. The tasks of the support crew relieve us of the preparation and disposal duties. Oh, how we could have done with these boys in the days of steam!

There were some characters among them, as I found out to my cost. I once made the mistake of leaving my camera in the support coach on one trip and, after finishing the film, I left it at the local chemist for developing. When I called to collect the photographs I was ushered into the back of the shop and quizzed by the young lady assistant as to the identities of the three persons exposing their bare backsides, and more. I suppose that I could have held an identity parade to find the culprits, but no thanks! If the support crews have been a bit short-staffed I have helped out, particularly with the disposal duties, having had the benefit of a lengthy slog in the disposing link at Lostock Hall dealing with 30 engines a week, which equates to dealing with the fires of more than a thousand engines during that time. Unbelievably the 'Duchesses' were not fitted with rocking grates except the last two, Nos 46256 and 46257, but I always enjoyed the occasional participation in assisting with the fire-cleaning of No 6233 and a few of the other locos, including No 850 *Lord Nelson*. One or two members of the support crew were permitted to travel with us on the footplate, some of them showing an interest in learning the art of firing, and to them I gave suitable encouragement and tuition.

When making my maiden voyage on a locomotive, my first port of call was always the support coach for a chat with the guys who looked after the engine. They were always more than willing to pass on any helpful tips and information or foibles about their steed, giving me a boost in confidence for firing their engine. Once I became acquainted with the engine I would offer the shovel to those interested when working on the easier stretches; some were complete novices, while others had some experience on preserved railways or had only fired that particular engine. Over the years I would like to think that I may have contributed to some of these guys eventually making the grade, including Simon, who is now one of the regular firemen on No 6233. I recognise at least eight of the current list of registered firemen at West Coast Railways who have been 'Fletcherised' – well done! In fact, many of the young firemen at West Coast have ventured into the job at a young age, similar to my background in the 1960s, and all credit to them for adapting to main-line firing so soon in their careers.

Among the numerous places I have visited as the fireman on No 6233 are Holyhead, Bristol, Worcester, Leicester, Scarborough, Carlisle via Shap, and Oxford. A trip to Blackpool was memorable as it was the first time that a member of the class had been allowed over the line from Preston. We had an enjoyable trip from Crewe, not spoiled by the lack of turning facilities at Blackpool North. It was a lovely summer's day as we travelled light engine tender-first to Preston, then slowly and reverently past my old depot at Lostock Hall, whistling a lament before completing the triangular move at Farington Junction and returning to Blackpool tender-first. Upon our return word had evidently been passed about this rare event and we were greeted by a healthy turn-out of former Fylde footplatemen, each of them applying the traditional single

shovelful of coal to the box to say that they had actually fired the 'Lizzie'. Locomen never referred to these engines as 'Duchesses' – to us they were 'Lizzies' and the originals referred to as 'Old Lizzies' (after the second Stanier 'Pacific' to appear, No 6201 *Princess Elizabeth*). (I do hope that I am not confusing the present-day generation of steam enthusiasts by occasional lapsing into repeating myself with loco descriptions.) The day's events were captured by that doyen of Fylde railway photographers, Peter Fitton.

I completed my firing on No 6233 with a three-day stint working the return 'Scarborough Spa Express' to Crewe. I have just realised that I have actually fired the engine in all three of its liveries – maroon, black and, my own personal favourite, green. I am a lucky boy!

The lack of turning facilities for these big 'Pacifics' reminds me of plans to transfer some of the class to the Southern Region when they became surplus to requirements in 1963/64, this bold suggestion being

With driver Bill Andrew on board No 6233 *Duchess of Sutherland* in maroon livery at Crewe, with driver Mick Rawling and the black livery at Hellifield, and with driver Christopher Cubitt at Scarborough, with the loco in green. *Author's collection (2)/ Adrian Scales* thwarted by the lack of turntables of suitable length.

I had no involvement with No 46229 *Duchess of Hamilton*, which had returned as a museum exhibit just before I resurrected my own main-line footplate career. It certainly looks resplendent in its streamlined form, regularly cleaned and polished by a handful of dedicated volunteers, among whom are two personal friends, Rob Tibbits and Adrian Scales, both of them a fountain of knowledge regarding Stanier 'Pacifics'. They both recently arranged for me to be the guest speaker at the annual reunion of the 46229 group, when I was asked about my first involvement with a 'Duchess' 'Pacific'. I think my reply made them sit up a little when I told them it involved taking one for scrap – No 46226 *Duchess of Norfolk* (ironically the last one I copped as a trainspotter). It was hauled by No 73128, a Caprotti valve gear 'Standard 5', which was in far worse condition than the condemned 'Pacific'!

If you should visit the home of No 46233 *Duchess of Sutherland* at the Midland Railway Centre in Butterley, you can view a short film in the museum taken on a journey with Bill and myself in charge of the engine. Crewe Heritage Centre is also worth a visit, and include a look round the former signal box if you go, as well as ride on the miniature railway, where you may actually have illustrious former main-line drivers Bill Andrew, Frank Santrian or Brian Williams at the controls, still keen lads spending eight days a week helping to run this Cheshire tourist attraction.

A lot of the jobs that we had were on routes that I worked over in the 1960s, and when I was asked to go on loan as a fireman with a fledgling main-line steam-operating company working trains from London I readily agreed to take up an opportunity of firing on foreign metals, and spent the next four years firing locomotives for Merlin Rail. Among other work at Merlin Rail was the contract for the 'Cathedrals Express' using the coaching stock known as the 'Green Train', a rake of Mark 1 coaches hauled by one of four locomotives, either No 34067 *Tangmere*, BR 'Standard 5' No 73096, No 34016 *Bodmin* or No 35005 *Canadian Pacific*, although the latter two were rarely available. The company had only three fireman on its books, so there was plenty of work, fitted in between running the shop and driving trains for the NYMR. I was therefore kept pretty busy, but enjoyed doing all three jobs, particularly the main-line footplate work. Living in Grosmont, it was a bit of a trek down to London and the other places to work these jobs, but I often broke my return journey by staying with my train driver son in Birmingham.

25 In praise of No 73096

My first job for Merlin Rail, which later became Fragonset Merlin, then finally FM Rail, was a Sunday return from Exeter St David's to London Victoria with BR Standard Class 5 4-6-0 No 73096, looking resplendent in its green livery at the head of ten matching coaches standing in the Riverside Yard near the station. Having not met my driver before, we introduced ourselves. He was Brian Dudley-Ward, and this was to be the first of many days on the footplate with this friendly and unflappable chap. After exchanging some 'Standard 5' dialogue with the engine's support crew, who appreciated the fact that I did have some experience of working this class of loco, we soon backed the coaches into Platform 3 of St David's station to await departure time at 16.40.

Obviously I was unfamiliar with the route ahead of us, although I had once footplated a 'Castle' Class loco from Taunton to Bristol. One of the first things I did when starting with the company was to purchase a British Rail gradient profile book, photocopying and laminating the relevant page for the journey and sticking it to the cab roof above my head at the fireman's side. According to this, when we left Exeter we had a 20-mile pull ahead of us to the summit of Whiteball. Luckily we had a nice cool summer's evening for the early part of our 170-mile return run to the capital.

As departure drew near it was time to prepare the fire. Putting the shovel into the coal for the first time, I immediately sensed that the tender shovelling plate was

slightly higher on this 'Standard 5' compared with others I had fired, bringing this to the attention of our support crew friend riding with us on the footplate.

A happy trio: driver Brian Dudley-Ward, myself and the incomparable BR Standard Class 5 No 73096 at Taunton. *Author's collection*

'Yes, fireman, you're right. It's about 2 inches higher, because the tender frame is not the original – it's an ex-LMS frame – but you are the first fireman to notice the difference, which confirms you as having some previous experience of these engines.'

I intended to repay the confidence they obviously had in me, and set about putting on a traditional sloping fire with a good back end with a little down the front until we escaped the confines of this important former Great Western junction station.

With a full pot of water we drew our ten-coach train on to the up main line as Brian closed the cylinder drain cocks. At the same time I fully wound open the back damper while the front one was given just one turn. Then I partially closed the firehole doors to help generate some heat, and the chimney emitted a light brown haze, reflecting the newly formed fire. We were soon passing Cowley Bridge Junction and, not having worked with Brian before, I was taking note of his driving style. He must have sensed my thoughts for he called me across, telling me that he would have to thump her a bit as our path was only 15 minutes ahead of an HST, which I interpreted to mean 'Get shovelling, Fletch, because we're going to motor!'

The Standard's pull-out regulator was now fully open, the handle acting as an armrest for Brian as we ascended Whiteball, using a 45% cut-off. The front end on this modern example of steam motive power had no blows or leaks, with four even beats, albeit a little on the loud side, as her 6ft 2in driving wheels begin to eat up the gradient. Meanwhile on my side of the footplate things were going equally well. I had been busy with the shovel for the last few minutes, so the fire was nicely built up and burning well all around the box. Then, after lifting the flap, it was further built up to that level, avoiding the need to partially close the doors. She was loving this treatment, pressure remained a solid 220lb, and the larger injector was in use, maintaining a steady three-quarters of a glass of water.

We were now on the approaches to the once important Tiverton Junction station, its sad demise cutting off the tracks to a number of places, including Hemyock, which must rank as the most popular branch line in the history of railway modelling! A few minutes later and 15 minutes into the climb, we blasted through the modern replacement of Tiverton Junction station at Tiverton Parkway, our passage being greeted by some incredulous looks from the waiting HST travellers. For the next 4 miles the gradient became stiffer at 1 in 115, so Brian lowered the cut-off to 50% to compensate. Firing remained steady, with plenty of steam and water, man and machine being complete masters of the job. We topped Whiteball and entered the tunnel at just short of 60mph, with both injectors pumping away to bring down the steam pressure as we began the 10-mile descent to Taunton.

No 73096 began to accelerate down Wellington bank, some of which is at 1 in 90, and we quickly reached the 75mph permitted maximum for our loco. Interestingly, if it had been a 'Black 5' our maximum would have been 60mph, imposed by Network Rail because of the engine's 6-foot driving wheels – so being 2 inches smaller can make a big difference! This makes me wonder how they justify this limitation, as these engines ran at speeds up to 90mph, and normal-day-to-day work saw us running at up to 75/80mph just to keep time with them.

Brian was constantly braking to keep our galloping steed to 75mph, which made me think of that day way back in 1904 when GWR 4-4-0 *City of Truro* supposedly achieved the first 100mph for a steam locomotive while descending this bank. For what it's worth, my thinking is that the loco could very well have achieved that speed; it was public knowledge that an attempt was going to be made, the train was the lightly loaded 'Ocean Mails', and the loco had topped Whiteball at 60mph-plus, giving a good start down the 10-mile decent to Taunton, which includes some straight stretches and long sweeping curves. Also, having had the pleasure of working on that fine machine, we found that if you unleashed it, it was off, and it rides superbly. Having been on the footplate of various engines coming down this hill, 100mph would be achievable with the right locomotive, although I have to say that we have obviously never attempted to do this in current conditions. So the speed set by No 3440 and recorded by Mr Charles Rous-Martin remains safe; incidentally, it was authenticated by a second person, travelling on and timing the train, postal worker William Kennedy.

Our modern machine was also giving us a quite thrilling run, riding the canted curves at 75mph. I was relaxing and leaning out of the cab window with an early evening summer breeze blowing in my face as we travelled through some rich Somerset countryside; it's real rural territory around here. But then my few peaceful moments were disturbed by the unmistakable sound of the vacuum brake being applied as Brian checked our speed and we rattled over the junctions for the erstwhile Barnstaple and Minehead lines at Norton Fitzwarren, arriving at Taunton a few minutes early in Platform 5 for our booked stop.

Brian had a look around the cab – the fire, the water, the cleanliness of the footplate – and said, 'Well, you got that bit right, mate. Only another 140 miles to go now!' which meant a lot to me, because it is part of the fireman's lot to work with the driver.

The last time I had been on the footplate at Taunton was in 1962, and I told Brian about when I had been down the Minehead branch, but my reminiscing was suddenly halted when the HST that had been trailing us roared past on the adjacent through road, causing a slight blow-back from our firebox. We would not see him again, as he would take the Bristol line at Cogload Junction while we would go via Castle Cary. Apart from a 7-mile pull to the top of Brewham, the route to there looked reasonably level on my gradient profile chart, and this proved to be the case After passing Castle Cary I was anxious for Brian to point out just where my favourite Somerset & Dorset line once crossed this former Great Western line. Disappointment was the word I would use when he pointed out where it had been, as no bridge remained, and very little of the embankment from which Ivo Peters occasionally managed to capture the simultaneous passing of S&D and GWR trains.

The village of Cole was visible in the distance. The station was actually named 'Cole for Bruton', acting as a feeder for the well-known private school. When we passed through Bruton station itself the demands of the steep gradient prevented me from getting more than just a glimpse of the place, but my task was soon over as we surmounted Brewham.

As the old saying goes, 'What goes up must come down,' and sure enough we are soon speeding downhill through Witham station. This was some engine we had, and it was a pleasure to be on board as we were using very little coal and water, the small injector maintaining boiler water level except when hill-climbing, when I switched to the large. The riding was excellent, and all the BR Standard engines were built with the fireman's controls at his side of the footplate and likewise for the driver. To test the engine's steaming capabilities – and my own – when halfway up the climb to Brewham with my mate using full regulator and 50% cut-off I purposely allowed the steam pressure to drop back to 175lb before springing into action with the shovel, firing coal around the box then building up the back end with the flap. This must have taken about 4 or 5 minutes before I put the shovel down and turned to look at the pressure gauge for the results of my efforts. I had to immediately make a dive to put on the large injector as she was about to lift her valves and blow off at the maximum 225lb on this 1 in 85 gradient with a ten-coach train and the speedometer reading just short of 50mph. They must have been able to hear our progress at the nearby East Somerset Railway and, thinking that they themselves would like some of that, we ran a special to that line not long afterwards.

The still important railway junction of Westbury was our next stopping place, and watering point, giving us a well-earned 20-minute break for tea and sandwiches. The support crew were busying themselves checking bearings and oil levels, and kindly drawing coal forward for me in the tender, and very soon the RO reported that all was well with No 73096 and away we went, all feeling suitably refreshed.

We had one more lengthy climb between here and London, although the 18 miles of uphill running before topping Savernake is a slightly easier ascent than from the opposite direction when coming from Reading. This was to be my maiden voyage over this route, which is better known as the Berks & Hants, a railway with which I was to become more than familiar over the next four years. Brian hadn't said much to me except for conversing about the route and relaying signal aspects where necessary; in fact, he had just left me to get on with it, giving a thumbs-up at intervals. Anyway, the footplate of a steam engine at speed is not exactly conducive to conversation, nor is such needed. This engine was reasonably free of rattles and draughts, and it rode well, so all credit was due to the guys who maintained her.

The late evening sun was a bonus to the awaiting photographers at Savernake summit, and just before topping the climb I flashed a final round of coal into the box, giving off a nice smoke effect for the benefit of the cameras, followed by an 'Ilkley Moor' on the whistle, which seemed to please them all. There was just time for a quick exchange of friendly waves and we were gone from their sight, the engine achieving another commendable 60mph when topping the lengthy incline.

Engine whistles are a

Whistle-happy: as we top the bank at Wilpshire I couldn't resist giving a blow on the chime whistle of 'Britannia' 'Pacific' No 70013 *Oliver Cromwell* hauling the 'Cumbrian Mountain Express'. Three miles further back from here is Langho, scene of the train fire described in Chapter 15 *Author's collection*

passion of mine, as I strongly believe that the whistle should complement the engine to which it is attached; the one we had on this engine pleased me, being bright, cheerful and audible over some distance. Some of the class were fitted with chime whistles similar to those on their big brothers the 'Britannia' Class, and you know what I think of those! To me, an obvious mismatch of engine and whistle is on the 9F, a monster with the voice of a midget. The ex-LNER 'A1', 'A2' and 'A3' whistles are like a pea on a drum; mercifully they did fit an alternative chime whistle to new-build 'A1' No 60163 *Tornado*, my choice when working this engine.

Travelling downhill from the summit, I always give a lengthy whistle when flashing through Hungerford; this has nothing to do with a gunman going on the rampage, but just the opposite really, as I happen to know the railway enthusiast vicar there who is usually standing on the platform as we pass. He does remind me of the clergyman in *The Titfield Thunderbolt*, and I did once ask him to say a prayer for me whenever he saw us on the climb up to Savernake.

We had a water stop at Newbury Racecourse station, and as we came to a stand the tanker was waiting for us with the hoses in position. The support crew leapt into action, I topped up the boiler with water as the tanker filled up the tender to its 4,000-gallon capacity, and in between all this we paid a visit to the support coach behind the engine for a quick wash and brush-up and to attend to the needs of the inner man. This station is a busy place on race days, but was more so in steam days and captured forever in that GWR promotional photo showing three members of the 'King' Class in the station at the head of their return special trains. All these have long gone, including us after a 15-minute break taking on board some best Berkshire water, which would be more than sufficient for the remaining 50 miles to the capital.

The railway around Reading is unrecognisable from just a few years ago. The power signal box staff gave us a clear run through their patch at this off-peak time, and away we went. The fire was still in decent condition, but nonetheless I gave the front and back grates a rocking before building up a fresh one. Everything was in order – steam and water just how I wanted them – so it was time for a few miles of relaxation on the slightly falling gradient on Brunel's masterpiece. Sonning Cutting flashed by, the fading light obscuring a better view of this well-known scene, and we were up to our maximum 75mph as we left Twyford behind. Our 'Standard 5' was really hot, and the need for more fuel was unwarranted for the next 10 miles, which was a welcome relief as tiredness was just beginning to creep in after the 140 miles from Exeter. One more good fire should see us right from Slough until leaving the main line at Acton.

The engine whistle was brought into life as we passed our sub-shed at Southall, alerting a lone figure in hi-vis clothing. Three stations further down the line Brian shut off for the restriction on the tight curve at Acton Main Line leading us up the incline to Acton Wells Junction. The coal was well back in the tender now, but she would still need feeding for this short but heavy pull up to the top, then around all the curves at Willesden and North Pole Junction before dropping down the few miles and coming to a stand at the once important but still imposing station of Kensington Olympia.

Then, following the obligatory autograph and photograph session, our guard whistled up and gave us a green, which Brian acknowledged and set our green train in motion for the very last leg of the day's outing, In due course we crossed the Thames and passed what was left of that once famous hallmark to steam at Stewarts Lane. Shortly after this we were faced with that last awkward half-mile steep pull that has caught out numerous firemen who have suffered the embarrassment of not having enough steam available, having misjudged the effort required by the engine to drag a heavy train over Grosvenor Bridge before dropping down into Victoria, complicated by the strict ruling regarding the emission of smoke and blowing-off steam in the confines of the station. Fortunately, this never happened to me and I like to think that it was down to good cooperation with the experienced drivers that I worked with – a team effort.

Driver Dudley-Ward brought No 73096 to a stand the regulation length from the buffer stops in No 2 platform at 22.50. We had been on the go for more than 6 hours, our loco had consumed more than 5 tons of coal and drunk nearly 8,000 gallons of water, but our efforts seemed to be appreciated by our leaving passengers, with plenty of 'thank you' comments. As I leaned out of the cab a £10 note was pushed into my hand, which was passed on to the support crew as a donation towards the teas and coffees with which they had kept us supplied.

Our footplate work was not finished yet, however, as the engine and stock were based on the Mid-Hants Railway, which involved a 50-mile tender-first run to Alton, the slight saving grace being that the whole train would be dragged there by the diesel loco that had been waiting patiently in the sidings for us. The clock on Alton station read 00.40 as we came to a stand, our 225-mile stint on No 73096 over. The Mid-Hants support crew took charge of proceedings from here to their Ropley depot, and our hotel was but a few minutes walk away. So we said goodbye to the men and their machine – what a superb engine they had. All credit to them.

Over the next few years I had the pleasure of working all over the South of England with this engine, which was utterly reliable and capable of hauling 12-coach trains without any assistance – it would certainly outperform a 'Black 5' and was far easier to work with than a Bulleid. It has the conventional Walschaerts valve gear; 30 of the class fitted with the Caprotti gear were not as popular and didn't seem to have the same power output. Speaking of which, I was always praising the achievements of the engine to the support crew and it was one of them who told me that when they restored No 73096 the cylinders were bored out an extra inch to 'Britannia' size. My only regret was that this former Patricroft engine never returned north, instead spending all its subsequent life confined to the south of the country.

Actually, this is just what seemed to be happening to me in the 12 months that I had been on loan to the company, working trains over former Great Western, Southern, Eastern and Great Eastern metals. I couldn't get enough of it, and did eventually join Merlin Rail. Obviously I had regrets at leaving West Coast Railways, as they were a great set of people with whom to share your working life. But the opportunity of firing a variety of locomotives over many different routes to places of which I had only read about in railway journals proved irresistible. Over the next few years the company expanded and gained more work, which of course required the need for more locomotives, and I could not have wished for a more varied pool of motive power on which to test my firing capabilities. We had ex-Great Western Nos 6024 *King Edward I*, 5029 *Nunney Castle*, 4936 *Kinlet Hall*, ex-Southern 34045 *Ottery St Mary* (actually *Taw Valley*), 850 *Lord Nelson*, 30777 *Sir Lamiel*, ex-LNER 60009 *Union of South Africa*, 60007 *Sir Nigel Gresley*, 4464 *Bittern*, ex-LMS 45231, 6233 *Duchess of Sutherland*, BR 71000 *Duke of Gloucester*, 'Mogul' 76069, and the regulars 34067 *Tangmere* and BR Standard 73069.

26 The Duke

Plucking one locomotive at random from the fleet, No 71000 *Duke of Gloucester* was rather cruelly referred to by its shortened name of the 'DOG' by my former footplate colleagues who worked on the engine in its BR days. It was built as a replacement for the former 'Turbomotive' No 46202 *Princess Anne*, which was wrecked in the 1952 Harrow crash. First, I think it is only good manners to say a few words about the guys who looked after No 71000, this unique piece of engineering, i.e. the support crew, as they had my utmost respect in ensuring its reliability and performance levels. I knew them all personally, in particular Adrian Meakin. The initial restoration must rank as an act of sheer bravado in the face of overwhelming odds as it was virtually just a boiler on its wheels and frames. I had no contact with it during its BR days other than to recall seeing it passing through Preston, usually hauling 'The Mid-Day Scot'. It amused me one day to see that some wag had written in chalk under the engine nameplate 'THE MINER'S FRIEND'. I am pretty sure that it must have been the handiwork of one of the top-link firemen.

The first of my many firing turns on this handsome fella came about when we worked a 'Cathedrals Express' to the home town of England's most illustrious bard – Stratford-upon-Avon. The 12 coach train arrived diesel-hauled at our starting point at Willesden sidings. We replaced the diesel on the front and during the 10 minutes it took for our guard to do a brake test I began to build up the fire. Our route to Shakespeare's birthplace would take us via Denham, High Wycombe, Beaconsfield, Princess Risborough, Aynho Junction, Banbury, Leamington Spa and Hatton Junction, branching to the left there and through Wilmcote to our destination. This 110-mile route was completely new to me, but I had my trusty gradient profile chart taped to the front cabside window, having studied it carefully the night before and calculated that approximately 45 miles would be spent on hill-climbing, including Saunderton. Our booked stops were Beaconsfield, Banbury (for water) and Warwick.

My driver was the company's Operations Manager, Peter Kirk, but he and I were no strangers, having worked together for a number of years, and I like to think that we were a good team. He was an ex-Derby man and a former traction inspector: I had the utmost respect for him and I know this was reciprocated. The third man in our team, as on so many other occasions, was guard Mike Hollingsworth, a dedicated and utterly reliable railwayman whose experience came to the fore when working these specials, as they involved some complicated shunting manoeuvres.

Mike completed the brake test and gave Peter the train loadings and timings, so we were almost ready for departure. My first firing stint was 50 around the box, particularly the back corner. This loosened me up a little and covered most of the grate, so I stuck my head out of the cab and

No 71000 *Duke of Gloucester* with driver Peter Kirk at Crewe on a Holyhead out-and-back job. *Author's collection*

breathed in the London air as we departed from Willesden sidings. For the first time I heard the six strong beats from the double chimney of 'the Duke' (a much more apt name for our engine and one that I shall use in future). By Greenford the engine was beginning to respond to my strategy of allowing him time to warm through, the fire was hotting up and all seemed well, as I wanted to be ready for the 7-mile pull up to Beaconsfield, which began after we pass Denham. However, I had to be careful not to overdo the firing because of the station stop at Beaconsfield, after which we had 5 miles downhill to High Wycombe. So I began a steady firing rate and relaxed after feeding him a round of 40 shovelsful.

Halfway up the climb the steam began to drop back, and it was with some reluctance that I flashed a 20-shovel burst down each side of the box before partially closing the doors. A quick look at the smoke coming from the chimney told me that my actions were justified, a view backed up by the pressure gauge almost on the red mark. Bringing the injector into action curtailed any chance of lifting the safety valves. Incidentally, the boiler pressure gauge is the fireman's sole responsibility, and is just one of 14 different gauges fitted in the cab of 'the Duke' – but of course they are all practically

meaningless if the fireman cannot maintain the steam pressure!

Just a couple of minutes later Peter pushed the regulator forward from the fully open position to fully closed as we topped the climb and drifted down the short distance to our first stop at Beaconsfield – when drifting with an engine fitted with Caprotti gear, the regulator must be in the closed position. We came to a stand with room in the boiler to keep her quiet in the once busy station, but now devoid of its centre roads. The platform was on the driver's side and Peter was talking to some chap holding an expensive-looking camcorder. He beckoned me across and told me that his company were on the train doing a promotional film that centred around a wedding party who were travelling with us throughout, and asked if he could come aboard during the water stop at Banbury for a filmed interview with us. Peter told him to come up and see us when we reached there, and to bring with him his cab pass; meanwhile he had better hurry up and get back on board as we were now due away.

The next five miles of descent to High Wycombe were spent shovelling coal methodically into the back corners and down the sides, then finally filling up under the door of this near-50-square-foot firebox, prompting Peter to ask, 'Is everything all right, mate?' as he took a glance at the fire and the boiler water level. Now, I have worked on the footplate of steam locomotives since 15 years of age and during that time I have picked up the real meaning of a driver's casual comments like that. 'Can we go for it?' is what he was really asking and, after getting the thumb- up from me, 'the Duke' was given his head and responded with a burst of power as we hurtled through the curve at High Wycombe at the bottom of the 8-mile climb to Saunderton.

We were going strongly and accelerating hard, 25 miles out from London, and I had become more confident of man and machine working together on my maiden voyage on the engine. It was also my first time on this route, which was taking us over parts of the former GW&GC main line, the scenery of which I took in while relaxing in the fireman's seat as our unique 'Pacific' ate up the gradient with ease. My only physical effort was to push down with my foot on the engine whistle lever, bringing to life that beautiful chime as we topped the climb to Saunderton with both injectors singing away, the fire not having been touched throughout the climb.

A glance up at the gradient chart told me that the next piece of real action involving the fireman was not for another 15 miles, but there were plenty of little jobs to keep me busy meanwhile. In between watching the road ahead and signal sighting, as well as looking back along our train as per safety rules, the footplate needed a sweep and a swilling down. I waited until we passed through Brill Tunnel before beginning to build up the fire, as we were only 4 miles away from another climb of 8 miles to beyond Ardley, then it was through the tunnel and over the viaducts and a descent to Aynho Junction.

It took me 10 minutes to fire 50 shovelsful of coal into the belly of this 8P giant; it is essential to balance out your workload to avoid over-firing and wasting steam, bearing in mind the station stops, tunnels, permanent way restrictions, unexpected signal checks, and general running delays, all of which make it essential that there is good teamwork between driver and fireman. We were given a clear run through Aynho Junction. My judgement of the fire was that it would do us to our water stop, but as the troughs beyond Kings Sutton no longer existed, a stop had to be made shortly, and a few miles further on we came to a stand under the protection of the semaphore signals that still existed at the former Great Western Banbury station, 65 miles from London.

We were greeted by the film crew, who had a cab pass to come aboard to conduct an interview, then to film the remainder of the journey on the footplate to give an insight into the working of the steam-hauled 'Cathedrals Express', the completed film is often shown on sky TV. Sitting in our respective seats, Peter and I answered some of their questions regarding locomotive matters. I must say that they were very naïve, and one question they asked of me was my opinion of the Caprotti valve gear. I teasingly replied that my side of the engine had Walschaerts gear; he looked a little embarrassed before blurting out, 'Oh, does it? I must have my facts mixed up.'

I told him that he must have been reading too many Ian Allan books, but in all seriousness over the years I spent firing 'the Duke', on its day I considered it to be equal to a 'Duchess', particularly when hill-climbing. Its 6ft 2in driving wheels, as opposed to the 6ft 9in of the 'Duchesses', helped to balance out the slight difference between the engines in supposed tractive effort; furthermore, the 'Duchesses' did have the advantage of having another 37 stablemates to compare performances, whereas 'the Duke' was a lone wolf. Having previously poured scorn on the 'Black 5' and

'Standard 5' locos fitted with the Caprotti valve gear, it would appear to have been of no disadvantage when fitted to this large 'Pacific' locomotive with 80% cut off. But two things are absolutely essential in the working of these Caprotti engines. First, the regulator must always be closed when coasting, and second, when reversing from any cut-off in fore gear, it is necessary to wind the reversing screw right back to full back gear position. Similarly, when reversing from any position in back gear, the indicator must be traversed to full forward gear position. Finally, to obtain the best results, work the engine as much as possible with a fully open regulator.

I cannot leave Banbury without mentioning a pleasant encounter that took place in the 1960s at Lostock Hall when I was asked by running foreman Ken Law to show around the shed two visitors, one of whom, a Mr Tom Rolt, had written books about railways and canals. During our conversation he seemed pleased that I knew of him, having read one of his books, *Red for Danger*. it then transpired that we both had a similar passion for vintage cars, each of us having an Alvis 12/50. Then, after mentioning an interest in canal boating, his visit lasted almost 2 hours! But he did tell me an enlightening story of his former steam boat *Cressy* moored at Banbury on the Oxford Canal – he was a very interesting chap.

So, with departure time approaching from Banbury it was time for action again and I began to busy myself with the shovel, having placed the cameraman on the fireman's seat to enable him to film the footplate action and the road ahead. It was not a high-speed railway between Banbury and Leamington Spa, and we only fleetingly touched our maximum 75mph. The trailing truck under the footplate ensured an excellent riding quality from our 101-ton 'Pacific'.

I once spent more than 5 hours at Leamington Spa driving steam trains in and out and through the impressive station, thoroughly enjoying myself. This was, of course, when operating trains on the magnificent O-gauge model railway of the station owned by Pete Waterman. Today's station is a much slimmed down version in comparison with Peter's steam age depiction, and we passed it on time. Driver Kirk shut off steam to allow 'the Duke' to drift through and down into the dip before the short climb into Warwick, where we come to a stand at this Chiltern Railways station. Our 12 coaches had no chance of fitting into the platform, but Peter drew forward to ensure that the guard's brake van was on the platform. Some passengers joined us here, the train stewards welcoming them and showing them to their reserved seats.

We occasionally had a Leamington stop, from which it was so much easier to get away, departing downhill, as against today's 3-mile heavy pull as we left Warwick and headed up Hatton bank to the junction. There we would head onto the single line through Claverdon and past the former junction station at Bearley, now just an unstaffed halt where a branch line to Alcester once met the Stratford-upon-Avon to Hatton line.

This would be my last heavy firing stint to get us up the ruling gradient of 1 in 103; 40 times I swung the shovel, which was about the average amount for each firing session on this loco. There was no point in getting up from your seat for anything less, for 'the Duke' was a sure-footed engine and rarely slipped, partly due to the smaller driving wheels.

As we left Warwick and dug into the bottom of Hatton bank, the loco's front end was making some beautiful three-cylinder music and Peter was working on full regulator and 60% cut-off, while our cameraman was in raptures, leaning out of the fireman's cab window to capture this giant of steam in full cry, toying with the 450 tons trailing behind the tender. I could listen all day to the sound coming from the double chimney and watch the rotary motion of the Caprotti gear mechanism at the same time.

'The Duke' is an immensely popular engine with the railway fraternity, and many of the lineside photographers had followed us from London to this stretch of railway. The simple act of closing the firehole doors created the special effects they so craved as our exhaust blackened the Warwickshire skyline, ensuring some great photographs. Just to complete the scene, we brought that beautiful chime whistle into song, which was greeted with a spontaneous thumbs-up and applause from the camera boys on the grassy embankments and overbridges on this warm and sunny spring day. However, shortly after passing there we had regretfully to shut the regulator just as the speedometer touched the 50mph mark, which was not bad from a standing start just 3 miles down the bank – but what bank! 'The Duke' didn't seem to notice it!

Just a quick word here regarding railway photographers, who are often derided – possibly due to the actions of a small minority of them. My photograph albums are full of their handiwork, which has been given or sent to me during my 15 years of firing steam locomotives on the main line. So thank you, boys – I just wish that the camera equipment and videos you have today had been available when I was firing for good old British Railways, a little upmarket from the Brownie 127!

We left the main route and took the single line through Claverdon and Bearley; with less than 15 miles to our destination, little firing was required. The final couple of miles into the terminus are down a 2-mile 1 in 75 gradient, which is much more interesting coming the other way. I was reluctant to bring the coal pusher into life, but the RO was on board and gave me the nod to do so; this piece of kit is a godsend to firemen on a large 'Pacific' locomotive. It is just a pity that the equipment wasn't fitted to all the engines with 50-square-foot fireboxes, as this was considered to be the maximum size for manual firing. A 'mechanical fireman' (stoker) was experimentally fitted to a few 9F engines, but not extensively.

Our train was now on the outskirts of Shakespeare's home town and we made a gentle approach to the curved platform line at this former through station, terminus of the line since 1976. The station is unmistakeably of Great Western origin, although a little cramped for handling long trains like ours. What happened next all depended on whether the signaller could give us a path to turn the engine; as no turntable existed there we needed to travel light engine tender-first to Hatton Junction triangle, and this could take up to a couple of hours to complete. On this day we had to wait for a path, so used the time to service the engine and take on coal and water, by which time the relief crew had arrived, thus freeing us from the engine-turning move.

That therefore brought to an end my maiden voyage on the engine. However, it was only the beginning of a three-year association with 'the Duke', during which time we visited a wide variety of places and departed from various London stations, including King's Cross, Victoria, Waterloo and Kensington Olympia working trains to Weymouth, Exeter, Chichester, Canterbury, Portsmouth, Lincoln, Ely, Norwich, Bristol, Bath, Winchester, Alton, Salisbury, Alresford, Stratford-upon-Avon, York and Newcastle, as well as from Crewe to Carlisle and, my favourite destination, Holyhead. Plenty of hill-climbing was involved in reaching some of these places; we have done battle with the likes of Shap, Savernake, Saunderton, Sapperton, Stoke, Honiton, Upton Scudamore and Bincombe. 'The Duke' has put up some remarkable performances and achieved record climbs for steam traction on a couple of these notable gradients, including topping Savernake at 75mph with 11 coaches in tow – there was little chance of viewing the scenery on that day, I can tell you! The finest of which occured on 20th July 2005 with Peter Kirk as the driver. When taking water at Newbury, we had discussed with the support crew the possibility of flattening Savernake with the *Duke*. I gave him a good breakfast of 100 shovels full around his nearly fifty square foot firebox beforeleaving to attack the hill. We soon passed Hungerford at our maximum of 75mph.After that it was a case of holding it back for the remainder of the climb. I am convinced that knowing the engine so well he could have maintained 85mph throughout the climb, had regulations permitted. We were told at the time that the *Duke* had acheived what was believed to be a record power output for a British Steam Locomotive equating to 3,5000i hp. But it wasn't until 2016 when Steam Railway magazine printed performance comparisons on the westward ascent to Savernake that the *Duke* received due credit for his achievement on that day. Incidently, the *Duke* consumed another 50 shovels full on the climb.

I am sometimes given the impression that the running of these steam specials in modern times is looked upon as a bit of a jolly for the crews compared to the days of the steam age. This might be the case on a few of the shorter hops, but there are not many of these on the network because, to make the job profitable, it is necessary to run lengthy trains and it is not unusual to have up to 13 coaches behind

the tender, together with a diesel trouble-shooter, making it a tare load equivalent to 16 coaches. Any suggestion that the diesel assists the working of the train is a myth, as it is only there for emergencies and shunting purposes. On occasions we have taken these loads with the most powerful of engines, including the 'King', 'Duchess' and 'the Duke', and it is heavy going, just as it was in the 1950s and '60s. It is still nearly 200 miles from York to King's Cross, it is still 170 miles from *Weymouth* to Waterloo, and Preston and Glasgow are still 200 miles apart. The gradients are just the same from the days of steam and, while the morning departure times for these trains at around 08.00 or 09.00 may seem quite sociable, we have usually been on duty very much earlier to work the empty coaches into London, spending time in Battersea loop, for example, awaiting our path into Victoria or elsewhere. So I think it fair to say that you certainly do earn your corn on long-distance steam work.

An interesting point when standing in Battersea loop was the request by the staff of the adjacent dogs' home to keep the noise down whenever possible because the rousing of just one single mutt could set off another hundred of his mates, treating everybody to an early-morning barking chorus!

No 30777 *Sir Lamiel* stands in Battersea loop with driver/inspector Ron Smith. The dogs' and cats' home is adjacent to us on the left, so quiet please! *Author's collection*

27 Holyhead trips and two routes to Blaenau

Having claimed the Crewe to Holyhead road as being a favourite, I must explain that in addition to the absence of any 'chicken mesh' to spoil any of the views, it has the capability for some sustained spells of maximum-speed running combined with the fresh breezy coastline, the holiday towns, Conway Castle and the Menai Bridge. Our usual water stop on these jobs was Llandudno Junction, and it was there one Saturday with No 71000, while performing that task, that among the guests we had invited onto the footplate was a fellow who talked over everybody until he was finally given a hearing – he actually made me sound interesting! He told us that he was an ex-footplateman from Crewe who had started there as a cleaner in 1954 and was passed for firing in 1956, and that over the next five years he had fired every one of this class, and in his opinion 'the Duke' was the best of the lot! Peter and I hadn't the heart to tell him that it wasn't a 'Brit'…

He then came out with another gem just as he was leaving the footplate when he loudly informed all and sundry that he had gone on loan to Doncaster and that he had fired all the streamliners there, and in his opinion the best of them all was No 60009 *Union of South Pacific*! At least it made a change from the usual comment that all steam footplatemen have had said to them by members of the public over the years who have come up to the engine to tell you that their dad or grandad or uncle used to drive the *Flying Scotsman*. I have on occasions enquired of them what depot these men had worked from, and the replies I got would have entailed reprinting the Ian Allan *Locoshed Book* for the 'A3' Class locomotives – I cannot recall any of the 'A3s' being based at Grimsby, Barnsley, Motherwell, Shrewsbury or Lancaster Green Ayre!

The Conway Valley line runs from Llandudno Junction to Blaenau Ffestiniog, and we had a few summer jobs on this steeply graded branch line under the banner of the 'Welsh Mountaineer'. To be honest, not many crews relished the challenge of the outward leg of the journey, which originated from Carnforth, calling at Preston, Warrington, Chester, and Llandudno Junction, and concluding with the 1 in 47 gradient up the branch with seven coaches in tow behind 8F No 48151. This required an all-out – and I do mean all-out – effort from the 2-8-0 and its crew.

Another problem with this turn was the inconvenience of having to run round the train at Chester, then travel tender-first to Llandudno in order to run engine-first up the branch. The use of an 8F loco was also not ideal for main-line passenger work, although it was the essential motive power bearing in mind the load and the grade; previous steam specials had come to grief due to underestimating the severity of the grading and curvature. It required locomotive handling of the highest calibre, so only a few drivers signed for this road, but those who did proved their worth.

I was fortunate to have either Bill Andrew or Peter Kirk on the regulator, and an 8F was no stranger to me, so between us there was enough experience to avoid any trouble each time we tackled the hill. Credit must go to an engine able to perform this task, albeit having to use full regulator and

65% cut-off, then demanding full forward gear for the final stretch; it was vitally important to keep a good 'tump' of coal under the door throughout the climb. We certainly cleared any scale off the tunnel roof as we topped the gradient, easing shortly after entering the tunnel to give the engine a well-earned breather on the short leg into the slate capital of Blaenau Ffestiniog. Our arrival at the station, jointly shared with the narrow gauge boys, usually coincided with an early-afternoon entrance of a Ffestiniog service. It always amused us to see the look of incredulity from its passengers upon sighting a full-size steam locomotive and train standing in the station – and telling them that this was their service back to Porthmadog!

On the subject of working trains back from Blaenau, this never happened to me with the 'Welsh Mountaineer' as I always had the tougher outward leg, only ever travelling back downhill in the service train. But let's be honest and admit that I thoroughly enjoyed the challenge of that big hill.

My love of everything railways has taken me on tracks of all gauges, and on the Ffestiniog Railway I had my only experience with an oil-fired locomotive. It all started when I became friends with a few Ffestiniog footplate lads who had joined the loco department at the NYMR. A couple of them were qualified drivers on their railway, and my role as a footplate inspector was to help guide them through our railway's promotional ladder. Of course, it was reciprocated with a request to share the footplate with them on their railway!

The day came one summer Saturday, when Jacqueline and I had already been in her home country for a few days at Aberystwyth, where if you remember I told you that her grandfather had been a steam raiser at 89C. So it was from there that we drove north in our Beauford Tourer, arriving at Boston Lodge shed at about 09.00 to be greeted by Adrian and his mate, our crew for the day on board 2-4-0ST *Linda*, originally an 0-4-0ST running on the Penrhyn Quarry Railway. My first impression was just how much room there was on the footplate of this diminutive-looking tender engine. Adrian had obtained a cab pass for me and, once the loco had been prepared, I was given a tour of the works while my wife took the car to the station prior to joining us in the train. Coming off the shed and over the Cob gave me my maiden voyage on a narrow-gauge locomotive, the sunshine reflecting off our immaculate machine.

A few miles into the journey, and under instruction, I was entrusted with the firing and, following the usual banter of how best to keep the oil balanced on the shovel, it soon became apparent that the colour of the exhaust from the chimney gave an indication of the accuracy of one's oil-firing skills. The driving technique was little different from a standard gauge loco, as was the braking. During the round trip over this highly scenic line I was treated to a professional performance by the crew and locomotive.

Before heading for home I wished to visit a particular spot, but was unsure of its location. Having read a biography of former King's Cross driver Bill Hoole's railway career, and knowing that he was buried in this area, I wanted to visit the last resting place of that esteemed footplateman. My enquiries led me to the cemetery at Minffordd, a short distance from Boston Lodge. We had actually passed the site on the train journey, but finding the grave wasn't going to be that easy among the many hundreds of headstones, all in Welsh marble – and there was no one to ask. We were able to drive in and park at the far end of the cemetery near the railway line. I suggested that we split up to begin a search, but Jacqueline pointed to the first headstone we saw, which uncannily proved to be Bill's grave. Part of the inscription aptly summed up his ability: 'Engineman Extraordinaire'.

28 *Tangmere*

Moving on to a class of locomotive that I am sure Bill probably never handled, but whose valve gear was just as unconventional as that of 'the Duke', No 34067 *Tangmere* was constructed in 1947, designed by Oliver Bulleid with chain-driven valve gear. This was not my first experience of these engines, having worked on Nos 34010 *Sidmouth* and 34072 *257 Squadron* on the NYMR. They were not everyone's cup of tea, and my first main-line turn with *Tangmere* was a round trip from London Victoria to Whitstable and Folkestone and back to Victoria, the driver being Peter Roberts, who had joined the company a few months earlier.

Peter was no stranger to this class of locomotive, having worked on the Southern at Nine Elms depot. I once asked him why the Southern favoured numbered names for some of their engine sheds, such as Three Bridges and Nine Elms, and was there a shed at Sevenoaks! After steam finished Peter turned to diesels, becoming an instructor and finishing as a driver/instructor for Eurostar. We had come to know each other over the previous few months when he had been familiarising himself again with steam traction under the auspices of operating manager and driver Peter Kirk.

I was also not a total stranger to the route, having traversed it on a number of occasions, but my trusty gradient profile chart and Peter's long experience of working trains in this part of the country gave me confidence of a good trip ahead of us around the scenic Kent coast with the 'Man of Kent' on this bright summer day. We had a comfortable departure time of 09.55 from Victoria's Platform 2. The inspectors there tended to leave us to our own devices as they had no knowledge of steam locomotives, or our Mark 1 coaching stock; to them we were just a bunch of old geezers reliving our youth by playing about with obsolete traction, so provided we left to time and didn't make any smoke or noise they didn't interfere.

The inspector rang us out, and the signal at the end of Platform 2 turned green, the same colour as our loco and 11-coach train. No 34067 was opened up, and at the same time the Class 55 'Deltic' diesel No 9016 *Gordon Highlander* on the back of our train began to bank us up the hill out of the station; he was not coupled to the train and left us at Grosvenor Bridge, by which time *Tangmere* would be into its stride. The 'Deltic', in its rather garish Porterbrook purple livery, had previously brought the empty stock into Victoria from where it was based on the Mid-Hants Railway. Our company also had a small fleet of vintage Class 31 and 33 diesels, and we occasionally also used a Class 73 electro-diesel to perform these tasks.

The first hour of our journey to the seaside was a real roller-coaster ride. First we had a 5-mile pull to Sydenham, including the cosmopolitan suburb of Brixton with good views of its main shopping street from our elevated position on the 1 in 100 gradient. I took care not to over-fire the engine because once we topped Sydenham Hill we were downhill through Penge Tunnel, and 11 miles out from the capital we had our first stop at Bromley South. Tickets for our train had all been pre-booked, with reserved seats in the respective coaches, each having an onboard steward. These chaps were pretty slick in their duties, which helped to keep station stop times to a minimum; however, it limited my time with the shovel to bring her round for another spell of 1 in 100 climbing to St Mary Cray Junction.

These engines had a reputation for slipping, but not with our experienced Southern man on the regulator, so *Tangmere* kept her feet and we dug into the climb, leaving behind the home town of H. G. Wells and one-time railway photographer and personal friend David Idle. She was a pretty free-steaming engine provided you followed the rules of firing a wide-firebox locomotive, and did not neglect the back corners, this being the ideal engine on which to implement the 'Digby Hesketh' firing technique. Having covered more than 25 miles and reached the top of Sole Street bank, this would be the first chance to blow the cobwebs off No 34067 as we made a full-speed descent of the 5 miles of 1 in 100 before crossing the River Medway, checking our speed as we passed through Rochester.

Just a few words here regarding working trains in the up direction, when it was not possible to have a run at the bank. The fireman must have the engine prepared for what lies ahead. I learned this very quickly during my four years working this route with a variety of motive power, always remembering that old adage, 'Be prepared'. This particular 1 in 100 is unlike the genteel Settle & Carlisle route, for here we were running on a very busy main line and the operators would not appreciate delays to an intensive train service caused by a steam locomotive that has failed to maintain its

booked time climbing the gradient. One of my regrets is that no member of the famous 'Schools' Class three-cylinder 4-4-0 had main-line certification, for this was the home ground of many of this class and it would have made my day to have done battle with my old friend from the NYMR, No 30926 *Repton*, with a full load behind the tender, just as it would have been in the heyday of her life when at 73B Bricklayers Arms.

Rochester was one of the Medway towns that we passed through, and within the next 3 miles of our journey we would pass through three tunnels and the other Medway towns of Chatham and Gillingham. I would urge anyone with a little time on their hands at Chatham to pay a visit to the historic dockyard and particularly the destroyer HMS *Cavalier*, which saw service in the Arctic during the war, all operations being controlled from the ship's open bridge! This makes our complaints of tender-first running seem a little trivial by comparison.

Our speed through Gillingham was rather less than we usually travelled through the other Gillingham in Dorset (pronounced with a hard 'G'), a rather thrilling maximum of 75mph being the norm at that passing place, which always seemed faster when running on a single line.

Our Bulleid 'Pacific' was handling the load well and not devouring too much coal per mile as we approached Sittingbourne, home of the 2ft 6in-gauge Bowaters steam railway – I cannot imagine their footplate crews calculating similar performance figures! This tourist railway has thankfully recovered from some severe operating challenges and is now running a train service again.

The branch line to Sheerness-on-sea diverges at Sittingbourne West Junction; we traversed this unspectacular line on a number of occasions using steam and diesel traction – actually a Class 73 electro-diesel – all of which I captured on film from the cab. Prior to departure with that train, the driver explained the three-position main control lever: push forward for electric traction, pull right back you have diesel power, and with the switch in the middle you have – and here I interrupted him and suggested 'steam'! He laughed before informing me that it was actually the neutral position. Much of the route down to Sheerness is hardly a tourist attraction, with scrapyards, run-down industrial units and dual carriageways, so it came as no surprise to be told that the locals often referred to the place as, Sheer-mess-on-sea!

The smell of hops indicated that we were on the approaches to Faversham, home of Britain's oldest brewer, Shepherd Neame. We had taken special trains here, usually at festival times, departing from London Bridge station, renaming *Tangmere* as No 34066 *Spitfire* and carrying 'The Spitfire' headboard in recognition of one of the firm's best-selling beers. Some of the brewery directors usually travelled with the train, gathering at the front of the engine with the support crew for publicity photos before departure from London Bridge. On one such occasion I posed a question to them all: what connection does our locomotive No 34066 *Spitfire* have with an overbridge situated just 4 miles into our journey today? Surprisingly it was one of the directors who gave me the answer, but he did have the advantage of being a resident of Lewisham, although he was not aware that the original *Spitfire* had been the loco involved in Britain's third worst railway disaster there in November 1957, and that our train would pass under the bridge erected as a temporary replacement structure and still in use today! I was asked if we would hang on to the whistle on our approach to the scene of the crash so they could pay their respects.

We occasionally branched right at Faversham to take the direct route to Dover via Canterbury East, but as we were 'The Man Of Kent' we ran through non-stop to take the coastal route via Whitstable, Herne Bay, Margate and Ramsgate to Dover. The former engine shed of 73E, Faversham, was still standing, albeit derelict, on our right as we accelerated away, leaving behind the aroma of hops and steam engine exhaust permeating the air of that brewery town.

The day was getting warmer and likewise so was I. The footplate of these Bulleid engines can become almost unbearably hot, so if you want to lose a bit of weight spend a hot summer's day on one of them – the mobile version of an Atkins diet! Although the engine was well maintained, an inherent design fault of the class is the position of the injectors, low and to the side of the fireman's seat, operated by circular serrated control handles that have a tendency to jam shut; maybe I have been spoiled working with LMS injectors all these years!

We soon came to a stand in Whitstable station, bang on time at 12 noon, and our 'Spam Can', having covered more than 60 miles, was ready for a drink, and her crew likewise, so it was out with the flask and a lid full of special brew for me – dehydration powders in blackcurrant juice. We had 20 minutes here to extract the 3,000 gallons of water required from our supply tanker; once empty he would hotfoot off to his base for topping up and meet us in the afternoon at Paddock Wood, our next booked water stop. I just have time to tell you about one of the first public railway lines built in this country, as long ago as 1830, which ran from here to Canterbury. Sometimes colloquially referred to as the 'Crab & Winkle Railway', the route is now a public footpath and cycleway.

At Whitstable our faithful and diligent support crew were busy giving *Tangmere* a quick servicing, checking the tyre pressures and cleaning the windows (only joking). The coal supply was brought forward and all bearings and oil levels, including the oil bath, checked and, with everything fresh, driver Roberts set *Tangmere* in motion towards the seaside town of Margate, which some folk reckon to be the equivalent of Blackpool, but how can it be when the place is full of bleeding Southerners! It does still retain its imposing station building, although the trackwork is much truncated, and we passed through on the curved platform road at the restricted 30mph, whistling our presence, which somewhat startled the holidaymakers waiting on the opposite platform for their train back to civilisation in London. Ten minutes further on saw our green train drifting through sister station Ramsgate, with the adjacent Traction Maintenance Depot built on the site of the former carriage sheds and loco depot of 73G.

One of my former footplate colleagues at the NYMR, Julian (Jack) Twyman, was a fireman based here in the 1950s. He featured in an article in *Trains Illustrated* by railway author Cecil J. Allen, who rode with them on a Cannon Street-Dover express on board No 34022 *Exmoor*, a 'West Country' sister to 'Battle of Britain' *Tangmere*. The author praised him for his firing skills in maintaining the steam pressure throughout, despite having a tender full of small coal and dust. RIP Jack – you were a true pro.

We now had an interesting 15 miles in front of us. The first three were down the 1 in 100 gradient running inland to the triangular junction at Minster, followed by 7 miles on the level passing through the Cinque ports of Sandwich and Deal before tackling the next 5 miles of some tough hill-climbing with a ruling gradient of 1 in 64 to the summit of Martin Mill. Despite the odd grumble, I do really enjoy working on this scenic coastal route, firing Southern engines on Southern metals.

We were tightly timed over this next stretch, giving us only 20 minutes to cover the 14 miles between Sandwich and Dover Priory. The old Southern signal box at Deal had its semaphores clear as we blasted past at the foot of the bank. I had an absolute

roaster of a fire covering the entire 38 square feet of the firebox, and *Tangmere* was responding to my efforts and rewarding us with steam pressure remaining rigid, the needle just short of the red mark at 245lb against the injector, which had to be kept on while working on full regulator and 60% cut-off. Peter was really putting our Bulleid 'Pacific' to the test dragging this 11-coach, 400-ton train.

The slightly disappointing thing about these engines is that when they are making an all-out effort like this they do not sound as though they are doing so, in comparison to the sharp exhaust of a 'Britannia' or a 'Black 5'. But let me assure you that No 34067 was a master of hill-climbing and required only a secondary 30-shovel round of coal at the halfway point, giving me the bonus of a few minutes to take in the scenery before topping this climb and plunging into Guston Tunnel. Emerging from there, we were running downhill and around the curves before entering the other Cinque port on our journey at Dover Priory station. It lacks the grandeur and interest of the former Dover Marine terminus, closed by British Rail in 1994 following the opening of the Channel Tunnel and the consequent demise of the once illustrious boat trains, but the building remains in use as a cruise liner terminal.

We had a 2-minute booked stop in Priory, the time being spent on assessing the condition of the fire. I ran a heavy fire iron over the grate, testing for any clinker that may have accumulated, which could effect the steaming as we had another long pull immediately after leaving the confines of Dover on the 10-mile ascent through Folkestone to Sandling Tunnel, followed by some fast downhill running between Westenhanger and Ashford. The coal we had was of decent quality, although our tender was now half empty. The hot fire iron was stacked safely away as I had satisfied myself that the fire was still in reasonable order. So we slowly worked our way out of this very busy port, our support crew guy pointing out to us the spoil excavated from the Channel Tunnel, which had lengthened not only the Dover shoreline but, according to him, had actually increased the length of the British Isles – just thought I should share this with you!

We now traversed what is probably one of the best known locations on the entire Southern as we climbed out of Dover up to Shakespeare Cliff Tunnel, entering through those unique portals. This was the first of five tunnels on our climb up to Westenhanger. There are strict regulations about working steam locomotives through tunnels. The sounding of whistles before entering a tunnel has been rescinded, as all maintenance work in tunnels is now regulated, and the engine

blower is to be applied and firehole doors closed to prevent a blowback of fire. It is important that all crews know the locations of all tunnels on a line – another instance of where the partnership between driver and fireman working together is essential. The driver will have signed a route card confirming his intimate knowledge over that route, including tunnels, stations, signals and speed restrictions, and he shares that information with his fireman during the course of the journey.

We were doing quite well and were halfway to Westenhanger with plenty of steam and water, our engine having been warmed through climbing Martin Mill. Coming into view through the cab window was Folkestone East, which was then the junction for the Folkestone Harbour branch.

'Battle of Britain' Class No 34067 *Tangmere*, suitably adorned, is about to tackle the 1 in 30 incline up the branch from Folkestone Harbour to Folkestone Junction. *Author's collection*

I cannot pass here without referring to a special day in 2009 when we worked a closure special on this line with *Tangmere*. We left Southall depot with empty stock for Victoria at 06.59, ten coaches with a Class 47 on the rear. With a full complement of passengers, we departed from London at 08.28, routed via Selhurst, Purley, Redhill and Paddock Wood, and arriving at Folkestone East Train Road at 10.58. The Class 47 led the procession down the 1 in 30 incline to the Harbour station, where many hundreds of enthusiasts and locals had turned out to witness the two round trips headed by a steam locomotive, which looked absolutely splendid displaying the full 'Golden Arrow' regalia of headboard, arrows on the boiler sides, flags, and Southern headcode discs. Our driver was Peter Roberts, with Pete Hanson and I sharing the day's firing. None of us had worked over a line with a 1 in 30 gradient, which had required up to four banking engines in the days of the boat trains from Folkestone Harbour. Obviously diesel assistance would be required, but it was agreed to work *Tangmere* to its absolute limit climbing what could best be described as a ski slope, and No 34067 did not disappoint the crowds – I am sure that all-out full regulator and full forward gear display of steam power would forever live on in their memories of this unique branch line, which closed completely a short while later.

Meanwhile, back on board 'The Man of Kent' we had topped Westenhanger with the prospect of some fast running ahead of us to Ashford. My knowledge of this route back to London was reasonable, which helped to avoid energy being wasted by possibly over-firing the engine. It is a busy route and as we had to maintain our pathing times it could be a little frustrating being limited to the maximum of 75mph; certainly *Tangmere* was capable, and was often desiring to rid itself of this tight restriction, but a trip out

on a present-day steam special is no occasion for high-speed running. Peter was holding her back to what may have seemed a little on the slow side to him in comparison to his days driving a Eurostar, which incidentally I was hoping to catch a glimpse of as we approached their territory around Ashford.

The up through road was showing greens all the way for us, I had boxed up a good fire, and the injector was maintaining a steady three-quarter glass of water, giving me a few minutes of freedom to survey the scene as we neared the station. My vigilance was rewarded with the sighting of a Eurostar standing in the down platform. It was my intention to announce the presence of our British steam express to any foreign tourists or asylum-seekers on the platform by hanging on to the whistle as we tore through the station at our maximum 75mph.

As we drew level with the platform ends at Ashford I began the long-drawn-out whistling, which had the desired effect of creating much excitement and waving from the crowds on the platforms, obviously thrilled by the experience, including a brief wave and a blast of the warning horn from the Eurostar driver. Peter glanced across the cab to see if he recognised the Eurostar driver, and I mouthed to him, 'Which would you rather be driving – the Eurostar or *Tangmere*?' His reply meant a lot to me when he said, 'On here with you, Fletch.' This made me feel quite proud to be firing for a guy who was qualified to drive a locomotive with its roots set in the Victorian age as well as what was then the most up-to-date form of traction on the network, as well as driving it in another country – now that's street cred for you!

With another 20 miles ahead on reasonably level track to our water stop at Paddock Wood, we hurtled through Headcorn, prompting Peter to check our running times against his watch. He put up three fingers followed by a thumbs-up, signifying that we were 3 minutes to the good passing there. My driver did have some connection with this place, as he lived not that far away; he often drove here and journeyed into London by train to sign on duty. He also had a further interest in Headcorn, for one day hopefully it might be reconnected to the Kent & East Sussex Railway, where just for a change and to get away from trains Peter goes on his days off to drive trains! It's just a shame that we never got paired up when I was working for them.

Our arrival at Paddock Wood had the station staff a bit worried as to whether we would overstay our allotted 20-minute allowance to take on water, but our support crew were a pretty slick gang. Mention should also be made of the professionalism of the tanker drivers in finding the sometimes obscure water stops and also arriving on or before time, bearing in mind the traffic situation in and around the London area. We were totally reliant on them, for a steam engine cannot proceed very far without water, or that other essential, coal. This is often taken on en route or at the halfway point, the one difficulty sometimes being finding a place where the coal wagon can get alongside the tender to load up.

The station inspector was smiling to himself and looking at his watch as we bid farewell to the great metropolis of Paddock Wood a full 2 minutes before our booked time, having ushered from the footplate the usual throng of photo-hunting enthusiasts who had been enjoying a chat with us. The scenery from here begins to transform into typical John Betjeman suburbia, although my viewing of it would be somewhat restricted due to being required for firing duties for the next 20 miles of uphill work to Knockholt, passing through Sevenoaks and Polhill tunnels on the climb. The next station to be graced with our presence was Tonbridge, where we left the line for Redhill and diverged to the right on our route back

in to London. Tonbridge Wells is now home to the Spa Valley Railway, which has taken over the former loco shed there and reinstated more than 5 miles of line back to Groombridge, linking up with the network at Eridge. Do pay them a visit if you are in the area, as they are a friendly lot.

The support crew member sharing the footplate with us was John Gibbins, who was keen to learn the art of firing. I had been nurturing him on the easier stretches over a period of time, and now felt confident enough to give him a go on the shovel when the engine was working that much harder. I would work the injectors and watch the road, leaving him to concentrate on the shovelling. I instructed him in the art of firing into the back corners of a wide-firebox engine, with the standard warning that is given to any of my trainee fireman –if they make a balls-up of the firing, they cannot look to me to take over and bail them out. Actually, over the many years of training novice firemen none have ever let me down, as I have always been able to assess each individual's capabilities beforehand.

My protégé was doing just fine. *Tangmere* was making the right music on the approach to Sevenoaks Tunnel, Peter had taken the precaution of applying the sanders and the blower, firing temporarily ceased and the firehole doors were closed while we negotiated this damp dark hole, hoping that the 6ft 2in driving wheels would retain adhesion on the rising 1 in 144 gradient. On entering the tunnel Peter was off his seat with both hands firmly gripping the regulator to immediately counteract any sign of slipping, but our 'Pacific' remained surefooted throughout.

Naturally the daylight and fresh air were very welcome as we emerged from the tunnel. I really cannot stress enough upon a layman the unique environment and atmosphere of a steam locomotive working hard and passing through the confines of a tunnel, particularly if it's a single bore. The danger of slipping to a stand is very real, having experienced this myself on two occasions, and being forced onto hands and knees with a wet handkerchief over my face, gasping for air through the floorboards – definitely no place for the faint-hearted!

I could never pass through Sevenoaks without thinking of the experiences that my dear Uncle Bob related to me about his footplate days working on the four-cylinder L&Y 4-6-4 'Baltic' tank locomotives and their propensity to roll at speed, which was found to be a feature of certain other large tanks and a contributory factor to the fatal crash near Sevenoaks in 1927 involving a Southern 'River' Class tank locomotive, after which the entire class was rebuilt to become the 'U' Class 2-6-0 tender locomotives.

We were now approaching Knockholt, a summit approached through a tunnel from both sides. First Polhill was negotiated, then once over the top and through the station we entered Chelsfield Tunnel and drifted down to the busy junction station of Orpington after Petts Wood, where we swung to the left and rejoined our outward route at Bickley Junction to complete the Kent circle and follow our morning route back to Victoria.

We had a booked pathing stop at Kent House, giving me time to inspect the handiwork of our apprentice fireman. I picked up the shovel that he had been using and immediately let go of it, jokingly telling him that the handle was still hot! We inspected the fire, which he had allowed to burn through nicely and would require only minimum attention for the 8 miles of running back into Victoria. There had been no blowing-off and wasting of steam, we had a full pot of water and the footplate was swept and swilled; he had done very well and deserving the praise from Peter and me.

The last leg of our journey took us downhill from Sydenham Hill through West Dulwich and Herne Hill, then the ever-

colourful Brixton followed by a punctual 15.30 arrival into our usual Platform 2 in Victoria. Almost without exception we were privileged to receive favourable comments from our day-trippers as they passed the footplate. It had been a long day for them, but was nowhere near finished yet for us and the support crew, as again we had a 50-mile run back to the Mid-Hants Railway, followed by engine disposal. The purple 'Deltic' had been waiting patiently on Stewarts Lane depot for our return, and backed up to the rear of our train. Then we were soon away out of the suburbs and heading towards Alton. Our own day would amount to about 10 hours on the footplate, but occasionally it stretched to the maximum of 12 hours if working out and back into London.

I regret not having had an opportunity to fire one of the 'Merchant Navy' class, but how I envied those guys at 'ee, what a mess, it's EWS' who operated *Clan Line* on the once-a-week VSOE lunchtime train on a quick out-and-back to Guildford. That lovely piece of kit was only out of its box for about 8 hours, one day a week, in stark contrast to *Tangmere* or 'Standard 5' No 73096, which often ran many hundreds of miles each week. My involvement with these locos took me almost everywhere, both on the Southern and Western regions, clocking up thousands of miles in the process. Having already stated that the wonderful 'Standard 5' never featured in any northern running, the same cannot be said of No 34067, for we partnered each other on numerous outings 'up north', including 'The Scarborough Spa Express', but regretfully the Crewe-Carlisle road eluded me.

Before closing this account of *Tangmere* I am going to relate a less than happy – indeed, perhaps the most disappointing and frustrating – day ever spent on the footplate, and it was no fault of the engine. The fateful day was 23 March 2006 and the train was 'The Somerset & Dorset', a Minehead-

The ill-fated 'Somerset & Dorset' railtour, with No 76079 running as 76009 and No 34067 *Tangmere* pictured taking water at the former Tiverton Junction station prior to the Exeter debacle. *Author's collection*

Taunton-Exeter-Yeovil Junction-Bath-Minehead special to commemorate the 40th anniversary of the closure of the S&D line. It was double-headed throughout by assistant loco BR Class 4MT 2-6-0 No 76079, running as No 76009 and crewed by driver Peter Kirk and fireman Andy McKenna, while the train engine, SR 'BB' Class 4-6-2 No 34067 *Tangmere*, was crewed by driver Chris Hopcroft and me.

Things went wrong shortly after we relieved the West Somerset crew at Bishops Lydeard, when a problem was discovered with the paperwork for one of the locos. By the time we had run round the train in Taunton station we were more than an hour late with our 13-coach train, and immediately faced a 10-mile pull to the top of Whiteball with a gradient of 1 in 80 near

the summit. We made an all-out effort and entered the tunnel in fine style, certainly not losing any time, but were unable to regain any time on the descent due to the 60mph restriction imposed on the assistant loco, before being turned into the loop at the former Tiverton Junction to take on water. This gave us time to assess the situation. Some of the coaching stock was not fitted for steam heating on this very cold day, so we walked back along the old platform, pausing at each compartment window and, after wiping away the condensation, apologising to the passengers inside. We should have had a diesel loco on the rear to provide heating and also assist us up the hills, particularly on the 1 in 37 climb from Exeter St David's to Exeter Central, then the pull up Honiton. Efforts were made to obtain diesel assistance from St David's, but the driver did not have the route knowledge up to the Southern station so we were on our own.

We requested Exeter power box to keep us at Cowley Bridge until they had a clear road for us through St David's up to Exeter

Central. The 15mph restriction leading on to the 1 in 37 gives you virtually no chance of having a run at it, particularly when you are being watched, as we were, by the power box signalmen leaning out of the windows encouraging us on. Both drivers waited patiently while our long train snaked through the junction restriction, then it was a case of sanders on, regulators in the roof and cut-offs set almost at maximum, keeping that little bit in reserve as every good driver does. Initially everything went fine for both engines, just feathering at the valves, indicating maximum working pressure. They made a fine sight and sound as we came out of the tunnel rounding the curve onto the final part of the climb and just 400 yards from our goal, but we were down to walking pace when Chris gave *Tangmere* the final 10% cut-off that he had kept in reserve, at the same time making the ominous remark, 'It's going to be touch and go.'

The station platforms at Exeter Central now loomed just 200 yards away up the last part of the tortuous 1 in 37 incline, with both engines now down to a laboured single exhaust blast, but we should just about make it provided both engines kept their feet. But then, disaster! The 'Pocket Rocket' suddenly lost adhesion and went into an almighty wheelslip, then another and another. With momentum lost, we came to a complete stand with no chance of recovery.

The telephone wires were soon hot with suggestions for a solution to the problem. We could not go forward nor could we reverse down the hill. My driver suggested that he make his way back to St David's and conduct the diesel driver on to the rear of our train, then assist the two steam locos onto level ground in the safe confines of Exeter Central station. However, this could not be done as the loco was stabled in the Riverside Yard and the problem was getting Chris to the site. Eventually permission was given to set the train back down to the former Great Western station, a tricky move undertaken in communication with the signaller, with our guard at the rear relaying signal aspects, enabling us to safely complete the move and come to a stand in the platform. There we stood for another hour until the decision was made to curtail the train and send everybody home via the Network Rail services.

Just to confirm our opinion that the train was overloaded for the rostered motive power, a former 83C Exeter driver approached the footplate and remarked that in his day, with the 'Z' Class 0-8-0 bank engines, we had the equivalent of a three-engine load. I was not asked to attend the subsequent enquiry, but they requested my written report, in which I condemned the tour company for the failure to provide adequate motive power on the day for banking and heating purposes, a verdict shared by the enquiry. As a footnote, I can reveal that the entire incident was captured on film from the footplate of the Bulleid, but this was not used at the subsequent enquiry.

29 More Southern tours

Continuing with the theme of Bulleid 'Pacifics' on the Southern gives me the pleasure of relating one of my journeys with a rebuilt version on a sunny September Sunday in 2004, with 'West Country' Class No 34027 *Taw Valley*, running as No 34045 *Ottery St Mary*, working the down 'Cathedrals Express', renamed 'Atlantic Coast Express', from London Waterloo to Exeter St David's. Sharing the footplate with me on the 170-mile journey to Exeter

was one of my regular drivers, Peter Kirk, with locomotive owner, the evergreen Bert Hitchin, keeping an expert eye upon his Bulleid beauty. The only slight downside to the day was the forecast of high temperatures, so I was well stocked up with flasks of rehydration fluids.

With the thermometer already reading more than 80 degrees on the footplate, we departed from Waterloo for the West promptly to time at 08.00 and, being a

On one of the hottest days of the summer of 2004 we are about to leave Waterloo for a 170-mile jaunt to Exeter with the 'Atlantic Coast Express' hauled by No 34027 *Taw Valley* running as No 34045 *Ottery St Mary. Author's collection*

Sunday, we had been given a path down the former London & South Western main line to Woking rather than our normal midweek route via Barnes, Staines and Virginia Water to Byfleet. The tour operator had included pick-up stops at Clapham Junction, Wimbledon and Woking, with a booked stop after 88 miles for water at Salisbury. To compensate for the absence of water troughs, the Southern Railway built engines with tenders that held plenty of water, an added advantage when operating present-day steam charters.

No 34045 had her feet nicely on the move as we steamed past the site of the former Nine Elms depot, which brought the engine whistle into action for the first time on our journey. Shortly afterwards we reached the country's busiest railway station at Clapham

A Geoff Rixon gem as he captures us passing Esher with 'the Duke' on a Weymouth-bound 'Cathedrals Express'. *Geoff Rixon*

Junction, with plenty of custom awaiting our arrival for a 3-minute booked stop. Firing was nice and steady at the moment, with nothing too strenuous, for I knew from past experience that this was a very free-steaming loco, with not a blow anywhere on her body. We disturbed the slumbering residents of leafy Wimbledon from their Sunday morning lie-in as we departed from the station, the three-cylinder exhaust beat of our Bulleid 'Pacific' making a much more musical sound than any alarm clock. Well, I think so!

We were 17 miles away from our next stop at Woking, and as our machine needed feeding I counted 20 down each side and

the back corners, finishing off with 10 under the door, making 50 in total. A quick glance at the exhaust told me to partially close the firehole doors, and I reckoned that there was enough in the box to get us to Woking. Surbiton station took on a different form on this quiet Sunday morning, but I would be paying more attention to the next station we passed through, Esher, for this was the regular haunt of my all-time favourite railway photographer, Geoff Rixon, and by prior arrangement there he was, poised on the platform, his expert eye focusing on the right angle and pressing the shutter just at the correct moment. We exchanged a quick friendly wave before disappearing from sight.

Geoff was held in high esteem by many footplatemen for he had that unique gift of having a railwayman's eye for that special shot. Not for him the standard three-quarter view from the lineside. As an example of his camera skills, if someone were to show me a hundred photographs of steam locomotives, with just one of them taken by Geoff, I would be confident of picking it out. He was of the old school of photographers with a pedigree dating back to the halcyon days of steam. Much of his talent for locomotive photography regularly appears on the front cover of the magazine *Steam World*, and his work adorns a variety of railway, tram and bus books.

As we drifted towards Woking I could somehow not resist a look on the left-hand side at the magnificent Shan-Jahan mosque; it is certainly more picturesque than the railway station, although I do have a soft spot for the disused 1930s signal box, which is now Grade 2 listed. There is always a good turn-out of enthusiasts at the station whenever a steam charter is running, and over the years I have got to know many of them who are generous in handing out photos of the locos and crews. But there was not much time for pleasantries that day as we had 64 miles of running before our next stop at Salisbury, and we were booked fast line to Basingstoke, so it was a case of head down and action with the blade.

The railway is on a gradual rise for the 30 miles to Oakley, so there was no chance of any easing back on the regulator; moreover, we wanted to show what *Ottery St Mary* was capable of doing if given the road. Four miles out and passing Brookwood our loco was getting into its stride; it was certainly far livelier than the residents alongside us in the sprawling cemetery, which once sported its very own railway line and station. The important Junction of Pirbright followed; this was the cut-off point on our many trips back and forth to our outpost at Alton, but not today, as Peter lifted our train over the slight knoll from there and we gained speed, passing through Farnborough with 75mph showing on the speedometer.

This really is a lovely stretch of main-line railway, over which we were timed at a mile a minute. It would have been easy to let our Southern 'Pacific' recreate the near three-figure speeds achieved between here and Hook, particularly on the up road, but we had to be content with present-day limits imposed upon steam traction. Basingstoke was ready for us, which was a treat for the keen photographers who had gathered at the station on that Sunday morning; they were rewarded with a steam-hauled train passing at full speed with whistle accompaniment throughout. Oh, how we enjoyed that!

Our speed remained unchecked as we rapidly approached my all-time favourite location on the Southern at Worting Junction, home of the famous Battledown flyover, where the routes to Salisbury and Southampton divide. The thrill of coming over with a steam-hauled express from Southampton and maintaining the speed through Basingstoke is something that will remain in the minds of all footplatemen who have shared the experience.

Continuing our journey, just a few short miles from here we began the descent to the former Andover Junction, nothing holding back our free-running loco as Peter had her under control with a series of steady touches on the brake to keep us within the permitted speed. We passed through Whitchurch and over the trackbed of the former Didcot, Newbury & Southampton Railway, which closed in 1963. At Andover was the junction for the 'Sprat & Winkle' line, which ran from here to Redbridge until closure in 1967.

My aim was to fire the engine just once more between here and Salisbury to surmount the 5-mile climb to Grateley. It was a pleasure to keep this machine on the move, with steady firing as and when required, which was just as well when working in this 90-degree heat, the only relief coming from leaning out of the cab and taking in the cool country air in this very pretty part of Wiltshire. The ancient and historic city of Salisbury was approached at slow speed through Laverstock and Fisherton Tunnel, running into the curved station trackwork before coming to a stand at this important junction.

We still had a further 85 miles to Exeter, with a water stop at Yeovil Junction. Had we been terminating at Salisbury, we would have turned our loco on the Milford Junction triangle (wasn't Carnforth portrayed as Milford Junction in the film *Brief Encounter*?) My claim to fame in Salisbury is having stayed on a number of occasions, courtesy of Merlin Rail, in the same hotel as Buddy Holly when he appeared for one night only at the Gaumont Theatre in the town on 22 March 1958 during his only tour of the UK.

The hands on the large station clock at Salisbury were showing 10 minutes past 10 and, having topped up the tender and drawn the coal forward, we were ready to depart. We had also topped ourselves up with a bacon butty each and a brew, before tackling the 17 miles of hill-climbing that lay ahead to the summit at Semley – one of the four stations that was closed between Salisbury and Yeovil Junction when most of this line was singled in 1967.

Once out of the confines of Salisbury, Peter opened up *Ottery St Mary* and filled the three cylinders with superheated steam. She responded with a burst of power and attacked the 1 in 115 on the early part of the climb, the music coming from the front end in complete contrast to the distant ringing of bells from the beautiful Salisbury Cathedral! I have to say that the performance of these Bulleid rebuilds is everything that he had hoped for from the originals, an opinion shared by many ex-Southern men I have had

the pleasure of knowing and working with, so I will leave it at that.

Running on a single-track main line such as this, which had once been double track, always gives me a surreal feeling, taking a while to adapt to the wide clearances in cuttings and under bridges, particularly in places where the single track has not been slewed across to the centre. The only time you get a true feeling of how fast you are travelling is when you pass any large structures, or hurry through stations, which we were about to do. Having just 'flattened' the climb to Semley, we now rapidly descended the 1 in 100 towards Gillingham station and its passing loop. We were spoiled of a fast run through because we had to pay a visit for pathing purposes from 10.42 until 11.18, to allow a London-bound train to pass on this busy single line.

To those who know me and my interest in a certain railway that once met the Southern line at the next station, it will come as no shock if I wax lyrical about the Somerset & Dorset! For until that line's closure in 1966 Templecombe was a very useful junction, even if transferring a train from one line to the other might not have been too easy! And it was the complex and costly arrangements needed to allow easy interchange of passengers and goods that was the Achilles heel of the link between the Southern and the S&D. The station was closed by BR, but reopened in 1983 due mainly to pressure from a local group, which continues to support the enterprise. The signal box was divided in half with a waiting area, the signalman doubling as a booking clerk selling tickets via a hatch in the partition. Alterations in 2012 resulted in the closure of the box for signalling purposes, but the ticket office remains open. The former 82G Templecombe engine shed is fortunately still intact in the centre of a typical industrial estate, but is not accessible to the public.

We now regained double-track working

just beyond the station, which in May 1967 went only as far as Sherborne, being single from there to Yeovil Junction. However, in October of that year the old down line was restored, and double-track working was extended to Yeovil, our next stop. Arriving there, our support crew were soon in action performing the necessary jobs. Bert was checking the bearing temperatures, oiling points and lubricator levels – fortunately there was no oil bath to fuss about with on this loco – while others were busy connecting the water hoses. Our passengers had a little time to stretch their legs and a few of them left the train here, to be picked up at 18.00 on our return leg, some no doubt visiting the adjacent Yeovil Railway Centre.

This was set up by local enthusiasts, aimed at the servicing of main-line steam locomotives; it is situated in the old down yard and includes the original locomotive depot turntable. The centre has been the site of a number of enthusiasts' events as well as being a calling-point for many steam-hauled excursions. I can personally vouch for the competence and professionalism of the staff, having used the turntable and servicing facilities on numerous occasions with a variety of locomotives. It fascinates me to think that Yeovil once had three railway stations, two of them still trading, the other, Yeovil Town, closed in 1967. We have visited Yeovil Pen Mill when working from Westbury or for engine turning on the triangle when on the Weymouth jobs, as no turning facilities remain at Weymouth.

My break from firing was spent by treating myself to a wash and brush-up in the support coach – I have to admit to feeling the 100-degree heat on the footplate on this roaster of a day. But fortunately my special brew staved off the risk of dehydration. (How many times have I mentioned this?) Returning to the footplate, my first task was to build up the fire. Picking up the shovel and opening the firehole doors gave me a

pleasant surprise – someone had beaten me to it, and put a fire on for me while I had been away, and that someone was obviously experienced in the art of firing a Bulleid 'Pacific'. I questioned Peter as to my benefactor's identity. He said that he was asked by a chap from the Railway Centre if he could have a look on the footplate, and told Peter that he was a retired driver on the Southern and asked if he could put a fire on for me.

The guard's whistle disturbed our chatter, and as we began to pull away from this Southern oasis Peter called me across the footplate and pointed out my phantom fireman standing outside the Railway Centre. We exchanged a friendly thumbs-up before joining the single line to the passing loop at Chard, where we were booked inside again for pathing purposes. We were tightly timed throughout the single-line running on this busy railway line, with just 19 minutes running time start to stop to clear the 17-mile section, half the distance being on gradients varying from 1 in 120 to the 3 miles of 1 in 80 climbing up through Crewkerne. There was also a tunnel to deal with on that stretch before topping the summit, followed by a fast 6-mile descent to Chard. It was at Crewkerne that 'Merchant Navy' No 35020 *Bibby Line* suffered a serious failure in 1953 when the crank axle on the centre driving wheel fractured while passing through the station at speed. Miraculously no one was injured, but the entire class was quickly withdrawn from traffic, and the incident resulted in a redesign and replacement of the crank axle.

It did make a pleasant change for me to sit back and take in some of the lush Somerset scenery, thanks to my Yeovil benefactor, whose firing skills got us to within a few miles of the summit. The former station at Chard Junction is still virtually intact, despite having been closed to passenger traffic in 1966. We never seemed to have enough time here to inspect the station, where recent proposals for reopening did not receive the support of the local council. South West Trains now operates the line, and after one of its services passed us we were given a clear road ahead, with no more stops over the 32 miles to Exeter St David's, although there was the little matter of a 6-mile thrash up Honiton incline!

Crossing the border into Devon, the name of our next station is known worldwide for the manufacture of its carpets, but Axminster was also the junction for the Lyme Regis branch until that closed in 1965. The impressive Axminster station building, designed by the LSWR's architect Sir William Tite in mock Gothic style, still serves its purpose. The climb to Honiton starts at Seaton Junction, or at least what remains of it. This once busy junction station for the Seaton branch is now a depressing sight; where once four tracks existed between the platforms, just an isolated single track now suffices for both up and down working on the former West of England main line. The main station building is now a private residence, and eerily the station's concrete footbridge still links the intact platforms. This former busy junction station ideally lends itself to be portrayed in model form, with its main-line platforms and through roads, the branch line platform and trains, the expresses and local services, and the dairy traffic.

It is still possible to travel by rail on part of the Seaton branch, on the Seaton Tramway between Colyton and Seaton, which I can thoroughly recommend, as I would a visit to 'Pecorama', the home of model railways situated nearby. The location of Seaton Junction station created a major problem for heavy westbound trains stopping here, since it was situated at the start of the 6-mile climb at 1 in 80 to the summit at Honiton Tunnel, but that should not be a problem to us today, as my driver

had adopted the same attitude as shared by most steam drivers when working this part of the route. *Ottery St Mary* was given her head and, with a long wailing warning whistle, we tore through at full speed to give us the momentum for an all-out assault on Honiton.

It may seem to you that I have been spending too much time talking and not concentrating on building up the fire for Honiton, but let me assure you that I can do both at the same time, as those of you who know me personally will testify! The last 15 minutes had been spent transferring the black stuff from tender to firebox, and we had a boxful on as we hit the bottom of the bank, which with proper control of dampers and firehole doors should provide us with enough steam to reach the halfway point of the climb before having to pick the shovel up again. Only those who have worked on these engines in this heat on the main line can imagine the environment; I was wearing a long-sleeved footplateman's jacket with leather gauntlets to protect my hands and arms when firing into the back corners.

My previous experience on this incline proved my judgement to be correct as we passed milepost 150 from London with a further 3 miles of climbing to the summit. Our speed was still a very creditable 55mph, with the power output from the disguised *Taw Valley* giving us the impression of being double-headed with its pseudonym! Just one more lengthy stint on the shovel should see us over the top, and the speedometer was reading a very creditable 30mph as we entered the tunnel on the last bit of the climb.

Emerging into the Devon sunshine, I slumped back into the fireman's seat, content with my efforts and looking forward to the downhill running to Exeter. It is always a relief to see the back of this incline, having had a few tussles previously on this Southern equivalent of Shap. The important difference between the two is that Honiton is now a single line where the surrounding vegetation and overhanging trees have been allowed to encroach over the trackbed, creating adhesion problems, particularly in the cuttings. This is not any problem to the local units operated over the line by South West Trains, but slightly different with 400 tons behind the tender and no diesel on the rear. In fact, should you come to grief here, there is nothing available to come and rescue you, and this was before steam charters were being given regular back-up diesel power.

What goes up must come down, as the old saying goes (I have said that before!), and we certainly did. Once through the summit tunnel our speed rapidly increased as we hurtled down the 1 in 90 before passing through our next landmark, which has been known by several different names over the years. From 1874 to 1967 it was Sidmouth Junction, with branch lines to Sidmouth and through Budleigh Salterton to Exmouth, all closed in 1967, followed by demolition of the station buildings. However, the station reopened in 1971 as Feniton, with a 'bus shelter' sufficing for passenger comforts. Most railway folk still refer to the place as Sidmouth Junction, which in its heyday was an important detachment point for coaches from the Atlantic Coast Express'. Incidentally, 5 miles along the Sidmouth branch the first station was Ottery St Mary, so I considered it to be quite apt to be hanging on to the engine whistle as we passed through the former junction station of the line that led to our engine's 'home town'.

Viewed from the footplate, much of the countryside along this single line to Whimple resembles a long green tunnel due to the overgrown lineside vegetation, although the place was considered important enough to be commemorated by Bulleid 'Pacific' No 34025. My apologies to the good folk of Whimple, but that nameplate must warrant the title of being one of the least inspiring names ever bestowed upon a steam locomotive, and not much improvement upon its original name of *Rough Tor*.

Ten miles further on we passed what was once a very important site in railway history, and a reminder of my youthful days of engine spotting at this premier Southern Region motive power depot, 72A Exmouth Junction. The site, now a shopping complex, was once home to the pride of Southern steam, employing more than 400 staff prior to its sad demise in 1967. Still intact is the junction for the rather uninspiring Exmouth branch, in particular its terminus, although the seafront area is worthy of a visit. Well, that's next year's holiday sorted; we shall probably travel by train and alight here at Exeter Central, as did many of our passengers as we arrived with the 'Atlantic Coast Express' on this glorious sunny Sunday in 2004.

Our final leg would be down the 1 in 37 to Exeter St David's, requiring a lot less effort from our Bulleid 'Pacific' than was required of sister engine *Tangmere* in attempting the climb two years later. All that was required was for my driver to release the brakes and away we went down the hill from the Southern onto the Western at St David's, arriving there punctually at 12.59, having travelled through five counties – Surrey, Hampshire, Wiltshire, Somerset and Devon – to complete our 5-hour, 170-mile excursion from London Waterloo.

Our relief crew were a welcome sight standing at the end of Platform 3. In less than 4 hours the engine needed to be turned, serviced, coaled and watered before returning to London. But for me, after a wash and a change of clothes, I had a 350-mile rail journey ahead, but I had enjoyed every minute of the trip from London, and would be reliving it all on the long journey back home to downtown Grosmont.

30 *Sir Lamiel* and *Lord Nelson*

Reference has been made to difficulties in operating steam locomotives on the ascent of Honiton incline, both instances having occurred during the autumn leaf fall season, when no blame could be attached to either loco or the crews involved. In both instances what saved the day was the driving skills of Pete Roberts on the regulator of loco No 30777 *Sir Lamiel*, which had slipped to a stand a couple of times, each time being coaxed back to life before eventually clearing the summit. This all happened before the introduction of the modern Sandite trains, and no blame could be attached to the last surviving 'King Arthur'.

No 30777 was a popular engine among the main-line steam fraternity, including me. This gutsy machine had always been well maintained by its Great Central Railway support crew. While not quite a 'Black 5' in terms of power output, it does have the advantage of larger driving wheels, at 6ft 7in, permitting running at 75mph, although capable of higher speeds in its heyday. Apparently these were the first British locomotives ever to carry smoke deflectors, which I feel do add to their handsome lines.

The 'King Arthur' Class engines belong to that generation of 1920s passenger locomotive designs that include the 'Lord Nelsons', GWR 'Kings' and the original straight-boiler LMS 'Scots', very different from the more modern machines of the 1930s and '40s, such as the LNER 'A4s', the LMS 'Coronation' Class, the rebuilt 'Scots' and the Bulleid 'Pacifics'. The fireman of a steam locomotive has to be able to adapt to whatever motive power is rostered for the duty; indeed, this is a challenge to his capabilities while at the same time hopefully stimulating interest in his job.

Initially, my own experience of firing a 'King Arthur' amounted to nothing – it was just another engine to add to the other 77 different classes of locomotives that I fired during a long footplate career, and just like all the others it had my total respect, and I wanted to master it. Over the years I have personally witnessed acts of overconfidence and cockiness by some firemen, who think they have completely mastered the art of firing; however, the footplate of a steam locomotive can be a great leveller and, let's face facts, all of us have had that rough trip! If I was offering advice to any fireman, whether a novice or experienced hand, it would be to gain as much knowledge as possible regarding the working of that particular locomotive – its likes and dislikes.

If you are a main-line fireman, you will benefit from a chat beforehand with the relevant support crew, which I did before leaving Stewarts Lane depot on my maiden voyage with No 30777 to Salisbury. And, lo and behold, I was made aware of something immediately important regarding the injector steam valves, which need to be turned clockwise to open them, which is the opposite of the injector steam valves on our 'S15' No 30841, known as the 'Goods Arthur', which is based on the NYMR.

My firing technique would have to be

adjusted slightly to allow for the lower working pressure of 200lb against the more common 225lb or more, to avoid any unnecessary blowing-off. At Waterloo station our 11 coaches just fitted into Platform 19 next to the Eurostar platforms, but with no room for *Sir Lamiel*, who was standing just behind the platform starter signal. There was just time for a quick photo at the front of the engine with my driver, Peter Roberts, then we were away, pulling up the slight grade out of Waterloo on our way to Salisbury. By chance a Eurostar came alongside us on his way to Paris; we wished each other 'bon voyage', but couldn't catch up with him!

Having already described in detail a journey over this route, I am going to fast forward to my experiences with another Southern loco, but not before telling you that *Sir Lamiel* always did what was demanded of it each time that I had the pleasure of being a member of the footplate crew.

My finale with Southern steam power would not be the favourite choice of every fireman; in fact, I know some who positively dislike No 850 *Lord Nelson*, but this vintage four-cylinder Maunsell locomotive had the highest tractive effort in Britain when built in 1926, with crank settings of 135% instead of the more normal 90%, giving it that unmistakable 'eight beats to the bar'. To me this was a fireman's engine, which demanded all your skills and experience for main-line operation. Another way of putting it is that if you were not prepared to graft hard, stay well away from this machine! Those who do master it will be rewarded with a real powerhouse on wheels. I could never get enough of it, yet that does not mean that it was a favourite steam locomotive – but it was my all-time favourite challenge.

Our first date was on a 'Cathedrals Express' from Victoria to Canterbury and return. Unfortunately I do not have the timing details of that run, so I have chosen to describe a 'Bath & Bristol' return charter from Bristol Temple Meads to Haywards Heath on Saturday 23 June 2007.

Lord Nelson does require plenty of labour for servicing, and part of the afternoon was spent assisting the support crew on Barton Hill depot adjacent to Temple Meads station. As the loco is not fitted with a rocking grate, my forte was helping with the disposal duties, i.e. fire cleaning; it was not an easy task paddling out the clinker on an engine with a firebox nearly 11 feet in length!

Leaving Bristol at 17.33, our route back to Haywards Heath would take us via Bath, Westbury, Salisbury, Eastleigh, Chichester, Worthing, Hove, and Preston Park, finally arriving at Haywards Heath at 23.37, to be followed by empty stock to Redhill – a nice 175-mile jaunt! – by which time *Lord Nelson* and me will hopefully have become firm friends!

The 12-coach set was full, our passengers having spent the afternoon exploring Bristol and Bath. Peter Kirk was my driver and we departed on time from Brunel's masterpiece, having taken the greatest of care not to blacken out the station's lovely overall roof. The first leg was a steady 20 minutes of steaming on a gradual gradient to our first stop at Bath Spa, which should prove ideal to warm through our Southern machine. As the engine began to come to life, the novelty of having an eight-to-the-bar exhaust pulling at my overall trousers as I commenced firing was something unique in my footplate career. Other four-cylinder engines of which I have experience have the conventional crank settings of 90%, giving just four exhaust beats per revolution of the wheel.

Fortunately I had plenty of previous experience on engines with long fireboxes, and as I had done previously when firing this engine my aim was to build up a nice wedge-shaped fire the length of the box, which included the middle, as on the 'King' and 'Royal Scot' class engines, which have a similar length of firebox. I paused from firing while we passed through the two tunnels before Keynsham, 5 miles from Bristol, and just after there at Saltford the chimney was telling me that the fire should suffice for the time being. It pleased me to see the pressure gauge creep round to almost the red mark; the injector had been on all the time, so I needed to adjust the dampers and doors a little as we were actually making too much steam as we entered the castellated Twerton Tunnel.

Shortly after that Peter shut off power, as we were watched by a bevy of cameramen perched on the former Somerset & Dorset railway bridge that spanned the line here on its 1 in 50 climb out of Bath Green Park. That station is still very much intact, albeit partly in use as a Sainsbury's supermarket, which paid for its restoration. The present-day track layout at Bath Spa station, without the centre roads, gives it the air of slight dereliction, belying its importance on this busy route. We had a brief 5-minute stay at this Grade 2 listed building, giving me just about enough time to build up a decent fire, as I liked to catch a glimpse of the lovely Sydney Gardens as we headed towards Bathampton. It was a nice summer evening and the gardens looked a treat; people out for a stroll gave us a friendly wave as we passed. I had no real concern regarding any heavy work being required of me and our locomotive over the next 15 miles to Trowbridge, but from there we faced our sternest test of the day, with 9 miles of hill-climbing to Warminster, including the 3-mile ascent at 1 in 70 of Upton Scudamore just beyond Westbury.

Firing was just steady as we crossed into Wiltshire, giving me time to announce our presence with a lengthy pull on the whistle as we approached the closed but still intact Limpley Stoke station, which is now a railway bookshop. The proprietor is usually

hanging about on the old platform with a glass of beer to hand, wistfully hoping for a few customers whenever a steam special passes. This, of course, was once the junction for the Camerton branch, which passed under the Somerset & Dorset at Midford, the setting for the 1953 Ealing comedy *The Titfield Thunderbolt*. This really was a most pleasant and attractive stretch of railway as we passed through Bradford-on-Avon, but my sightseeing would have to come to an end soon as it was time to prepare the fire on *Lord Nelson* by first filling up under the door, then addressing the middle and finally, just before hitting the bottom of the bank, some lengthy swinging to the front gave me the ideal wedge-shaped fire. The injector had been on at the same time, giving us a full pot as we announced our noisy presence through Trowbridge.

On the first 4 miles of climbing to Westbury the ruling gradient is 1 in 120, which was not a big challenge to us, but what we were looking for was a clear run through this major junction. We approached on a right-hand curve and had two yellows, which was not looking good for a run at the bank, so we resorted to a bit of old-fashioned whistling to the bobby to alert him of our urgency for the road. Old habits die hard, and we were not put off by the mere fact that the present-day 'bobby' was probably ensconced in a soundproof multi-million-pound alien signalling centre situated in some car park – but wherever he or she was, our primitive communication method seemed to work, as yellows turned to green with 'feathers' for the left-hand route to Warminster and Salisbury. This gave us the chance of a run at the 1 in 70 Upton Scudamore bank, which would be upon us immediately we cleared the confines of Westbury station.

On the footplate we were grateful for having avoided the prospect of a standing start before tackling this nasty little-known gradient, although it was no stranger to Peter or me as we knew exactly just what effort was required from a locomotive to climb the steepest railway gradient in Wiltshire. This meant that we were both ready as we blasted through Platform 1 and around the sharp left-hand curve onto the incline at about 30mph, following a bout of heavy shovelling, then finishing off with 20 up the front.

Lord Nelson hit the bottom of the bank on full regulator and an initial 55% cut-off. Peter left it like that for the first mile. Steam and water were fine; in fact, she was feathering against the injector. Instinctively we both glanced back at the owner's rep travelling with us; he immediately read our thoughts and, with a nod from him, the cut-off was dropped down to 65%, and we physically felt a surge in power from our 80-year-old machine.

Working him like that, exerting almost every ounce of the 33,000lb tractive effort, did keep me pretty busy with the blade, but at no time did it get away from me and we maintained a three-quarter glass with simmering safety valves. With the top of the bank in sight we celebrated with a triumphant blast on the whistle, captured by a few of the more enterprising railway photographers aware of this location. One of these guys uploaded film of our 35mph topping of Upton Scudamore to YouTube (Steam Age Pictures, The Bath & Bristol 850 Lord Nelson), including scenes at Botley and Salisbury.

After the furore of the last 5 miles we had a gentle 20-mile downhill trot after Warminster to our first stop for water at Salisbury, 55 miles from Bristol. As previously mentioned, the lack of water troughs on the Southern meant that most of its tender engines had a large water capacity, but that left less space for the coal, which wasn't a great concern in the days of steam as there were plenty of depots to top-up the supply. *Lord Nelson* has a 5,000-gallon tender

with a coal capacity of 5 tons, which is not a lot, particularly when the engine is working long-distance steam charters.

With watering complete, we left Salisbury behind and, once we cleared Alderbury, we had plenty of easy running before diverging to the left at Romsey, which would take us through Chandlers Ford and on to our engine's birthplace at Eastleigh for a booked stop. Peter brought us to a stand adjacent to a station name board, so I nipped on to the platform with my camera and captured a photo of the engine and the Eastleigh board together. I have had the pleasure of visiting Eastleigh yard and shed with a variety of Southern engines on steam charters – quite a privilege for a Midland man.

Our next stop was at 21.00 for water at Botley, once the junction for a branch to Bishops Waltham. Quite a crowd had gathered to view the operation; it was probably the highlight of a Saturday night out in Botley watching us pulling coal down and watering the tender! My route knowledge from here to our next booked stop at Chichester via Fareham and Havant was reasonable, having worked into nearby Portsmouth, and it was not very taxing on the shovel. On this warm June evening plenty of folk were having a Saturday night stroll and were a little taken aback by our presence as we steamed through those places. Some of the stations along this line have been subject to an identical modernisation plan and Chichester is no exception, although we would not have much time to look around the place during our booked 2-minute stop.

The busy junction of Arundel was passed 15 minutes from Chichester, followed by the Sussex seaside towns of Goring-by-Sea, Worthing (a passenger stop) and Shoreham-by-Sea (now barely visible in the fading light) before coming to a stand in Hove, which still retains the magnificent canopies covering its entrance-way. Leaving there just before 11 o'clock, we diverged left, bypassing Brighton, to head north after the briefest of stops at Preston Park. Our destination was 10 miles further on, but before then we had to negotiate three more tunnels before finally arriving back at Haywards Heath at 23.40, our train having departed from there at 07.57. Everyone seemed to have enjoyed themselves, including us and the support crew, and *Lord Nelson* had behaved himself impeccably on his 350-mile excursion into Somerset. We had an empty stock movement to Redhill to complete the day's outing, lodging overnight before a Sunday afternoon departure returning the entire ensemble to Alton and the Mid-Hants Railway.

My last turn on No 850 *Lord Nelson* was a return Steam Dreams charter to commemorate the 40th anniversary of the ending of Southern steam, which ran on Sunday 8 July 2007 from Waterloo to Exeter via Yeovil Junction and return via Bristol. That weekend also saw other Southern steam-hauled specials; I had *Tangmere* on one on the Saturday, before travelling down to Exeter and staying there overnight to relieve the inbound crew of No 850 at St David's on the Sunday at 13.30. However, all was not well; the fireman told me that he was knackered and had not had a break from firing as it had been a rough trip after part of the brick arch had collapsed on to the fire, affecting the steaming.

We quickly shunted the coaches into the Riverside Yard, after which I offered my services to assist in the removal of the collapsed portion of the brick arch. Again my experience with the fire irons proved useful when using the long paddle assisted by a support crew member using the long bent bar to manoeuvre the bricks onto the paddle before pulling them back out of the long firebox to discharge them through the open cab doors. It was a tiring process, taking us more than an hour, by which time we could see that one third of the arch was missing.

My driver was Ray Poole, and between us and the support crew RO we made the decision to carry on and do our best to get the 12-coach train back to London, realising that it certainly would tax our capabilities, and no possibility of any diesel assistance. Added to this, we had a conductor driver for Ray, but fortunately he was not passed for steam, so with Ray doing the driving we would have an experienced hand on the regulator.

The first stage of our journey could not have been tougher – straight from the platform end at St David's we were faced with the 20-mile climb to the top of Whiteball with a ruling gradient of 1 in 80. Ray appreciated the fact that I did have good knowledge of our route to Westbury, which helped to overcome the possible conflict of route information advice given by the diesel conductor driver to the differing wants of a steam fireman. We managed to depart on time in the late afternoon from Exeter with a full head of steam, a good fire and a pot full of water, so let battle commence!

Ray is not known for hanging about, and he soon had the 'Lord' into its stride. I had purposely avoided starting off with the usual roaster of a fire, preferring instead to fire little and often to see how things went with the steaming, as my expectations were of a sluggish start until I could get No 850 warmed through, but patience was required due to the large hole in the arch. I tend to use the driver's-side injector when hill-climbing with this engine, finding that it will maintain a suitable water level. Of course, it cannot be turned off when working the engine hard, and as the conductor driver was standing behind Ray he was able to oversee the injector overflow pipe. As he was part of our four-man footplate team I explained to him the importance of the injector picking up cleanly, asking him to keep an eye on it.

Seven miles into the climb, as we passed through Silverton, at last *Lord Nelson*'s steam gauge began to rise, having been rock solid at a slightly worrying 170lb. The fire had been given my constant attention since departure, and by Cullompton, the halfway point of the climb, my strenuous efforts to increase the steam output seemed to have been rewarded as 210lb was registering on that most important gauge. But mysteriously we appeared to be losing the water level, which had dropped to less than half a glass. However, this was an artificial reading, due to the engine working on full regulator and 55% cut-off; a truer level was nearer to a quarter of a glass. My first instinct was to enquire of the conductor driver that the injector was working all right.

'Yes, it's OK, mate,' came his reply. 'Water is still coming out of the pipe.'

Ray heard him and quickly spun around, lifted the driver's seat and adjusted the injector overflow. At the same time I put on the fireman's-side injector, turning it off 5 minutes later when the water level was satisfactory again. It would have been unfair to have given the diesel driver a rollocking for his mistake – after all, his priority was as route conductor, and he accepted my apology, at the same time not realising the importance of the task.

We had a short 1-mile downhill dip passing through the former Tiverton Junction, and Ray took full advantage of this and we roared through Tiverton Parkway at 55mph, attacking the final 3 miles of 1 in 115 grade. The engine had now lost all the sluggishness displayed on the early part of the climb and was hot and eager, each turn of the 6ft 7in driving wheels bringing us ever nearer to that summit and the accompanying tunnel. As you can imagine, firing had been almost constant throughout, working this four-cylinder engine to its near maximum output, but all of us were loving it. What a thrill, what a pleasure it was for man to master the machine. Ray dropped down the cut-off another half-turn to 60% for the last

mile, bringing one continuous roar from the multiple-jet blast pipe of *Lord Nelson* as we topped the summit with safety valves feathering just short of the maximum 220lb, and half a glass showing on the gauge. This was quickly followed by the introduction of the second injector to bring up the level as we entered the tunnel, where the gradient changed to 1 in 80 down.

I have previously described the route from here to Taunton on board No 73096, and it was much the same with No 850 running to our maximum, but this time without a Taunton stop and taking the left-hand road from Creech through Cogload Junction to our water stop at Bristol. This is an almost level 45-mile hop to Temple Meads, but it was imperative that we keep the 'Lord' as hot as possible without any blowing off, for my fear was that we might not be able to revive him should the firebox temperature diminish. This demanded my total concentration in keeping all areas of the firebox covered and burning bright, which could only be achieved by firing little and often (quite often).

A very short break was taken as we whistled through Bridgwater, then Highbridge. We actually managed an on-time arrival into Platform 4 at Bristol, coming to a stand opposite the water hydrant. The support crew leader and loco custodian Jesse was the first of the gang to hit terra firma and began to wind out the first of the five hoses needed to span the gap between tender and hydrant. Jesse was Mr Lord Nelson during my time operating the engine, leading a small but dedicated support crew in the none-too-easy task of maintaining this elder statesman of the locomotive world. He owned at least two executive-class live steam models of *Lord Nelson* and it would be fair to say that without his dedication the engine would not have completed such a high main-line mileage. We were situated near the former

Southern Railway four-cylinder 4-6-0 No 850 *Lord Nelson* stands at London Victoria. My driver, Peter Roberts, changes the lamps while loco custodian Jesse looks relaxed as we prepare to depart with a special for Southampton and Salisbury. *Author's collection*

bay platform sidings, where some scenes were filmed for the Ealing comedy *The Titfield Thunderbolt*, with Bristol Bath Road shed in the background. This later became a diesel depot, but at the time of writing is just waste ground.

Ray and I were sitting on the platform enjoying a well-earned cuppa courtesy of the support crew when to our surprise a relief crew appeared in the form of driver Bill Andrew and fireman Brian ('Wizzer') Williams. We had been booked for relief at Westbury, but having heard about the brick arch problem they had decided to come to Bristol to help if required. After a few minutes discussion it was agreed that they should relieve us in Bristol, and with that sorted Ray jumped on the first service back

to Birmingham. The conductor driver was not now required, but I remained on the job to assist Brian to Salisbury, where I was booked in for the night before travelling into London on the Monday to work the engine and stock back to the Mid-Hants.

It took nearly an hour to top up the water due to the slow supply, during which time the loco had cooled down. Brian and I discussed the situation, and although he was an experienced fireman *Lord Nelson* was a bit of a stranger to him, so we decided to make it a joint effort to keep the engine on the move. I have previously described the route from Bristol to Westbury, and it is not the most taxing of lines, but any route can become troublesome if the engine is not behaving, which is exactly what happened between Bristol and Bath. Apart from cooling down, the engine had now developed the additional problem of leaking tubes, but we manage to keep time to Bath. From there it was a different story, for we are fighting to maintain sufficient steam and water along the undulating Avon Valley. Both Brian and I were trying every trick in the book, but could not punch the steam pressure beyond 150lb. Bill was driving the loco as gently as possible, and our aim was to make Westbury then assess the situation, when and if we reached there.

In front of us was a 4-mile pull from Trowbridge to Westbury on a gradient of 1 in 120. This was not a problem under normal circumstances, but it was on an engine with missing sections of brick arch causing flue tube leakage, which in turn was dowsing the fire at the front of the firebox. All of this was causing a shortage of steam, and on top of all that Jesse cast an expert eye around the box as we passed through Trowbridge and declared that we also had leaking crown stays. But we were still on the move as *Lord Nelson* gallantly attacked the climb to Westbury. Brian and I had experience of thousands of firing turns, and believe me we were being tested to the limit keeping No 850 on the move. If we came to a stand here it would be hours before they found something with enough power to drag us into Westbury.

On the final part of the climb, with the station in sight, our loco was still gallantly dragging a train weighing more than 425 tons with just 125lb of steam on the clock and 2 inches of water showing in the glass. We mustn't fail here, so it was off with the injector to help maintain the steam pressure. We were now down to a single blast and walking pace. Bill had the large ejector on, which was helping to keep the brakes off as we entered the station and managed to come to a stand with the entire train inside the platform road clear of all points. Bill expertly allowed the train to come to a stop without touching the brake, thereby eliminating the possibility of exposing the firebox crown.

The situation demanded a powwow between all parties – the Responsible Officer, support crew, loco crew, train manager and guard, together with Network Rail Control – but realistically the final say would be with Jesse, the loco's custodian. His main concern – nay, worry – was the leaking crown stays. While the predicament was being assessed, Brian and I had been trying to revive the fire against the profusely leaking tubes, and the water was winning, extinguishing at least a quarter of the fire grate. Having previously lost a third of the arch, together with the leaking crown stays, resulting in the engine having difficulty in raising steam even when stationary, I think we all knew the inevitable outcome was going to be engine failure. This was confirmed by Jesse, who was visibly upset and unaware at the time that this would be the finale of main-line operation for 'his' *Lord Nelson*.

The train was terminated at Westbury, passengers being ferried home courtesy of Network Rail. I was instructed to travel to Salisbury and stay overnight pending further developments; Bill and 'Wizzer' remained with the train until diesel assistance arrived to take it forward to London. On the Monday my services were obviously not required, resulting in me travelling home passenger to Grosmont. All of us involved with the return charter later received a communication thanking us for our efforts on the day.

Just as a footnote, it has occurred to me, reminiscing about my footplate days throughout the rail network, just how much hill-climbing was involved, and an interesting fact emerged linking together all of the inclines at Bincombe, Blea Moor, Buriton, Copy Pit, Diggle, Evershot, Honiton, Horsforth, Knockholt, Merstham, Ore, Rattery, Sapperton, Saunderton, Selling, Shepherdswell, Stoke, Upholland, Westenhanger, Whiteball and Wilpshire – all of them have a tunnel at or near the summit. Why? Answers on a postcard please to Mr I. K. Brunel, PO Box 13, Swindon…

31 Great Western trips, a funeral party, and a jaunt with 'SNG'

Mention of that hallowed place Swindon leads me in nicely to relate some of my main-line experiences with products manufactured by the Great Western Railway at those Wiltshire workshops. Having described my first experience of footplating a member of the 'Castle' Class when I rode as a working guest in 1962 aboard No 5094 *Tretower Castle* from Taunton to Bristol, it was to be more than 40 later before I was able to renew my acquaintance with another member of the class, No 5029 *Nunney Castle*. This engine became a regular sight working the 'Cathedrals Express' and we became good friends.

So let's wind the clock back to Wednesday 24 August 2005 when we were together on a Bristol-bound 'Cathedrals' charter with driver Peter Kirk. The run to Bristol was one of my favourites, particularly when we travelled direct along Brunel's main line from Reading rather than via the Berks & Hants and Savernake. The engine and coaches had been stabled at Old Oak Common depot, which was still quite busy at that time, although only one of the original four turntables was still operative. We made use of it before going off shed and travelling via the Greenford loop line, eventually arriving at London Victoria for an 08.53 departure. The train comprised the standard

formation of 12 coaches, all in green livery, and with a green locomotive at the head – what more could you ask for?

No 5029 *Nunney Castle* has been turned at Old Oak Common and is ready to leave the depot to work a Bristol charter with Peter Kirk as driver. *Author's collection*

Before departure from the lengthy Platform 2, an important job was to ensure that we were displaying the correct headcode. We had two authentic Western headlamps, one over each buffer, signifying an express; one of them had been cleverly modified to battery operation to conform with the requirements of displaying an electric light. To complete the scene No 5029 was carrying an authentic 81A shed plate, where it had spent most of its working life.

Promptly at 08.53 Peter opened the regulator and brought *Nunney Castle* to life on this sunny but very breezy summer morning, and we began the short climb out of the station, a diesel giving us a push to Grosvenor Bridge. Then we were on our own travelling via Stewarts Lane to our first pick-up point at Kensington Olympia. Many of our passengers preferred to travel from there to avoid congestion and the parking difficulties around Victoria. Ahead of us we had a short but stiff climb to Mitre Bridge before passing through the myriad of lines through Willesden. We then descended from Acton Wells to Acton, where we joined the Great Western main line. On the footplate were two members of the support crew as well as Peter and me; in order to give each of us some room, the support crew boys positioned themselves in each doorway with the warning that they were to hang on tight once we were under way, as these GW tender engines have just a flimsy chain across the gap instead of cab doors. I have said this before – footplate promotion must have been pretty rapid on the old Great Western!

Ten minutes was allowed for the 'Kenny O' stop, which gave me time to build up a decent fire to climb the road ahead to Mitre Bridge. We attained 30mph as we hit the bottom, then attacked the hill on full regulator and 60% cut-off. The gradient dragged us down to walking pace and single blasts – anyone residing in the adjacent yuppie flats received a noisy wake up call, but

No 5029 had the climb in its pocket and I had my head out of the cab window enjoying the music while at the same time looking along the boiler and admiring the fine lines of this handsome locomotive, adorned with brass and copper work.

As the fireman you are always thinking of the road ahead, and we were about to join the main line, demanding strict timekeeping. But it was pointless building up the fire until we were assured of a clear road through Acton, followed by some green signals beyond there. We had 30 minutes running time to our first port of call at Maidenhead. It took us just over 10 minutes to pass the former 81C steam depot and our own sub-depot at Southall. The novelty of having two whistles to play with proved irresistible, Southall being the first of three places on the route that would be treated to my self-composed Swindon symphony, played out on each apparatus! The four cylinders on our 'Castle' Class were also in good voice, and this smooth-running machine had our train nicely on the move. As the needle on the speedometer nudged past the 60mph mark, all was well on the footplate: we had steam and water aplenty and were gaining speed on this straight and true former broad-gauge main line.

I love the architecture and the very functional layout of the stations on this route. For instance, Slough – or to use Will Hay terminology, 'Sluff' – is one of three stations between Southall and Reading that was a junction station for a former branch line; a facsimile still exists at Maidenhead, where the branch train to Marlow is still affectionately known as 'The Marlow Donkey'. Entering Maidenhead we passed over another Brunel masterpiece, his bridge over the River Thames, where the railway is carried over the river on two brick arches. At the time of building they were the widest and flattest in the world; interestingly, the right-hand arch is also known as the

Sounding Arch because of its spectacular echo effects. Our station stop at Maidenhead was booked from 10.19 to 10.20, which was simply impossible to achieve with this 12 coach steam charter train, but thanks to some sharp work by the train stewards and guard we left at 10.23.

The railway has a slight gradient of 1 in 1320 (!) from here to our next stop at Reading. Anxious to make up a little of the lost time, Peter gave 'Nunney' its head, which I had anticipated, having spent the station time building up the fire, so the job was under control as we passed Twyford, 6 miles out from Maidenhead, doing a creditable 70mph. We would therefore not be taking the Henley-on Thames branch, which diverges with a 25mph speed limit!

When I was a young boy, railway books of the day invariably contained photos of the next place that we were now rapidly approaching; it seemed to be a Mecca for the likes of railway photographers such as Maurice Earley, E. R. Wethersett and George Heiron. I never thought that one day it would be me firing a Great Western steam locomotive through the iconic Sonning Cutting and having photographs taken by the bevy of present-day lineside cameramen. The mini-thrash from Maidenhead had blown the cobwebs off our steed, and we entered the busy confines of Reading station precisely to time at 10.35.

Because of pathing problems on the main line, the usual route for steam trips from here to Bristol is over the Berks & Hants line, rejoining the main line at Bathampton, but today we would carry straight on out of Reading and down the main line to our next booked stop at Swindon, the birthplace of our locomotive some 70 years earlier. But before this we would visit the loop at Challow to quench the thirst of engine and crew. The railway climbs gently for the next 40 miles to the loco's birthplace, so we said goodbye to Reading with the intention of reaching and maintaining the 75mph required of us to maintain time on this busy stretch of railway. The coal had been pulled forward by the support crew and I was digging into this with a vengeance to keep up with the demands for steam. Peter is a good steady driver who doesn't knock the engine about, although it was a little cramped on the footplate, with the addition of the air brake apparatus and the support crew. The ability to fire an engine left- or right-handed is an advantage, and is less strenuous for me.

We roared through Didcot, that other bastion of Great Western practice, with whistles screaming out a warning to stand well clear of the platform edge. The working museum here once housed our locomotive. After languishing for some 12 years in Woodham's Barry scrapyard it was bought by a consortium of the Great Western Society and became the last loco to leave the yard by rail. The museum encompasses the former steam depot and is well worth a visit, although my wife and I had an interesting experience on the day of our visit a few years ago. It was mid-week and the museum appeared to be closed, with no one about, when a lady appeared in a hi-vis jacket escorting a small party, so we tagged along on the end, coming to a halt when we reached a locomotive in the engine shed. The lady then turned around and asked us if we were related to the deceased. We had only tagged on to the end of a burial party, who were planning to put the ashes of the poor departed into the firebox of his favourite engine!

On the approach to Challow my driver shut off in good time in order to sight the exact position of the water tanker, which should be waiting for us on a road overbridge adjacent to the derelict former down platform. It was imperative that he was there, because we were down to less than 500 gallons in the tender. But we needn't have worried, for he was in position and had been for some time, being a regular man who knew the importance of his task; he sometimes had to link up with us three or four times a day in separate locations, maybe in remote settings, demanding excellent knowledge of all areas. Our timings allowed for a 15-minute stop for water, which was a bit tight considering the amount of hoses needed to link up from tender to tanker, but our support crew were a well-organised bunch, who also examined the engine and topped her up with lubricants where required, in addition to supplying us with fresh tea.

Away we went promptly at 11.35, and I was firing with renewed vigour following our tea break, which kept me engrossed for the next few miles. Having left behind the four-track section of main line, we were now running on double track only. One of the support crew reminded me that we were at Uffington, and to look out for the prehistoric hill figure of the famous White Horse, formed from deep trenches filled with crushed chalk and a notable landmark for miles around. Shortly afterwards we crossed the border from Oxfordshire into Wiltshire before arriving at our locomotive's birthplace of Swindon for a 9-minute pathing stop, mimicking the days up to 1895 when every train stopped here for at least 10 minutes to change locomotives.

We had hardly come to a stand before the footplate was thronging with some past employees from the works, which at its zenith employed more than 14,000 personnel. It must be heartbreaking for those who are left from those days living in a Swindon devoid of its heart. It was with great reluctance that we had to ask these professional railwaymen to vacate the footplate, but we were due away and I had to physically wrestle the shovel from one old boy who insisted on giving me a demonstration on how best to fire one of 'his'

'Castle' Class locomotives – and no doubt he could, if we had the time.

The other route that we often took from this junction station was to Gloucester via Kemble, down Sapperton bank; if you fancy a trip over the line come with me on 'King' Class No 6024 on a return Gloucester-London job later in this chapter.

One of the benefits of present-day communications, mobile phones, etc, is that people are much better informed. An example of this being put to good use was the number of Swindon folk who were occupying vantage points along the lineside as we departed from their station, all of them aware of the presence of our steam charter train headed by one of their locomotives, once the pride of Swindon. And *Nunney Castle* did not disappoint them. Peter gave her full regulator, setting off a cannon-like exhaust beat that reverberated around the former works site, and amid much whistling and waving we left town.

For the next 25 miles the railway is a bit of a roller-coaster by Isambard's standards, with 3 miles of almost level running, 5 miles of gentle downhill cruising to Wootton Bassett, a sudden drop of 1 in 100 to Dauntsey, a little up and down for the next 10 miles to Corsham, the 2-mile-long Box Tunnel on a descent of 1 in 100, and a final 6-mile gentle stroll into Bath. Since leaving Swindon the weather had changed and a strong breeze was blowing, creating a vortex in the tender coal space and disturbing the coal dust, but easily dealt with by the use of the slacker pipe. When operating steam locomotives I always have a preference for working on routes devoid of overhead wires; when working under the 'chicken mesh', entering the tender or otherwise is forbidden, as is the use of the slacker pipe, hence the 'cleanliness' of some footplate crews at the end of a journey. Another downside is the visual aspect of the catenary apparatus, a real blight on the countryside.

I did not need to touch the fire after passing Dauntsey, confident of reaching Bath without picking up the shovel again. Anyhow, we had a 5-minute station stop at the Spa city, giving me enough time to build up the black stuff in the 30-square-foot firebox. Drifting down towards Bath, our loco rode steadily at the maximum 75mph, all was well with the world for the time being and, as is my wont, this rare moment of relaxation was allowing my mind to think back to just a few weeks previously on this stretch of line when I was the fireman on board one of my all-time favourite class of steam locomotive, an 'A4' 'Pacific', and my old friend No 60007 *Sir Nigel Gresley*, working a return Bristol-London charter with Mr Raymond Churchill occupying the driving seat.

On that day we had left Temple Meads late, so time needed to be made up if possible, but the 40 miles separating us from Swindon were all uphill apart from the dip through Chippenham. To give you some idea of just how hard we were working, if I was to say that some three weeks later I was still very wary of putting my head out of the cab of *Nunney Castle* on this same stretch of track to avoid the risk of being burned by sparks still descending from the double chimney of the 'A4'! Riding with us that day as part of the support crew was a fireman from the NYMR, Gary Stainburn, who I am sure after watching the proceedings could just not comprehend the gulf between firing on a preserved railway and firing steam locomotives on the main line. Just as a matter of interest, Ray got us back to time!

It is always a pleasurable experience on the run-in to Bath, giving us an elevated view of those Georgian sandstone properties. One of my many claims to fame is having been inside a house with the most prestigious address in the city at Royal Crescent, home to the doyen of Somerset & Dorset Railway photographers Ivo Peters. He made our family most welcome one Sunday morning,

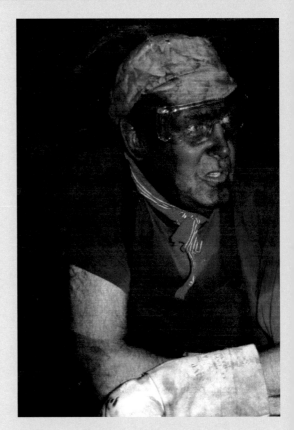

Mucky me: arriving at King's Cross with 'A4' 'Pacific' No 60007 *Sir Nigel Gresley*, having worked in a 230 mile special from Scarborough. *Author's collection*

giving us a viewing of his films of the S&D and apologising that some of them had been sent to the BBC to put on some newfangled thing called 'video'! Oh, how I would love to have lived at Bath in those halcyon steam days, but Ivo did sign my copy of his book *The Somerset & Dorset Railway*.

Anyway, back to the tale. We had enjoyed an enjoyable and fast run from the capital, arriving on time at this ancient Roman city. The timetable said that we were allowed 19 minutes for the last 11 miles on the slight descent to Bristol, but given the road we could and often did cut a few minutes off those timings. No 5029 was already nice and warm, waiting patiently for the off at the end of Platform 1. Precisely at 12.41 we had a green from our guard, I relayed this to Peter, and he gave her the gun with a repeat of the Swindon departure. *Nunney Castle* noisily announced our leaving and on through the busy suburbs of downtown Bath, attracting the attention of customers at the nearby busy shopping malls and no doubt providing them with a talking point aside from mundane duties.

When I next looked up from my firing we were on the approaches to the Tudor-style Twerton Tunnels, time to close the firehole doors and on with the jet, or blower to some. Emerging from the tunnels we were running almost parallel with the former Midland Railway Bath to Bristol line, part of which has been preserved as the Avon Valley Railway from Bitton, but nothing was running there today so it was time to feed 'Nunney' with a short final burst of coal as we passed through Keynsham, now devoid of any of its Great Western heritage buildings, passengers having to wait in a common brick shelter. Until 1980 there was a connection here to Fry's chocolate factory at nearby Somerdale.

We ran unchecked from Bath and were now approaching North Somerset Junction on the outskirts of Bristol. Fortunately they were ready for us and we got a clear run in, coming to a stand in Platform 13 under Mr Brunel's masterpiece with the hands on the station clock at 12.57; 16 minutes was not bad for a start-to-stop time, allowing for negotiating the speed restrictions on the station approaches. Although a nice finale to the 118-mile journey, it did not match the timings of the erstwhile 'Bristolian', but that was a lightweight train that ran with only seven or eight coaches.

We have already had the story of No 5972 *Olton Hall*, or the 'Harry Potter Hall', so let's now relate a tale of a trip I made on sister engine No 4936 *Kinlet Hall* double-headed with No 5029 *Nunney Castle* on the 'Three Choirs Express', steam-hauled

from Stourbridge Junction to Gloucester via Worcester, Hereford and Newport on Saturday 4 October 2008.

The charter was organised by Past Time Rail and left Nottingham at 06.00 diesel-hauled by Brush Sulzer No D1775 resplendent in two-tone green. I knew some of the route on this lengthy trip, having been to Worcester with 'Duchess' No 6233, and visited Gloucester a few times with No 6024 *King Edward I*. The charter would normally have been covered by firemen from Tyseley depot, where the two engines were based, but with some not available I accepted the chance to pair up again with a driver with whom I always enjoyed working, and who has a passion for anything Great Western, Mr Raymond Churchill.

My weekend started on the Friday, travelling from Grosmont to a hotel adjacent to the Tyseley depot, meeting Ray and the crew of the assisting loco at about 07.30. It was nice to be given a brief guided tour of this former BR steam depot ,prompting me to think that only a select few of them now remain to turn off steam locomotives half a century after BR closed them to steam. Also included with Tyseley are the depots at Southall, Stewarts Lane and Old Oak Common, all of which I have worked from with steam traction during my time based in London, and of course Carnforth back home in Lancs. Following my tour of 84E my feelings were that Tyseley still embodied the spirit of a Great Western steam depot, and take that as a compliment coming from a northerner.

Stepping aboard the immaculate No 4936 *Kinlet Hall*, a warm welcome was given me by the support crew and the Responsible Officer for the day, Tyseley supremo Bob Meanley, whose son Alistair is a top-notch fireman at the depot, so I needed to be at my best, being a stranger to both route and engine. We were the leading loco, with No 5029 behind us, and we left the depot with the support coach and headed for Stourbridge Junction, the tour's changeover point for steam.

The weather was reasonable, but with a threat of rain later in the day we had a tarpaulin sheet covering the gap between the cab roof and tender; while this made it a little claustrophobic for the four of us on the footplate, it would help to keep us dry. Moreover, when beneath the overhead wires it served as a reminder not to climb above footplate level. Although it was a little cramped to have four on this class of engine, it was usually the decision of the fireman as to how many support crew could ride on the footplate, my only ruling being that I was given the space to do my work. Four has always been the norm with me – after all, it is their engine and they are doing the job free gratis.

Having had experience of firing a right-hand-drive engine way back in my BR days, when I taught myself to fire from either side of the footplate, this proved useful aboard this Great Western engine. As many firemen from those days will tell you, it was a case of having to be adaptable on the shovel, otherwise you could incur the wrath of some drivers who would not let you shovel coal from their side of the footplate, a kick up the rear not being entirely unknown! A somewhat greater inconvenience was that the driver of No 5029 did not sign for all of the route, but this was not a safety issue as he was not in control of the train, just the locomotive; Ray, of course, was the driver and signed for the entire route, having previously briefed his colleague regarding the road, with instructions 'to drive off our chimney', which is standard practice when working double-headed. The term simply means that the assisting driver must watch and also listen to the exhaust from the leading engine as that will tell him when to apply or shut off steam. As a fireman I did have concerns, of course, that the larger engine, No 5029, might not always do the fair share of the work, as it was a powerful four-cylinder engine and could handle the ten-coach train without assistance. However, more about that later.

At Stourbridge Junction we had time for a cuppa while awaiting the arrival of the 'Three Choirs' (be careful how you say that!). Being a nosey beggar, I just could not resist a quick visit to the statuesque former GWR signal box, the friendly incumbent having agreed to my request when I rang him first on a lineside phone. We talked of the short but steep branch line of less than a mile leading to Stourbridge Town, and he related six accidents of runaway trains over the years, also telling me that a day's shift for the present train crew is 11 round trips, prompting me to remark that they must be rather dizzy by the end of that shift.

Back on the footplate I began to take stock of the situation, not having fired this particular member of the class, so the run down from Tyseley had broken me in somewhat. In addition, a chat with the support crew and a review of the road ahead with Ray meant that I was ready for action when we backed on to our train, which had run in on time behind No D1775. This loco would remain at Stourbridge until we departed, then would travel light engine to Gloucester to work the return leg back to Nottingham.

The station clock moved to 09.27, both engines whistled up, and away we went on the first leg of our 160-mile journey. *Kinlet Hall* came complete with the obligatory Great Western firing shovel, which is larger than a standard Lucas and slightly larger than my Southern/GWR hybrid, but I was soon swinging it like a veteran – come to think of it, that is probably what I am now! The road ahead was not too taxing and we soon made a stately passage through Kidderminster, home of the preserved Severn Valley Railway, exchanging a friendly greeting on the whistle with one of their engines standing at the head of a train to Bridgnorth. The station pub here is famous for my favourite multi-award-winning Bathams bitter. However, I digress, but can report that *Kinlet Hall* appeared to be steaming well and responding to what I call my standard Great Western fire, having concentrated on keeping under the door and the middle of the firebox well built up, lifting and lowering the flap at each charge, and leaving the firehole doors open.

I had been absorbed so much with footplate happenings that, shortly after passing through a short tunnel, when next I looked out we were approaching Worcester, which was still sporting semaphore signals. The surroundings of this busy interchange are a bit cramped, and much of the railway infrastructure has gone, although the lovely viaducts remain. We would be doing some chuffing for the next 10 miles with a ruling gradient of 1 in 80 to the summit at Colwall, but before that, at Malvern Wells, the line became single to pass through the tunnels at Colwall and Ledbury, the latter notorious for its bad atmosphere, the result of its unusually narrow bore combined with a steep gradient and a bend at the north end.

Ray kept me well informed beforehand of any upcoming changes in gradient, so I was well prepared for the thrash ahead. He does like to hear the engine talk and making them go a bit, but I was ready for him as he dropped *Kinlet Hall* down the rack and she responded with that lovely crisp beat typical of Great Western engines, devoid of any ejector exhaust, the vacuum pump manfully fulfilling that role. On the footplate as we climbed the Malvern Hills we had a real team affair keeping things spot on: the two support crew boys were enthusiastic in helping out with trimming the coal, watching injector overflows and keeping the footplate clean, as well as forming a natural barrier as a draught excluder when standing on either side of the footplate.

Having had experience over the years working double-headed trains, I do know when one engine is working harder than the other, and this had definitely been happening throughout the morning. My thoughts were backed up by the travelling support crew, not to mention that on my part it was taking some extra grafting with the shovel! The 3 hours spent on the footplate since leaving the depot had given me sufficient time to form an opinion of *Kinlet Hall*; obviously comparisons with an LMS 'Black 5' were going to be made, as they shared the same size of driving wheel at 6 feet, limiting them to the present 60mph restriction. However, our 'Hall' has slightly larger cylinders, giving a higher tractive effort. Factors not in its favour are the spartan cab devoid of side windows and a side spectacle plate, and the open-back tender, the shape of which makes coal trimming doubly hard. Having only one gauge frame is not the inconvenience it must have been in steam days, when a burst gauge class could be a menace, more so if it happened at night when on the move. Fitting lubricators on the footplate is far from ideal, but I think I have grumbled about these things before, as steam footplatemen have to have a grumble about something, so let's move on to the positives of No 4936.

First, what I love about GW engines is their injectors, which are ultra-reliable. The boilers are usually free-steaming and all locos should have those simmering Swindon safety valves. Moreover, when you open the regulator they move without fuss – but their riding qualities vary. This loco rattled along a bit, but 60mph was only a cruising speed and comfort was not a problem, for despite being due for an overhaul, I was told, she had certainly lost none of her hill-climbing capabilities, having just effectively flattened the last 3 miles of 1 in 80 up to Colwall. This gave me a short welcome break on the 5-mile descent to Ledbury, a passing place on this single line, which was once the junction of a line to Gloucester, which closed entirely in 1965. This very rural area commands only a single line, so it was a little upsetting passing through so many closed country stations, most of them very much intact with friendly inhabitants waving and photographing us as we recreated the rare sight of a steam train passing through their station once more.

Steaming onwards we approached the outskirts of the city of Hereford, which was to be our water stop. Having been there before I did know the location of the hydrant, which was situated at the south end in the car park of the superstore adjacent to the station. We hoped that no one had parked a car in the way! We were signalled down the centre road in Hereford station, so no time was wasted in hooking off the engines; then to prove me wrong the signalman put us in the back road for water and not the car park siding. We were enjoying this sandwich break, feeding the inner man, although I think some Desperate Dan nut-and-bolt soup would have been more appropriate to revive me, having toiled away for the past few hours seemingly dragging ten coaches plus one dead steam locomotive, as No 5029 had definitely not

been doing its share of the work.

We discussed what lay ahead on the route to Abergavenny and Newport, which wasn't entirely strange to me, having been over that territory on a few occasions. I just needed to be well prepared in time for climbing to Llanvihangel, and the lesser pull to Pontypool Road. In our favour was that both these climbs were more severe from the opposite direction. Getting away from this cathedral city, we entered double track again onto the Welsh Marches line. There is an immediate sharp rise for a couple of miles, but we were prepared for it, followed by a 7-mile downhill stretch, giving us a good chance of a run at the 6 miles of climbing to Llanvihangel. Suitably refreshed from the break, I was throwing the shovel about with renewed energy, as Ray charged into the bottom of Llanvihangel with *Kinlet Hall* announcing its presence into Wales on full regulator and cut-off set at 50%.

As we left Herefordshire behind, this was heavy digging, prompting me to look back to see what effort was actually being made by *Nunney Castle* – the answer was not much. I managed to catch the attention of the fireman leaning out of the cab, scenery-

A nice pairing of Great Western motive power as we drift to a stand for the Hereford water stop with Nos 4936 *Kinlet Hall* and 5029 *Nunney Castle*, having worked in with a Stourbridge Junction-Gloucester railtour on Saturday 4 October 2008. *Author's collection*

viewing. I gesticulated to him with my arm lifting an imaginary regulator, he got the message and a much stronger exhaust emerged from our four-cylinder companion. Apart from this incident, I was enjoying the day travelling through some gorgeous countryside with plenty of semaphore signalling and old stations, a real throwback to how the railways once were, nowhere more so than the former Pontypool Road station, now renamed Pontypool & New Inn.

The railway here once dominated this entire area. As a young teenager it was familiar to me when I travelled from my home in Preston on one of our regular visits to my aunt and uncle living in Cardiff. The number of trains that passed through this railway junction station was unbelievable! It had its own engine sheds and a 50-road marshalling yard, but guess what is left today. Yes, just a bus-type shelter standing on a single platform. Sometimes it doesn't do to have memories. I have only been back to Cardiff once since those days, when I lodged overnight prior to working a Saturday Swansea-Crewe charter over the tortuous Sugar Loaf mountain route double-headed with Ian Riley's 'Black 5s' Nos 45407 and 44871. Unfortunately I did not have sufficient time on the Friday to go out to the suburb of Fairwater to visit the area where my aunt once lived.

The junction at Maindee was still quite a busy place as we passed, having drifted down the 15 miles from Pontypool Road, and within a few minutes we drew to a halt in Newport station. Here we were paid a visit by the RO, Bob Meanley, who hopped onto the footplate and took a quick look at the coal we had left in the tender, before carrying out the same inspection on No 5029. Raised voices could be heard, which was not Bob's style, but he then returned to inform us that we had burned twice as much coal on *Kinlet Hall* as they had used on *Nunney Castle*, confirming my suspicions of

events since leaving Stourbridge Junction. However, he told us that they had been instructed to share the workload for the remainder of the day.

Departing from Newport we passed some interesting places along the way on the more or less level 50 miles to Gloucester. First was Severn Tunnel Junction, which still occupied plenty of railway land, although the sheds and banking engines were long gone. The experience of travelling through that tunnel on board a steam locomotive is unforgettable, although on today's journey we would miss out on that thrill as we were taking the Chepstow route at the junction. What remained of the station buildings at Chepstow was hardly inspirational to the traveller; of more interest is the railway bridge over the River Wye, or 'The Great Tubular Bridge', built to the instructions of I. K. Brunel in 1852. As we passed over the bridge it was noticeable that big brother at the back was doing plenty of shoving; he was almost trying to climb over our tender in an effort to make up for hours of inadequacy!

We were soon at the former junction station of Lydney, home of the preserved Dean Forest Railway. Not far from here can be seen the remains of the once mighty Severn Railway Bridge; two barges collided with it in 1960 in thick fog and a strong tide, causing its closure and eventual demolition in 1970. The weather had turned a bit grim for us in the late afternoon, somewhat spoiling our views as we ran parallel to the Severn estuary.

Our arrival at Gloucester was about 20 minutes late, which wasn't too bad considering the adventurous route we had taken. Following a short spell of good-natured banter discussing the day's events with the crew of No 5029, no time was then lost in the loco change and we soon headed back to Tyseley depot via the circuitous route of Swindon, Didcot and Oxford, a good day having being had by all.

32 And now a 'King'

The GWR 'King' Class locomotive No 6024 *King Edward I* featured on our rosters for a number of years, giving me the opportunity to become acquainted with the ultimate of Swindon motive power. Not for them a fleet of 'Pacific' locomotives; this class of 4-6-0s had in theory the edge on power over an LMS 'Duchess' and most other top-end 'Pacific' classes. In my possession are the timings for a run we made with No 6024 on Saturday 12 March 2005 working 1Z28, a Chester-Minehead charter, steam-hauled from Gloucester to Minehead. The job entailed the usual overnight stay in the Bristol Ibis hotel on the Friday, before reporting to Barton Hill depot at 05.00 on the Saturday, and departing from there with engine and support coach up the former Midland main line to Gloucester.

This almost routine operational move was not without incident when, on the outskirts of Standish Junction and travelling at 60mph, some nice twat threw a brick at us from a road bridge, shattering, but not breaking, the fireman's cabside window. It was no coincidence that a travellers' camp was situated in the adjacent field, but we carried on, although it certainly woke us all up.

Arriving at Gloucester, more trouble ensued due to a signalman in the power box being unfamiliar with the necessary and preplanned propelling movements in order to turn the locomotive and coach on the triangle. Although he had worked in the

box for a number of years, the move was alien to him; the situation was stalemate until a senior controller agreed to sanction the move, but for the engine only. This highlights some of the problems when running heritage trains on the national network, where the majority of modern-day signalmen have no experience with shunting movements, propelling movements, wrong line movements, or banking or assistant locos. All they handle are complete trains and fixed units, which is not their fault of course – in fact, some of them have gone out of their way to be helpful to keep the job moving.

As we stood in the station sidings awaiting the arrival of our charter, I was looking out for my train driver son, who was on his way from Birmingham to travel with us on the special. He worked for Central Trains (now London Midland) and right on cue he arrived at the station and made his way down to us, but not without first chatting up the young female driver who had brought him from New Street. One thing that none of our sons three sons suffer from is shyness – I don't know where they get that from!

A few minutes later at 09.05, with John Lloyd safely ensconced in our support coach, we were greeted by the arrival at the lengthy Platform 4 of our Class 50-hauled 12-coach charter from Chester. We replaced the diesel on the front of the train, and it ran round and hooked onto the rear. Following a satisfactory brake test, the '50' would take no further part hauling the train except in an emergency, leaving us to drag him to Minehead – plus the 12 coaches, of course! The other two members of the footplate crew were both regulars, with Chris Hopcroft driving us to Bristol, where Peter Kirk would be on the throttle, and guard Mike Hollingsworth was in charge of the train. It was Mike who came to the footplate and, with a broad grin on his face, announced that the gross train weight was more than 600 tons, which ended any further conversation between us! So I busied myself with the shovel, feeding the lengthy firebox.

Promptly at 09.30 the sound of the guard's whistle brought a halt to my labours. I relayed the right away to Chris, then for the first time we heard the bark of a 'King' as No 6024 got hold of the weight and began a sure-footed drag up the 1 in 108 to Tuffley Junction, then onto the 1 in 104 up to Standish Junction. Throughout the climb the loco was working on full regulator using 50% cut-off. The 'King' was certainly announcing his presence, making all this effort with not the slightest hint of a slip as the Golden Valley line bore off to the left at Standish Junction (I will describe a run up there with the 'King' later).

We were now gaining speed as the cut-off was brought up the rack and we travelled downhill to the former junction station for the Dursley branch at Coaley. Passing there both engine and crew were now suitably warmed up, although this was no time for any relaxation, as my gradient profile chart was telling me that we had a 10-mile climb coming up once clear of Berkeley Road. Travelling this line I was more than a little excited to be firing over the route of the 'Pines Express', once destined for Bath and Bournemouth on my favourite Somerset & Dorset Railway, although regrettably that would not be happening today, nor would an engine of the 'King' Class have been heading

the train. It would much more likely have been a Midland 4-4-0 similar to loco No 714, which was in charge of the 10.00pm down Bristol passenger and mail express on this very stretch of track, and like us was approaching Charfield. But thankfully there the similarity ends.

On that fateful foggy October night in 1928 the driver missed both the Down Distant and the Outer Home signals protecting Charfield, which were both set at danger, and his train collided with the 9.15pm GWR down goods being shunted in the station. The impact caused the down express to crash into the 4.45am LMS up goods train that was passing through the station, before finally coming to rest underneath the road bridge to the north of the station. The train being gas-lit, fire broke out almost immediately and it seems likely that the majority of the 14 passenger fatalities occurred due to this fire. Among the dead were the remains of two small children, who were never identified. They are buried in St James churchyard in Charfield and, according to local accounts, from 1929 until the late 1950s an unknown woman dressed in black used to regularly visit the graves.

Returning to 2005, we managed a safe passage through the closed Charfield station, the main building and station master's house now standing rather forlornly surrounded by modern industrial buildings. Just to prove wrong my earlier comment about inclines and tunnels, we were now on the 10-mile climb at 1 in 281, which actually has a tunnel halfway up the hill rather than at the summit at Yate! All was well on the footplate as we emerged from the 1,401-yard Wickwar Tunnel, the location of the well-known painting of 'The Devonian' double-headed by two 5XPs, the leading one being No 45682 Trafalgar. Our Great Western representative is putting on a fine display of hill-climbing, giving us no trouble whatsoever in what was being asked of him hauling this decent load. The support crew were happy with the way we were handling their prized possession, which did look at its best in fully-lined green – it seemed such a shame to get it dirty. It was certainly not as resplendent as when first I saw it in 1962 standing forlornly out of traffic at its final depot of Cardiff Canton.

The South Gloucestershire station of Yate flashed by us. This was formerly the junction for the Thornbury branch, closed to passenger traffic as long ago as 1944, but remaining open until 2013 to serve the needs of Tytherington Quarry. Our rapid progress towards Bristol received a setback when we were cautioned on the approaches to Westerleigh Junction, Chris bringing us to a halt at the signal protecting the junction to allow a Virgin Trains express to go by. The signal then cleared for us, permitting *King Edward I* to pull our train forward off the former Midland main line and over this important junction, but halfway across we all heard the sound of a brake application, causing our usually sure-footed four-cylinder giant to lose his feet, and despite the best efforts by Driver Hopcroft No 6024 slipped to a stand. We quickly checked the brake equipment in the cab – no fault there, and likewise in the support coach. Our guard called us to confirm that the communication cord had not been activated. The only place left was the cab of the Class 50 diesel. Over the radio the maintenance crew swore their innocence, but just as mysteriously the brakes suddenly came off again, full brake pressure was restored and away we went, anxious to make up the 4 minutes lost while we scratched our heads at Westerleigh Junction.

Our charter train was made up of air-braked stock, which negated the time-honoured problem when changing locomotives working vacuum-braked trains with Great Western motive power; the latter operated with 24 inches of vacuum as against the 21 inches used by all other engines, necessitating the time-consuming task of pulling the strings on all the vacuum cylinders. My son was handily placed to film the action from the support coach behind the engine as we passed over the truncated Midland line, now singled, which once continued through Mangotsfield.

Compared with the earlier panoramic view of engines on the LMS Barrow Road sheds, the present-day contribution to the Bristol steam scene was the welcoming sight of No 5029 *Nunney Castle* standing on Barton Hill depot as we drifted past and entered the lengthy Platform 4 at Temple Meads, coming to a stand at our booked time of 10.34. The support crew leapt into action to complete the watering and maintenance tasks within our allotted 40 minutes. On some of these steam charter trains our passengers do not get an opportunity to view and photograph the engine or chat to the crew, etc, but on today's outing they were spoiled for time, both at Gloucester and here during our only booked stop of the journey. An orderly queue formed on the platform of people wanting to visit the footplate for photographs of themselves in the driver's seat, or with the crew. We always try to oblige, as by travelling with us they are actively supporting main-line steam operation, and we are more than happy to answer their questions about the locomotive, provided we know the answer! If in any doubt, then it is always wise to refer them to the support crew boys.

Our 40-minute break flashed by and our visitors vacated the footplate, giving me the chance to swing the shovel and get a back end on before departure. The firebox of our 'King' is 11ft 6in long, making it the longest of all the engines in the main-line steam fleet, and it takes a practised swing to reach the front end of it with fuel.

At 11.13 we said goodbye to Bristol

with Peter now on the regulator. We had been fortunate to have occupied the main Platform 4 for so long on a busy Saturday morning without causing any delays, although unlike in the days of steam most platform lines at main-line stations are now bi-directional. Some early chuffing soon livened up the fire as we steamed past the site of the former GWR Bath Road engine sheds and negotiated the pointwork at the station throat leading us out on to the down main line. We passed a stationary northbound Virgin express with the driver capturing the scene on his mobile phone camera – a regular occurrence with national network drivers when we pass their oncoming trains.

We were given a 50-minute slot for the 45 miles to Taunton, climbing for the first 5 miles to Flax Bourton, then relaxing for 5 miles downhill to Yatton, where we should achieve our maximum 75mph and maintain this on the 35 miles of almost level track to Taunton. Not anticipating any signal checks before then, I built up the fire accordingly, leaving the front end until last to avoid creating smoke in the station. As was the case in the early part of the non-stop stretch of running, I was kept quite busy getting things in order on the footplate, so much so that we were approaching Yatton when I next looked up from my duties. But my labours had been rewarded; *King Edward I* was showing a rock-steady 240lb of steam and displaying the standard three-quarters of a glass of water in the single gauge frame as we hurtled through the station, our 75mph creating a vortex of air under the platform canopy of this former Great Western station, junction for the Clevedon and Congresbury lines. Five minutes later we whirled through Worle, not visiting the loop line to Weston-super-Mare on this day, although we had taken His Majesty down there previously.

All was well on the footplate, and we were having a good trip. Firing the 'King' consisted of a burst of 25 shovelsful of coal, lifting and lowering the flap after each charge in true Great Western tradition, and he was loving it – for mile after mile our speed remained constant at 75mph, requiring no adjustment of the controls from Peter. It was as though the engine was locked in at that speed, prompting engine custodian Steve Underhill to remark that this was often the case, not only with No 6024 but with most of the main-line fleet of locomotives, which became accustomed to running for mile after mile at that speed, and likewise with those restricted to 60mph running. Confirmation of our thoughts of how easily the loco was handling the 600-ton train came later, when my son played back the film he had taken of our journey from the first coach – on this stretch the engine's exhaust was hardly audible.

The once important Somerset town of Highbridge was coming up and I aimed to remind the nearby residents of its connection with the steam locomotive and my love for the railway that once passed through their town; I also reminded myself that it was the home town of my old boss at Lostock Hall MPD, Mr Harold Sedgebeer. Having given prior warning of my intentions to Peter, who stuck his fingers in his ears, I opened up both whistles as we hammered through the station, leaving behind us echoes from the steam era at this once important railway town.

The area around here is known as the Somerset Levels, the railway reflecting this, giving me a reasonably easy passage with the shovel, but at the same time being extra cautious to avoid blowing off steam. Fortunately the safety valves on these Great Western locos begin with a gentle simmer, unlike for instance LNER locos, which explode into life upon reaching full working pressure, which can be a shock to the system to anyone nearby. The very issue of firemen and safety valves is a touchy subject. If we go back to my BR days, it wasn't uncommon for firemen to face disciplinary action from the inspectorate, charged with lacking boiler control management. In my opinion blowing off steam can be avoided, as there is no excuse for an experienced fireman, who knows both the loco and the route, allowing this to happen, particularly in a station area. I accept that sometimes unplanned delays and signal checks can happen; we all make mistakes, but I still feel a sense of shame and embarrassment when I know that I may have been at fault.

The outskirts of Bridgwater now appeared. Unfortunately this is not the Bridgwater featured on my S&D layout, but the still largely intact GW station, still sporting its original footbridge, so I suppose that deserved a whistle of acknowledgement as we passed through, treating a healthy crowd of camera-wielding enthusiasts who had gathered on the platforms on this bright but chilly March Saturday.

The flying junction at Cogload is where trains from Bristol start to share tracks with those from Castle Cary. The distinctive girder bridge always reminds me of the OO-gauge model that Airfix produce. We rattled over this and past the site of the water troughs and Creech Junction, our speed now reduced for the entry into Taunton where it was once possible to continue your journey to Minehead or to Barnstaple. With the ending of these services, Taunton station has been reduced accordingly, with the bay platforms for the branch services now lying derelict. Thankfully Platform 2 was still in use and we drifted along, stopping only for operational purposes to pick up a conductor driver who would take us to Norton Fitzwarren Junction; there he and a West Somerset Railway fireman would take the train forward to its destination at Minehead.

We journeyed for a couple of miles on the relief line before coming to a stand at Norton Fitzwarren Junction, where we took our leave of No 6024 after briefing the West Somerset fireman of the 600-ton load behind the tender. That figure went straight over his head, as the heaviest train he had worked was less than half that weight, so I had a couple of minutes with him regarding the firing before they pulled away to Bishops Lydeard. Some 20 minutes later we were informed that the train had unfortunately come to a stand due to a shortage of steam, requiring banking assistance from the Class 50 diesel.

A little earlier, while standing at Norton Fitzwarren Junction with the 'King', conversation turned to fellow member of the 'King' Class No 6028 *King George VI*, which had been involved in a fatal crash here in 1940 when the driver misread the signalling and track layout, causing him to drive through the trap points at the end of the relief line at 40mph, killing 27 people. The inquest was told that the house belonging to the driver had been bombed the night before, but that he had gone to work as usual.

Now, as threatened here is a further instalment of 'the King and I', which took place on a very hot summer Saturday when working a return charter train from Gloucester, but this time heading back to London Paddington with steam coming off at Old Oak Common. (There is a moral in this short tale, which will be revealed later.) I have neither the date nor the timings for this job, but the driver was Chris Hopcroft; we met at Gloucester in the early afternoon after I had arrived there from Grosmont.

We had 2 or 3 hours to spare before departure, and spent the entire time in the station sidings entertaining all and sundry who visited the footplate. As stated, it was a roaster of a day with no breeze. We left Gloucester at about 16.00, our route back to London being via Sapperton and the beautiful Golden Valley line to Swindon, where we joined the main line to Didcot,

Driver Chris Hopcroft, myself and 'King' Class No 6024 *King Edward I* await the arrival of our London-bound charter at Gloucester. *Peter Skelton*

before our first stop at Reading. (Oh, how I would dearly have loved to have travelled on a Gloucester-Chalford auto-train in steam days, hauled by a diminutive GWR 0-4-2T – what better way to admire the passing Cotswold scenery?)

Once away from Gloucester we were faced with a tough 20 miles of hill-climbing to the summit at Sapperton. With a ruling gradient of 1 in 60 it was a case of 'be prepared' for some serious shovel-swinging hauling this 12-coach train. Although this route was not new to me, I was looking forward to the first part of our journey through the Cotswolds, although I must admit to being more familiar with the Standish Junction near Wigan than the Standish Junction that we were passing some 8 miles out from Gloucester, sending us off in the direction of Stroud.

As the gradient increased Chris gave the 'King' another 10% cut-off, the loco responded accordingly and began digging into the climb with some gusto. The fact that I had some time to take in the views confirms that all was well on the footplate. Oops, spoke too soon! Chris interrupted my firing, shouting 'Signal check, Stroud!' and closing the regulator at the same time. A couple of miles later we were brought to a

stand by a big fat red signal, the telephone for which was at my side, so I climbed down and duly reported to the bobby, who apologetically informed me that in front of us was a freight, struggling up Sapperton bank and taking a while to clear, but he would give us the road once he had cleared the section.

This spoiled all our plans for topping Sapperton in some style. We followed the freight all the way up, only getting a clear road after Kemble, making us some 20 minutes late at Swindon. Chris laid into it from there and we soon attained our running speed, but it was about this time when I began to feel unwell, sweating profusely and with stomach cramps. The owner's rep, Steve Underhill, was on the footplate and asked if I had been drinking plenty because of the heat. I must admit that I probably had not, prompting him to remark that I was as white as a sheet and maybe suffering from heat exhaustion or dehydration. Certainly I felt quite weak, but managed to keep the job going, even brightening up slightly when passing Cholsey, where No 3440 *City of Truro*, with NRM custodian Ray Towell on the footplate, was running round its train, prompting an exchange of Great Western whistling as we roared past.

When we reached the outskirts of Reading I was feeling terrible, but luckily for me Steve was a qualified fireman and, following a short discussion, it was agreed that I would travel in the support coach and that Steve would take over the firing back to London. After spending most of the journey ensconced in the support coach toilet, a taxi was waiting for me at Old Oak to take me straight to my hotel, were I showered and went straight into bed until 9 o'clock on Sunday morning. After a hearty breakfast, I informed my superiors that I felt fit enough to travel home. The moral of this story is to ensure that you have a sufficient intake of fluids if working in a hot environment; it certainly taught me a lesson, and only happened once in hundreds of firing turns, but that was enough. Since that day I have always carried a flask containing Boots rehydration treatment in a blackcurrant flavour or similar.

Just briefly, a few weeks later we had another job with the 'King', this time to Oxford, preparing the train on Old Oak shed. It was decided to give the coaches a clean by propelling them through the carriage washing plant, which seemed like a good idea until the water and brushes could not be turned off before we passed through with the locomotive, drenching everybody and everything! Fortunately it was a hot day and we soon dried out – and it did save me the task of watering the coal in the tender.

It was with the King that I had my maiden voyage over the South Devon banks to Plymouth on Saturday 13 November 2004, working 'The Devonian' 07.00 Ealing Broadway-Plymouth charter train. We arrived at Bristol 6 minutes early, top-and-tailed by Class 47 diesels Nos 47200 and 47316, then it was steam-hauled from Bristol to Plymouth and return, with driver Peter Kirk.

Having already related a journey between Exeter and London, I shall describe the 50-mile voyage between Exeter and Plymouth, and what a spectacular 50 miles of railway that is. Once away from Platform 4 at Exeter, the first 20 miles are on almost level track, making it not that taxing as regarding firing duties, with a relatively light load of nine coaches, imposed upon us by Network Rail for operational purposes. The real heavy work would start beyond Newton Abbot.

Once away from St David's, few people on the train were aware that there had been a third railway station in Exeter, the rather humble St Thomas station, the buildings of which are now a nightclub and Chinese restaurant. Then within a few short miles the picture was a nice coastal view as we skirted the sea from Starcross to Dawlish Warren. The seafront and pathways are a magnet for holidaymakers at Dawlish, and driving trains over this line must be a real privilege for the lucky few; but I can't complain because on this Great Western engine the fireman gets the best views from his side.

We had a few temporary speed restrictions while traversing this section of line. The railway and the sea are at odds with each other in this area, involving a constant battle for the engineers to keep the infrastructure fit enough to let the services operate. Our 4-6-0 'King' Class engine did not like some of the curves, which restrict speeds to 60mph, and from experience a 'Pacific' locomotive with the trailing truck rides better. Never having been a diesel enthusiast, and it may come as a shock to those who know me, but I was pleased to see that the HST units still bore the brunt of passenger services on this line; they have been a remarkable design and if they all dropped to bits tomorrow they would not owe the railways a single penny.

One of these units, sporting its First Great Western colours, was departing from Platform 3 as we arrived at Platform 1 at Newton Abbot. We had a booked water stop here from 12.21 to 12.39, which was not quite as rushed as we had arrived 6 minutes up on schedule. Here we had a change of support crew member on the footplate, now having the company of the RO himself, Steve Underhill, who would ride with us to watch the performance of man and machine over the gruelling South Devon banks that lay just ahead of us.

My first task was to jokingly offer him a drink from my flask of special brew mixture and to thank him for standing in for me at Reading, at which he actually thanked me for giving him the rare opportunity to fire the engine. Then followed a brief discussion regarding the driving and firing of the locomotive over the Dainton and Rattery inclines, all of us being slightly disappointed that our loading had been restricted to just the nine coaches by Network Rail.

At 12.39 we left Newton Abbot behind in bright autumn sunshine, making rail conditions almost perfect. The 'King' had a full lunch of coal under the door and in the middle of his firebox, and once we were around the corner passing Aller Junction, where the Torquay line branches off, it was time to start feeding the front end. At the same time Peter gave him full regulator and 60% cut-off as we began the assault of the mighty Dainton incline, almost 3 miles of slogging to the summit tunnel with a ruling gradient of 1 in 36.

Part way up at Stoneycombe we were in great shape; the boiler was responding to my steady feeding of the fire, steam remained rigid against the injector at 245lb and, as though the King was out to prove a point, he was romping up and 'flattening' his old stamping ground. I had been concentrating so much on the firing that when Peter shouted 'Tunnel!' it did not register with me that we had reached the summit in what seemed no time at all. My last act before

The 'King' in full cry on the 1 in 36 of Dainton with 'The Devonian', and managing to knock 9 minutes off the scheduled timings. Driver Peter Kirk is on the regulator. *Mike Hollingsworth*

entering the tunnel was to leap across the footplate and turn on the other injector to ensure a good level of water when we emerged from the 291-yard tunnel and descended the almost equally steep 5 miles to Totnes. We passed there 7 minutes early at 12.49, having covered the 9 miles in just 10 minutes! Now for Rattery!

After exchanging greetings with the crew of the South Devon Railway 'Prairie' tank while passing through Totnes on the middle road, we were immediately faced with a gruelling 8 miles of uphill work to the summit of Wrangaton. The initial 4 miles have a ruling gradient of 1 in 46 to Rattery, but I had not been idle and daydreaming while descending Dainton. Far from it – the handle on my firing shovel was almost red hot, such had been my labours in building up the fire, hoping to extract all 40,285 lb of tractive effort from this former doyen of Great Western motive power.

The clear run through Totnes gave us the momentum on the early stages of the climb. It is important on this loco, and on the 'Castle' Class engines, to have the fire built right up under the door, giving the heavy blast from the exhaust something to bite on. If you lose this back end you can expect steaming troubles. Fortunately we were having none of that, and all of us on the footplate were enjoying the engine's performance. Steve kept himself busy pulling the coal forward for me in the tender while I steadily fed the grate, expending plenty of energy in reaching the front end of the 11ft 6in firebox.

Accompanying me on many firing trips was my trusty video camera, enabling me to capture scenes from the footplate aboard a wide variety of locomotives. Sometimes the filming was done by a member of the support crew when I was otherwise engaged, but regretfully no filming was done aboard No 6024, although I was planning to issue a DVD in 2017 covering some of my main-

line journeys. Oh, how I would love to have captured the double-chimney exhaust music coming from the copper-capped chimney as we ascended this South Devon bank, passing the site of Rattery signal box, then over the viaduct before blasting our way into the single-bore Marley Tunnel.

Brent was the next landmark. At one time this had been the junction for the tranquil branch to Kingsbridge featured in one of the *Railway Roundabout* films shown on BBC TV in the late 1950s, which meant for me a quick dash home after school to watch it on our black and white telly. One scene in the film showed some Scouts swimming in the river at Gara Bridge, the second station down the line; how envious I was of those people staying in the camping coach there! I visited the site a few years ago, but everything has gone apart from bits of the station. The pleasures of life were that much simpler in the 1950s. Oh, do stop drifting off the tale, Fletch, and get back on board your engine!

We were now within a mile of Wrangaton summit, then it was all over and I could sit back and watch the road ahead. Peter let out the cut-off and we topped the hill on full power, the toil over the South Devon banks complete once again for 'the King and I', but what a performance from him! We had steam and water aplenty after leaving Newton Abbot, and a quick check of our running schedule revealed that the 'King' had knocked an incredible 9 minutes off the timings allowed for climbing these hills, fully justifying our belief that an 11-coach train was within the engine's capabilities and, hopefully, that of the footplate crew!

Rolling downhill to Plymouth we passed through a modern Ivybridge station and crossed the first of three viaducts between here and Hemerdon. This is the gorgeous Ivybridge Viaduct, a listed structure that replaced Brunel's original wooden bridge when the line changed from broad gauge in

1892; the granite piers of the original are still visible. Five miles of further downhill running brought us to Hemerdon, the summit for up trains on the almost 'gentle' 3 miles of 1 in 42 from Plympton, which will be facing the crew on board the 'King' with the return 'Devonian' to Bristol later in the day. By my calculations, No 6024 *King Edward I* would then have completed more than 25 miles of arduous hill-climbing on the toughest stretch of railway in the country.

At 13.15 we arrived at the curved Platform 7 at Plymouth, the station announcer stating that we were the 13.28 charter train arrival from Ealing Broadway; this brought a ripple of applause from passengers on the adjacent platform awaiting a late-running express for the capital! Still, I don't suppose many trains arrive at Plymouth 13 minutes early. My family have some connections with the city as Jacqueline's father was based here with the Marines and the family lived here in the 1950s, so we have been back a number of times visiting. I have always admired the work of railway enthusiast and poet laureate Sir John Betjeman, and his description of the rebuilt Plymouth station as 'the dullest of stations and no less dull now it has been rebuilt in copybook contemporary' is very apt.

Although we had some 3 hours before the return departure, the train had to be shunted, then cleaned and its water tanks topped up, and the loco needed turning, coaling, watering and servicing, all to be fitted in between the arrivals and departures at this busy station. We first shunted the coaches, then headed tender-first to Laira, turning the engine on the triangle there, then a moment of pure nostalgia as we took the 'King' on to 83D, once the home to nine members of the class. His presence created much interest among past and present Laira shed staff while he was serviced, and we were

Having completed the outward leg of 'The Devonian', our mighty steed rests at Laira shed, former home of some of its classmates. *Author's collection*

in the mess block servicing ourselves. Our final act was to bring him off the shed light engine to the station in time for the 16.45 return departure of 'The Devonian'.

The 'King' had to head off back towards London, as these engines were barred from running to Cornwall due to weight restrictions, unlike me, who will now relate my only foray into true 'Worzel' territory. So, if you are sitting comfortably I will begin. During my 15 years working as a fireman for both West Coast Railways and Fragonset Merlin, I was fortunate in being able to work on all three of the main-line-registered 'A4' 'Pacifics', Nos 60007 *Sir Nigel Gresley*, 60009 *Union of South Africa* and 60019 *Bittern*, so let's first relate a tale or two involving the latter.

33 *Bittern* in Cornwall and King's Cross

The date was Sunday 19 September 2010, two days prior to which I had been on duty in the bargain shop at Grosmont engine shed, giving a customer some discount! I received a call from Andy Taylor, the Southern Area Operations Manager and driver for West Coast Railways, wanting to know if I could help him out over the weekend because one of his experienced fireman had injured his arm and was unable to work his turn. As it happened I was free, so without first asking him what the job was I verbally agreed to cover the turn, and he told me that he would be the driver. Andy arranges the jobs in the south, so I didn't expect to be working on my doorstep; however, I didn't anticipate him asking me if I would just nip down to Par, Cornwall, on the Sunday, and work back to Bristol with an 'A4'! I think it must have slipped his mind that I lived a few miles away from Par, so it was agreed that I would travel down to Bristol on the Saturday and lodge there overnight. Just before he hung up a thought occurred to me – had he actually said that it was an 'A4' on the job, because as far as I was aware no 'A4' had ever worked into Cornwall? Imagine my delight when he confirmed that No 60019 *Bittern* had replaced No 5029 *Nunney Castle*, and that Network Rail had agreed to the request for it to work beyond Plymouth, but not to an increase of the eight-coach load that had been allocated to the 'Castle'. So the stage was set.

After nipping off to Par, all 415 miles

from downtown Grosmont, I duly linked up with Andy on the incoming 'Cornishman' (the 08.05 from Bristol Temple Meads) when she ran in at 13.15. The incoming fireman was Chris Yates, who was also a member of the engine support crew who shared my adulation for the 'A4' 'Pacific'. He had enjoyed a trouble-free run from Bristol over the South Devon banks and the steep 15-mile climb from Plymouth to Doublebois, exchanging with me in time-honoured fireman's jargon the comment 'You can't keep her quiet' as he left the footplate. Our diagram included shunting the stock, then light engine to the former 83E St Blazey depot for servicing and turning.

All was going well until we got on to the turntable. We got about a quarter of the way round then realised that the loco was fouling the iron safety railings surrounding the turntable. The Network Rail guy in charge of proceedings was perplexed by this and said that they had no problems turning a steam locomotive there a few weeks previously; it was then pointed out to him that not all engines are the same length, but in his defence nobody had told him that the engines had been swopped and that this one was longer than a 'Castle'.

An attempt was then made to dismantle the railings by unscrewing the nuts and bolts securing all the posts, but they had become rusted together over the years due to lack of maintenance, so the only solution was to burn the heads off all the bolts and dismantle the railings. The guy was on his own, although the support crew were assisting; what we really needed was the outdoor maintenance gang, who would have the equipment, but this was a Sunday. He attempted to contact them by mobile phone, but they were at home watching the big football match, Man Utd v Liverpool. The situation was becoming farcical; time was getting on, the engine had to be turned as we could not run tender-first back to Bristol, and there was no back-up diesel power. But just when all seemed lost a Network Rail pick-up truck came roaring through the gates with three big lads in the cab and, more importantly, some oxy bottles and burning gear. Half an hour later the railings had been dismantled and *Bittern* was facing the right way, and had been serviced and coal taken on while the problem was being sorted

The delay also gave me the chance to inspect what was left of this former steam shed, now used DB Schenker. The main building is the sole surviving semi-circular roundhouse, although much of the building has been converted into industrial units. St Blazey does not have a permanent allocation of locomotives, but many are out-based here for use on local freight services. I didn't cop anything!

We managed to arrive back light engine at Par station in time for our 16.45 departure with the return 'Cornishman', reporting number 1Z20. We had booked stops at Bodmin Parkway (16.54-16.58), Liskeard (17.09-17.12), Plymouth (17.37-18.29, for water), Exeter St David's (19.52-20.29, also for water), and Taunton (21.06-21.09), arriving at Bristol at 21.56. My trusty gradient profile chart taped to the cabside would be consulted regularly

between here and Plymouth, as both the engine and fireman will be making their maiden voyage on this return route.

The first couple of miles should warm the engine up a little on the 1 in 62 pull up to Treverrin Tunnel, then the same mileage took us downhill and through Lostwithiel before we faced the stiffest challenge on the route back to Plymouth by tackling the 9 miles to the summit at Doublebois. The gradient is 1 in 58 for part of the climb, interrupted by the station stop at Bodmin Parkway. I had every confidence in a trouble-free run as regards the capabilities of our 'A4' locomotive, having worked all over the country on all three preserved engines. In my opinion they are without equal when it comes to power output, size for size, pound for pound, against any other class of steam locomotive I have known.

We left Par after having built up what I call my standard 'A4' fire – both back corners and under the door full of fresh coal. Once away from the station confines I opened the damper then fired to the sides followed by a scattering to the middle and the front of the grate, all done using a lightweight Lucas shovel, not my usual

The offending handrails round the St Blazey turntable, prevented the turning of 'A4' 'Pacific' No 60019 *Bittern*, are being removed. *Author's collection*

hybrid SR/GWR tool, due to the narrow LNER-type 'rat-trap' firehole door. My trusty leather gauntlets allowed me to reach further into the firebox with the shovel, and believe me if the firing is done correctly these 'A4s' love this treatment. Added extras are being able to control the amount of secondary air to the fire by the positioning of the flap on the firehole door, and I always leave the blower cracked open a little to counteract the possibility of a blowback of fire. Finally, where possible I keep a strict adherence to a maximum of 230lb boiler pressure; there is no need to be running about with steam pressure at or near the maximum 250lb, which risks committing the cardinal sin of lifting the ear-shattering safety valves. These engines will perform just as well if you treat 230lb as being the red mark on the gauge. My weakness with these locomotives is the whistle, of course; it intrigues me that the very action of pulling such a short 4-inch operating lever on the footplate can bring into life such a melodious, almost tear-jerking response, entirely befitting a relation of the world's fastest steam locomotive. My first opportunity of whistle-blowing was as a warning before entering Treverrin Tunnel, met by a shaking of the head from Andy, followed up by his premonition that it was going to be a long journey back to Plymouth!

Not having touched the fire until we passed through Lostwithiel, it needed building up again for the climb ahead, but not the 'full monty', of course, due to the station stop 4 miles ahead at Bodmin Parkway. It was thus a case of 'back corners and under the door' followed by a quick dozen around the box. While engaged in these duties Andy beat me to the whistle on the approach to Brownqueen Tunnel, this being the setting chosen by railway artist Don Breckon for his inspirational 'Manor at Brownqueen' painting.

The weather on this mid-September evening was bright and a little breezy as we enter a crowded Bodmin Parkway station, which is the junction for the Bodmin & Wenford Railway. There had been a good turn-out of folk at most vantage points along the line, most of them now using digital cameras to capture this rarity of motive power that has ventured into their county. Then lo and behold, I recognised one of the 'Worzels' standing on the platform as a volunteer driver on the NYMR, who lives in this area. He wanted to be able to say that he had fired an 'A4' in Cornwall, so I invited him aboard and he flashed a few shovelsful around the box to achieve his ambition. Then we bid farewell to him and Bodmin, with Andy taking great care in getting us away without a slip on the 1 in 85 curve, each turn of the driving wheels taking us just a little bit further on our journey back to Devon.

My driver was not from the old school of former BR steam men on the books of West Coast Railways; he was one of a number of drivers and fireman with a background in diesel traction who had adapted themselves to becoming competent steam men after expert tuition from the old boys in the handling of these temperamental machines, that being the only way to fill the gaps left by the retirement of men from the steam age – including me! What I will say is that these new boys are a pleasure to work with, being devoid of the idiosyncrasies of some footplatemen that we had to put up with in the days of steam.

What did impress me about this route was the number of handsome viaducts we were traversing on our ascent of Doublebois; in the last 4 miles alone we had crossed no fewer than seven, many of them having replaced the original wooden structures from broad gauge days. Westwood Viaduct was the last of these as we topped the climb and descended towards Liskeard. I had not yet broken into a sweat on firing duties; No 60019 was the complete master of the load and road, steadily getting fed around the box, with plenty of coal in the back corners. This had kept pressure rigid at 230lb with the injector being on throughout, and Andy had used full regulator with a 50% cut-off for almost all the climb.

A glance at my gradient chart told me that we were rapidly approaching the first and possibly the finest of all 11 viaducts between Par and Plymouth, the statuesque Grade 2-listed Moorswater Viaduct, which has attracted a bevy of snappers from the trackbed of the Looe branch below. Coming to a stand in Liskeard station following the short climb from the viaduct brought back memories of a family holiday in Cornwall and a visit to the now defunct Dobwalls Adventure Park. Within its grounds was a magnificent miniature railway, part of it depicting Sherman Hill, Wyoming, with a complement of live steam American locos including a huge model of a 4-8-8-4 Union Pacific Railroad 'Big Boy'. Upon closure, much of the railway went to a site in Dorset, since when all was shipped out to Australia for a venture next to the 'Puffing Billy Railway'.

Our 3-minute stop at Liskeard was over at 17.12, and away we went again, a short pull over three smaller viaducts taking us onto the fireman's easy part of our journey, with almost 15 miles of downhill running to Plymouth, allowing us 25 minutes to negotiate the many curves, including the 15mph crossing of the Royal Albert Bridge. The importance of keeping the footplate clean was instilled in me as a junior fireman – the hand brush is an essential part of the fireman's kit – and I was kept busy with this while taking a break from firing duties. I also brought the slacker pipe into use, both on the footplate and in the tender coal space. Perhaps my only grumble with LNER engines is their noisy injectors and the slacker pipe operating solely from the driver's-side injector, but I suppose it does

encourage the regular use of both injectors as shown in the firing manual.

Almost a classroom full of children were on the platform at the quaint but unstaffed St Germans station as we sailed through, with me treating them to an almost unique sound in the whole of Cornwall, that of the chime whistle fitted to *Bittern*!

All day long I had been thinking about what would be happening just 5 miles down the line from here when we reached Saltash, and took part in the unprecedented event of an 'A4' 'Pacific' returning from Cornwall and crossing the River Tamar on Brunel's masterpiece, the Royal Albert Bridge. As expected, when we arrive the place was awash with folk, and the event was being filmed from the footplate of *Bittern* as, amidst much cheering and whistling, we proceeded slowly onto the bridge, passing under the first tower that proudly and boldly proclaimed 'I. K. Brunel Engineer 1859'. A lump came into my throat when I thought that the masterpiece of another brilliant engineer, Sir Nigel Gresley, was proudly traversing Brunel's iconic Victorian structure.

So we said goodbye to Cornwall, having seemingly provided the Sunday evening entertainment for almost everyone in the immediate area, judging by the amount of folk lining the trackside as we negotiated the last few miles of railway leading into Plymouth station. There we would have almost an hour awaiting our path forward, and during that time the engine would be watered and receive any servicing required. Surprisingly, when we came to a stand we were visited by a few dyed-in-the-wool ex-Great Western Laira footplatemen, who said they just happened to be passing the station and, hearing the chime whistle, had come along to investigate! A likely story, particularly when one of the station staff told us that the three of them had been on the platform for over an hour waiting for us, prompting Andy to remark that it was

The unprecedented event of a visit to Cornwall by an 'A4' 'Pacific', No 60019 *Bittern*, is seen from the footplate on the return leg about to cross the River Tamar on Brunel's masterpiece, the Royal Albert Bridge.

either that, or they had exceptional hearing to have heard the engine whistle an hour before, when we were at Par! Nay, they had just come to see what a proper steam engine looked like. I remember them remarking on the plush bucket seats, enclosed cab, the exhaust sound from the ejector, the large speedometer, and, totally alien to them, the firehole door. That had now to be opened to enable me to prepare the fire for our imminent departure once our honoured guests had vacated the footplate after being indoctrinated into the benefits of an 'A4' 'Pacific' over GW motive power!

Andy took it steady with *Bittern* on the short climb out of the Pilgrim Fathers' station so that the few miles to Tavistock Junction give me the chance to build a good fire for the 10-mile drag up the hill to Wrangaton, not forgetting of course

that the first few miles to Hemerdon had a gentle 1 in 41 ruling gradient. Our LNER stranger was making all the right noises as she steamed past that former bastion of the Great Western era, 83D Laira, allowing me to temporarily leave off firing duties to announce on the whistle the presence of a locomotive making a sound alien to all machines that were ever built at Swindon, that of a three-cylinder express passenger steam locomotive! And what a pleasing sound, as Driver Andy dropped the cut-off well down the rack and gave No 60019 full regulator to take every advantage of the short dip before hitting the bottom of Hemerdon Bank.

This was serious stuff, and taxed man and machine alike, but I was ready for it. There was no time for whistling for a while as total concentration was required for the job in hand – injector on and shovel in hand, methodically feeding given areas of the fire to my set pattern. I prefer to remain standing when not shovelling, and had given up the fireman's seat to our support crew guy;

placing him there gave me complete freedom of space when swinging the shovel. It was not necessary to look out of the cab to view the engine's exhaust – the one instrument on the footplate that was controlling my actions was the needle on the boiler pressure gauge. My sole aim was to keep it at 230lb – no more and no less.

Many folk assume that the best asset of an 'A4' is speed, but let me assure you that, despite having 6ft 8in legs, they are excellent hill-climbers. Giving off that lovely Gresley beat, derived via his own conjugated valve gear, No 19 *Bittern* was treating the 1 in 41 grade like an everyday occurrence, reaching Hemerdon Sidings at a healthy 30mph and giving us the momentum to top Wrangaton 3 minutes early. It was then siesta time for the run down Rattery, through Totnes at 60mph, and we were halfway up Dainton before we noticed the climb.

With a clear run through Newton Abbot, we could settle down for some steady running along the picturesque coastline for the next 20 miles, bringing us to our next water stop at Exeter St David's. There we had a change of drivers, Ray Poole taking over from Andy, who rode back to Bristol in the train. Water had been taken at Tiverton Junction on the down run, and we passed there in fine style on the climb to Whiteball before coming to a stand in a dark and almost deserted Taunton station at 21.06.

Leaving here I blotted my copybook somewhat in allowing the engine to blow off for the first and only time that day, caused by misreading the pressure gauge due to the glare from the fire. Anyhow, Ray soon used up the excess with one of his trademark spirited runs, ensuring that we made an on-time arrival at 21.56 at an unusually quiet Temple Meads station, followed by some slick shunting of coaches and locomotive, so that by 23.00 all six members of that day's footplate crew were to be seen enjoying well-earned pints in the hotel bar. *Bittern*

was no doubt contenting itself with a tender full of fresh water and black victuals, well satisfied with its day's foray into previously unexplored territory.

My next tale relates a trip with *Bittern* on Saturday 25 July 2009, working 1Z51 from York to King's Cross, booked as a non-stop test run, using two tenders designed to eliminate any water stops. Departure was scheduled for 16.55, passing Peterborough at 18.53 and arriving at King's Cross at 20.32. David Blair was the driver, with Bill Andrew travelling as inspector/driver overseeing events and driving the first leg to Peterborough.

No 60019 had worked up from 'the Cross' in the morning and had experienced lubrication problems. Repairs took place at York, and when we booked on in the afternoon they continued almost to departure time, the last job being the coaling and watering of the tenders to their 14,000-gallon capacity. We had a 10-coach train plus the additional tender, making it equal to 12 coaches, and left to time on our 188-mile journey, carrying the headboard 'The Brighton Belle' to publicise the launch of the 'Brighton Belle' restoration project by the 5BEL Trust. *Bittern* soon had the job in hand, touching 70mph as we diverted to the left at Colton Junction, and it was time to pick up the shovel for the first time since leaving York with a well-prepared fire. Obviously plenty of thought had been given beforehand regarding the firing on this non-stop run, 230lb maximum pressure being my benchmark figure, with a 200lb minimum on the easier stretches to save energy and steam on this 3½-hour firing stint.

The first leg of the journey to Doncaster, our locomotive's birthplace in 1937, was certainly not comparable with the original route from Chaloners Whin via Selby, which was riddled with speed restrictions due to mining works. No such problems existed on this new stretch, and our streamliner was loving the freedom of the rails, effortlessly eating up the miles. The centre road was cleared for us to pass through Doncaster, which was treated to a melody on the chime whistle from this home-town girl as we roared through on this sunny evening, evoking memories of steam from days gone by at that great centre of industry, universally known as 'The Plant'. The East Coast Main Line, unlike the West Coast, is devoid of excessive gradients, 1 in 200 being about the average, which ensures plenty of fast running throughout.

The slight hump between Rossington and Bawtry was taken without any drop in our speed, and my knowledge of the route was sufficient for firing purposes although, had we been running in the dark, it would have needed regular consultation with the driver, outlining the route ahead. The firing was regular and steady; having opted to remain standing between each charge, the plush fireman's seat was occupied by our support crew laddie. Our constant 75mph running was eating up the miles, although not as rapidly as other forms of traction on this busy route, with express trains passing us at 125mph (almost as fast as sister engine *Mallard!*) – we were actually the slowest passenger train on the line that day!

On the approach to Retford I increased the firing rate in preparation for the added output needed to ascend the 4-mile climb through Gamston to the summit at the short Askham Tunnel. Then it was downhill to Carlton, followed by 5 level miles to Newark, the start of the 20-mile climb to Stoke summit. I should admit to having a slight affinity with Retford going back to my youth, for among my large collection of vinyl records was a slight variation to the pop music theme when I purchased a number of Argo Transacord EPs and LPs, with the sounds of the steam locomotive captured by Peter Handford. My favourite were his recordings of 'A4' and 'A3' 'Pacifics' hurtling

All prepared and ready to leave the NRM at York for a good day out on the 'SSE', with a good engine and a good mate, driver David Blair – what more could you wish for in life? *Author's collection*

through Retford South Crossing, with the 'A4' chime whistles contrasting with the bells ringing out from the nearby Ordsall church on a Sunday morning in 1956. This was captured on the EP *Gresley Pacifics*, the cover of which depicts No 60034 *Lord Faringdon* passing No 60007 *Sir Nigel Gresley* under the girder bridge by Peterborough station. These records were played almost as much as my Buddy Holly collection!

The gradient to Stoke summit is roughly the same from each side, giving ample time on the level stretches to prepare the fire. Up to now Bill had been using a reasonably short cut-off, but on the approach to Newark this all changed to full regulator and 35% cut-off to ensure a flat-out speed to give us a run at the long climb ahead, and for the first time on our journey we are treated to the sound that attracted Peter Handford to the lineside, the 'Gresley beat'. We had been climbing for the last 15 miles and all was well on the footplate, despite the swirling coal dust; as already mentioned, one of the hazards of working steam locomotives 'under the wires' is not being able to use the slacker pipe to combat this.

We were now on the approaches to another former East Coast centre of steam at Grantham, and our speedometer was reading the maximum 75mph; this was strictly adhered to by all our drivers, who were far too professional for any acts of bravado. Indeed, a glance around the cab revealed there to be more than 100 years of footplate experience operating this locomotive! I enjoyed firing these engines as my efforts were always rewarded by the free-steaming qualities for which these 'A4s' are renowned. and that day was no exception as we battened down the hatches and blasted our way through Stoke Tunnel to top the summit doing a creditable 70mph.

It was descending the hill from there to Peterborough that Messrs Duddington and Bray gained worldwide recognition for the London & North Eastern Railway on that July day in 1938 on board No 4468 *Mallard* when they established a record speed for steam traction of 126mph. Now, on this July day some 70 years later we were content with a speed of 50mph less than that, as we are booked to run on the slow line to Peterborough with a matching 75mph speed restriction.

By New England on the outskirts of Peterborough we had covered more than 110 miles non-stop, but despite being on time we were brought to a stand by adverse signals to allow a late-running express to take our booked path from Peterborough. Our support crew lightened the disappointment by appearing on the footplate carrying

teas and coffees, having negotiated the obstacle course of two corridor tenders. Being stationary for a short while allowed them an opportunity to have a quick check around their charge; fortunately we had not suffered the same fate as *Mallard* when it arrived at Peterborough all those years ago, but unbeknown to us there was to be trouble ahead before we reached our destination!

We left Peterborough feeling most frustrated with Network Rail allowing a National Express service take our path. David had taken over the driving and 5 miles further, passing Yaxley, we were cruising at a steady maximum on almost level ground. We did not notice the slight climb to Abbots Ripton – in fact, the next 20 miles of running was well within our timings to Biggleswade, followed by 10 miles uphill to Stevenage, and it was on this stretch that *Bittern* began to sound a little off-beat. It was hardly noticeable at first, but between Stevenage and Potters Bar the engine was definitely limping and down on power.

The RO was summoned to the footplate, and he agreed to continue to Potters Bar, where we had a 2-minute booked stop, giving us an opportunity for engine examination. Within minutes of coming to a stand, the problem was diagnosed as broken valve rings, and a decision was made to limp along to Finsbury Park, where the train would terminate and a diesel pilot from King's Cross would haul us and the train to Southall. Not the ideal end to a supposed non-stop run – shades of 1938, in fact – but unlike in 1938 there was no 'Atlantic' loco to work our train forward to King's Cross. With apologies all round, we headed off for Southall depot, arriving there well after midnight, then shunted the train before finally arriving at the Heathrow hotel in the early hours. Just as a footnote, it was to be some months before *Bittern* was able to 'fly' again.

34 Union of South Africa to Inverness, and London

Let us now change footplates on to sister engine No 60009 *Union of South Africa*. As the song goes, 'I've been everywhere man,' and that is true, as we have been all over the country together to, among others, Weymouth, Stratford-upon-Avon, Norwich, York, London, Bristol, Lincoln, Carlisle, Edinburgh, Perth and Inverness, usually in the company of engine owner John Cameron. So where would you like to go? Scotland, did you say? Well, all right, Scotland it is.

I have been fortunate to have worked over most of the routes permitted for steam operation in Scotland, visiting Glasgow, Edinburgh, Dundee, Aberdeen, Ayr, Oban, Kyle of Lochalsh, Thurso and Keith. I obviously cannot describe all of

'A4' 'Pacific' No 60009 *Union of South Africa*, on a test run from Carnforth, heads towards Hellifield at Giggleswick after an overhaul. *David Bradley*

these journeys, so I am just choosing one at random. On Saturday 4 July 2009 this was a special organised by the Scottish Railway Preservation Society from Polmont to Inverness, steam-hauled from Perth with No 60009. I travelled from home to Perth the day before and linked up with my driver and West Coast Northern Operations Manager Peter Walker, who is a native of the country with extensive route knowledge of the area. Our overnight accommodation was in the plush Station Hotel where, after a hearty evening meal, we retired in readiness for an early start on our 118-mile journey over the arduous Highland main line to Inverness.

Scottish kippers formed my breakfast at 7.00am, sunshine greeted us at the station, the support crew had been busy since the early hours, and our 'Streak' looked a treat! I always have a selection of headgear with me, varying from a grease-top to a beret, but due to the warm weather today's choice would be something favoured by many 1960s BR firemen, a 'knotted handkerchief'. Our day's excursion had departed for Polmont at 06.42 hauled by Class 37 diesel No 37676, arriving in Perth on time at 07.58 and immediately detaching from the nine-coach train to stand in the station sidings and await our return at 20.36 that evening. We backed up with the engine and support coach and completed the obligatory brake test before departing at 08.36 with ten coaches in tow.

This route is not for the faint-hearted. The first 52 miles are mostly on adverse gradients, including the 17-mile climb from Blair Athol to the summit of Druimuachdar, with a further 12 miles between Aviemore to Slochd with a ruling gradient of 1 in 60. This line was once the domain of double-headed 'Black 5s', my only previous foray over it having been a recreation of one of those runs; maybe there could still be a banking engine languishing at Blair Athol shed to help us up Druimuachdar!

We began to eat up the miles, passing through scattered hamlets and small villages with sparse communities and closed stations. The first sign of any railway life was at Dunkeld & Birnam, where the signal box was still intact and controlled the passing loop; we had a couple of minutes here for token exchange. On stretches between Dunkeld and Pitlochry the main A9 road runs parallel with the railway, and we were being pursued by a variety of classic cars including an extremely rare Hispano-Suiza, often referred to as the Spanish Rolls-Royce. It may have been just

Photographer Eddie Bobrowski is well known on the steam scene and here he captures West Coast Railways driver and Northern Operations Manager Peter Walker and myself about to depart from York with 'Britannia' 'Pacific' No 70013 *Oliver Cromwell* working forward to Edinburgh with the annual 'Great Britain' charter tour. *Eddie Bobrowski* a coincidence having the cars for company, or an organised local rally – either way it was much appreciated by the multitude of onboard cameramen leaning out of carriage windows.

Our arrival at Pitlochry saw a healthy turn-out of townsfolk, the footbridge linking the two platforms providing the ideal vantage point. We had a few minutes there, giving me time to appreciate the contrasting stone-built station building with the traditional timber-built structures on the opposite platform. We made a steady start, getting away from there on the 1 in 85 grade, Peter allowing the engine to find its feet. Speed built up gradually as we topped the 2-mile climb without a slip and descended through a short tunnel, emerging into the Pass of Killiecrankie 4 miles from Blair Athol.

Until now the route had not been too taxing; firing and steaming had been steady over the last 35 miles, but both engine and fireman were about to liven up as we began the 17-mile slog taking us to the highest point on a British main line at Druimuachdar summit, 1,484 feet above sea level. At Blair Athol much remained of this once important Highland Railway outpost, including the former loco shed and yard; I captured a few photos of the old depot as we passed, before returning to footplate duties, building up the fire for the assault on Druimuachdar.

From Blair Athol for the next 35 miles to Dalwhinnie the railway changes from single to double track, but there was not much chance of a run at the bank. However, Peter managed to coax 35mph from our Scottish-based 'A4' 'Pacific' at the beginning of the climb at 1 in 80, and we soon settled down to a steady rhythm using full regulator and 45% cut-off. The higher we climbed the more rugged the countryside became. Dwellings were a scarcity – just the odd isolated farmhouse, although the A9 was visible at times, but no sign of the classic cars

now. Perhaps it was a bit too steep for them!

This railway line has been a tough challenge for man and machine over the years and today would be no exception. In steam days our ten-coach train would have had banker assistance from Blair Athol, but our engine was manfully handling the load, firing was steady at 30 shovelsful of coal each charge, and the live steam injector was being used in preference to the sometimes temperamental exhaust injector. To give some indication of the length and severity of this climb, we passed Blair Athol at 09.37 and our timings indicated that we should pass Druimuachdar summit at 10.23, allowing 46 minutes to climb the hill, but to our credit we passed the famous summit board at 10.14, and 10 minutes later we regained civilisation after some welcome downhill running and passed through the populous (118) village of Dalwhinnie. The station is a lifeline at this remote spot, famous for its whisky, and according to the village road sign it is twinned with Las Vegas!

For the next 45 miles we would be on a single line again, but more importantly we now had 12 miles on a falling gradient to Kingussie, giving me the chance of a welcome breather from the lengthy firing stint in surmounting Druimuachdar. My thoughts briefly wandered back to the story related to me by former Nine Elms footplateman Bert Hooker when in 1948 the newly formed British Railways conducted a series of locomotive trials and exchanges that saw Bulleid 'Pacific' No 34004 *Yeovil* performing a similar task to ours over the Highland main line between Perth and Inverness with Bert on the shovel. No 34004 was fitted with an LMS tender complete with water scoop, and put in some outstanding performances, leading to BR introducing the design of a new Class 6 locomotive and the emergence of the 'Clan' 'Pacifics' for use in Scotland.

We were given a clear run through Kingussie, but were scheduled for a 15-minute visit to the loop at Kincraig, although the station here closed in 1965. We followed this with a 40-minute stop at Aviemore to take on water; having covered some 80 miles from Perth, the tender was ready for a drink. Our presence here attracted the attention of visitors to the adjacent Strathspey Railway, who arrived with a service from Broomhill behind a well-presented 'Austerity' saddle tank. Our own passengers, many of them members of the Scottish Railway Preservation Society, congregated on the platform, patiently awaiting a visit to our footplate, while Peter and I adjourned to the coach for lunch, leaving the support crew to market their machine.

At 12.08 Peter slowly and skilfully pulled open the regulator of this stranger to the Highlands, and No 60009 responded with a steady start, the Kylchap exhaust softening the blast on my newly formed fire as we gradually accelerated, having preplanned to attack the first couple of miles of 1 in 350 to gain a foothold on the 'slog to Slochd', 10 miles of heavy digging as we headed north to the summit with a ruling gradient of 1 in 60. No scenery-watching on this stretch for me, with just a 25-minute margin from a standing start to clear Slochd, with my tried and tested 'A4' footplate procedure in place. The RO was in the fireman's seat, allowing me room to work, and the live steam injector was set to maintain three-quarters of a glass of water and giving me use of the slacker pipe. I fed 25 shovelsful of coal at each charge, feeding the back corners, sides and under the door with just a scattering to the front to ensure the grate had the correct amount of covering; keeping the steam pressure no higher than 230/235lb was easy by adjustment of the firehole door flap and the damper – the 'A4s' love this treatment! Another useful tip passed on to

me by the old boys was to familiarise myself with the route by use of the mileposts. For instance, the summit of Slochd is at milepost 95, allowing me to control the firing as we progressed with the climb. No 60009 got us over the top in fine style and we headed off downhill for the remaining 22 miles to Inverness.

As I have said before, what goes down must come up, and they don't come up much longer and steeper than the southbound climb out of Inverness to attain 1,315 feet at the summit of Slochd. To achieve this you must traverse 22 miles of tortuous climbing with a ruling gradient of 1 in 60, which commences just a mile from Inverness station; to put it into perspective, the climb is twice the length of the infamous Beattock bank.

Coming down off the mountain we passed through the closed stations of Tomatin, Moy, Daviot and Culloden Moor, all succumbing to the Beeching axe in 1965. Fortunately we could still traverse the magnificent 29-arch Culloden Viaduct, the longest masonry viaduct in Scotland. It was near here that a 'slight skirmish' occurred in 1746 between the Jacobite army and the Government army, the site of which is now a visitor centre.

From Daviot to Inverness it is double track, and just outside the Highland capital we joined the line from Aberdeen at Milburn Junction, the final stretch into the station taking us past what remains of the once extensive sidings together with the former Highland Railway Lochgorm Locomotive Works, which now is the Inverness Maintenance Depot. Much of the daily shunting duties here involve propelling movements around the station and, unlike the signaller at Gloucester mentioned in a previous chapter, the signallers at Inverness are quite adept at the procedure.

Although we had terminated there on that day, on other occasions we have worked to the Far North at Wick and Thurso with steam and visited Kyle of Lochalsh with No 61994 *The Great Marquess*. Also, in 2009 with 'The Great Britain' we traversed the line from Inverness to Aberdeen, then to Dundee and via the Tay Bridge back to our starting point at Perth, having steamed over Druimuachdar two days previously, with motive power being double-headed 'Black 5' Nos 45231and 45407. The final part of that tour was from Edinburgh with No 60009 *Union of South Africa* to York, where diesel haulage took over the last leg to King's Cross. I will give you a few snippets of 'A4' memories to conclude, including my first firing turn for a driver who had been at Copley Hill depot in steam days, following in the footsteps of his father who likewise had been a 56C man.

Ron Smith had joined the company as an inspector a few months previously, having taken early retirement from driving on the national network at Leeds. He came with a reputation as a bit of a stickler and a disciplinarian, but actually once you got to know him his bark was worse than his bite. His driving and knowledge of the job were a compliment to his many years of service and we always got on well together. Our maiden voyage was on Saturday 17 March 2007 with a return York-King's Cross (Finsbury Park) charter made up of 13 coaches, then ECS to Old Oak Common. Both of us were pleased to have an 'A4', No 60009 being diagrammed for the 200-mile job.

I arrived early at York depot to assist with loco preparation and overseeing the coaling of the tender after lining the entire grate with about half a ton of coal. Having previously described a similar journey with an 'A4' between York and King's Cross, the main difference between the two runs was the heavier load and a headwind, resulting in greater coal consumption and an arrival on shed at Old Oak Common with little more than a ton left in the tender. Nevertheless a very creditable 65mph was achieved at Stoke summit, a testimony to the hauling capabilities of this class, considering that we were dragging the weight of at least three more coaches than was the norm for the class, except for the war years, which saw these engines sometimes hauling 20-coach trains!

35 Scarborough, Carlisle, Carnforth, Canterbury, Redhill, Ely, Norwich, Sheerness...

By coincidence I was Ron's mate on his maiden voyage on No 34067 *Tangmere* when it came north to work the 'Scarborough Spa Express'; we were routed via the much more scenic run from York to Scarborough via Knaresborough, Harrogate and Leeds. Although Bramhope Tunnel was a lengthy, wet, mucky hole that dirtied the engine and stock every time we passed through, the climb out of Leeds and a fast descent to Church Fenton made up for it. It was the same partnership again for Ron's maiden voyage with No 6233 on a York-Carlisle charter over the S&C accompanied by fellow new-boy and work colleague of his, Mick Rawling, who was diesel-qualified and training on steam traction.

All went well on the day as far as Hellifield, the RO being pleased with Ron's handling of what was a strange locomotive to this Eastern man. During the water stop at Hellifield we all had a good chat – in fact, rather too good a chat on my part, as for once I boobed with my preparation time and broke the golden rule of 'Be prepared'. Consequently I had nowhere near enough fire or steam when we departed, although we rallied a little on the downhill stretch to Settle Junction, but I knew she wasn't warm enough and we only managed to keep a reasonable pace up to Ribblehead thanks to the combined efforts of Mick bringing coal forward in the tender, me shovelling for England, and Ron's skilful handling of the situation – all this caused by me yapping

too much! Needless to say, I never again neglected my own motto. On a brighter note, it didn't put Mick off his ambition to make it as a steam driver, as he went on to become a 'natural' when driving this form of traction.

Ron Smith and I were involved in making a little bit of railway history on the morning of 30 August 2011, all of which happened purely by chance when we were booked to take 'Black 5' No 44932 from the NRM at York to Carnforth, hauling a couple of support coaches. After ringing off the depot we passed through the station heading towards Church Fenton; neither of us gave any thought to the morning departure from York of another West Coast job, the 'Scarborough Spa Express', until we saw his tail lamp when we were a couple of miles out of York. The 'Britannia'-hauled charter was beginning to get into its stride when Ron and I decided to give chase.

So began some cat-and-mouse parallel running to Church Fenton, with us on the up Leeds line and the 'SSE' express on the fast line. We claim this to be the first occasion of parallel running on the main line by two steam locos since steam ended in 1968, and much of what happened was filmed by the passengers in the train and from the road bridge overlooking Colton Junction. And guess what? Yes, it's on YouTube!

Some firemen at West Coast became qualified for guard duties. I very much enjoyed this responsible role and was on such a job with Mick Rawling as driver on the annual special organised by the company's doctor Rob Dallara; that year we visited Canterbury on this popular three-day outing. Departure from Saltburn-by-Sea on the Friday was followed by an early evening arrival at Canterbury, then the stabling of the 12-coach set top-and-tailed by Class 47 diesels in the little-used down siding at the back of the West station until Monday's return working to North Yorkshire. We were off duty on the Saturday and Sunday and stayed in a nearby hotel, but visited our train a couple of times and voiced our concern at the lack of security at the site. Our fears proved correct, for during our Sunday morning examination we found the locos had graffiti on the bodywork. The coaches had escaped the attention of the 'artist', who may have been disturbed by the lone security guard. Either way, it was generally agreed that whoever had done it had not just daubed on the paint, but had shown some artistic talent. Apparently all graffiti artists identify themselves with some sort of personal signature, and company boss David Smith was a little disappointed to be told that this artwork was definitely not a highly prized 'Banksy'!

Some diesel turns required a second man on board, and such was my role on a NENTA charter that arrived at York from King's Cross, and which we worked forward to Northallerton, then down the Wensleydale branch to mark the 6-mile extension of the line from Leyburn to Redmire, which made it a total of 25 miles. The 12-coach train was top-and-tailed by two Class 47 diesels, and we departed from Platform 10 at York with the indicator board unable to display our destination of Redmire; the best it could do was to list the calling points as Northallerton, then NLRTREV, then NLRTWDR.

Trouble arose when we entered the

The best attempt by the York indicator board to display our destination as Redmire! *Author's collection*

little-used loop line at Northallerton, as the adjacent hawthorn hedgerow had not been cut back for ages and was now encroaching over the rails. It was therefore with some reluctance that we entered the loop after gaining assurance from Network Rail Control that compensation would be forthcoming to cover the costs of removal of scratch marks from the side of the coaches and the two locomotives. We had a conductor driver to guide Peter Kirk down the branch, which was occupied by hundreds of pheasants; all survived our passing and likewise on the return, partially because of our 25mph speed restriction. There was a great deal of excitement as we left Leyburn, venturing on to the new section to Redmire for the first time, where I envisaged a whole community awaiting our arrival at this new tourist venture. So imagine my huge disappointment when we arrived and saw just a handful of folk standing on the single platform next to the station house, this being the only building at the new terminus. A railway journalist asked what we thought of Redmire and seemed to like my reply: 'There couldn't have been much here when there was something here…' But do pay the Wensleydale Railway a visit – I can assure you of a friendly welcome amidst some fine scenery on this up-and-coming rural railway.

The destination of our NENTA tour was Redmire – there couldn't have been much there when there was something there! Peter Kirk is the driver. *Author's collection*

Ely was a popular destination for the 'Cathedrals Express', originating either from King's Cross via Hitchin or from Liverpool Street via Bishops Stortford. 'The Duke' was usually the motive power on the former, ensuring an all-out effort to maintain fast-line running to Hitchin for a brief stop, then off to the right via Letchworth to the Cambridge stop before a final burst on to Ely. The Liverpool Street departure was one of my regular outings, but was not without its operational problems due to the almost underground environment that exists since the station was built over at the country end; strict rulings apply regarding the operation of steam locomotives at this station. There must be absolutely no emission of smoke or blowing-off otherwise we would be instructed to leave the station and stand outside in a siding with our engine. As we usually had about an hour waiting in the station before leaving at lunchtime, I had a procedure that eliminated any possibility of breaking the rules. It involved keeping the dampers and blower closed and boxing up the fire under the door and the middle of the box, allowing the fire at the front end to go out but keeping the steam pressure at about 200lb with boiler water in the top nut. When given the 'right away', I closed the firehole doors, opened the

damper and blower and had a fire iron ready; then, once clear of the station confines, I opened the doors and, using the iron, spread some of the fire to the front of the grate, then ran the iron through the remainder as I withdrew it, finally partially closing the firehole doors and sitting back for a minute until she warmed through.

The departure from Liverpool Street is on a rising gradient, not dissimilar to the other London termini from which we have operated. These also enforced the same strict regulations regarding the steam locomotive, but I can honestly state that by rigidly sticking to my tried and tested departure procedure we managed to avoid any conflict with the authorities.

The route to Ely with 'The Cathedrals Express' was hardly the most demanding of our schedules; in fact, if ever I was to come back on this earth and work again on the footplate it would be as the regular fireman on 'The Fenman', the principal express that traversed most of this route with almost billiard-table levels. Having said that, we did actually climb steadily for 30 miles to the summit at Elsenham on an average gradient of about 1 in 300! To reach there we travelled via Bethnal Green, Seven Sisters, Edmonton Green on the Southbury loop

The claustrophobic confines of the country end of Liverpool Street station, captured by photographer Ed Hirst, aptly demonstrate the need to keep the emission of smoke and steam to an absolute minimum as we await departure with our stalwart 'Standard 5' No 73096 with a 'Cathedrals Express' for Norwich. *Ed Hirst*

to Cheshunt, Harlow Town and Bishops Stortford. Two stations we passed through were of some interest: White Hart Lane was obviously a bit busier whenever Tottenham Hotspur football club (I could have written Spurs and saved ink) was playing at home, and in the goods yard at Southbury there was a tender locomotive complete with smoke deflectors that appears to be of Norwegian origin, its purpose being to promote a local timber merchant.

The usual motive power employed on the job was either a 'Black 5' or the 'Standard 5', so take your pick. However, as I have the timings for a run we made with 'Black 5' No 45231 on Wednesday 21 December 2005 with the aptly titled 'Cathedrals Express Carol Concert Express', you are welcome to travel with us.

We departed from Liverpool Street's Platform 5 at 12.07 on the fast line with a handy 10-coach load on our tail. Immediately faced with the climb of Bethnal Green bank, this livened up the fire nicely for firing to begin, first by filling up the back end and under the door, then up with the flap and build the coal up to this level before covering the remainder of the grate. All 'Black 5s' love this treatment and, after

a couple of minutes digesting this, you will be rewarded with an upward movement of the boiler pressure gauge, by which time you need to bring into action the live steam injector before sitting yourself down in the fireman's seat for a well-earned breather. Incidentally, as far as I am aware no main-line-registered 'Black 5s' are fitted with an exhaust injector.

Working on the footplate with me that day were driver Brian Dudley-Ward and footplate inspector Peter Kirk, with locomotive owner Bert Hitchen acting as the RO. Although the route was none too taxing, I did enjoy this 'Cathedrals Express' as we were booked non-stop over the 70 miles to Ely. A slight disappointment was the 60mph maximum allowed with our 'Black 5' as opposed to the 75mph with the 'Standard 5', but interestingly no allowance was made in the timings for this discrepancy.

Our good progress on this bright winter's day was halted after 25 miles when we were brought to a unscheduled stand by adverse signals at Harlow Town. Here Bert decided to use the opportunity to adjourn to the support coach, having been on duty since the early hours in charge of the loco preparation at Ropley on the Mid-Hants Railway. We

'Black 5' No 45231 was a regular on the 'Cathedrals Express', and here we see engine owner Bert Hitchen sharing the footplate with us at Ely. *Author's collection*

had worked the 50 miles into London with the empty stock, leaving Alton at 07.30. Bert's replacement was fellow NYMR footplate inspector and neighbour of mine, Stuart Whitter, whose railway pedigree stretched back to 'Deltic' days when in charge at Gateshead depot, later performing the same role in charge at North Pole depot. As he climbed aboard, bringing his own Lucas firing shovel, I decided to entrust this fellow Lancastrian with the firing duties to Cambridge.

We had a few more minutes awaiting the road, during which time my deputy built up the fire in anticipation of Brian resorting to some 'catch-up running' after we left Harlow Town 4 minutes late at 13.07. Our next timing point was at Elsenham, 10 miles ahead, being due through there at 13.22, after which it was more or less downhill running to Cambridge. It was at Elsenham on 3 December, less than three weeks earlier, that a heartbreaking incident had occurred when two young girls were killed on the foot crossing by a Stansted express; a footbridge now gives pedestrian access to the staggered Cambridge platform.

Between each passing place throughout the journey recovery time was built into the train timings; for instance, between Elsenham and Ely a total of 5 extra minutes was allowed for any out-of-course checks. Cambridge was once the hub of a number of branch lines in East Anglia, which became one of the first areas to experiment with the early BR diesel trains until finally succumbing to the Beeching cuts. Prior to this I did actually travel on a couple of these lines, including the Mildenhall branch behind the country's last working 2-4-0 locomotive No 62785, now happily preserved as part of the National Collection.

An instantly recognisable landmark on the approaches to Cambridge is the famous Addenbrookes Hospital, which we passed at 13.49, just 1 minute behind time. All was well on board No 45231, and my apprentice fireman had done such a good job that he was asked to continue on the shovel over the final 15 miles on level track to Ely. Following a punctual arrival at our destination, and after shunting the empty train into the sidings, we headed light engine to Ely North Junction, thence taking the Peterborough line as far as Manea, where we reversed back through the crossover then the Ely West curve for the loco to face the right way for our 17.43 departure back to Liverpool Street, arriving at 19.58. This round-trip steam excursion encompassed just over 8 hours, making it a popular day trip. When we had worked the inaugural train the previous year with No 73096, upon arriving at Ely the train had been greeted by the town's Mayor and Mayoress.

A longer journey over these metals took us to Norwich from Ely travelling via Brandon, Thetford and Wymondham (pronounced 'Windum'). This journey was a real throwback to the steam age: modernisation had not yet reared its head, with stations in almost their original condition, together with the nine signal boxes, crossing gates, semaphore signalling, telegraph poles, platelayers' huts, and 60-foot rails giving that 'jiggerty-can-jiggerty-can' rhythm so beloved of my youth! Our return route to London from Norwich, via Diss, Ipswich and Colchester for water, was spoiled by the presence of the overhead wires, which destroyed any semblance of a vintage atmosphere although the railway allowed us 75mph running on a line with no noticeable gradients throughout. This was

a very popular 'Cathedrals Express', leaving Liverpool Street at 11.10 and arriving back in the capital 10 hours later at 21.11, such timings ruling out 'Black 5' haulage.

However, we had plenty of other routes and destinations suitable for the use of Mr Stanier's finest design, including an interesting working with 'The Spitfire' charter on Sunday 3 September 2006 hauled by No 45231, which started with empty stock from Haywards Heath to Brighton, then visited Eastbourne, Ashford, Hastings Faversham, Sheerness and return to Faversham. Some of this route was alien both to myself and my regular drivers, thus requiring a conductor for some of the journey, the difficulty being the non-availability of a qualified steam driver with the route knowledge. The problem was only overcome at the 11th hour when we hired in a South Central Trains driver in his late 20s, who had never been on the footplate of a steam loco but was highly enthusiastic when given the opportunity to do so. His role would not involve the handling of the locomotive, but to instruct the steam driver in the position of signals, stations, speed restrictions, tunnels, gradients, etc.

The 08.55 Sunday departure from Brighton to Eastbourne would not have been popular with local residents as we climbed away from the station faced with a ruling gradient of 1 in 100, immediately demanding an all-out effort from our Class 5 hauling the 10-coach load plus a dead Class 31 diesel. The heavy exhaust beat would have ruled out

We were honoured by the presence of the Mayor and Mayoress upon arrival at Ely with the inaugural 'Cathedrals Express'. The Mayor is on the footplate with driver Brian Dudley-Ward, an interesting quartet for the cameras. *Author's collection* a peaceful Sunday morning lie-in for a few locals living close to the line for the first 4 miles. My predictions proved to be true, the sight and sound of our steam-hauled special creating an incredulous response from the natives of Brighton as No 45231 topped the climb to Falmer Tunnel in fine style. As driver Peter Kirk eased off the regulator I brought the other injector into use to top up the water and we began a swift descent of the 1 in 88 for 4 miles to Lewes, the county town of East Sussex.

We had a brief stop there to top-up our passenger levels, the period feeling of this former London, Brighton & South Coast station being somewhat spoiled by simply infilling the trackbeds of the disused bay platforms with ballast.

The platform clock showed 09.15 as we said goodbye to Lewes; it would be more than 12 hours before we returned at 21.50. Our next port of call was Eastbourne, which we reached by branching to the right just beyond Polegate, reaching the terminus station at 09.51. There our diesel loco on the rear began to earn its keep by dragging us the 40 miles from Eastbourne to Ashford, and as we had only a 9-minute allowance to crank up the diesel and complete a brake test, there was little time to become acquainted with the citizens of this Victorian seaside town. But wait a minute – someone had just come to the engine asking me how things were in Grosmont? I recognised him immediately as Kieran, the former manager of Grosmont Co-op, who now lived in Eastbourne and worked in the station's booking office!

We bid farewell as we left Eastbourne behind, and being towed tender-first we would provide assistance only where required. It is reasonably level track to Ashford, apart from two short but nasty climbs, the 3 miles of 1 in 60 from Hastings to Ore, which should get the Class 31 coughing and spluttering a bit, followed by 2 miles of 1 in 100 just before Ashford. In between I took the opportunity to capture the events on film as we had been joined on the footplate by Andy Johnson, a fellow fireman and diesel driver who wanted to swing the shovel to Ashford.

I particularly wished to capture on film the signal box coming up shortly with the enchanting title of Bopeep Junction, which controlled the junction of the Tonbridge and Hastings lines. Satisfied with my camerawork – apart from not being able to find the sheep – we entered Bopeep Tunnel, emerging into the aptly named St Leonards Warrior Square station before immediately plunging into Hastings Tunnel, finally arriving in the relative safety of Hastings station itself, all of which must have been an operational nightmare in steam days. After a few miles filming the route it quickly became obvious why this area was so popular with residents and holidaymakers alike. It really is a very pleasant coastline.

Our 15-minute station stop saw the final batch of charter passengers joining our train, but also gave fireman Andy sufficient time to get a fire going for the assault on Ore incline as the Class 31 diesel had no chance of taking the load without our assistance. The lineside over the next 3 miles was well patronised with camera-wielding enthusiasts keen to capture the rare spectacle of a heritage diesel being banked by a steam locomotive: 'A Roar on Ore' was how one steam magazine described the occasion. We had a 42-minute allowance to reach Ashford, this former South Eastern & Chatham route being now known as the Marshlink Line. The 15-mile section between Ore and Appledore is single line, with Rye providing a passing place; it was here that existed a full-size concrete version of the Hornby-Dublo OO-gauge Southern Railway footbridge.

Although nothing much remains here of the former Rye & Camber narrow-gauge railway, built to transport golfers and their caddies to the new course at Camber, the steam railway also took fishermen from Rye to their fishing boats moored opposite Rye Harbour village. The line's promoters cunningly decided to build the railway on private land to avoid the necessity of having to obtain an Act of Parliament, the 3-foot gauge line surviving until 1939.

Leaving Rye, the line is as flat as a fluke to Appledore; according to National Rail the station's official name is Appledore (Kent), despite the other Appledore station in Devon having closed in 1917! On official documents and railway company websites, the station is also referred to as Appledore (Kent), although the locals must surely know it as just 'Appledore'! The station was once a junction for the line to Lydd, Dungeness and New Romney, which is now closed to passengers but still needed for freight to Dungeness Power Station

The only passenger trains on offer at the coast now are on the narrow-gauge Romney, Hythe & Dymchurch Railway. I can thoroughly recommend visiting this, having had the pleasure of a footplate ride after becoming friends with one of the railway's drivers when he shared the footplate with me on the NYMR. This led to me coming out of Hythe station driving No 9 *Winston Churchill* with 13 coaches behind the tender, and what a thrill that was! It was a totally different atmosphere when a Lostock Hall driver was there for a while during the Second World War manning the railway's armoured train.

There has been another change of station name for our next port of call at Ashford, which following rebuilding is now known as Ashford International. The Class 31 diesel drew to a halt with our train precisely at 11.48. Our route conductor/driver left us here, but not before having a few photos

of himself (now known as 'selfies') taken on board No 45231 to show his young son and envious workmates back at his modern traction depot!

We were more or less straight in and straight out of Ashford, but I returned to firing duties as it was but a short 15-minute hop to our water stop at Wye, the first station on the line to Canterbury West. With this in mind it would be a case of little and often regarding the firing, giving me just enough time to capture on film what was once the South Eastern Railway's locomotive works at Ashford as we passed. The last Wainwright 'C' 0-6-0 to work there now lives on the Bluebell Railway and ventured to King's Cross early in 2016 for some filming work.

Arriving at Wye we rendezvoused with our road tanker, the driver not at all confused by the proximity of Wye to Rye, just 20 miles separating the two. So it was all hands to the pump, so to speak, as we only had an allotted 8 minutes to perform the task, but these boys were seasoned professionals and all duties, including engine examination, were completed to time, and just 15 minutes later 'The Spitfire' charter rolled to an unceremonious halt in Canterbury West station with no sign of a Mayor or Mayoress to greet us, and the Archbishop probably a bit too busy on a Sunday!

Forward from there we were booked non-stop around the coast, taking in Margate, Ramsgate and Herne Bay, to Faversham, then we visited Sheerness before returning to Faversham and retracing our route back into Brighton at 22.15. We were not finished yet, as the empty coaches needed to be taken to Haywards Heath for overnight stabling. It had certainly been a value-for-money 13-hour, 200-mile Sunday excursion for our passengers.

36 Back to the West Coast, and Nos 6201, 45231, 46115 and 5690

As previously stated, the Fragonset Merlin company never reached the dizzy heights achieved by West Coast Railways in working heritage charter trains, and the enterprise eventually folded without too much impact on job losses, as most of the staff, including me, worked part-time on an 'as-required' basis. But the experience gained from working almost the length and breadth of the country on the footplate of practically every main-line-registered steam locomotive is never likely to be repeated, and it was with this under my belt that I applied for and was accepted for employment back at West Coast Railways, coming home to Carnforth in Lancashire. Within a few months of my return I had added four more locomotives to the roster of first-time experiences on the main line, beginning with a class of engine that I missed in my BR days, a 'Princess' Class 'Pacific', or in locomen's speech an 'old Lizzie', No 6201 *Princess Elizabeth*. I also fired No 46115 *Scots Guardsman* on just a single occasion, and to those could be added the two 'Britannias', Nos 70000 and 70013 *Oliver Cromwell*, which I worked on only at the NYMR.

Dealing with the 'Princess' first, my maiden voyage was to Carlisle with a Christmas Saturday charter on 8 December 2007, steam-hauled from Preston with a well-known ace on the handle, Paul Kane. The engine was stabled overnight at Bury on the East Lancashire Railway, and we lodged in a hotel nearby on the Friday night, not getting the best night's sleep due to revellers at a Christmas party – the lucky devils! 06.30 was the wake-up call for the taxi to the depot, the hotel supplying us with a pack-up of sandwiches, etc.

We met the support crew at the depot and carried out the usual pre-flight checks before leaving with the engine and support coach for Preston at 08.00. On the way the RO bemoaned the fact that the engine had not been steaming well for the past few weeks, but claimed that we should be all right today with two old hands in charge; this restored some confidence in man and machine although I have to admit that engine and support coach working would not test us unduly! We came to Preston via the circuitous route of Salford, Chat Moss, Warrington and Wigan, and awaited the arrival of our train from the south in No 9 platform, taking on water from the nearby hydrant.

Our 12-coach train arrived in the adjacent No 8. We swapped locos and while our guard was carrying out the brake test I began to fill up the firebox of our 'Pacific'. In theory this has slightly more power than a 'Duchess' because of the smaller driving wheels, but its smaller 45-square-foot firebox was also of benefit to me. Having fired for Paul to his home town of Carlisle on a number of occasions, I knew that his driving technique would be to go all-out on the 5-mile climb from Preston to Barton and Broughton, hopeful of reaching 60mph passing there before pulling back the cut-off on the short downhill stretch to Brock, then passing Garstang & Catterall at our maximum 75mph with the regulator now in first valve and cut-off at 25%, 'just blowing the smoke off the chimney' as he would say! We should be able to maintain this for the next 10 miles of level running before easing off for the descent through Lancaster, and the initial heavy burst of power should have given us an early indication of the engine's steaming capabilities.

By departure time I had done my preparation work; the all-important back corners and sides of the firebox had been covered, while under the door coal was built up over the flap, allowing me just enough space to fire down the front but avoiding any smoke or blowing-off before we were given the 'right away'. We had a full glass of water and the CWA (carriage warming apparatus) was pumping out 60psi. The platform inspector relayed the guard's 'right away' signal, but I knew that we would not move until Paul got confirmation from his fireman that he too was prepared for departure. With a nod from me, my driver lifted the big handle and brought No 6201 to life, allowing just a few exhaust beats before closing the cylinder drain cocks to avoid covering the rails in steam, as it can be quite tricky getting away cleanly on the 1 in 90 grade out of Preston.

After passing under the wide Fishergate Hill bridge, I leapt into action with the shovel, concentrating on covering the front of the grate. Paul gave a whistle and a wave to the signallers watching our departure from the Preston power box, which stands on the site of the former MPD. I briefly glanced up through the cab roof as we passed the tallest spire of any parish church in England, that of St Walburge's, which stands between the lines to Blackpool and Lancaster. I lost sight of the church as we passed under Maudland Road bridge, the heavy exhaust beat from a full regulator and 50% cut-off almost dislodging the brickwork, while the coal was disappearing off my shovel into the firebox with the greatest of ease!

Passing the site of Oxheys cattle yard, the scene of the gauge glass incident of some 45 years before, I decided that my 40-shovel burst would suffice for the time being before partially closing the firehole doors. A glance at our smoky exhaust reassured me that all should be well; the water had just come into sight at the top of the glass, so I reached to put on the exhaust injector and at the same time took my first look at the boiler pressure gauge, expecting it to read near full working pressure of 250lb. But something wasn't right, as the gauge was stuck rigid at 210lb, so I postponed the injector idea and examined the fire instead. I used my shovel to deflect the glare and

A happy crew with a slightly unhappy engine: on 8 December 2007 LMS Stanier 'Pacific' No 6201 *Princess Elizabeth* stands in Preston station waiting to work forward with a Christmas special to Carlisle, the home town of driver Paul Kane. *Eddie Bobrowski* flames, and was satisfied that all appeared well, with plenty of heat being generated and the chimney giving off exhaust of the correct colour. I decided to leave things alone for a few minutes, apart from a slight adjustment of the dampers by opening the front one to the first notch, the back one being fully open.

Shortly afterwards, with the water now dropping to just over half a glass and no upward movement of steam pressure, the injector would have to go on as the actual water level was lower than that, and should Paul shut off steam the true level would be only about an inch from the bottom of the glass. The engine was displaying all the signs of being stiff for steam, despite there being a bright fire, which encouraged me to fire around the box – but not too heavily – and to try my luck with a lighter fire. The downside of this was the admission of cold air into the box with the injector pumping water into the boiler at the same time. The plus factor was that we were about to pass Barton & Broughton, where Paul quickly closed the regulator and in the same movement reopened it to full first valve, winding the 'Princess' back to the 20% mark on the reverser. Then, pointing to the 62mph reading on the speedometer, he gave me a cheeky grin that didn't disappear despite me pointing to a steam gauge reading 160lb with the water 'just bobbin''. Nonchalant? Well, maybe so, but this guy was a veteran of struggles with the steam locomotive over this tough route, his 50-year career having spanned the steam, diesel and electric ages operating from the Carlisle depots. I was in good hands!

We decided to run an iron through the fire, then to give it the 'little and often' treatment and switch from the exhaust to the live steam injector. This had some effect, and 10 miles on we passed Bay Horse in better nick with 200lb on the clock and three-quarters showing in the gauge

glass, the theory being not to fire when the injector was on if at all possible. Carnforth was often the stopping point for taking on water on these charters, but on this day we were only booked in after 70 miles at Penrith, which meant that we would have to be ready and able to pass through Carnforth prepared for the 30 miles of almost relentless hill-climbing ahead of us to the summit of Shap.

Once past the loops at Oubeck, Paul was able to shut off and coast through Lancaster, enabling me to top up the boiler and build up the back corners and sides of the box. It was while passing here that the vibration caused the vacuum brake gauge to come loose and hit Paul on the head, causing a little amusement but no damage to gauge or man, although Paul did temporarily register 21 inches of vacuum on his head! The gauge was quickly fixed back in place by the travelling RO, who incidentally passed the comment that we were doing well in keeping No 6201 on the move and running to time.

With Lancaster behind us and passing over the River Lune bridge, my driver asked if I was ready for the challenge ahead and, with full pressure and a full boiler, he got the nod from me and No 6201 was given full regulator with the cut-off lengthened accordingly. Seven minutes later we hammered through Carnforth at the full 75mph, whistle blowing and waving to our mates at the depot as though all was well; steam locomen, of course, never like to admit to having a rough trip! Our big 'Pacific' rode just as well as a 'Lizzie', with little difference in power output; in fact, some locomen prefer this 'old Lizzie' as the smaller firebox helps the fireman's labour – although in her present condition she seemed to be suffering from the same frailties as a Midland 4F in that she was steaming like a witch – until you put the ruddy injector on!

However, I continued with my little-and-often firing policy and not firing when the injector was on, which was hard graft with this 45-square-foot firebox, but we managed to top Grayrigg with half a glass and 180lb on the clock. That was not bad considering that I had been forced to mortgage water for steam and vice versa since Carnforth. All this huffing and puffing was amusing Paul, who knew that I would rather die than give up the struggle; he told me that he would let the engine drift through Low Gill and Dillicar to be in some sort of 'shape for Shap'.

I made more use of the fire iron while both injectors were singing away, then it was off with those and the CWA – sorry, folks, as it's beginning to snow, but you can have the heat back on again once we're over the summit. Now with the iron away, the shovel was in action again, sending the black stuff around the box. My labours were briefly halted by Paul hanging on to the engine whistle and jokingly telling me that he was whistling for the bank engine to be ready for us at Tebay! But we managed to attain a healthy 50mph and hit the bottom of the bank with a full pot and 230lb on the clock.

The RO offered to make himself useful and pull down the coal, enabling me to concentrate on the steam and water situation. The benefit of having a full pot at Tebay was that it enabled us to cover the first 2 miles before needing to use the injector, but once brought into use it would have to remain on throughout the climb. Another mile into the climb we passed the former outpost of Scout Green, where in steam days, according to legend, Carlisle men used to go on their days off to watch Crewe men struggling up Shap! We were also labouring a bit now at just 25mph, down to half a glass and 180lb, with just a few hardy souls recording our passage on this snowy December Saturday; then Father Christmas himself suddenly appeared at my side of the footplate in the form of driver Paul Kane,

telling me to watch the road ahead while he had a go on the 'fuel transfer tool'.

Although three score years and ten, Paul was a fit fella who still enjoyed the art of firing and finished his stint on the shovel with the summit in sight. But we had water worries, with just an inch showing in the glass, forcing me to bring the other injector into life, lowering the steam to just 150lb. Paul had no option but to drop the cut-off to full forward gear, enabling us to top Shap at a heady 20mph in the swirling snow with just one lone photographer braving the elements; I recognised him as the former Chairman of the NELPG, Maurice Burns, who later forwarded me a print.

But the work wasn't over just because we had topped the summit, for I knew that Paul would be wanting to make up some of the lost time on the 13 miles of downhill running to our water stop at Penrith. We were fortunate that the steam pressure was kept from dropping below 150lb, as at about 140lb the brakes would have begun to rub, but we had recovered nicely and passed Eden Valley Junction at 75mph with a full pot, 200lb and the CWA doing its job again at 60lb. We reached Penrith having clawed back 3 of the 11 minutes of late running.

The water stop gave us the chance to query the support crew regarding the locomotive's disappointing performance. They admitted to being somewhat baffled, having tried and eliminated all the usual steam engine faults on its last few outings – in fact, they had not been that hopeful of us being able to surmount Shap! Needless to say, the remaining 20-mile downhill hop to Carlisle was completed in less than the booked time, our arrival being just a few minutes late and not too inconvenient for our Christmas shopper passengers, who would return south later in the day with a relief crew on board No 6201.

Paul was a resident of the Cumbrian capital, so we said our farewells, wishing each other the season's greetings, after which I travelled back home to downtown Grosmont via Newcastle, Darlington and Middlesbrough.

A few weeks later I was Paul's fireman again, and he informed me that our relief crew on the 'old Lizzie' had a nightmare run back, losing time and having to stop for a blow-up. The good news was that the cause of the steaming problems was found to be the misaligned blast pipe. The next time I had the engine, with the steaming problems sorted thanks to the expertise of the support crew, she showed us her true colours as the regular engine on the Fridays-only 'Scarborough Flyer', the 07.30 Crewe to Scarborough calling at Wilmslow, Stockport, Denton (for water), Huddersfield, Wakefield, Milford Loop (also for water) and York. A couple of times during the first weeks of working this job we were stopped out of course at Sandbach (no, not to ask if we knew the road to Hartford – 1963 and all that!) where we were informed that a hot axle box detector had been activated; the signaller had been most surprised to be informed that it was a steam engine heading the train, and maybe that was something to do with it!

As we drifted into Stockport past the site of the former 9B engine sheds and the town's football ground, the links to the past continued with the signal boxes in the area dating from the 1870s. Network Rail was still putting off the replacing of these antiquities, even flying in 12 signal engineers from India for a few weeks' experience in the refurbishment of the mechanical interlocking mechanism still in existence in the five signal boxes. Once over the mighty Stockport Viaduct we ventured off to the right at Heaton Norris Junction for the Stockport-Stalybridge line, stopping at Denton for water. This station is famous for having just one train a week in one direction only, christened 'The Denton Flyer', and would you believe it runs on a Friday morning near our booked time for water here.

So, not relishing the possibility that we might delay the one and only service, we always managed to leave before he appeared. At Guide Bridge station evidence still remained of the former 1,500V DC Woodhead route. That useful diversion route, closed entirely in 1970, is remembered for the use of the EMI Bo-Bo electric locos; I once owned the highly collectable Trix OO-gauge model. Once we joined the main Lancs to Yorks line and passed through Stalybridge station, famously situated on the Transpennine Real Ale Trail, we began the 8-mile 1 in 125 pull up to Standedge Tunnel. This was the highlight of the journey, whether heading to the east or in the return westbound direction, with *Princess Elizabeth* 'flattening' this Yorkshire incline. The 3½- mile tunnel was the only lengthy level stretch of line between Manchester and Leeds, so let's put a set of water troughs in there! These were situated at the Leeds end, almost at the tunnel portal, and could be an operational nightmare for any foreign crews searching for the position of the troughs, not to mention the difficulties encountered by the maintenance staff for the tunnel on this busy route, which was, as you can imagine, rarely smoke-free.

Three miles after our Huddersfield stop we passed the reinstated Bradley Wood Junction, the route we took with 'Black 5s' Nos 44871 and 44894 working 1Z78 on 4 August 1968, referred to previously. I partially retraced that run in 2010 on 'Black 5' No 45231 as the fireman to former Rose Grove man Mick Kelly on his driving exam for West Coast Railways, which he passed with flying colours. This was a reunion of two ex-L&Y men over Copy Pit, then on past the site of Rose Grove MPD (whistling accordingly). From Blackburn we took the old route to Bolton through Sough Tunnel with relief at Manchester Victoria, the train continuing over the Oldham loop as one of the last steam runs before its rebirth as the Metrolink.

At Mirfield the former engine sheds were awaiting demolition, but an even sadder sight came into view shortly after with the remnants of the once extensive marshalling yards at Healey Mills, only constructed in 1963. This yard and the combined diesel depot are now but history, a similar fate befalling 55E Normanton shed a little further down the line, now just waste ground with a single platform remaining of the once extensive station, which we frequented on the midweek 'Scarborough Spa Express'. Fortunately Rugby League is still played at Castleford, with free viewing of the action from the adjacent railway embankment. The stretch between here and our next water stop at Milford was once a favourite for cable thieves, causing extensive disruption; they were well organised and versed in railway safety regulations, wearing hi-vis clothing and correctly acknowledging our warning whistle, then standing clear next to their white Transit van, which they had suitably lettered in authentic Network Rail transfers! The railway police eventually nabbed them, a suspended sentence being their only punishment. The police would dearly love to see a charge of endangering life for those offences.

Working this Friday steam job to Scarborough was one of my favourite turns and would have been even better had we been relieved at York instead of going through to Scarborough. Sometimes water was taken at Bootham instead of Milford, after which we were Scarborough next stop, missing out the once busy junction station of Malton. The big 'Pacific', having a trailing truck, could negotiate with ease the tight curves between York and Malton. That station's claim to fame was the means adopted to allow passengers to access the second (island platform); instead of a footbridge or barrow crossing, the NER installed a moveable section of platform in the form of a wheeled trolley running on rails set at right angles to the (single) running line, and interlocked with the signals giving access to the platform. When a train had to use the platform, the trolley was wheeled back under the up (York) platform.

The NYMR was a recipient of much useful equipment from Malton goods yard and its S&T department when they closed; prior to their demolition a small team of us spent almost a week dismantling and transporting much of the large variety of heritage items. The station was once the junction for the Pickering and Driffield lines, the latter closing in 1958. The junction for the Pickering line was at Rillington, where nothing much is left now apart from a row of cottages. Even if the junction had still been in place, there is no way we could have taken our 160-ton beauty down the line, being much too heavy for a jolly to Pickering.

At Seamer Junction we were joined by the line from Bridlington and Hull coming in on the right. Bridlington station was still winning awards for its floral displays and its restored buffet and bar set in the 1930s; with its real ales it is a magical place, sporting a wide range of railwayana – visit it! Scarborough station has lost a lot of its former grandeur, but unusually in these modern times it still retains a Railway Staff Club. Most of the large semaphore signal gantry that once controlled the station throat now resides at Grosmont in full working order, while the signal box itself has been preserved. Members of the Scarborough Railway Club help maintain the station gardens, and were kind enough to invite me to put on a slide show on more than one occasion, with a few views depicting the operating turntable in the yard, which attracts much attention whenever a steam special appears in the town.

I had not set foot on No 46115 *Scots Guardsman* since working the 18.00 Preston North Union Yard-Warrington Arpley freight with driver Colin Shaw shortly before its withdrawal in 1965, at which time some of the class were still operating services in our London link. What a transformation it was the next time the loco and I came together! It looked absolutely resplendent, having just had a full restoration by the West Coast Railways team, and there was nobody more proud than me to be rostered to work the southbound 'Cumbrian Fellsman' from Carlisle, sporting a 'Thames-Clyde Express' headboard on the smokebox, with another S&C veteran on the regulator, the redoubtable Gordon Hodgson.

LMS 5XP No 5690 *Leander* stands at Hellifield with legendary Carlisle driver Gordon Hodgson waiting for another tussle up the hill with a northbound 'Fellsman' charter. *Eddie Bobrowski*

As with Paul Kane and John McCabe, this was Gordon's railway, which he had known man and boy during a long railway career on the footplate working out of the Carlisle depots. He was a fit fella for his age, one of his interests being fell walking, and there are plenty of them in this part of the country! He wasn't the tallest in stature, but that's maybe because of all the walking, so once he put the engine's regulator in the roof it usually stayed there as it was a long reach for him to ease it down; nor did the engine's cut-off receive that much attention! Consequently Gordon was not known for losing time when working a steam locomotive! His firing skills were also still first-class, and if for any reason I had to briefly leave the footplate he was on the shovel, putting me a fire on; or if he had a conductor driver over the route I wouldn't be able to prise the shovel off him. We also shared an interest in classic cars as he owned an Austin 7 and a 1960s Saab, so as you can imagine that I enjoyed my days as his fireman.

On the day in question, 7 February 2009, we relieved the incoming crew of Bill Andrew and Frank Santrian at Carlisle, then turned and serviced the engine before departing to Manchester, steam-hauled to Hellifield with the return working. One notable difference with the engine since my days on the class in the 1960s was the reduced height of the cab roof for safe working under the overhead wires, but one thing that was the same was that long firebox, similar to that of a Southern 'Lord Nelson'. But when rebuilt, the 'Scots' were worlds apart from the original straight-boiler version; how often I used to see one arriving on time at Crewe with 15 on, having manfully replaced the unavailable rostered 'Lizzie' on a Euston-Glasgow express! During the 1948 Locomotive Exchanges a rebuilt 'Royal Scot' proved capable of matching the performance of the much larger LMS 'Coronation' Class. In fact, the only derogatory opinion of them was their susceptibility to some rough riding at speed, possibly due to the absence of a trailing truck to steady the ride! This forced some drivers to take drastic measures for that little bit of extra comfort by removing their false teeth!

We left Carlisle mid-afternoon for the 30-mile first leg to Appleby, arriving there a few minutes early for our booked water stop. I also had a water stop, and returned to the footplate to find Gordon in action with the shovel. Meanwhile a chap came up to the cab remarking on our headboard and telling me that he had been a regular traveller on the original 'Thames-Clyde Express' in the 1950s with a 'Scot' when it used to top the 17½-mile ascent to Ais Gill summit in just 24 minutes from Appleby. My first thought after he told me was that I just hoped Gordon hadn't heard him!

With watering completed we had the 'right away' from Appleby and, as Gordon cracked open the regulator on No 46115, he looked at me with a mischievous grin asking, 'Did that bloke just say it took 24 minutes to top Ais Gill?' Instead of answering him I just thought it wise to just get busy on the shovel as quickly as possible in anticipation of my driver attempting to blow the smokebox door off its hinges for the next 17½ miles. After having taken advantage of the short dip to Ormside Viaduct, we were in full cry as we entered Helm Tunnel, which gave me a quick breather from the firing. After emerging it was a case of continually feeding the fire around the box over the flap with no need for any hefty swinging to reach the front end of the long box – the heavy exhaust saw to that. The water level was holding at a near full glass, and the injector had no chance of any inactivity while the

On a cold 7 February 2009 we storm through Kirkby Stephen station with 'Royal Scot' Class 4-6-0 No 46115 *Scots Guardsman* with a southbound 'Thames-Clyde Express'. Our 24-minute climb to the summit of Ais Gill was later claimed as a record for the load and loco class; the driver was Gordon Hodgson on his own turf. *John Shuttleworth*

engine was being worked with the regulator fully open and a long cut-off. In fact, I was having to introduce the live steam injector in short bursts as we roared through Kirkby Stephen on that cold but sunny February Saturday afternoon. The few enthusiasts on the snow-covered fells who had braved the elements were enjoying the ideal light conditions, perfect for capturing some great shots of a steam locomotive doing battle on this hill of all hills.

Not that I had any chance to take in the magnificent scenery, nor was the cold bothering me as Gordon was keeping my circulation going very nicely as he gave me a quick thumbs-up to attack the last leg from Mallerstang. He dropped the cut-off down the rack and, with a wide-open regulator, the response from our three-cylinder double-chimney rebuilt 'Scot' to this all-out action was to increase the pace and begin to feather at the safety valves! This proved yet again the capabilities of these rebuilt engines, whose performances in BR days earned them the utmost respect from locomen. And there was nothing wanting from this performance by No 46115 *Scots Guardsman* some four decades after withdrawal from traffic by its previous owner. A quick burst on the Stanier hooter announced the topping of Ais Gill summit at 45mph, but with few witnesses to the sight at this Mecca for steam enthusiasts. The 25-mile descent to Settle Junction was achieved without the use of the firing shovel, while from the junction to Hellifield only a brief salvo was required to take our train into the up loop, where fell-walker Gordon brought his hill-climber to a stand ready for a well-earned drink from the water column.

While taking on water I was summoned by our guard, who told me that a couple of passengers in the second coach wanted to have a quick word with me. So, leaving Gordon in charge of the watering, I walked back along the ballast and spotted two men leaning out the corridor window of the second coach looking quite excited and calling me towards them. One of them was the chap I had spoken to at Appleby.

'You did it!' he exclaimed. 'That was a record climb so far as we are aware, taking you just 24 minutes from Appleby to Ais Gill summit'!

'Oh, I'm pleased to hear that our efforts have maybe created a little bit of history,' I replied, and turned round to walk back to the engine. But had he got his facts right? I was certain that he said it took the 1950s 'Thames-Clyde Express' 24 minutes for the climb, so I questioned him.

'Yes,' he replied. 'Your timings today matched the 1950s run but with just one slight difference in that he was pulling 385 tons whereas you had 470 tons behind the tender!'

For aficionados of YouTube some film exists of the final leg between Mallerstang and Ais Gill summit. Comments posted likened the sound reverberating off the hillsides to that of an approaching jet, but others bemoaned the fact that they had missed us due to us being 17 minutes early! But let me state quite clearly that at no time was the engine thrashed; yes, it worked hard, proving to the owner just what a powerhouse on wheels he had available to him in his fleet. In fact, I will further state that during my 15-year stint working on main-line steam, no engine was ever knocked about or driven with brazen bravado and without thought as to its historic stature. That was worlds apart from their role in the true days of the steam locomotive, when each shed had its own small allocation of rough devils on the regulator!

The culmination of the 2009 season came in the September with a three-day outing to Scotland with the 'West Highlander', featuring three locomotives, Nos 5690 *Leander*, 61994 *The Great Marquess* and 62005. Gordon and I had the 5X on the Friday, leaving Carnforth at 08.36 with the

10-coach ECS to Preston, then away from there at 10.11 to Glasgow Central before taking the ECS to Cadder via Springburn, arriving there at 19.44, a nice 12-hour 250-mile day out with Grayrigg, Shap and Beattock to surmount during the course of the trip.

After a pleasant two-day break we returned from Cadder with the 5X at 16.36 on the Monday, arriving at Preston at 22.49, then ECS to Carnforth. No 61994 handled the Glasgow-Fort William- Cadder leg, while No 62005 worked Fort William-Mallaig and return. The lengthy voyage into Scotland on the Friday entailed three stops for water at Oxenholme, Lockerbie and Abington; this was my first visit to Glasgow Central with steam since being thwarted on World Cup Final day in 1966.

The real highlight of our 2009 journey was the all-out performance of No 5690 *Leander* hauling ten coaches on the 10-mile 1 in 60 up Beattock. She was overloaded for a 5X, and had this been the 1960s a banker would have been taken with anything over eight coaches. But it was of no use whistling up for one as everything, including the shed and station at Beattock, had been swept away, including the branch line to Moffat! We had been given a none too generous 17 minutes to climb the 10 miles to the summit with 400 tons behind the tender, which to a layman may seem reasonably achievable, but the Stanier 5X is not the ideal hill-climber. Nevertheless *Leander* and our crew, including Danny, our young apprentice on tender duty, gave it everything and topped Beattock in just over the allotted time with the engine still in its stride doing a creditable 25mph.

Awaiting departure time at Preston with the 10-coach 'West Highlander' three-day charter for Glasgow and a tour of Scotland, with a further variety of motive power. *Author's collection*

37 Epilogue

When I look back to what we did that day it would be hard to recall anything in my career that could better that particular achievement with a steam locomotive. Interestingly, when we worked the same train with No 5690 the next year, changes had been made and the loading reduced to just eight coaches with a Liverpool Lime Street departure and a return from Glasgow via the former Glasgow South Western route through Paisley and Dumfries. However, the permanent way along this line was not to the liking of our 5X, resulting in some heavy rolling and rough riding until we rejoined the main line at Gretna. I should just mention that I knew the very last station master at Beattock, Mr Carl Snaith; we became good friends when he transferred to Preston, working with us at our signing-on point as a senior clerk.

The other two locomotives involved with the 'West Highlander', 'K1' No 62005 and No 61994 *The Great Marquess*, are both capable of punching above their weight and thus ideal for working the 'Jacobite' service or a turn over the Settle & Carlisle. In particular, the 'Marquess', with 5ft 2in driving wheels and three cylinders developing more than 36,000lb tractive effort, boasts a higher power output than a 'Scot'. Driving it was always a pleasure with everything responding to the touch, not to mention that beautiful six-to-the-bar beat. The engine is out of traffic at the moment awaiting overhaul.

I had limited experience firing the other two main-line-registered ex-LNER locos Nos 4472 *Flying Scotsman* and 'V2' No 60800 *Green Arrow*, amounting to just a couple of turns on the latter versatile workhorse, and just a single trip on the 'A3', neither loco being in good nick at the time, shortly before their withdrawal.

My own footplate future both at West

What better way to end a firing career! Stanier 'Pacific' No 46233 *Duchess of Sutherland*, resplendent in green livery, awaits my attention before departing from Scarborough with a charter for Crewe on my last main-line footplate turn in 2013. *Adrian Scales*

Coast Railways and the NYMR was rapidly drawing to a halt by the summer of 2013, but not before a fitting finale to my firing career working the return leg of the summer-only Scarborough-Crewe excursion on three consecutive Friday evenings with No 46233 *Duchess of Sutherland*, resplendent in her green livery.

A change to our regular return route due to engineering works at Huddersfield saw us diverted via the Calder Valley line through my old stamping ground of Hebden Bridge, Littleborough and the summit tunnel with a stop at Rochdale. The big 'Pacific' would have looked a little out of place among the tank engines and 'Black 5s' in my day when working steam on this line. My last NYMR driving turn was on my favourite class of steam locomotive, the 'A4' No 60007 *Sir Nigel Gresley*, and I captured both last journeys on film.

Now, how do you sum up a footplate career that began at the age of 15 in 1962 without becoming too sentimental? I do recognise just how much I owe to my work colleagues over those years, men whom I have admired and envied for their natural talents and capabilities working the steam locomotive. Included among them have to be many of the present generation of footplate staff, whether on heritage railways or main-line operation, all of them dedicated to keeping alive that unique machine so wilfully discarded as being surplus to requirements half a century ago.

Keep smiling folks! Bye from Fireman Fletch!

Index

Further reading for enthusiasts...

A series paying tribute to the *Ian Allan Combined Volumes* so much revered by the trainspotters of the 1950s, 1960s, 1970s and beyond.

Running Out of Steam by David Mather and Barry Allan's *Schooldays and Steam Days*, the first two titles in the series, sold out within a few months of publication and have become much sought after.

The next in the series *The Glory and The Steam* by John Gilroy was published in response to readers asking for more and was centred on the North Eastern area.

Bearing in mind every 'Gricers' story is as different as the areas, locosheds and stations visited back in the days of steam, there has been no shortage of potential material for further additions to the series!

Stewart Warrington's memories of those younger days extended the series with not one but two volumes entitled *'Jubilees' and 'Jubblys' Parts 1 and 2*.

Next, also in two parts, came John Stretton's *Garratts and Guitars*. John's volumes are subtitled *Sixty*

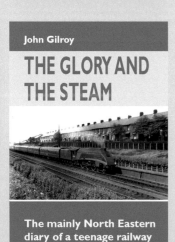

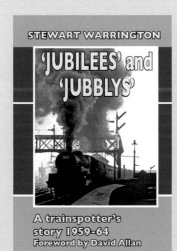

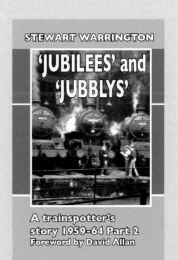

Trainspotting years and are autobiographical thereby including many other aspects of life alongside the railway memories.

These pocket-sized volumes are proving a big hit and we are developing further projects for the future.

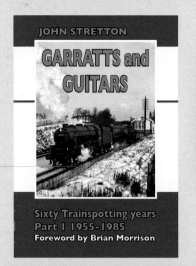

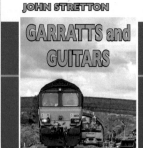

The North Eastern Locomotive Preservation Group was formed on 28 October 1966 in an upstairs room of theBridge Hotel, Newcastle, with the original intention of saving a 'J27' 0-6-0 tender engine, No 65894, at that time still in use by BR. The NELPG not only succeeded in that aim but also acquired another North Eastern workhorse, 'Q6' 0-8-0 No 63395. Both were restored to full working order and operated on the then embryonic North Yorkshire Moors Railway.The success of the NELPG led to 'K1' 2-6-0 No 62005 being presented to the Group in 1972 and this, too, was overhauled, to see a new lease of life on the NYMR, in 1974. That year saw the NELPG involved in the restoration of LMS 'Black Five' 4-6-0 No 44767, which culminated in all four locomotives participating

in the never-to-be-forgotten celebrations to mark the 150th anniversary of the Stockton & Darlington Railway, at Shildon, in1975.

That year was the precursor to main-line operations for both the 'K1' and the 'Black Five', and the 'K1' went on to become the most used locomotive on the highly successful steam service on the Road to the Isles between Fort William and Mallaig. In 1982 the NELPG acquired 'J72' 0-6-0 No 69023 of Railway Children fame, and this too was overhauled for use on the NYMR, as well as numerous other heritage railways around the UK.

Not content with overhauling and maintaining its own locomotives, the NELPG was also involved with the two 0-6-2 tanks Nos 5 and 29 from the National Coal Board system at Philadelphia, County Durham, 'Q7' 0-8-0 No 901 from the National Collection, and the two Gresley 'Pacifics', 'A4' No 60019 Bittern and 'A2' No 60532 Blue Peter. With the exception of Bittern, all were overhauled under the auspices of the NELPG to see further use on the NYMR and, in the case of the 'A2', the main line.

This unique book not only chronicles the 50-year history of the NELPG, augmented by a superb and varied collection of colour photographs, both before and after preservation, but gives a rare insight into what is actually involved in steam locomotive overhaul and maintenance. This is done through a series of remarkable pictures that graphically illustrate the many and varied technical processes involved in a way that words alone cannot adequately describe.